Brain-Computer Interfacing

The idea of interfacing minds with machines has long captured the human imagination. Recent advances in neuroscience and engineering are making this a reality, opening the door to restoring and potentially augmenting human physical and mental capabilities. Medical applications such as cochlear implants for the deaf and deep brain stimulation for Parkinson's disease are becoming increasingly commonplace. Brain-computer interfaces (BCIs) (also known as brain-machine interfaces or BMIs) are now being explored in applications as diverse as security, lie detection, alertness monitoring, telepresence, gaming, education, art, and human augmentation.

This introduction to the field is designed as a textbook for upper-level undergraduate and first-year graduate courses in neural engineering or brain-computer interfacing for students from a wide range of disciplines. It can also be used for self-study and as a reference by neuroscientists, computer scientists, engineers, and medical practitioners.

Key features include:

- Essential background in neuroscience, brain recording and stimulation technologies, signal processing, and machine learning
- Detailed description of the major types of BCIs in animals and humans, including invasive, semi-invasive, noninvasive, stimulating, and bidirectional BCIs
- In-depth discussion of BCI applications and BCI ethics
- Questions and exercises in each chapter
- Supporting Web site with annotated list of book-related links

Rajesh P. N. Rao is an associate professor in the Computer Science and Engineering department at the University of Washington, Seattle. He has been awarded an NSF CAREER award, an ONR Young Investigator Award, a Sloan Faculty Fellowship, and a David and Lucile Packard Fellowship for Science and Engineering. Rao has published more than 150 papers in conferences and leading scientific journals, including *Science, Nature*, and *PNAS*, and is the co-editor of *Probabilistic Models of the Brain* and *Bayesian Brain*. His research targets problems at the intersection of computational neuroscience, artificial intelligence, and brain-computer interfacing. His not-so-copious spare time is devoted to Indian art history and to understanding the ancient undeciphered script of the Indus civilization, a topic on which he has given a TED talk.

Brain-Computer Interfacing

AN INTRODUCTION

Rajesh P. N. Rao

Department of Computer Science and Engineering &
Neurobiology and Behavior Program
University of Washington, Seattle

CAMBRIDGE
UNIVERSITY PRESS

CAMBRIDGE
UNIVERSITY PRESS

University Printing House, Cambridge CB2 8BS, United Kingdom

One Liberty Plaza, 20th Floor, New York, NY 10006, USA

477 Williamstown Road, Port Melbourne, VIC 3207, Australia

314-321, 3rd Floor, Plot 3, Splendor Forum, Jasola District Centre, New Delhi - 110025, India

79 Anson Road, #06-04/06, Singapore 079906

Cambridge University Press is part of the University of Cambridge.

It furthers the University's mission by disseminating knowledge in the pursuit of education, learning and research at the highest international levels of excellence.

www.cambridge.org
Information on this title: www.cambridge.org/9781108708012

First published 2013
3rd printing 2018
First paperback edition 2019

A catalogue record for this publication is available from the British Library

Library of Congress Cataloging in Publication data
Rao, Rajesh P. N.
Brain- computer interfacing : an introduction / Rajesh P. N. Rao.
    pages   cm
Includes bibliographical references and index.
ISBN 978-0-521-76941-9 (hardback)
1. Brain- computer interfaces.   I. Title.
QP360.7.R36   2013
573.8´60113–dc23   2013009994

ISBN 978-0-521-76941-9 Hardback
ISBN 978-1-108-70801-2 Paperback

Additional resources for this publication at bci.cs.washington.org

To Anu, Anika, and Kavi

Contents

Color plates follow page 176.

Preface

"Scientists demo thought-controlled robots" (*PC Magazine*, July 9, 2012)

"Bionic vision: Amazing new eye chip helps two blind Brits to see again" (*Mirror*, May 3, 2012)

"Paralyzed, moving a robot with their minds" (*New York Times*, May 16, 2012)

"Stephen Hawking trials device that reads his mind" (*New Scientist*, July 12, 2012)

These headlines, from just a few weeks of news stories in 2012, illustrate the growing fascination of the media and the public with the idea of interfacing minds with machines. What is not clear amid all this hype is: (a) What exactly can and cannot be achieved with current *brain-computer interfaces* (BCIs) (sometimes also called *brain-machine interfaces* or BMIs)? (b) What techniques and advances in neuroscience and computing are making these BCIs possible? (c) What are the available types of BCIs? and (d) What are their applications and ethical implications? The goal of this book is to answer these questions and provide the reader with a working knowledge of BCIs and BCI techniques.

Overview of the Book

The book provides an introduction to the field of *brain-computer interfacing* (the field also goes by the names of *brain-machine interfacing, neural interfacing, neural prosthetics*, and *neural engineering*). Several extremely useful edited volumes have been published on this topic over the past few years (Dornhege et al., 2007; Tan and Nijholt, 2010; Graimann et al., 2011; Wolpaw & Wolpaw, 2012). There has, however, been a growing need for an introductory textbook aimed specifically at those who do not have an in-depth background in either engineering or neuroscience. This book aims to serve this need. It can be used as a textbook in upper-level undergraduate and first-year graduate courses on brain-computer interfacing and neural engineering. It can also be used for self-study and as a reference by researchers, practitioners, and those interested in joining the field.

The book introduces the reader to essential ideas, concepts, and techniques in neuroscience, brain recording and stimulation technologies, signal processing, and machine learning before proceeding to the major types of BCIs and their applications. Exercises and questions at the end of each chapter provide readers with the opportunity to review their knowledge and test their understanding of the topics covered in the chapter. Some exercises (marked by the expedition icon ⚲) allow the student to go beyond what is discussed in the textbook by following leads in research publications and searching for new information on the Web.

The book is organized as follows: Chapters 1 through 5 of the book provide the necessary background in neuroscience and quantitative techniques to understand the terminology and methods used in building BCIs. In Chapter 6, we begin our journey into the world of BCIs by learning about the basic components that go into building a BCI. The next part of the book introduces the reader to the three major types of BCIs classified according to degree of invasiveness. Chapter 7 describes invasive BCIs, which utilize devices implanted inside the brain. Chapter 8 describes semi-invasive BCIs, which are based on nerve signals or devices implanted on the surface of the brain. Chapter 9 covers noninvasive BCIs such as those that record electrical signals from the scalp (EEG). Chapter 10 reviews BCIs that stimulate the brain in order to, for example, restore lost sensory or motor function. Chapter 11 introduces the most general type of BCIs, namely, BCIs that both record from and stimulate the brain. In each case, examples of classic experiments as well as the state-of-the-art technologies (circa 2013) are presented. Chapter 12 reviews some of the major applications of BCIs, and Chapter 13 considers the ethical issues pertaining to the development and use of BCI technology. We conclude in Chapter 14 with a summary of some of the limitations of present-day BCIs and speculate on the future of the field. The book also includes an Appendix that provides basic mathematical background in linear algebra and probability theory useful for understanding and implementing BCIs.

Web Site

The Web site for the book is bci.cs.washington.edu.

Since BCI is a rapidly growing field, the Web site will maintain a periodically updated list of useful links related to BCI research.

Additionally, given that this book contains upward of 101,000 words, it is very likely that errors and typos have crept in unbeknownst to the author. Therefore, any errors or typos brought to the notice of the author by discerning readers will be maintained in an up-to-date errata on the book Web site.

Cover Image

The image on the book's cover depicts a human brain in action when controlling a cursor with an electrocorticographic BCI (see Section 8.1). The bright red region on the brain indicates increased activity in the hand area of the motor cortex when the subject imagined hand movement to move the cursor toward a target on the computer screen. The image was generated by Jeremiah Wander, Bioengineering graduate student and member of the Grid Lab and Neural Systems Lab at the University of Washington.

Acknowledgments

I would like to thank Lauren Cowles of Cambridge University Press for her encouragement and continued support for this project despite many missed deadlines. Thanks are also due to the Center for Sensorimotor Neural Engineering (CSNE) and the BCI group at the University of Washington (UW), especially my collaborators Jeffrey Ojemann, Reinhold Scherer (now at TU Graz), Felix Darvas, Eb Fetz, and Chet Moritz, for numerous leads and many enriching discussions. Students in the Neural Systems Laboratory were a constant source of inspiration and new ideas in BCI research – I thank them for keeping me on my toes: Christian Bell, Tim Blakely, Matt Bryan, Rawichote Chalodhorn, Willy Cheung, Mike Chung, Beau Crawford, Abe Friesen, David Grimes, Yanping Huang, Kendall Lowrey, Stefan Martin, Kai Miller, Dev Sarma, Pradeep Shenoy, Aaron Shon, Melissa Smith, Sam Sudar, Deepak Verma, and Jeremiah Wander. Pradeep was a teaching assistant in an early BCI course that I taught and helped organize the structure of the course, which provided a foundation for this book. Sam was a teaching assistant in a later offering and provided valuable feedback on course material. Kai helped establish the early collaboration with the medical school in BCI research and played a key role in launching our electrocorticography-based BCI research.

A number of funding agencies and organizations supported my research as well as the writing of the book: the National Science Foundation (NSF), the Packard Foundation, National Institutes of Health (NIH), the Office of Naval Research (ONR) Cognitive Science Program, the NSF ERC for Sensorimotor Neural Engineering (CSNE), and the Army Research Office (ARO) – I thank them for their support. Parts of the book were written at the scenic Whiteley Writing Center at Friday Harbor Laboratories, which provided just the right environment for jump-starting the writing process when the need was acute.

For providing a solid mathematical and scientific foundation for a future career in research and teaching, I am grateful to my school teachers at Kendriya Vidyalaya Kanchanbagh (KVK) in India, my undergraduate professors at Angelo State University in Texas, my doctoral advisor Dana Ballard at the University of Rochester, and my postdoctoral advisor Terry Sejnowski at the Salk Institute. To my parents, I owe many thanks for their long-standing support and for piquing my scientific curiosity at an early age with a houseful of books. To my children Anika and Kavi, I owe an apology for not having given them as much attention during this book project as their unconditional love deserves. Last but not least, my wife Anu provided the inspiration and steadfast support that have kept me going through the many years of writing – this book would not have been possible without her.

Introduction

Our brains evolved to control a complex biological device: our body. As we are finding out today, many millennia of evolutionary tinkering has made the brain a surprisingly versatile and adaptive system, to the extent that it can learn to control devices that are radically different from our body. Brain-computer interfacing, the subject of this book, is a new interdisciplinary field that seeks to explore this idea by leveraging recent advances in neuroscience, signal processing, machine learning, and information technology.

The idea of brains controlling devices other than biological bodies has long been a staple of science-fiction novels and Hollywood movies. However, this idea is fast becoming a reality: in the past decade, rats have been trained to control the delivery of a reward to their mouths, monkeys have moved robotic arms, and humans have controlled cursors and robots, all directly through brain activity.

What aspects of neuroscience research have made these advances possible? What are the techniques in computing and machine learning that are allowing brains to control machines? What is the current state-of-the-art in brain-computer interfaces (BCIs)? What limitations still need to be overcome to make BCIs more commonplace and useful for day-to-day use? What are the ethical, moral, and societal implications of BCIs? These are some of the questions that this book addresses.

The origins of BCI can be traced to work in the 1960s by Delgado (1969) and Fetz (1969). Delgado developed an implantable chip (which he called a "stimoceiver") that could be used to both stimulate the brain by radio and send electrical signals of brain activity by telemetry, allowing the subject to move about freely. In a now-famous demonstration, Delgado used the stimoceiver to stop a charging bull in its tracks by pressing a remote-control button that delivered electrical stimulation to the caudate nucleus in the basal ganglia region of the bull's brain. At around the same time, Fetz showed that monkeys can control the activity of single brain cells to control a meter needle and obtain food rewards (see Section 7.1.1). Slightly later, Vidal (1973) explored the use of scalp-recorded brain signals in humans to implement a simple noninvasive BCI based on "visually evoked potentials" (Section

6.2.4). The more recent surge of interest in BCIs can be attributed to a confluence of factors: faster and cheaper computers, advances in our knowledge of how the brain processes sensory information and produces motor output, greater availability of devices for recording brain signals, and more powerful signal processing and machine-learning algorithms.

The primary motivation for building BCIs today is their potential for restoring lost sensory and motor function. Examples include sensory prosthetic devices such as the cochlear implant for the deaf (Section 10.1.1) and retinal implant for the blind (Section 10.1.2). Other implants have been developed for deep brain stimulation (DBS) to treat the symptoms of debilitating diseases such as Parkinson's (Section 10.2.1). A parallel line of research has explored how signals from the brain could be used to control prosthetic devices such as prosthetic arms or legs for amputees and patients with spinal-cord injuries (e.g., Section 7.2.1), cursors and word spellers for communication by locked-in patients suffering from diseases such as ALS (amyotrophic lateral sclerosis) or stroke (Sections 7.2.3 and 9.1.4), and wheelchairs for paralyzed individuals (Section 12.1.6). More recently, researchers have begun exploring BCIs for able-bodied individuals for a host of applications (Chapter 12), ranging from gaming and entertainment to robotic avatars, biometric identification, and education. Whether BCIs will eventually become as commonplace as current human accessories for sensory and motor augmentation, such as cellular phones and automobiles, remains to be seen. Besides technological hurdles, there are a number of moral and ethical challenges that we as a society will need to address (Chapter 13).

The goal of this book is to serve as an introduction to the field of brain-computer interfacing. Figure 1.1 illustrates the components of a generic BCI. The aim is to translate brain activity into control commands for devices and/or stimulate the brain to provide sensory feedback or restore neurological function. One or more of the following processing stages are typically involved:

1. **Brain recording**: Signals from the brain are recorded using either invasive or noninvasive recording techniques.
2. **Signal processing**: Raw signals are preprocessed after acquisition (e.g., by bandpass filtering) and techniques for artifact reduction and feature extraction are used.
3. **Pattern recognition and machine learning**: This stage generates a control signal based on patterns in the input, typically using machine-learning techniques.
4. **Sensory feedback**: The control signal from the BCI causes a change in the environment (e.g., movement of a prosthetic arm or a wheelchair, change in the grip of a prosthetic hand). Some of these changes can be seen, heard, or felt by the user but in general, one can use sensors in the environment such as tactile sensors, force sensors, cameras, and microphones, and use the information from these sensors to provide direct feedback to the brain via stimulation.

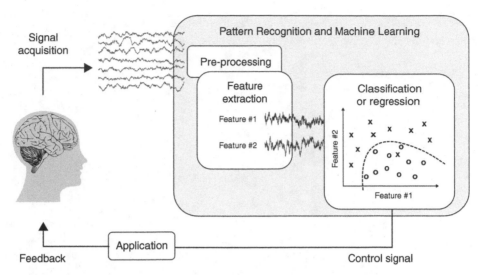

Figure 1.1.   **Basic components of a brain-computer interface (BCI).** (Adapted from Rao and Scherer, 2010).

5. **Signal processing for stimulation**: Before stimulating a particular brain region, it is important to synthesize an activity pattern for stimulation that mimics the type of activity normally seen in the brain region and that will have the desired effect. This requires a good understanding of the brain area being stimulated and the use of signal processing (and potentially machine learning) to home in on the right stimulation patterns.

6. **Brain stimulation**: The stimulation pattern received from the signal processing component (5) is used in conjunction with invasive or noninvasive stimulation techniques to stimulate the brain.

It is clear from the stages of processing listed above that to begin building BCIs, one must have a background in at least four essential areas: basic neuroscience, brain recording and stimulating technologies, elementary signal processing, and basic machine-learning techniques. Often, beginners in BCI come with a background in one of these areas but usually not all of them. We therefore begin our journey into the world of BCIs with Part I (Background), which introduces the reader to basic concepts and methods in these four areas.

Background

Basic Neuroscience

Weighing in at about three pounds, the human brain is a marvel of evolutionary engineering. The brain transforms signals from millions of sensors located all over the body into appropriate muscle commands to enact a behavior suitable to the task at hand. This closed-loop, real-time control system remains unsurpassed by any artificially created system despite decades of attempts by computer scientists and engineers.

The brain's unique information processing capabilities arise from its massively parallel and distributed way of computing. The workhorse of the brain is a type of cell known as a *neuron*, a complex electrochemical device that receives information from hundreds of other neurons, processes this information, and conveys its output to hundreds of other neurons. Furthermore, the connections between neurons are plastic, allowing the brain's networks to adapt to new inputs and changing circumstances. This adaptive and distributed mode of computation sets the brain apart from traditional computers, which are based on the *von Neumann architecture* with a separate central processing unit, memory units, fixed connections between components, and a serial mode of computation.

In this chapter, we provide a primer on neuroscience. Starting from the biophysical properties of neurons, we explore how neurons communicate with each other, how they transmit information to other neurons via junctions called synapses, and how synapses are adapted in response to inputs and outputs. We then explore the network level architecture and anatomy of the brain, learning how different areas of the brain are specialized for different functions.

2.1 Neurons

A neuron is a type of cell that is generally regarded as the basic computational unit of the nervous system. As a crude approximation, the neuron can be regarded as a leaky bag of charged liquid. The membrane of a neuron is made up of a lipid bi-layer (Figure 2.1) that is impermeable except for openings called *ionic channels* that selectively allow the passage of particular kinds of ions.

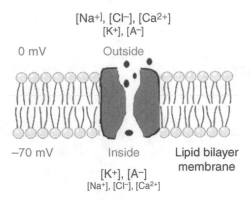

Figure 2.1.   **The electrochemical dance of ions in a neuron.** The diagram depicts the larger concentration of sodium, chloride, and calcium ions outside the neuron and the larger concentration of potassium ions and anions inside the neuron (maintained by active pumps), resulting in a "resting" potential difference of approximately −70mv across the lipid bi-layer membrane. Proteins known as ionic channels, which are embedded in the membrane, act as gates regulating the flow of ions into and out of the neuron.

Neurons reside in an aqueous medium with a larger concentration of sodium (Na+), chloride (Cl⁻), and calcium (Ca^{2+}) on the outside of the cell and a greater concentration of potassium (K+) and organic anions (A⁻) inside the cells (Figure 2.1). As a result of this imbalance, there is a potential difference of approximately −65 to −70 mV across the neuron's membrane when the neuron is at rest. There exist active pumps that work to maintain this potential difference by expending energy.

2.2 Action Potentials or Spikes

When the neuron receives sufficiently strong inputs from other neurons (see Section 2.4 below), a cascade of events is triggered: there is a rapid influx of Na+ ions into the cell, causing the membrane potential to rise rapidly, until the opening of K+ channels triggers the outflow of K+ ions, causing a drop in the membrane potential. This rapid rise and fall of the membrane potential is called an *action potential* or *spike* (Figure 2.2), and represents the dominant mode of communication between one neuron and another. The spike is an all-or-one stereotyped event with little or no information in the shape of the spike itself – information is thought to be conveyed instead by the *firing rate* (number of spikes per second) and/or the timing of spikes. Neurons are therefore often modeled as emitting a 0 or 1 digital output. Similarly, in extracellular recordings typically done in awake animals (Section 3.1.1), a spike is often represented as a short vertical bar at the time the spike occurred.

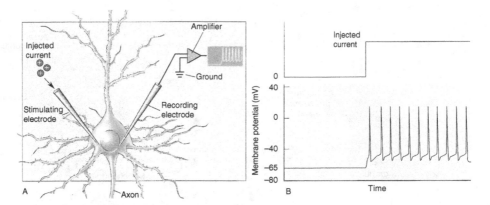

Figure 2.2. **Generation of spikes or action potentials.** (A) depicts the experimental procedure of injecting a current (positive ions) into the cell body of a neuron using a stimulating electrode and recording the change in membrane potential of the cell using a recording electrode. (B) shows the result of injecting a sufficiently large amount of current, which results in a sequence of spikes or action potentials. Each spike has a stereotypical shape that rises rapidly above 0 mv and falls again. After each fall, the constant injection of current causes the potential to ramp up again until a "threshold" of slightly below −40 mv (for this neuron) is reached, which causes the cell to fire again (from Bear et al., 2007).

2.3 Dendrites and Axons

Neurons in different regions of the brain have different morphological structures, but the typical structure includes a cell body (called the *soma*) connected to a tree-like structure with branches called *dendrites* and a single branch called the *axon* that emanates from the soma and conveys the output spike to other neurons (see Figure 2.3). The spike is typically initiated near the junction of the soma and axon and propagates down the length of the axon. Many axons are covered by *myelin*, a white sheath that significantly boosts the speed of propagation of the spike over long distances. The terms *white matter* and *gray matter* correspond respectively to the myelinated axons connecting different brain regions and the regions containing the cell bodies.

2.4 Synapses

Neurons communicate with each other through connections known as *synapses*. Synapses can be electrical but are more typically chemical. A synapse is essentially a gap or *cleft* between the axon of one neuron (called the presynaptic neuron) and a dendrite (or soma) of another neuron (called the postsynaptic neuron) (see Figure 2.3). When an action potential arrives from a presynaptic neuron, it causes the release of chemicals known as neurotransmitters into the synaptic cleft. These chemicals in turn bind to the ionic channels (or receptors) on the postsynaptic neuron, causing these channels to open, thereby influencing the local membrane potential of the postsynaptic cell.

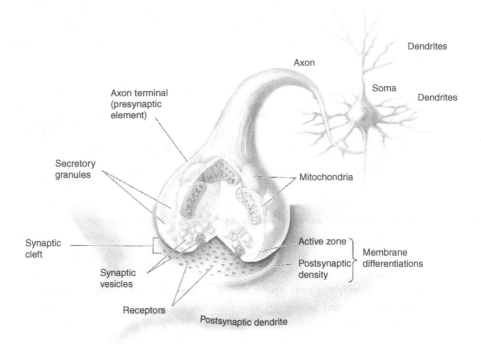

Figure 2.3. **Dendrites, soma, axon, and synapse.** The figure depicts a connection from one neuron to another. The dendrites, cell body (soma), and axon of the first neuron are shown, along with the synapse this axon makes on the dendrite of a different neuron. A spike from the first neuron causes the release of neurotransmitters stored in synaptic vesicles in the "presynaptic" axon terminal. These neurotransmitters bind with receptors in the "postsynaptic" dendrite, causing the ionic channels to open. This results in the influx or outflow of ions, changing the local membrane potential of the postsynaptic neuron (adapted from Bear et al., 2007).

Synapses can be excitatory or inhibitory. As the name suggests, excitatory synapses cause a momentary increase in the local membrane potential of the postsynaptic cell. This increase is called an excitatory postsynaptic potential (EPSP). EPSPs contribute to a higher probability of firing a spike by the postsynaptic cell. Inhibitory synapses do the opposite – they cause inhibitory postsynaptic potentials (IPSPs), which temporarily decrease the local membrane potential of the postsynaptic cell. A neuron is called excitatory or inhibitory based on the kind of synapse it forms with postsynaptic neurons. Each neuron forms only one kind of synapse, and therefore if an excitatory neuron is to inhibit a second neuron, it must excite an inhibitory "interneuron," which then inhibits the desired neuron.

2.5 Spike Generation

The generation of a spike by a neuron involves a complex cascade of events involving sodium and potassium channels as described above. However, in many cases, this process can be simplified to a simple threshold model of spike generation. When the neuron receives sufficiently strong inputs from its synapses for its membrane potential to cross a neuron-specific threshold, a spike is emitted (Figure 2.2B). This makes the neuron a hybrid analog-digital computing device: digital 0/1 inputs are converted to analog changes in the local membrane potential, followed by summation of these changes at the soma, and a spike if the summation of changes exceeds threshold. This simplified model of course ignores the complex and potentially important forms of signal processing associated with dendrites, but the threshold model of a neuron has proven to be a useful abstraction in neural modeling and artificial neural networks.

2.6 Adapting the Connections: Synaptic Plasticity

A critical component of the brain's adaptive capabilities is the ability of neurons to change the strength of the connections between themselves through synaptic plasticity. Numerous forms of synaptic plasticity have been experimentally observed, the most studied being *long-term potentiation* (LTP) and *long-term depression* (LTD). Both involve changes to a synapse that last for hours or even days. More recently, other types of plasticity have been characterized, including *spike timing dependent plasticity* (STDP), where the relative timing of input and output spikes determines the polarity of synaptic change, and *short-term facilitation/depression*, where the plasticity is rapid but not long-lasting.

2.6.1 LTP

One of the most important forms of synaptic plasticity is long-term potentiation or LTP (Figure 2.4). In its simplest form, LTP involves an increase in the strength of a synaptic connection between two neurons caused by correlated firing of the two neurons. LTP is regarded as a biological implementation of Donald Hebb's famous postulate (also called Hebbian learning or Hebbian plasticity) that if a neuron A is consistently involved in causing another neuron B to fire, then the strength of the connection from A to B should be increased. LTP has been found in a number of brain areas including the hippocampus and the neocortex.

2.6.2 LTD

Long-term depression or LTD (Figure 2.4) involves a decrease in the strength of a synaptic connection caused, for example, by uncorrelated firing between the two neurons involved. LTD has been observed most prominently in the cerebellum, although it also coexists with LTP in the hippocampus, neocortex, and other brain areas.

2.6.3 STDP

Traditional experimental protocols demonstrating LTP/LTD involved stimulating a presynaptic neuron and a postsynaptic neuron simultaneously. These protocols

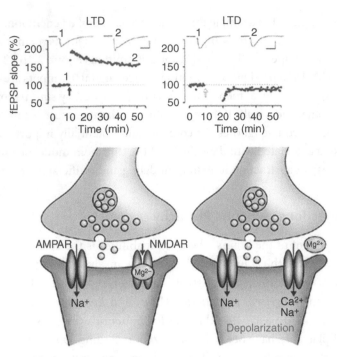

Figure 2.4.   **Synaptic plasticity.** (Top) Experimental data demonstrating long-term potentiation (LTP) and long-term depression (LTD) in the hippocampus. Synaptic strength was defined in terms of the slope of the excitatory postsynaptic potential (labeled fEPSP). The left panel demonstrates LTP, a long-lasting increase in synaptic strength, caused by high-frequency stimulation (100 Hz stimulation for 1 s; black arrow). The right panel shows LTD caused by low-frequency stimulation (5 Hz stimulation for 3 minutes twice with a 3 min interval; open arrow). Scale bar: 0.5 mV; 10 ms. (Bottom) A proposed model of synaptic plasticity. AMPAR and NMDAR are two types of ionic channels. During weak stimulation (left panel), Na+ flows through the AMPAR channel but not through the NMDAR channel because of the Mg^{2+} block of this channel. If the postsynaptic cell is depolarized (right panel), the Mg^{2+} block of the NMDAR channel is removed, allowing both Na+ and Ca^{2+} to flow inside. This increase in Ca^{2+} concentration is believed to be necessary for synaptic plasticity (adapted from Citri & Malenka, 2008).

manipulate the firing rate of pre- and postsynaptic neurons but not the timing between presynaptic and postsynaptic spikes. Recent studies have revealed that the precise timing of pre- and postsynaptic spikes can determine whether the change in synaptic strength is positive or negative. This form of synaptic plasticity has been termed spike timing dependent plasticity (STDP). In one form of STDP, known as Hebbian STDP, if the presynaptic spike occurs slightly before the postsynaptic spike (e.g., 1–40 ms before), the synapse is strengthened, whereas if the presynaptic spike occurs slightly after (e.g., 1–40 ms after), the synaptic strength is decreased. Hebbian STDP has been observed in the mammalian cerebral cortex and hippocampus. The opposite phenomenon of anti-Hebbian STDP, where the synapse is strengthened for presynaptic spike occurring after postsynaptic spike and vice versa, has also been observed in some structures, particularly in inhibitory synapses such as those in cerebellum like structures in weakly electric fish.

2.6.4 Short-Term Facilitation and Depression

The types of synaptic plasticity discussed above are called long-term plasticity because the changes they cause can last for hours, days, or even longer periods of time. A second form of plasticity with more ephemeral effects has also been discovered. This type of plasticity, known as short-term plasticity, causes the corresponding synapses to act as temporal filters on input spiking patterns. For example, in short-term depression or STD, which has been observed in neocortical synapses, the effect of each successive spike in an input *spike train* (sequence of spikes) is diminished compared to the preceding spike. Thus, if the neuron receives a burst of spikes as input, the first spike in the burst has the most effect with each successive spike causing lesser and lesser changes in the membrane potential until an equilibrium point is reached and all subsequent input spikes have the same diminished effect on the postsynaptic neuron. Short-term facilitation or STF exhibits the opposite effect, where each successive spike has a larger effect than its predecessor, until a saturation point is reached. Both STD and STP play important roles in regulating the dynamics of cortical networks by gating the effects of input spike trains on postsynaptic neurons.

2.7 Brain Organization, Anatomy, and Function

The design of a brain-computer interface typically involves choices regarding which brain areas to record from and, in some cases, which brain areas to stimulate. This section provides a brief overview of brain organization and anatomy. The reader is referred to neuroscience textbooks such as those by Bear et al. (2007) and Kandel et al. (2012) for a more in-depth treatment.

The human nervous system can be broadly divided into the *central nervous system* (CNS) and the *peripheral nervous system* (PNS). The PNS consists of the somatic nervous system (neurons connected to skeletal muscles, skin, and sense organs) and the autonomic nervous system (neurons that control visceral functions such as the pumping of the heart, breathing, etc.).

The CNS consists of the brain and the spinal cord. The *spinal cord* is the main pathway that conveys descending motor-control signals from the brain to muscles all over the body and ascending sensory feedback information from the muscles and skin back to the brain. Besides conveying information to and from the brain, neurons in the spinal cord are also involved in local feedback loops that control reflexes such as the rapid withdrawal of your finger when you accidentally touch a hot item.

The brain is composed of many different nuclei (clusters of neurons) and regions (Figure 2.5). At the base of the brain are the *medulla, pons*, and the *midbrain*, which together constitute the *brain stem*. The brain stem conveys all the information

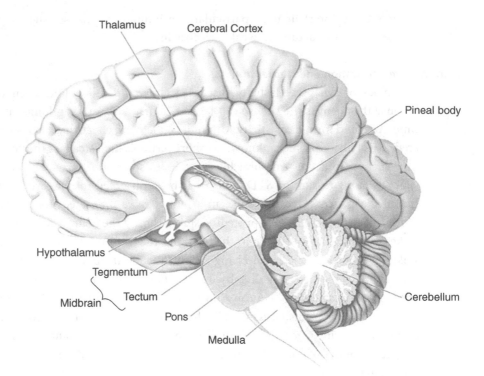

Figure 2.5.   **Major brain regions.** The diagram depicts some of the major regions of the human brain. The medulla, pons, and midbrain together comprise the brain stem and are involved in conveying most of the information from the brain to the body. The thalamus and the hypothalamus comprise the diencephalon; the former is involved in relaying sensory information to the brain while the latter regulates basic needs. At the base of the brain is the cerebellum, which plays an active role in the coordination of movements. At the top is the cerebral cortex, which includes the neocortex and the hippocampus, and is involved in a variety of functions ranging from perception to cognition (see Figure 2.6) (adapted from Bear et al., 2007).

from the brain to the rest of the body. The medulla and pons are involved in basic regulatory functions such as breathing, muscle tone, blood pressure, sleep, and arousal. A major component of the midbrain is the *tectum*, which is composed of the *inferior* and *superior colliculus*, and is involved in the control of eye movements and visual and auditory reflexes. Also in the midbrain is the *tegmentum*, composed of the *reticular formation* and other nuclei, which modulates muscle reflexes, pain perception, and breathing, among other functions.

The *cerebellum* ("little brain") is a highly structured network of neurons located at the base of the brain (see Figure 2.5) that is responsible for the coordination of movements.

Farther up from the base of the brain is the *diencephalon*, which includes the *thalamus* and the *hypothalamus*. The thalamus is traditionally regarded as the main "relay station" that conveys all the information from the sensory organs to the neocortex (one exception is the oldest of all senses, olfaction or the sense of smell, which bypasses the thalamus and feeds directly into the olfactory cortex). Recent research on the thalamus has revealed that it may not merely be a relay station but may also be involved in active feedback loops with the neocortex via the many cortico-thalamic feedback connections known to exist between these two regions of the brain. The other major part of the diencephalon, the hypothalamus, regulates basic needs of the organism such as feeding, fighting, fleeing, and mating.

Furthest from the base of the brain are the two *cerebral hemispheres*, consisting of the *neocortex*, the *basal ganglia*, the *amygdala*, and the *hippocampus*. The basal ganglia play an important role in motor control and action selection while the amygdala is involved in the regulation of emotion. The hippocampus is known to be critical for memory and learning, besides spatial cognition.

The neocortex is the convoluted surface that resides at the top of the brain (see Figure 2.5) and is about one-eighth of an inch thick. It consists of about 30 billion neurons arranged in six layers, each neuron making about 10,000 synapses with other neurons, yielding around 300 trillion connections in total. The most common type of neuron in the cortex is the *pyramidal neuron*, populations of which are arranged in columns oriented perpendicular to the cortical surface. The surface of the cortex is convoluted, with fissures known as *sulci* and ridges known as *gyri*.

The neocortex exhibits functional specialization (Figure 2.6) – that is, each area of the cortex is specialized for a particular function. For example, the occipital areas near the back of the head specialize in basic visual processing while the parietal areas toward the top of the head specialize in spatial reasoning and motion processing. Visual and auditory recognition occurs in the temporal areas (toward the sides of the head) while frontal areas are involved in planning and higher cognitive functions.

Inputs to a cortical area predominantly come into the middle layers whereas the outputs from an area leave from the upper and lower layers. Based on these input-output patterns, it is possible to regard the cortex roughly as a hierarchically organized network of sensory and motor areas. For example, in the case of visual processing, information from the retina reaches the cortex via the visual region of the thalamus (the lateral geniculate nucleus or LGN). This information first reaches the middle layers of the primary visual cortex (also called cortical area V1 or area 17). V1 contains neurons selective for primitive features such as moving bars and edges. Further processing involves progressively more complex types of processing, involving visual areas V2, V4, and IT (inferotemporal cortex) along one visual pathway (the "ventral stream") and areas MT, MST, and parietal cortex along another pathway (the "dorsal stream"). The ventral stream is specialized for processing the form and color of objects and is involved in object and face recognition. The dorsal stream motion and reasoning about spatial relations. Despite these functional differences, the different areas of the cortex are remarkably similar in their anatomical organization, leading to the suggestion that the cortex employs a prototypical

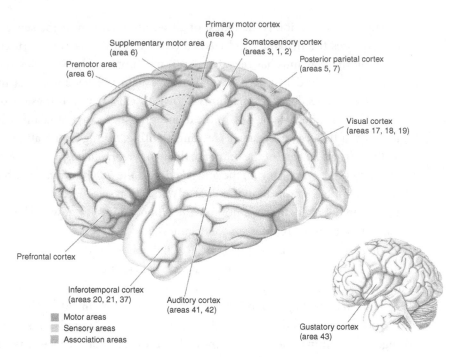

Figure 2.6.   **Major areas and functional specialization of the neocortex.** The figure depicts how different areas of the neocortex are specialized for sensory, motor, and higher order function ("association"). The major sensory areas are visual, somatosensory, auditory, and gustatory cortices. The major motor areas are primary motor, premotor, and supplementary motor cortices. Association areas such as those in inferotemporal and prefrontal cortices are involved in cognitive functions such as face recognition, language, and planning. Area numbers in parenthesis correspond to a numbering scheme for the cortex proposed by the neuroanatomist Korbinian Brodmann in 1909 (from Bear et al., 2007).

algorithm for processing information, and specialization occurs through differences in the types of inputs received in each area.

2.8 Summary

This chapter introduced you to the basic computing unit of the brain, the neuron. We learned how neurons use electrical and chemical processes to communicate with one another, transmitting information "digitally" through spikes or action potentials. We also learned how such communication is mediated by junctions between neurons called synapses. Synapses can adapt at different time scales in response to inputs and outputs. Long-term changes in synaptic strength are thought to be the basis of memory and learning in the brain.

As we shall see in subsequent chapters, the fact that information transmission in the brain is fundamentally electrical in nature opens the door to building a variety of BCIs that can record from and/or stimulate the brain. Additionally, the plasticity of the brain, as mediated by changes in synaptic strength, plays a crucial role in allowing novice BCI users to learn to modulate their brain activity in order to control novel devices.

2.9 Questions and Exercises

1. What is a typical resting potential difference across the membrane of a cortical neuron? Explain the biochemical mechanisms that allow the neuron to maintain this potential difference.

2. Describe the sequence of events that gives rise to an action potential. Start from a volley of action potentials arriving along the input axons to the neuron and trace the biochemical and electrical consequences leading to an output action potential.

3. What are four prominent types of synaptic plasticity observed in the brain? Explain how they serve to modify the effect of a presynaptic spike on the postsynaptic neuron.

4. What are the major components of the CNS and the PNS?

5. Describe the functions that have been ascribed to the brain stem and the cerebellum.

6. What are the major components and functions of the diencephalon?

7. What are some of the functions thought to be carried out by the basal ganglia and the hippocampus?

8. Approximately how many cells does the neocortex contain? How many synapses on average does a cortical neuron have with other neurons?

9. What are the major areas of the neocortex and what are some of their functions?

10. (⚑ Expedition) Is the cortex hierarchically organized? Discuss evidence for and against this hypothesis.

3

Recording and Stimulating the Brain

As described in the previous chapter, the brain communicates using spikes, which are all-or-none electrical pulses produced when the neuron receives a sufficient amount of input current from other neurons via synaptic connections. It is therefore not surprising that some of the first technologies for recording brain activity were based on detecting changes in electrical potentials in neurons (invasive techniques based on electrodes) or large populations of neurons (noninvasive techniques such as electroencephalography or EEG). More recent techniques have been based on detecting neural activity indirectly by measuring changes in blood flow that result from increased neural activity in a region (fMRI) or by measuring the minute changes in the magnetic field around the skull caused by neural activity (MEG).

In this chapter, we review some of these technologies that serve as sources of input signals for BCIs. We also briefly describe technologies that can be used to stimulate neurons or brain regions, thereby allowing BCIs to potentially provide direct feedback to the brain based on interactions with the physical world.

3.1 Recording Signals from the Brain

3.1.1 Invasive Techniques

Techniques that allow recording from individual neurons in the brain are typically invasive, that is, they involve some form of surgery, wherein a part of the skull is removed, an electrode or implant placed in the brain, and the removed part of the skull then replaced. Invasive recordings are typically taken from animals such as monkeys and rats. The recording itself is not painful because the brain has no internal pain receptors, but the surgery and recovery process can cause pain and involves risks such as infection. The recording procedure can be performed on both anesthetized as well as awake animals, although in the case of awake recordings, the animal is typically restrained to minimize artifacts resulting from large movements. In the case of humans, invasive recordings are taken only in clinical settings such as during brain surgery or when patients are being monitored for abnormal brain activity (e.g., seizures) prior to surgery. The time period available for recording may range from weeks and months to years in the case of some animals (e.g., monkeys) to a few days or minutes in the case of humans in a clinical setting. A major advantage of invasive recordings is that they allow recording of action potentials (the acknowledged output signals of neurons) at the millisecond timescale. This contrasts with noninvasive techniques, which measure indirect correlates of neural activity, such as blood flow, that occur at a coarser timescale (hundreds of milliseconds). Invasive recording in both humans and animals is based on the technology of electrodes.

Microelectrodes

A *microelectrode* is simply a very fine wire or other electrical conductor used to make contact with brain tissue. A typical electrode is made of tungsten or platinum-iridium alloy and is insulated except at the tip, which measures around 1μm in diameter (recall that a neuron's cell body diameter is in the range of tens of μm). In some cases (especially intracellular recordings – see next section), neuroscientists use a glass micropipette electrode filled with a weak electrolyte solution similar in composition to intracellular fluid.

Intracellular Recording

The most direct way of measuring the activity of a neuron is through *intracellular recording*, which measures the voltage or current across the membrane of the neuron. The most common technique, known as *patch clamp recording* (Figure 3.1), uses a glass micropipette with a tip diameter of 1 μm or smaller that is filled with a weak electrolyte solution similar in ionic composition to the intracellular fluid found inside a cell. A silver wire is inserted into the pipette to connect the electrolyte to the amplifier. Voltage is measured with respect to a reference electrode placed in contact with the extracellular fluid that exists outside the cell. To record from the cell, the glass microelectrode is placed next to the cell and, using gentle suction, a piece of the cell membrane (a "patch") is drawn into the electrode tip, forming a high-resistance seal with the cell membrane. Given the delicate nature of this procedure, intracellular recordings are typically performed only on slices of brain tissue ("in vitro") and seldom performed on the intact brains of living animals ("in vivo"). This technique has therefore not found much applicability in brain-computer interfaces compared to extracellular recordings.

Extracellular Recording

One of the most common types of invasive recordings, performed especially in the intact brains of animals, is *extracellular recording* of a single neuron (or single "unit"): a tungsten or platinum-iridium microelectrode with a tip size of less than 10 microns is inserted into the target brain area. The depth of the microelectrode is adjusted until it comes close enough to a cell body to pick up the electrical

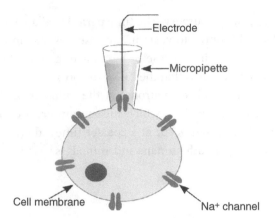

Figure 3.1.   **Intracellular recording using the patch clamp technique.** The technique allows measurement of ionic currents in a small patch of a cell membrane or the entire cell (image: T. Knott, Creative Commons).

fluctuations caused by action potentials generated by the cell (Figure 3.2). These voltage fluctuations are measured with respect to a "ground" or reference wire, often attached to a skull screw. The magnitude of the recorded signal is usually less than a millivolt and thus requires the use of amplifiers to detect the signal. The recorded signal looks like an action potential even though the electrode does not penetrate the cell because the voltage fluctuation is directly related to the action potential: when an action potential is generated, positively charged sodium ions rush into the cell, creating a negative voltage fluctuation in the area surrounding the cell relative to the reference electrode (see lower oscilloscope display in Figure 3.2). This fluctuation is picked up by the recording electrode. The signal from the amplifier is fed to a computer, which performs additional processing such as filtering noise and isolating the spikes (action potentials).

Tetrodes and Multi-Unit Recording

It is possible to record from multiple neurons simultaneously by using more than one electrode. One common configuration is called a *tetrode*, where four wires are tightly wound together in a bundle. The advantage of the tetrode is that each neuron in the neighborhood of the tetrode wires will have a unique signature for the four recording sites (determined by the neuron's distance to a recording site), allowing a potentially large number of neurons to be isolated and recorded from. For example, it may be possible to record from up to 20 neurons with a single tetrode by identifying the neurons' signatures.

Multielectrode Arrays

To record from larger numbers of neurons, microelectrodes can be arranged in a grid-like structure to form a *multielectrode array* of $m \times n$ electrodes, where

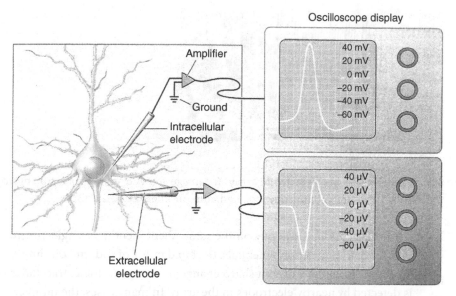

Figure 3.2. **Intracellular versus extracellular recording of spikes.** The two oscilloscope displays on the right compare action potentials (spikes) recorded using intracellular (top) and extracellular (bottom) recording. Intracellular recording measures the potential difference between the inside of the cell (tip of the intracellular electrode) and an external electrode placed in the solution bathing the neuron ("ground"). Extracellular recording measures the potential difference between the tip of the extracellular electrode (placed near but outside a neuron) and a ground electrode. When the neuron produces a spike, positive ions flow away from the extracellular electrode into the neuron, causing the initial negative deflection in the display. This is followed by a positive deflection as the action potential decreases and positive charges flow out of the neuron toward the extracellular electrode. Note the difference in scale between the intra- and extracellular signals. Extracellular spikes are usually represented simply by a short vertical hash mark at the time each spike occurs (e.g., Figure 7.5A) (from Bear et al., 2007).

the values of m and n typically range between 1 and 10 (Figure 3.3). Such arrays have been developed for in vitro as well as in vivo recordings. Here we focus on implantable arrays for in vivo recordings because these are the most relevant for brain-computer interfacing. The most common types of implantable arrays are microwire, silicon-based, and flexible microelectrode arrays. Microwire arrays use tungsten, platinum alloy, or steel electrodes and are similar to the tetrodes discussed in the previous section. Silicon-based arrays include the so-called Michigan and Utah arrays. The former allows signals to be recorded along the entire length of the electrodes, rather than just at the tips. Both of these arrays permit a higher density and higher spatial resolution than microwire arrays. Flexible arrays rely on polyimide, parylene, or benzocyclobutene rather than silicon for recording, thereby providing a better match to the mechanical properties of brain tissue and reducing the possibility of shear-induced inflammation that can be caused by silicon-based arrays.

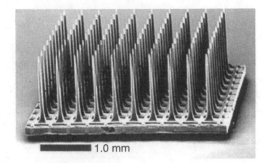

1.0 mm

Figure 3.3.   **Example of a multielectrode array.** The image shows a scanning electron micrograph of a 10 × 10 electrode Utah array (adapted from Hochberg et al., 2006).

Multielectrode arrays rely on the same phenomenon as single-electrode recordings for detecting action potentials: the rapid influx of sodium ions into a cell during an action potential causes a sharp change in voltage in the extracellular space that is detected by nearby electrodes in the array. In many cases, the number of neurons that can simultaneously be recorded from is 10 percent to 50 percent less than the actual number of electrodes in the array because some electrodes do not provide viable signals.

The major advantage of multielectrode arrays over more conventional single-electrode systems is increased spatial resolution; the ability to record simultaneously from several dozens of neurons opens the door to extracting complex types of information such as position or velocity signals that could be useful for controlling prosthetic devices.

Implantable arrays also have their disadvantages, especially if the implanted device remains in the brain tissue for a long time (as required for long-term control of prosthetics). In particular, non-neuronal cells known as glial cells surround the implanted device, leading to the formation of first *scar tissue* and then an insulating sheath around the array, increasing the impedance of the electrodes. This biological response to the implanted device can result in significant reduction in recorded signal quality over time, decreasing its usefulness in brain-computer interfacing. Ongoing research on biocompatibility of implants seeks to address these problems by coating the devices with polymers and other substances.

Electrocorticography (ECoG)

Electrocorticography (ECoG) is a technique for recording brain signals that involves placing electrodes on the surface of the brain. The procedure requires making a surgical incision into the skull to implant the electrodes on the brain surface (Figure 3.4). ECoG is typically performed only in clinical settings, such as in-hospital monitoring of seizure activity in epilepsy patients. Typically, a grid or strip of $m \times n$ electrodes is implanted, where the values of m and n vary between 1 and 8. ECoG electrodes can be tipped with carbon, platinum, or gold alloy, and are typically 2–5 mm in diameter.

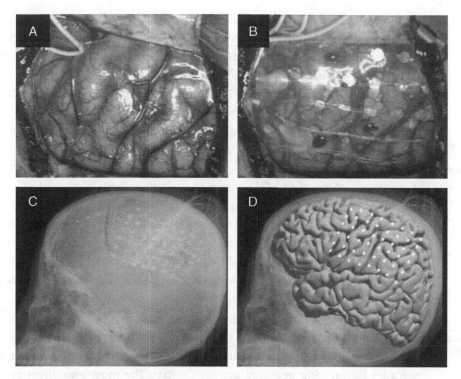

Figure 3.4.   **ECoG in a human.** (A) and (B) Implantation of an ECoG array. The brain is surgically exposed (A), and an electrode array (B) is placed under the dura onto the brain surface. The electrodes are 2 mm in diameter and separated from each other by 1 cm. (C) X-ray image of the skull showing the location of the electrode array. (D) Electrode positions shown on a standardized brain template (from (Miller et al., 2007).

The spacing between grid electrodes is usually 10 mm to 1 cm. The electrodes are flexible enough to accommodate normal movements of the brain.

Unlike single-cell electrodes or multielectrode arrays, ECoG electrodes can record the electrical fluctuations caused by the coherent activity of large populations of neurons (several tens of thousands). While ECoG electrodes do not directly measure spikes, the signal recorded is thought to be directly related to the input currents received by the dendrites of cortical neurons, particularly in the upper layers of the cerebral cortex.

ECoG has recently received attention from the BCI community as a partially invasive compromise between invasive multielectrode arrays and noninvasive EEG (see Section 3.1.2). Unlike multielectrode arrays, some forms of ECoG do not penetrate the blood-brain barrier and are therefore safer than arrays implanted inside the brain. ECoG electrodes may also be less likely to wear out compared to brain-penetrating electrodes which suffer from glial accumulation and scar tissue formation over time (see *Multielectrode Arrays* section above). Because it is closer to the neural activity, ECoG offers greater spatial resolution than noninvasive techniques described in Section 3.1.2 such as EEG (tenths of millimeters versus centimeters), broader spectral bandwidth (0–200 Hz versus 0–40 Hz), higher amplitude (50–100 μV versus tens of μV), and considerably less vulnerability to artifacts such as muscle activity and ambient noise.

Limitations of ECoG include: (1) it can currently only be used in surgical settings, (2) only surgically relevant portions of the brain can be recorded, and (3) there may be interference due to drugs or patient-related conditions such as seizures.

MicroECoG

One disadvantage of ECoG, namely, the relatively large size of ECoG electrodes (several mm in diameter) is being addressed by researchers using *microECoG* electrodes. These microelectrodes are only a fraction of a millimeter in diameter and spaced only 2–3 mm apart in a grid, allowing detection of neural activity at a much finer resolution than traditional ECoG. This opens up the possibility of decoding fine movements, such as the movements of individual fingers, or even speech, without actually penetrating the brain.

Optical Recording: Voltage-Sensitive Dyes and Two-Photon Calcium Imaging

A range of invasive optical techniques have been investigated over the past two decades for imaging neuronal activity in vivo. The most prominent of these are imaging techniques based on *voltage-sensitive dyes* and on *two-photon fluorescence microscopy*. Those based on voltage-sensitive dyes operate on the principle that once neurons are stained with a voltage-sensitive dye, their electrical activity can be imaged because the dye responds to changes in membrane potential by changing its absorption and/or fluorescence. As an example, styryl or oxonol dyes have been used to stain the upper layers of a rat's sensory cortex and a microscope objective used to image a region of the stained cortex using a photodiode array. Each detector in the array receives light from many neurons and thus the recorded optical signals correspond to summed responses from several simultaneously active neurons. Using this technique, researchers have been able to image populations of neurons in intact rat brains responding to visual, olfactory, and somatosensory stimuli (Figure 3.5).

Voltage-sensitive, dye-based optical imaging is particularly useful for imaging macroscopic features of the brain (such as feature maps in the cortex), but for more targeted imaging of neurons, the technique of *two-photon microscopy* has garnered much attention. A particularly fruitful technique has been *two-photon calcium imaging* (Figure 3.6). The technique is based on the fact that electrical activity in neurons is typically associated with changes in calcium concentration: for example, depolarization in neurons is accompanied by an influx of calcium ions due to the opening of various voltage-gated calcium channels in the membrane of the neuron. Additionally, calcium may also be released from intracellular calcium stores. Thus, one can get a window into the electrical activity of individual neurons by imaging the calcium activity caused by these electrical changes. The technique of two-

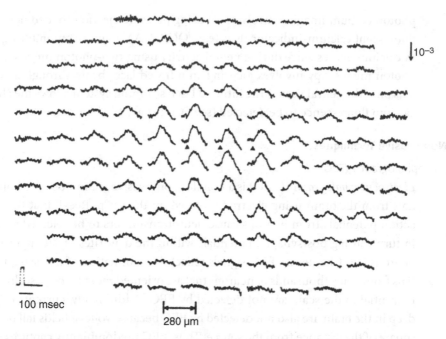

Figure 3.5.   **Optical imaging of somatosensory cortex of a rat.** Optical signals were detected by measuring fluorescence changes in somatosensory cortex of an anesthetized rat stained with a
styryl dye. Movement of a whisker caused the optical signals seen in the center of the field
(image: Scholarpedia http://www.scholarpedia.org/article/Voltage-sensitive_dye).

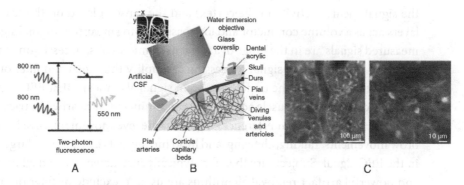

Figure 3.6.   **Optical recording using 2-photon microscopy.** (A) Illustration of the basic idea behind
2-photon microscopy showing two photons being absorbed to produce fluorescence. (B)
Diagram of the experimental setup, showing exposed cortex with sealed glass window and
microscope objective. The tip of the shaded triangle (drawn across the skull and dura) indicates location of two-photon fluorescence. (C) Two-photon imaging of neuronal and vascular
signals: (left) neurons stained with Oregon Green BAPTA-1 AM (OGB-1 AM) calcium-sensitive
dye; (right) transgenic mouse neurons expressing green fluorescent protein (GFP) (adapted
from Kherlopian et al., 2008).

photon calcium imaging involves: (1) using pressure ejection to load neurons with fluorescent calcium-indicator dyes (e.g., OGB-1 AM) and (2) monitoring changes in calcium fluorescence during neural activity using two-photon microscopy. Two-photon microscopy involves focusing an infrared laser beam through an objective lens onto the neural tissue. The infrared laser-scanning system allows the changes in calcium fluorescence to be detected (see Denk et al., 1990 for details).

3.1.2 Noninvasive Techniques

Electroencephalography (EEG)

Electroencephalography (EEG) is a popular noninvasive technique for recording signals from the brain using electrodes placed on the scalp. Recall that the spikes or action potentials from neurons cause neurotransmitters to be released at synapses, in turn causing postsynaptic potentials within the dendrites of the input-receiving neurons (see Chapter 2). EEG signals reflect the summation of postsynaptic potentials from many thousands of neurons that are oriented radially to the scalp. Currents tangential to the scalp are not detected by EEG. Additionally, currents originating deep in the brain are also not detected by EEG because voltage fields fall off with the square of the distance from the source. Thus, EEG predominantly captures electrical activity in the cerebral cortex, whose columnar arrangement of neurons and proximity to the skull favor recording by EEG. The spatial resolution of EEG is typically poor (in the square centimeter range) but the temporal resolution is good (in the milliseconds range).

The poor spatial resolution of EEG is caused primarily by the different layers of tissue (meninges, cerebrospinal fluid, skull, scalp) interposed between the source of the signal (neural activity in the cortex) and the sensor placed on the scalp. These layers act as a volume conductor and low-pass filter to smear the original signal. The measured signals are in the range of a few tens of microvolts, necessitating the use of powerful amplifiers and signal processing to amplify the signal and filter out noise. The weak amplitude of the underlying brain signal also means that EEG signals can be easily corrupted by muscle activity and contaminated by nearby electrical devices (e.g., 60 Hz power-line interference). For example, eye movements, eye blinks, eyebrow movements, talking, chewing, and head movements can all cause large artifacts in the EEG signal. Subjects are therefore typically instructed to avoid all movement, and powerful artifact removal algorithms are used to exclude or filter out portions of the EEG signal corrupted by muscle artifacts. Additional noise sources include changing electrode impedance and varying psychological states of the user due to boredom, distraction, stress, or frustration (e.g., caused by BCI mistranslation).

EEG recording involves the subject wearing a cap or a net into which the recording electrodes are placed (Figure 3.7A). In some cases, scalp locations may be prepared for recording by light abrasion to reduce impedance caused by dead skin cells. A conductive gel or paste is injected into the holes of the cap before placing the electrodes. The international 10–20 system is a convention used to specify standardized

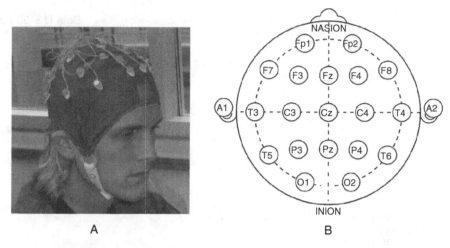

Figure 3.7. **Electroencephalography (EEG).** (A) Subject wearing a 32-electrode EEG cap. (B) International 10–20 system for standardized EEG electrode locations on the head. C = central, P = parietal, T = temporal, F = frontal, Fp = frontal polar, O = occipital, A = mastoids (image A courtesy K. Miller; image B from Wikimedia Commons).

electrode locations on the scalp (Figure 3.7B). The *mastoids* reference electrode locations behind each ear (A1 and A2). Other reference electrode locations are *nasion*, at the top of the nose, level with the eyes; and *inion*, at the base of the skull on the midline at the back of the head. From these points, the skull perimeters are measured in the transverse and median planes. Electrode locations are determined by dividing these perimeters into 10 percent and 20 percent intervals. The international 10–20 system ensures that the naming of electrodes is consistent across laboratories. The number of electrodes actually used in applications can range from a few (for targeted BCI applications) to 256 in high-density arrays.

Bipolar or unipolar electrodes can be used for measuring EEG. In the first method, the potential difference between a pair of electrodes is measured. In the latter method the potential of each electrode is compared either to a neutral electrode or to the average of all electrodes (*common average referencing* or CAR). In a typical setup, each EEG electrode is connected to one input of a differential amplifier, and the other input is connected to a reference electrode – for instance, nasion or linked mastoids (average of the two mastoids). The amplification of voltage between the active electrode and the reference is typically 1,000–100,000 times. The amplified signal is passed through an anti-aliasing filter and then digitized via an A/D (analog to digital) converter at sampling rates of up to 20 kHz depending on the application (typical sampling rates for BCI applications are in the range of 256 Hz–1kHz). After digitization, the EEG signal may be additionally filtered by a 1–50 Hz bandpass filter. This excludes noise and movement artifacts in the very low and very high frequency ranges. An additional notch filter is typically used to remove "line noise" caused by the electrical power supply (60 Hz in the United States).

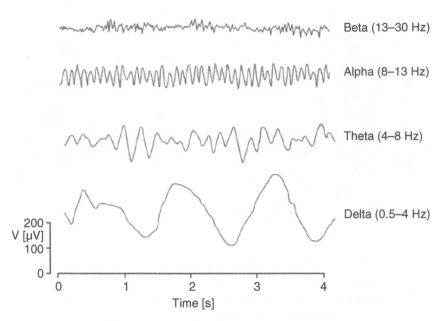

Figure 3.8. **Examples of EEG rhythms and their frequency range.** (Adapted from http://www.bem.fi/book/13/13.htm).

EEG recordings are well-suited to capturing oscillatory brain activity or "brain waves" at a variety of frequencies (see Figure 3.8 for some examples). These waves, arising for example from the synchronization of large populations of neurons, have characteristic frequency ranges and spatial distributions and are often correlated with different functional states of the brain. *Alpha waves* (or the *alpha rhythm*) are electrical fluctuations in the range 8–13 Hz and can be measured in EEG from the occipital region in awake persons when they are relaxed or their eyes are closed. A particular kind of alpha wave popular in BCI applications is known as the *mu rhythm* (8–12 Hz). It is found over sensorimotor areas in the absence of movement and is decreased or abolished when the subject performs a movement or imagines performing a movement.

Beta waves (13–30 Hz) are detectable over the parietal and frontal lobes in a person who is alert and actively concentrating. *Delta waves* have the frequency range of 0.5–4 Hz and are detectable in babies and during slow wave sleep in adults. *Theta waves*, with a frequency range of 4–8 Hz, are associated with drowsiness or "idling" in children and adults. *Gamma waves*, in the frequency range 30–100 Hz or more, have been reported in tasks involving short-term memory and multisensory integration. *High gamma* activity (70 Hz and above) has also been recently reported for motor tasks and used in ECoG BCIs (see Chapter 8).

Magnetoencephalography (MEG)

Magnetoencephalography (MEG) measures the magnetic fields produced by electrical activity in the brain using *superconducting quantum interference devices*

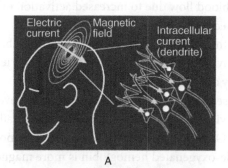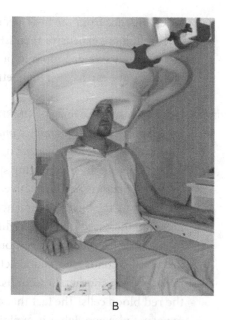

A   B

Figure 3.9. **Magnetoencephalography (MEG).** (A) Schematic diagram illustrating the orthogonal magnetic field generated by currents in dendrites of similarly oriented cortical neurons. (B) Example MEG system (image A: Wikimedia Commons; image B: http://dateline.ucdavis.edu/photos_images/dateline_images/040309/DondersMEGOle_W2.jpg).

(SQUIDs). Figure 3.9 depicts a typical MEG setup in which a subject sits in a chair and responds to stimuli on a screen by pressing buttons on a handheld device.

Both MEG and EEG signals originate from the net effect of ionic currents flowing in the dendrites of neurons due to synaptic inputs from other neurons. As shown in Figure 3.9A, these currents produce an orthogonally oriented magnetic field (as dictated by Maxwell's equations). To be detectable by MEG, these current sources need to have similar orientation (otherwise they would cancel out) and therefore, magnetic activity detected by MEG is believed to be the result of concurrent activity of tens of thousands of pyramidal neurons (Section 2.7) in the neocortex oriented perpendicular to the cortical surface. Since MEG detects the orthogonally oriented magnetic field, it is sensitive only to currents flowing tangential to the scalp. Thus it preferentially measures activity from cortical sulci (furrows in the cortical surface) rather than the gyri (ridges in the cortical surface), compared to EEG which is sensitive to both.

Like EEG, MEG offers high temporal resolution because it directly reflects neural activity, rather than metabolic activity as in the case of techniques such as fMRI, fNIR or PET described in the following sections. One advantage of MEG over EEG is that the magnetic fields produced by neural activity are not distorted by the intervening organic matter (such as the skull and the scalp), as is the case with electric fields measured by EEG. Thus, MEG offers better spatial resolution than EEG and independence from the head geometry. On the other hand, MEG systems are considerably more expensive than EEG systems, bulky and not portable, and require a magnetically shielded room to prevent interference from external magnetic signals, including the earth's own magnetic field.

Functional Magnetic Resonance Imaging (fMRI)

Functional magnetic resonance imaging (fMRI) indirectly measures neural activity in the brain by detecting changes in blood flow due to increased activation of neurons in particular brain areas during specific tasks.

When neurons become active, they consume more oxygen, which is brought to the brain by the blood. Neural activity triggers a dilation of local capillaries, resulting in an increased inflow of highly oxygenated blood that replaces oxygen-depleted blood. This hemodynamic response is comparatively slow – it appears several hundred milliseconds after neural activity and peaks at 3–6 seconds, before falling back to baseline in another 20 seconds. Oxygen is carried by the hemoglobin molecule in the red blood cells. The fact that de-oxygenated hemoglobin is more magnetic than oxygenated hemoglobin is exploited in fMRI to generate images of different cross sections of the brain showing increased activation in specific areas during a particular task. Given that it measures oxygenation levels in the blood, the signal recorded by fMRI is called the *blood oxygenation level dependent* (BOLD) response.

In typical experimental settings, subjects are made to lie down and their head is positioned inside the fMRI scanner (Figure 3.10A). Subjects may be presented with stimuli such as images, sounds or touch, and can execute simple actions such as pressing a button or moving a joystick.

A major advantage of fMRI is that its spatial resolution, typically in the 1–3 mm range, is much higher than other noninvasive techniques such as EEG and MEG. However, its temporal resolution is poor.

Functional Near Infrared (fNIR) Imaging

Functional near infrared (fNIR) imaging (Figure 3.9B) is an optical technique for measuring changes in blood oxygenation level caused by increased neural activity in the brain. This type of imaging is based on detecting near-infrared light absorbance of hemoglobin in the blood with and without oxygen. It thus provides an indirect window into ongoing brain activity in a manner similar to fMRI (see previous section). It is less cumbersome than fMRI, although it is more prone to noise and offers less spatial resolution.

Functional near infrared imaging relies on the fact that infrared light can penetrate the skull and enter a few centimeters into the cortex. Infrared emitters placed on the scalp send infrared light through the skull; this light is partly absorbed and partly reflected back through the skull, where it is detected by infrared detectors. Infrared light is absorbed differently based on the oxygen content of the blood, providing a measure of the underlying neural activity. Similar to EEG, using a number

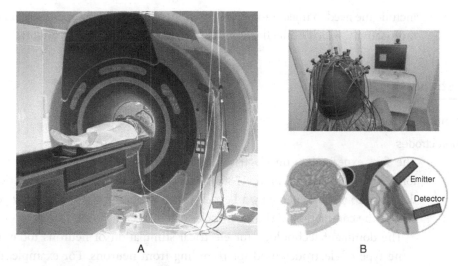

Figure 3.10. **fMRI and fNIR recording of brain activity.** (A) fMRI machine with a subject whose brain is being scanned while performing an experiment. The subject is holding a button-press device for indicating choices or outputs. (B) Top: subject wearing an fNIR cap. Bottom: illustration of how an fNIR system uses emitters and detectors for measuring changes in blood oxygenation level caused by increased neural activity (image A: Creative Commons; images B: http://neuropsychology.uni-graz.at/methods_nirs.htm).

of evenly spaced "*optodes*" (emitters and detectors) across the head allows one to construct a two-dimensional map of neural activity across the brain surface.

Functional near infrared imaging, however, is restricted by design to measuring neural activity close to the skull, unlike fMRI, which can image deep regions of the brain. On the other hand, unlike fMRI, subjects are not restricted in their movement as they are not lying down within an MR scanner. Functional near infrared imaging is not as susceptible to muscle artifacts (compared to EEG) because it relies on optical rather than electrical measurements. It is also much less expensive than fMRI and like EEG, is portable.

Positron Emission Tomography (PET)

Positron emission tomography (PET) is an older technique for measuring brain activity indirectly by detecting metabolic activity. PET measures emissions from radioactively labeled, metabolically active chemicals that have been injected into the bloodstream for transportation to the brain. The labeled compound is called a *radiotracer*. Sensors in the PET scanner detect the radioactive compound as they make their way to various areas of the brain as a result of metabolic activity caused by brain activity. This information is used to generate two- or three-dimensional images indicating the amount of brain activity. The most commonly used radiotracer is a labeled form of glucose.

The spatial resolution of PET can be comparable to fMRI, but the temporal resolution is typically quite low (on the order of several tens of seconds). Other drawbacks include the need to inject radioactive chemicals into the body and the rapid decay of radioactivity, which limits the amount of time available for experiments.

3.2 Stimulating the Brain

3.2.1 Invasive Techniques

Microelectrodes

The first experiments on electrical stimulation of the nervous system were performed by Luigi Galvani in the 1780s. In his now-classic experiment, electric current delivered to a spinal nerve by a Leyden jar or a rotating static electricity generator caused the contraction of the leg muscles of a dissected frog.

The dominant technology for electrical stimulation of neurons today uses the same type of electrodes used for recording from neurons. For example, the glass microelectrodes used for recording intracellularly from a cell can also be used to inject current into the cell to depolarize or hyperpolarize the cell (to increase or decrease the probability of spiking).

The platinum-iridium microelectrodes for extracellular recording can also be used for stimulation, although extracellular stimulation typically activates a local population of neurons near the electrode rather than a single neuron. Such electrodes have been used, for instance, in experiments where a monkey's decision in a decision-making task can be altered by stimulating neurons in a cortical area (Hanks et al., 2006). A more prominent example is *deep brain stimulation* (DBS) in which slightly larger electrodes, about a millimeter thick, are surgically implanted into the brains of Parkinson's patients. The electrical pulses, tailored to the patient, are delivered continuously to relieve symptoms such as tremors and gait problems (DBS will be discussed in more detail in Section 10.2.1). Arrays of microelectrodes are also used in cochlear implants to stimulate the auditory nerve (see Section 10.1.1 for further details). The use of stimulating microelectrodes in BCIs is beginning to grow, especially in studies involving monkeys where one set of such electrodes is used for recording and another set for stimulation. We will discuss such bidirectional BCIs in Chapter 11.

Direct Cortical Electrical Stimulation (DCES)

A semi-invasive method for stimulating neurons in the brain is to use electrodes on the surface of the cortex as discussed above for electrocorticography (ECoG). Electric current (typically less than 15 mA) is delivered across bipolar electrodes on the brain surface, usually in the form of short pulses of alternating polarity. The effect is limited to the several thousands of neurons in the local cortical tissue near the electrode pair. Stimulation effects are rapid in their onset and offset, coinciding with the duration of stimulation.

DCES can produce "positive" effects such as generating movements or causing particular sensations, or "negative" effects such as the disruption of a movement or behavior. DCES is typically used in a clinical setting for mapping the location of sensory, motor, memory, and language functions in the brains of neurosurgery patients. Its potential for providing direct feedback during brain-computer interfacing remains to be explored.

Optical Stimulation

It has been known since the work of Fork (1971) that *laser illumination* can produce excitation in a neuron. Later work demonstrated that *two-photon* laser illumination can be used to focus the laser light much more precisely than earlier techniques, allowing, for example, excitation of single neurons in brain slices from a mouse's visual cortex. Illumination is applied tangentially to the membrane of the cell. The excitation occurs at short latency and is modulated by both the intensity and wavelength of illumination. Although the exact mechanisms are unknown, it has been suggested that excitation occurs due to a transient perforation of the cell's membrane that is quickly re-sealed when illumination is discontinued.

An alternate approach, known as *optogenetic stimulation*, is to use genetic manipulation to make only certain neurons responsive to illumination. For example, one can express genes that code for specific elements of the invertebrate retina in hippocampal neurons. The retinal elements then produce a light-controlled source of excitatory current in the affected neurons, as they would in the retina. When exposed to light, the neurons transfected with the retinal elements depolarize and generate action potentials at latencies between one and several seconds. Further, increasing the light intensity tends to increase the firing rate of the neurons.

In summary, while two-photon laser illumination offers a method to selectively excite single neurons, optogenetic stimulation could provide a means to selectively excite only a specific class or classes of neurons that have been genetically altered using cell-specific methods. *Optogenetics* is a promising emerging technology but has not been explored much in the context of brain-computer interfacing because a majority of the studies to date demonstrating the technique have been done on brain slices or cultured cells rather than on intact brains of behaving animals. Research by Diester, Shenoy, and others (2011) is helping address this limitation.

3.2.2 Noninvasive Techniques

Transcranial Magnetic Stimulation (TMS)

TMS relies on the close relationship between electricity and magnetism and the process of *electromagnetic induction*: when current is passed through a coil of wire, a magnetic field is generated perpendicular to the current flow in the coil. If a second coil is placed within the magnetic field, a current is generated in a direction opposite the first flow. TMS exploits this phenomenon by placing a plastic-enclosed coil of wire next to the skull to produce a rapidly changing magnetic field oriented orthogonal to the plane of the coil. The magnetic field passes unimpeded through the skin and skull and, by the principle of electromagnetic induction, produces an electric current in the brain that activates populations of neurons.

The magnetic field produced by TMS is believed to penetrate to a maximum depth of about 3 to 5 centimeters into the brain, in the area directly adjacent to the coil. The technique is therefore suitable only for activating neurons in the superficial layers of the brain. A major advantage of TMS is that it is noninvasive and its use is not restricted to patients. Its disadvantages include the relatively high power requirements and poor localization of the area of stimulation compared to invasive techniques such as microelectrodes and DCES.

Transcranial Ultrasound

A more recent technique for noninvasive stimulation of brain circuits is transcranial pulsed ultrasound. Ultrasound is a mechanical pressure wave (sound wave) having a frequency above the range of human hearing (>20 kHz). Ultrasound has the favorable property that it can be transmitted through solid structures, including bone and soft tissues, making it well suited for noninvasive medical applications. It is known that high-intensity ultrasound (> 1W/cm^2) affects neural activity through thermal effects, but such stimulation can cause tissue damage. Fortunately, researchers have found that low-intensity (< 500 mW/cm^2) *pulsed* ultrasound can also influence neural activation but without thermal effects or tissue damage. For example, Tufail et al. (2010) showed that low-intensity pulsed ultrasound (frequency of 0.35 MHz, 80 cycles/pulse, with a pulse repetition frequency of 1.5 kHz) stimulation of intact motor cortices of mice increased the spiking frequency of motor cortical neurons and evoked muscle contraction and movements in 92 percent of the mice tested.

The exact mechanisms underlying the effects of ultrasound on neural activation are unknown, but it has been suggested that ultrasound may affect neural ion channels with mechanically sensitive gating kinetics or produce fluid-mechanical effects on the cellular environments of neurons, thereby affecting their resting membrane potentials. Pulsed ultrasound may offer an advantage over TMS in terms of spatial resolution in that it can stimulate brain regions 1–2 mm in diameter, compared to 1 cm or greater in the case of TMS. It remains to be seen whether it can be used as part of a noninvasive BCI system for delivering targeted feedback to specific brain areas in closed-loop BCI tasks.

3.3 Simultaneous Recording and Stimulation

Although most current BCIs only record ongoing neural activity to control devices and provide visual or tactile feedback, some researchers are exploring the possibility of simultaneously recording neural signals and providing direct feedback through neural stimulation. Two possible approaches being explored include using arrays of

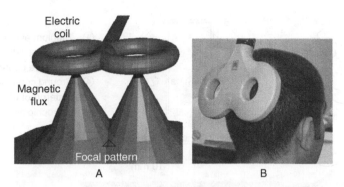

Figure 3.11. **Transcranial magnetic stimulation (TMS).** (A) Schematic illustration of electrical stimulation produced by electromagnetic induction using a "butterfly" coil. (B) TMS of visual cortex of a subject using a butterfly coil (images: Creative Commons, http://www.princeton.edu/~napl/).

microelectrodes and more sophisticated implantable chips, such as the Neurochip, that implement signal processing and other algorithms, processing neural activity and delivering stimulation within the chip itself rather than being tethered to a computer.

3.3.1 Multielectrode Arrays

As described above, microelectrodes used for recording spiking activity can also be used to deliver depolarizing or hyperpolarizing current to excite or inhibit neurons. Thus, in a multielectrode array, some electrodes can be set aside for recording and others may be used for stimulation. We will explore such a use of multielectrode arrays in Chapter 11.

3.3.2 Neurochip

The Neurochip (Figure 3.12) is an example of an integrated chip that records from one or more neurons, performs useful signal processing and other computation on-board the chip, and, based on the results of these computations, delivers appropriate stimulation to one or more neurons (Mavoori et al., 2005). The chip is thus a self-contained unit, allowing the implanted subject to roam freely and engage in natural behaviors. The battery-powered chip has an array of twelve moveable tungsten microwire electrodes (diameter 50 mm; impedance 0.5 MV; interelectrode spacing 500 mm). The chip contains a microprocessor that can perform spike sorting (Section 4.1) on signals from one set of electrodes and instruct a stimulator circuit to deliver electrical pulses via another set of electrodes. Short segments of recorded signals and desired stimulation patterns can be stored to the on-chip memory.

The Neurochip has been used in monkeys to demonstrate that consistent activation of a group of neurons in correlation with the activation of another can cause a

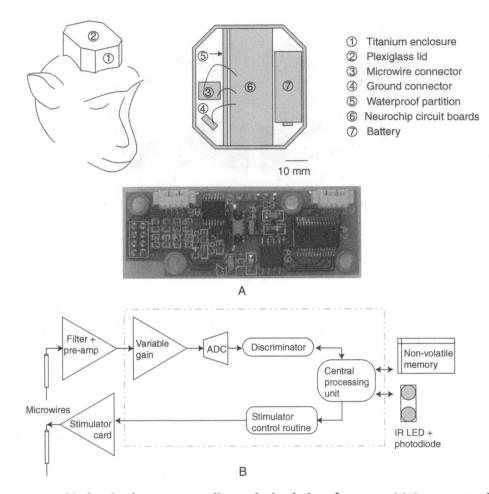

Figure 3.12. **Neurochip for simultaneous recording and stimulation of neurons.** (A) Components of the implant containing Neurochip. (B). Architecture of the Neurochip, showing analog and digital components, on-chip memory, and IR LED and photodiode for wireless communication of up to 1 meter (adapted from Mavoori et al., 2005).

strengthening of connections between the two groups of neurons. We will examine the use of the Neurochip for BCI applications in Chapter 11.

3.4 Summary

This chapter introduced some of the major methods available today to record from and stimulate the brain. Invasive methods typically employ one or more microelectrodes implanted inside the brain to record electrical activity in the form of spikes. Newly developed techniques exploit a combination of genetic manipulation and optical imaging to record activities of large populations of neurons.

Semi-invasive techniques such as ECoG record the combined electrical activity emanating from large populations of neurons from the surface of the brain.

Noninvasive techniques have been developed to record electrical activity from the scalp (EEG), magnetic field fluctuations caused by electrical activity in the brain (MEG), and changes in blood oxygenation level occurring as a result of neural activity (fMRI and fNIR). In subsequent chapters, we examine in more detail the ability of these techniques to provide useful signals for BCI applications.

3.5 Questions and Exercises

1. What are the techniques currently available for invasive recording of brain signals? Specify for each technique whether they can record spikes from individual neurons.
2. Explain the difference between intracellular and extracellular recording. Which of these techniques is typically used for recording in awake, behaving animals?
3. State whether the following statements are true or false:
   a. Intracellular recording allows the membrane potential of an individual neuron to be recorded.
   b. The patch clamp technique is an example of an extracellular recording technique.
   c. The tip of a microelectrode is usually about 10^{-6} m or less in diameter.
   d. A tetrode can be used to record from at most four neurons at the same time.
   e. Multielectrode arrays can be used for simultaneously recording the spiking activity of dozens of neurons.
   f. Electrocorticography (ECoG) involves recording electrical potentials from the surface of the brain.
4. Discuss the relationship between the signal recorded by an ECoG electrode and the neural activity underneath that electrode.
5. Compare and contrast the strengths and weaknesses of using a multielectrode array versus an ECoG array for recording brain activity.
6. What is the approximate voltage range of the neural signal measured using a microelectrode versus an ECoG electrode?
7. Explain how voltage-sensitive dyes can be used to image the activities of populations of neurons.
8. Describe the principle behind two-photon imaging of neural activity based on fluorescent calcium-indicator dyes.
9. What component of neural activity does EEG measure? What region of the brain contributes the most to the EEG signal?
10. What is the 10–20 system used in EEG?
11. Describe the frequency range and brain phenomena associated with the following EEG waves:
    a. Alpha
    b. Beta
    c. Gamma

      d. Mu

      e. Theta

12. Enumerate the strengths and weaknesses of MEG compared to EEG as a noninvasive brain recording technique.

13. Describe the relationship between the signal measured by fMRI and the underlying neural activity.

14. What are some of the strengths and weaknesses of fMRI compared to EEG? Comment particularly on the spatial and temporal resolution afforded by these two methods.

15. Compare and contrast fNIR imaging with fMRI for recording brain activity.

16. Describe two invasive and two noninvasive techniques for stimulating neurons in intact brains. Explain the trade-off between specificity in stimulation versus invasiveness.

17. What are the benefits offered by an implantable chip such as the Neurochip for simultaneous recording and stimulation, compared to using a standard array of microelectrodes?

4

Signal Processing

In this chapter, we review the signal-processing methods applied to recorded brain signals in BCIs for tasks ranging from extracting spikes from the raw signals recorded from invasive electrodes to extracting features for classification. For many of the techniques, we use EEG as the noninvasive recording modality to illustrate the concepts involved, although the techniques could be applied to signals from other sources as well such as ECoG and MEG.

4.1 Spike Sorting

Invasive approaches to brain-computer interfacing typically rely on recording spikes from an array of microelectrodes. The goal of signal-processing methods for such an input signal is to reliably isolate and extract the spikes being emitted by a single neuron per recording electrode. This procedure is usually called *spike sorting*.

The signal recorded by an extracellular electrode implanted in the brain is typically a mixture of signals from several neighboring neurons, with spikes from closer neurons producing larger amplitude deflections in the recorded signal. This signal is often referred to as *multiunit hash* or *neural hash* (Figure 4.1A). Although hash could also potentially be used as input to brain-computer interfaces, the more traditional form of input is spikes from individual neurons. Spike sorting methods allow spikes from a single neuron to be extracted from hash.

The simplest spike sorting method is to classify spikes according to their *peak amplitude*. This works well when the extracellular electrode picks up strong signals from neurons at slightly different distances, resulting in different amplitudes. However, in many cases, the peak amplitudes may be the same for different neurons, making the method infeasible. A better approach, used in many commercial systems, is the *window discriminator* method in which the experimenter visually examines the data and places windows on aligned recordings of spikes of the same shape (Figure 4.1B). The method then assigns all future spikes crossing one or more of these windows to the same neuron. The method suffers from the drawback that the

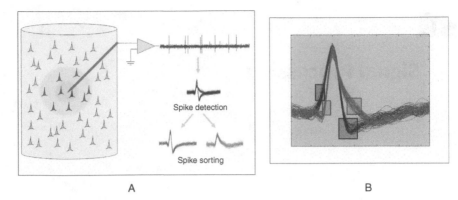

Figure 4.1.   **Spike sorting.** (A) Illustration of how extracellular recording can result in a signal (called multiunit hash) containing spikes from multiple neurons. These spikes can exhibit different amplitudes and shapes. (B) The commonly used method of window discriminators for spike sorting involves the experimenter placing different windows on example spikes to allow the computer to separate out the spikes (two in this case) according to the windows traversed (adapted from http://www.scholarpedia.org/article/Spike_sorting).

experimenter has to manually label spikes as coming from one neuron or another. The recent trend has been toward clustering spikes automatically into groups based on shape, where each group corresponds to spikes from one neuron. The shape of a spike is characterized by features extracted using wavelets or principal component analysis (PCA) (see Sections 4.3 and 4.5).

4.2 Frequency Domain Analysis

Noninvasive approaches such as EEG are based on signals that reflect the activity of several thousands of neurons (see Chapter 3). The recorded signal thus is able to capture only the correlated activities of large populations of neurons, such as oscillatory activity. For example, overt and imagined movements typically activate premotor and primary sensorimotor areas, resulting in amplitude/power changes in the mu (8–12 Hz), beta (13–30 Hz) and gamma (>30 Hz) rhythms in EEG/ECoG. The existence of such oscillatory activity makes analysis, such as Fourier analysis, of the signals in the frequency domain particularly useful.

4.2.1 Fourier Analysis

The basic idea behind Fourier analysis is to decompose a signal into a weighted sum of sine and cosine waves of different frequencies. Consider the example in Figure 4.2. Suppose you are given a step function that is a constant positive value for some time and then becomes a constant negative value, followed by the original positive value again (Figure 4.2A). As shown in Figure 4.2B–F, you can approximate the step function by adding sine waves of different frequencies, each weighted by a

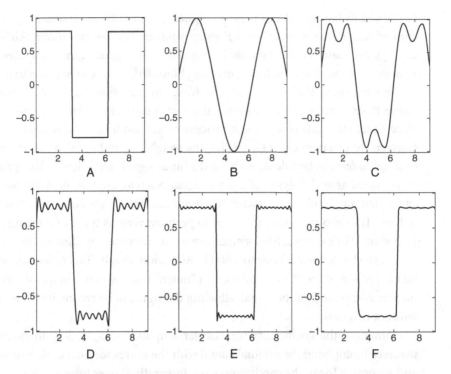

Figure 4.2.   **Approximating a step function with sine waves.** The figure shows how a step function
can be approximated as a weighted sum of sine functions of different frequencies and amplitudes. (A) Step function that alternates between a constant positive value (+0.8) and a constant negative value (-0.8). (B) sin(x). (C) sin(x) + (1/3)sin(3x). (D) sin(x) + (1/3)sin(3x) +
(1/5)sin(5x)+...+(1/11)*sin(11x). (E) sin(x) + (1/3)sin(3x) +...+ (1/51)*sin(51x). (F) sin(x)
+ (1/3)sin(3x) +...+ (1/151)*sin(151x).

different coefficient (amplitude). The step function can thus be decomposed into a
set of sine functions (a potentially infinite number of them) of specific frequencies
and amplitudes.

Fourier analysis involves decomposing a time-varying signal $s(t)$, defined over an
interval $t = -T/2$ to $t = T/2$, into a weighted sum of sine and cosine waves of different
frequencies:

$$s(t) = \frac{a_0}{2} + a_1 \cos(\omega t) + a_2 \cos(2\omega t) + \ldots + b_1 \sin(\omega t) + b_2 \sin(2\omega t) + \ldots$$

$$= \frac{a_0}{2} + \sum_{n=1}^{\infty} a_n \cos(n\omega t) + \sum_{n=1}^{\infty} b_n \sin(n\omega t) \tag{4.1}$$

$$= \frac{a_0}{2} + \sum_{n=1}^{\infty} a_n \cos(2\pi n f t) + \sum_{n=1}^{\infty} b_n \sin(2\pi n f t)$$

where ω is the angular frequency, defined as $\omega = 2\pi/T$, and f is the ordinary frequency
(measured in Hertz or cycles per second), defined as $f = 1/T$. The time interval T can

be viewed as the period of a periodic signal $s(t)$. The above expansion of $s(t)$ into a sum of infinite terms is called a *Fourier series* or *Fourier expansion*. Although we don't go into details here, it should be noted that the signal $s(t)$ needs to meet certain reasonable conditions (such as remaining bounded) for the expansion to exist.

We can regard the cosine and sine waves in Equation 4.1 as "basis functions." These basis functions can be summed up with different weights a_n and b_n to produce different kinds of signals, a process corresponding to "synthesis" of signals. Conversely, given an input signal $s(t)$, the weights a_n and b_n (also called *coefficients* or *amplitudes*) can be calculated from the input signal (see below) – this process can be regarded as an "analysis" of a given signal. Such an analysis is useful because the calculated amplitudes tell us what the dominant frequency components of the signal are. The decomposition allows us to perform various types of filtering based on frequency. For example, EEG signals are often corrupted by "line noise" around 60 Hz (in the United States) due to a 60 Hz AC power supply. This noise can effectively be filtered out of the EEG signal using a "notch" filter, which removes the 60 Hz frequency component of the signal, allowing the signal to be reconstituted or analyzed without this noise.

Estimating the coefficients (or Fourier amplitudes) a_n and b_n in Equation 4.1 involves multiplying the original signal with the corresponding cosine or sine wave and summing (or in the continuous case, integrating) over time:

$$a_n = \frac{2}{T} \int_{-T/2}^{T/2} s(t) \cos(n\omega t) dt$$
$$b_n = \frac{2}{T} \int_{-T/2}^{T/2} s(t) \sin(n\omega t) dt$$

(4.2)

One can regard these equations as basically performing a cross-correlation between the input signal and a cosine or sine wave of a particular frequency, with the strength of the correlation (the "similarity") being captured by the corresponding coefficient a_n or b_n.

For $n = 0$, we have $\cos(0 \cdot \omega t) = 1$. Thus, the first term $a_0/2$ in the Fourier decomposition (Equation 4.1) is simply the average of the input signal (the "DC" or zero frequency component) over the interval $-T/2$ to $T/2$:

$$\frac{a_0}{2} = \frac{1}{T} \int_{-T/2}^{T/2} s(t) dt$$

(4.3)

Similarly, the coefficient a_1 associated with the term $\cos(2\pi f t)$ captures the amplitude of the cosine component at frequency f, the coefficient a_2 captures the amplitude of the cosine component at frequency $2f$, and so on.

The Fourier decomposition of a signal into its frequency amplitudes thus provides a useful representation of the signal in terms of its frequency content rather than time. Figure 4.2 provides several examples of time-varying signals and their

Fourier decomposition. Notice how a signal that spans a short temporal extent (e.g., "Boxcar" or "Impulse") occupies a large or infinite extent in the frequency domain.

A simpler form of the Fourier series can be obtained by allowing the Fourier coefficients to be complex numbers. Recall that complex numbers are of the form $a + jb$ where $j = \sqrt{-1}$. Recall also the identity $e^{j\theta} = \cos\theta + j\sin\theta$. We can therefore define a single set of coefficients c_n as:

$$
\begin{aligned}
c_n &= \frac{a_n - jb_n}{2} \quad n > 0 \\[2mm]
&= \frac{a_0}{2} \quad n = 0 \\[2mm]
&= \frac{a_n + jb_n}{2} \quad n < 0
\end{aligned}
\tag{4.4}
$$

The Fourier series for a signal $s(t)$ then becomes:

$$
s(t) = \sum_{n=-\infty}^{\infty} c_n e^{jn\omega t}
\tag{4.5}
$$

where

$$
c_n = \frac{1}{T} \int_{-T/2}^{T/2} s(t) e^{-jn\omega t} dt
\tag{4.6}
$$

The transformation to the set of coefficients c_n given by Equation 4.6 is also called the *Fourier transform* (FT) of the signal $s(t)$. The transform is reversible: the original signal can be recovered given the coefficients c_n using Equation 4.5 – this is called the *inverse Fourier transform* (IFT).

4.2.2 Discrete Fourier Transform (DFT)

For BCI applications, the brain signals are typically sampled at discrete time intervals. The Fourier series discussed above can be modified to apply to a discretely sampled signal as well. The *discrete Fourier transform* (DFT) takes as input a time series $S(t)$ sampled at time points $t = 0, \ldots, T\text{-}1$ and transforms it to the corresponding complex Fourier coefficients:

$$
C(n) = \frac{1}{T} \sum_{t=0}^{T-1} S(t) e^{-jn\omega t} \quad n = 0, \ldots, T-1
\tag{4.7}
$$

where $\omega = 2\pi/T$ as before.

The *inverse discrete Fourier transform* (IDFT) is similarly defined as:

$$
S(t) = \sum_{n=0}^{T-1} C(n) e^{jn\omega t} \quad n = 0, \ldots, T-1
\tag{4.8}
$$

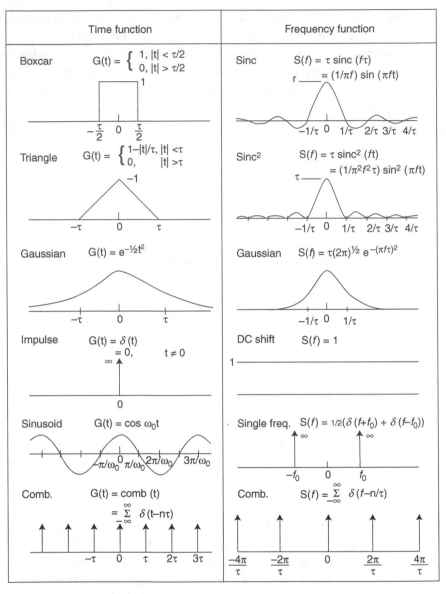

Figure 4.3. **Examples of time-varying signals and their Fourier transforms.** (Image: Creative Commons, http://wiki.seg.org/index.php/File:Segf19.jpg).

As in the previous section, the complex Fourier coefficient $C(n)$ captures both the amplitude and phase of the nth sinusoidal component. These can be recovered using the polar form of complex numbers as:

$$\text{Amplitude } A(n) = \sqrt{\text{Re}(C(n))^2 + \text{Im}(C(n))^2} \tag{4.9}$$

$$\text{Phase } \varphi(n) = \arctan(\text{Im}(C(n)), \text{Re}(C(n))) \tag{4.10}$$

where $\text{Re}(x)$ and $\text{Im}(x)$ denote the real and imaginary parts of x. The amplitude values $A(n)$ for $n = 0,\ldots, T\text{-}1$ define the *amplitude spectrum* of the signal while the $\varphi(n)$ values define the *phase spectrum*. In typical BCI applications, we are interested in the magnitude of changes in the different frequency components during the course of a task. While the amplitude spectrum can be used for this purpose, it is more common to square the amplitude values and use the *power spectrum* of the signal:

$$\text{Power } P(n) = A(n)^2 = \text{Re}(C(n))^2 + \text{Im}(C(n))^2 \qquad (4.11)$$

4.2.3 Fast Fourier Transform (FFT)

One can compute the DFT based on its definition above, but for a signal with T points, this takes approximately T^2 arithmetical operations. The running time of the algorithm is thus quadratic in signal size T. For very large T (e.g., in the millions), this can be quite slow.

The *fast Fourier transform* (FFT) is a more efficient way of computing the DFT. It runs in time approximately $T \log T$, which can result in huge savings in computation time for large sizes T. The most common FFT algorithm, the Cooley-Tukey algorithm, uses a "divide and conquer" strategy and recursively breaks down a DFT into many smaller DFTs. Most signal-processing packages come with an FFT implementation, making the FFT the most commonly used method for transforming a time-varying signal to the frequency domain.

4.2.4 Spectral Features

Many BCI systems rely on features extracted from the power spectrum of a brain signal such as EEG or ECoG over a time interval. The power spectrum is first computed using an FFT, and the power in a particular frequency band is used as a *spectral feature* in further analysis (such as classification). For example, given that motor movement or imagery is known to reduce the power in the mu frequency band (8–12 Hz), we could use the power in the mu band as a feature in a BCI to allow a subject to move a cursor using motor imagery. Another common approach is to use motor screening to find subject-specific frequency bands: the subject is asked to perform a variety of movements, and the frequency bands that exhibit robust changes in power during movement are then utilized in subsequent BCI experiments involving movement imagery. A more sophisticated approach is to utilize a bank of spectral features and allow a machine learning algorithm to automatically select features that enhance classification accuracy on test data.

4.3 Wavelet Analysis

The Fourier transform represents an original signal with a set of "basis" functions, namely, sines and cosines of different frequencies. However, because sines and

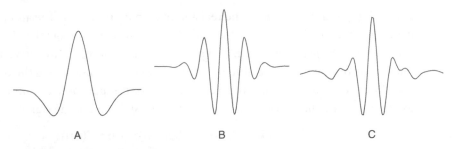

Figure 4.4.   **Different types of mother wavelets.** (A) Mexican hat. (B) Morlet. (C) Meyer. A linear combination of scaled and translated copies of a mother wavelet can be used to represent any signal.

cosines occupy an infinite temporal extent, the Fourier transform does a poor job of representing signals that are finite and non-periodic, or have sharp peaks and discontinuities. Furthermore, brain signals such as EEG are typically non-stationary (i.e., the statistical properties change over time), breaking the assumption of a stationary signal in Fourier analysis. One way of addressing this problem is to perform Fourier analysis over short-time windows, a procedure known as the *short-time* (or *short-term*) *Fourier transform* (STFT). The STFT however leaves open the question of the size of the window, with small windows providing good temporal but poor frequency resolution and large windows providing better frequency resolution but poor temporal resolution. This realization led to the development of the wavelet transform, which seeks to achieve the best tradeoff between temporal and frequency resolution.

Rather than using sines and cosines, the *wavelet transform* (WT) uses finite basis functions called *wavelets*, which are scaled and translated copies of a single finite-length waveform known as the *mother wavelet* (Figure 4.4). By using basis functions at different scales, the wavelet transform allows a signal to be analyzed at multiple resolutions, with larger scale components revealing coarse features in the input signal and smaller scale components revealing finer structure. Moreover, their finite extent allows wavelets (unlike the sines and cosines used in Fourier analysis) to represent signals that are non-periodic or have sharp discontinuities.

As in the case of the Fourier transform, the wavelet transform represents the original signal as a linear combination of basis functions, in this case, the wavelets (see Figure 4.5). Analysis of the signal is performed using the corresponding wavelet coefficients. Most current signal-processing packages include the wavelet transform as one of the available options and provide a variety of choices for the mother wavelet.

4.4 Time Domain Analysis

4.4.1 Hjorth Parameters

Hjorth parameters, introduced by B. Hjorth in 1970, provide a fast way of computing three important characteristics of a time-varying signal, namely, the mean power,

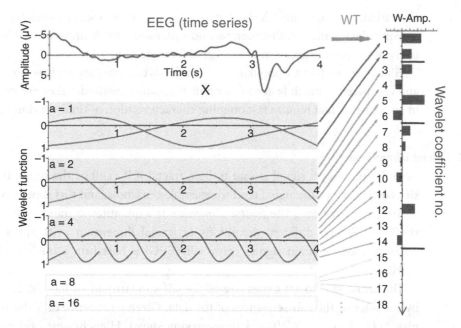

Figure 4.5.   **Example of the wavelet transform.** The EEG signal at the top is an average over several trials. This signal can be decomposed into a weighted linear combination of the wavelets shown below (wavelets for a = 1 to 4 are shown; those for 8 to 16 are not shown). Each wavelet is a scaled and translated version of a mother wavelet (two translated copies are shown at scale a = 1). The scaling factor is decreased by the index a, which is doubled at each step up to a = 16. This leads to 2 wavelets at a = 1, 4 at a =2, 8 at a =4, etc. The wavelet coefficients or weights, which represent the wavelet transform for this signal, are shown as bars on the right. Note that these coefficients capture various characteristics of the signal, e.g., the negative fluctuation between 3s and 4s is an "event related potential" (ERP) and is captured by the large coefficients for wavelets 5 and 12 (from Hinterberger et al., 2003).

the root-mean-square frequency, and the root-mean-square frequency spread. These parameters are also called "normalized slope descriptors" because they can be computed from the first and second derivatives of the signal.

Mathematically, the three Hjorth parameters, which are termed "activity," "mobility," and "complexity," are defined as follows:

$$A = a_0$$

$$M = \sqrt{\frac{a_2}{a_0}}$$

$$C = \sqrt{\frac{a_4}{a_0}}$$

(4.12)

where a_0 is the variance (or equivalently, the mean power) of the signal in the epoch under measurement, a_2 is the variance of the first derivative of the signal, and a_4

the variance of the second derivative of the signal. These measures can be shown to be equivalent to the zeroth-order, second-order and fourth-order moments respectively of the power spectrum of the signal (see Equation 4.11).

Hjorth parameters are popular in EEG analysis because they are based on variance and are therefore much faster to compute than other methods. They are thus useful in applications that require fast ongoing characterization of time-varying signals.

4.4.2 Fractal Dimension

Broadly speaking, a signal is said to be a fractal if it exhibits the property of self-similarity: parts of the signal tend to resemble the whole, and this similarity repeats in a recursive fashion. The *fractal dimension* is a quantitative measure of this self-similarity. Several different definitions of fractal dimension exist but a popular measure used for brain signals (especially EEG) is based on a method proposed by Higuchi.

The intuition is to get a measure of the self-similarity in an input data sequence by considering the sub-sequences of the data. Given a sequence of N discrete samples $X(1)$, $X(2)$, ..., $X(N)$ of a time-varying signal, Higuchi's method constructs sub-sequences by varying the time interval k between data samples:

$$X_k^m : X(m), \ X(m+k), \ X(m+2k), \ldots$$

for starting time $m = 1, \ldots, k$.

The goal is to compute the "length" $L(k)$ of the input signal at different time intervals k and estimate the *fractal dimension* D from the relationship:

$$L(k) \propto k^{-D} \tag{4.13}$$

The length of a particular X_k^m is estimated as:

$$L_m(k) = \frac{1}{k}\left(\sum_{i=1}^{M} | X(m+ik) - X(m+(i-1)k)|\right)\left(\frac{N-1}{Mk}\right) \tag{4.14}$$

where M is the largest integer less than or equal to $(N-m)/k$. For each interval k, the average length $\langle L(k)\rangle$ is calculated and plotted as a function of k on a log-log plot. If $\langle L(k)\rangle \approx k^{-D}$ for the input data, then the log-log plot should approximate a straight line with slope $-D$. Thus, the fractal dimension D can be recovered from the slope of the best fitting line using a standard least-squares fitting procedure. This method yields fractal dimensions between 1 and 2, with $D \approx 1$ for simple curves (e.g., flat line) and D closer to 2 for highly irregular curves that fill the whole two-dimensional plane.

The fractal dimension D for brain signals such as EEG can range between 1.4 and 1.7, with higher values signifying highly spiky activity such as seizures. In typical BCI applications, D values are calculated using a sliding window (e.g., 100 ms) and used as a local feature for characterizing the "complexity" of the time-varying brain signal.

4.4.3 Autoregressive (AR) Modeling

Autoregressive (AR) models rely on the fact that natural signals tend to be correlated over time (or even other dimensions such as space). Thus, it is frequently possible to predict the next measurement based on the values of the past few measurements. A traditional AR model uses a set of coefficients a_i to predict the current signal measurement x_t based on past measurements:

$$x_t = \sum_{i=1}^{p} a_i x_{t-i} + \varepsilon \qquad (4.15)$$

where ε is assumed to be a zero mean white noise process that accounts for the differences between the signal and its linear weighted sum approximation. The parameter p is called the *order* of the AR model and determines the window of past inputs used for predicting the current input. It is either chosen through an optimization process such as cross validation (Section 5.1.4) or fixed a priori to a small arbitrary number.

The traditional AR model assumes the statistical properties of the signal are stationary so that a single set of coefficients a_i can be used. However, brain signals tend to be non-stationary, and one consequently requires a time-varying set of coefficients $a_{i,t}$. This leads to an Adaptive Autoregressive (AAR) Model:

$$x_t = \sum_{i=1}^{p} a_{i,t} x_{t-i} + \varepsilon_t \qquad (4.16)$$

The time-varying coefficients $a_{i,t}$ can be updated on-line using a recursive least-squares optimization procedure such as Kalman filtering (see below). The coefficients $a_{i,t}$ capture the local statistical structure of the signal as it evolves over time and can be used as features in further processing (e.g., classification) in a BCI.

4.4.4 Bayesian Filtering

The time domain methods discussed above do not explicitly maintain estimates of uncertainty of the signal properties being computed over time. Maintaining a representation of uncertainty can be important in BCI because potentially disastrous actions based on poor estimates can be avoided if the amount of uncertainty associated with an estimate is taken into account before committing to a decision. *Bayesian filtering* techniques provide a statistically sound methodology for estimating signal properties and their uncertainty.

We begin by considering the definition of conditional probability of a random variable x given another random variable y (see Appendix, Equation A.10):

$$P(x \mid y) = \frac{P(x, y)}{P(y)} \qquad (4.17)$$

where $P(x,y)$ is the joint probability of x and y, and $P(y)$ is the probability of y. The same definition gives us:

$$P(y\mid x)=\frac{P(y,x)}{P(x)}=\frac{P(x,y)}{P(x)}$$

Therefore,

$$P(x,y)=P(x\mid y)P(y)=P(y\mid x)P(x)$$

This simple observation gives rise to one of the most important theorems in probability and statistics, namely *Bayes' theorem* or *Bayes' rule*:

$$P(x\mid y)=\frac{P(y\mid x)\ P(x)}{P(y)} \tag{4.18}$$

where $P(x\mid y)$ is called the *posterior probability* of x given y, $P(y\mid x)$ is called the *likelihood*, and $P(x)$ is the *prior probability* of x. The probability $P(y)$ can be computed by summing over x:

$$P(y)=\sum_{x}P(x,y)=\sum_{x}P(y\mid x)\ P(x)$$

Thus, Bayes' rule can be expressed as:

$$P(x\mid y)=\frac{P(y\mid x)\ P(x)}{\sum_{x}P(y\mid x)\ P(x)} \tag{4.19}$$

Bayes' rule has profound consequences for the statistical estimation of signal properties because it prescribes how evidence from measurements, represented by $P(y\mid x)$, can be combined with prior knowledge and beliefs, expressed as $P(x)$. For example, suppose y represents EEG measurements and x represents a stimulus that caused the brain response. For a BCI application, we are interested in finding the cause of a measured EEG signal, which corresponds to estimating the posterior probability $P(stimulus\mid EEG)$. This probability is hard to estimate directly but the probability $P(EEG\mid stimulus)$ can be estimated by exposing the subject to stimuli and collecting stimulus-response data from a number of trials. The prior probability of the stimulus $P(x)$ could be fixed a priori by the experimenter or can be estimated from data.

Bayes' rule can be extended to estimate posterior probability from a series of measurements made over time. Suppose we make the measurement y_i at time step i. We would like to know the posterior probability of the unknown state or event x, *given all the measurements* we have made so far, i.e., $P(x\mid y_1,\dots,y_t)$. We can again apply Bayes' rule to obtain:

$$P(x\mid y_1,\dots,y_t)=\frac{P(y_t\mid x,y_1,\dots,y_{t-1})P(x\mid y_1,\dots,y_{t-1})}{P(y_t\mid y_1,\dots,y_{t-1})} \tag{4.20}$$

The above equation can be simplified if one makes the reasonable assumption that the measurement y_t is conditionally independent of all previous measurements given the state x. This leads to the following *Bayesian filter* or update rule:

$$P(x \mid y_1, \ldots, y_t) = \alpha \, P(y_t \mid x) \, P(x \mid y_1, \ldots, y_{t-1}) \qquad (4.21)$$

where $\alpha = 1 / P(y_t \mid y_1, \ldots, y_{t-1})$ is the normalization constant. Note that the Bayesian filter equation is recursive: the estimate of the posterior at time t is computed by combining the previous estimate at time t-1 with the likelihood of the current measurement y_t.

A final addition to the Bayesian model above is to allow the state x to vary over time. This would correspond, for example, to the general case where the stimuli or other sources of the brain signal are dynamic. In the simplest and most common case, these dynamics are assumed to be Markovian, i.e., the probability of the next state depends only on the current state and not on previous states: this probability is given by $P(x_t \mid x_{t-1})$. To derive the general Bayesian filtering equation for x_t, we begin by considering Equation 4.21 we encountered above:

$$P(x_t \mid y_1, \ldots, y_t) = \alpha \, P(y_t \mid x_t) \, P(x_t \mid y_1, \ldots, y_{t-1})$$

This equation is simply an application of Bayes' rule, but it illustrates the "prediction-correction" property common to filtering algorithms: a prediction $P(x_t \mid y_1, \ldots, y_{t-1})$ is first made using past measurements, and this prediction is then corrected using the new measurement as given by the likelihood $P(y_t \mid x_t)$. The prediction itself can be computed recursively from the filter estimate at the previous time step:

$$
\begin{aligned}
P(x_t \mid y_1, \ldots, y_t) &= \alpha \, P(y_t \mid x_t) \, P(x_t \mid y_1, \ldots, y_{t-1}) \\
&= \alpha \, P(y_t \mid x_t) \sum_{x_{t-1}} P(x_t, x_{t-1} \mid y_1, \ldots, y_{t-1})
\end{aligned}
\qquad (4.22)
$$

Using the Markov assumption, we obtain the *general Bayesian filtering* equation:

$$P(x_t \mid y_1, \ldots, y_t) = \alpha \, P(y_t \mid x_t) \sum_{x_{t-1}} P(x_t \mid x_{t-1}) P(x_{t-1} \mid y_1, \ldots, y_{t-1}). \qquad (4.23)$$

This equation prescribes how information from a new measurement y_t should be combined with the previous posterior $P(x_{t-1} \mid y_1, \ldots, y_{t-1})$ to obtain the new posterior distribution at time t. As we will see, popular statistical filtering techniques such as Kalman filtering and particle filtering can be seen as specific instantiations of Equation 4.23.

More generally, Bayesian filtering can be viewed as performing probabilistic inference in a *Dynamic Bayesian Network* (DBN), which is a type of *graphical model* in which nodes represent random variables (in our case, states x_t and observations y_t) and arrows from a node to another node represent conditional probabilities (in our case, $P(x_t \mid x_{t-1})$ and $P(y_t \mid x_t)$). The interested reader is referred to the textbook by Koller and Friedman (2009) for further details on Bayesian networks and graphical models.

4.4.5 Kalman Filtering

The Kalman filter is perhaps the best known of Bayesian filtering algorithms. The filter is derived by assuming linear Gaussian models for both the dynamics and the measurement probabilities:

$$x_t = Ax_{t-1} + n_t$$
$$y_t = Bx_t + m_t \tag{4.24}$$

where n_t and m_t are zero-mean Gaussian noise processes with covariance matrices Q and R respectively (see Appendix for a review of vectors, matrices, covariance, and multivariate Gaussian distribution). These equations yield:

$$P(x_t \mid x_{t-1}) = N(Ax_{t-1}, Q)$$
$$P(y_t \mid x_t) = N(Bx_t, R) \tag{4.25}$$

where N denotes the normal (or Gaussian) distribution with mean and covariance as specified within the parenthesis. Suppose we begin with a Gaussian distribution $P(x_{t-1} \mid y_1, \ldots, y_{t-1})$. In the continuous case, the prediction distribution is obtained by replacing the sum over x_{t-1} with an integral:

$$P(x_t \mid y_1, \ldots, y_{t-1}) = \int_{x_{t-1}} P(x_t \mid x_{t-1}) P(x_{t-1} \mid y_1, \ldots, y_{t-1}) dx_{t-1} \tag{4.26}$$

Since both $P(x_t \mid x_{t-1})$ and $P(x_{t-1} \mid y_1, \ldots, y_{t-1})$ are Gaussian, the above equation implies that $P(x_t \mid y_1, \ldots, y_{t-1})$ is also Gaussian. The Bayesian filtering equation becomes:

$$P(x_t \mid y_1, \ldots, y_t) = \alpha \, P(y_t \mid x_t) P(x_t \mid y_1, \ldots, y_{t-1})$$
$$= \alpha \, P(y_t \mid x_t) \int_{x_{t-1}} P(x_t \mid x_{t-1}) P(x_{t-1} \mid y_1, \ldots, y_{t-1}) dx_{t-1} \tag{4.27}$$

Since $P(y_t \mid x_t)$ is Gaussian (as is $P(x_t \mid y_1, \ldots, y_{t-1})$), it follows that the posterior $P(x_t \mid y_1, \ldots, y_t)$ is also Gaussian and completely specified by a mean and a covariance:

$$P(x_t \mid y_1, \ldots, y_t) = N(\hat{x}_t, S_t).$$

The Bayesian filter in this case, also known as the *Kalman filter*, reduces to the following equations for recursively updating the mean $\hat{x}_t$ and covariance S_t at each time-step t (see, for example, Bryson & Ho, 1975 for a derivation):

$$\hat{x}_t = \bar{x}_t + K_t(y_t - B\bar{x}_t)$$
$$S_t = (B^T R^{-1} B + M_t^{-1})^{-1}$$
$$\bar{x}_t = A\hat{x}_{t-1} \tag{4.28}$$
$$M_t = AS_{t-1}A^T + Q$$

where $K_t = S_t B^T R^{-1}$ is called the *Kalman gain*.

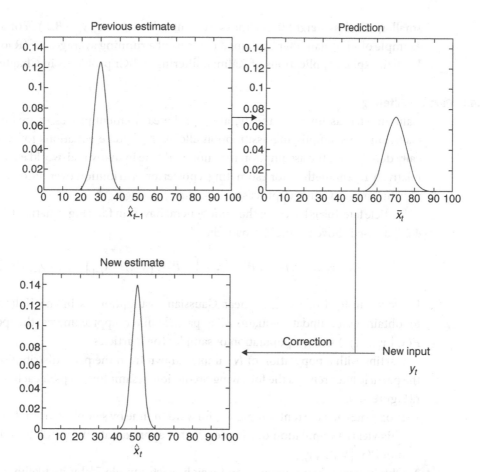

Figure 4.6.   **Kalman filtering.** The Kalman filter maintains an estimate of the hidden state of the environment as a Gaussian distribution specified by a mean and (co-)variance. The estimate for the previous time-step (with a mean of 30 in the figure) is used to make a prediction for the next time-step using the known linear equation for dynamics, resulting in a new Gaussian distribution (with a mean of 70 in the figure above and a larger variance). The predicted mean and variance are corrected using the new input at time t, resulting in a new estimate defined by the corrected mean and variance (adapted from Rao, 1999).

Despite their somewhat complex appearance, the Kalman filter equations (4.28) are actually quite easy to understand. Before making the measurement y_t, we have a prediction $\bar{x}_t$ of the mean and a prediction M_t of the covariance, computed from the Kalman filter estimates for mean and covariance at time step t-1. We then compute the prediction error $(y_t - B\bar{x}_t)$. The new estimate $\hat{x}_t$ is then obtained by adding the correction term $K_t(y_t - B\bar{x}_t)$ to the predicted mean $\bar{x}_t$. Figure 4.6 illustrates the prediction-correction cycle of the Kalman filter.

The Kalman gain K_t determines the amount of weight given to the new evidence y_t and is a function of the noise covariances Q and R for the dynamics and measurement processes. For example, if the measurement noise R is large, K_t becomes small, giving less weight to the measurement-related term $(y_t - B\overline{x}_t)$. For a simple example of a Kalman filter explained in terms of a running average, see (Rao, 1999). We will explore applications of Kalman filtering to BCI problems in Chapter 7.

4.4.6 Particle Filtering

Kalman filters assume that the dynamics and measurement processes are linear and Gaussian. This simplifying assumption allows the update equations to be analytically derived, but the assumption may not hold true in many real-world examples. A relatively recent method for estimating a posterior distribution over hidden state for non-linear non-Gaussian processes is *particle filtering*.

Particle filtering is based on the same general Bayesian filtering equation (Equation 4.27) as used above for the Kalman filter:

$$P(x_t \mid y_1,...,y_t) = \alpha\, P(y_t \mid x_t) \int_{x_{t-1}} P(x_t \mid x_{t-1}) P(x_{t-1} \mid y_1,...,y_{t-1}) dx_{t-1}$$

However, instead of using a linear Gaussian assumption as in the Kalman filter to obtain exact update equations, a particle filter approximates the posterior $P(x_t \mid y_1,...,y_t)$ using a population of samples (or "particles").

Starting with a population of N samples drawn from the prior distribution $P(x_0)$, the particle filter repeats the following prediction-resampling steps at each time-step t (Figure 4.7):

1. Propagate each current sample $\hat{x}_{t-1}^i$ forward in time by sampling from $P(x_t \mid \hat{x}_{t-1}^i)$. This yields a population of samples $\overline{x}_t^i$ that approximate the prediction distribution $P(x_t \mid y_1,...,y_{t-1})$.
2. Obtain new measurement y_t and weight each sample $\overline{x}_t^i$ by its likelihood value $P(y_t \mid \overline{x}_t^i)$.
3. Resample the population to generate a new population of N samples $\hat{x}_t^i$ where the probability that a sample $\overline{x}_t^i$ is selected is proportional to its weight. Note that the new samples $\hat{x}_t^i$ are unweighted.

It can be shown that samples computed by the particle filter algorithm above correctly represent the posterior probability $P(x_t \mid y_1,...,y_t)$ as the number of samples N tends to infinity. In practice, the number of samples used depends on the specific application and computational power available, with typical numbers in the 1,000–5,000 range.

4.5 Spatial Filtering

Spatial filtering techniques take as input brain signals recorded from several different locations (or "channels") and transform them in one of several ways. Possible goals include enhancing local activity, reducing noise that is common across channels, decreasing the dimensionality of the data, identifying hidden sources, or finding

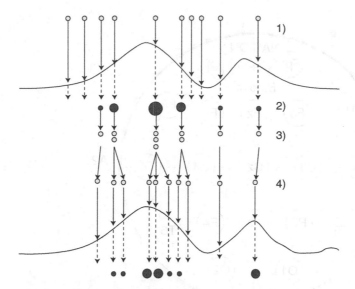

Figure 4.7.   **Particle filtering.** The steps 1 through 4 illustrate a full iteration of the particle filter from one time-step to the next. We start out with a set of particles (10 small circles of equal size in step 1) representing samples from the prediction distribution. In step 2, we make a new measurement and weight each sample by its likelihood value (different-sized circles in 2); the curve above with two peaks is the likelihood density). In step 3, we resample the particles with probability proportional to their weights. In step 4, each particle is propagated forward in time according to the transition probability distribution (the dynamics). This gives us a new set of particles (10 small circles of equal size in step 4) representing the prediction distribution, and the entire cycle (measurement-weighting-resampling-prediction) is repeated again (from Bellavista et al., 2006).

projections that maximize discrimination between different classes. We discuss some commonly used spatial filtering methods below.

4.5.1 Bipolar, Laplacian, and Common Average Referencing

For continuous-valued electrical brain signals such as EEG, it is common to use a simple form of spatial filtering based on re-referencing the recordings. Let s_i denote the signal from channel i. One can then extract *bipolar* signals $\tilde{s}_{i,j} = s_i - s_j$ to highlight the electrical potential differences between the two electrodes of interest (i and j).

A second spatial filter method, *Laplacian filtering*, extracts local activity at electrode i by subtracting the average activity present in the four orthogonal nearest-neighboring electrodes Θ:

$$\tilde{s}_i = s_i - \frac{1}{4}\sum_{i \in \Theta} s_i. \tag{4.29}$$

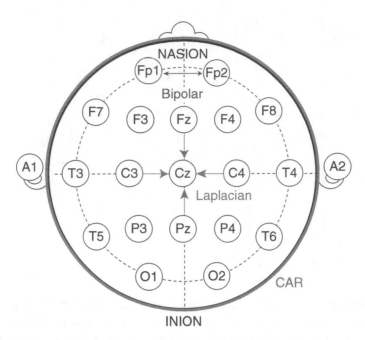

Figure 4.8.   **Basic spatial filtering.** Schematic diagram showing three basic spatial filtering techniques. Bipolar filtering involves taking the difference between two electrodes. Laplacian filtering involves subtracting from each electrode the average of four nearest-neighbor electrodes. Common average referencing (CAR; outer circle) involves subtracting the average over all electrodes.

This causes common activity such as muscle-related activity to be subtracted away from the electrode of interest. A closely related type of spatial filtering, *common average referencing* (CAR), enhances the local activity at electrode i by subtracting the average over all electrodes:

$$\tilde{\mathbf{s}}_i = \mathbf{s}_i - \frac{1}{N}\sum_{i=1}^{N}\mathbf{s}_i. \tag{4.30}$$

Figure 4.8 summarizes these three basic spatial filtering techniques.

4.5.2 Principal Component Analysis (PCA)

Suppose we have N data points, where each data point is L-dimensional. For example, a data point could be the vector of electrical brain signals (e.g., EEG) from L electrodes at a particular time t, and the data set could be N such L-dimensional vectors collected during an experimental session. The goal in *principal component analysis* (PCA) (also called the *Karhunen-Loève* or *Hotelling transform*) is to discover the underlying statistical variability in the data and reduce the data's dimensionality from L to a much smaller number of dimensions M ($M \ll L$). PCA achieves this goal by finding the directions of maximum variance in the L-dimensional data and

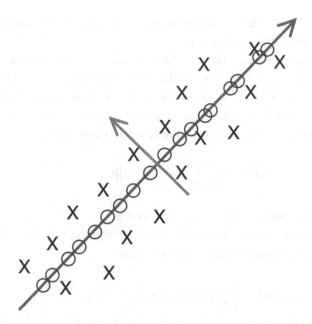

Figure 4.9.   **Principal component analysis (PCA).** The figure depicts the idea behind PCA, which finds the directions of maximum variance in the data. For the two-dimensional data shown (points marked x), the direction of maximum variance is along the diagonal vector (long arrow). The second directional vector found by PCA is orthogonal to the first and is shown by the short arrow. Since most of the variance is along the first vector, one can project all the data points onto this vector and represent the data with one-dimensional coordinates (circles) along this vector. This achieves a reduction in dimensionality from two dimensions to one (albeit with the loss of a small amount of information about the data along the vector given by the short arrow). Similar (but much greater) reductions in dimensionality can be achieved for higher-dimensional data such as images and multi-channel brain signals.

rotating the original coordinate system to align with these directions of maximum variance (see Figure 4.9). Coordinates corresponding to low variance directions can then be dropped, allowing significant reduction in dimensionality if the original data was redundant and contained only a few directions of large variance.

Most natural signals, including brain signals recorded from multiple locations, tend to be redundant and are therefore amenable to dimensionality reduction. For example, in the case of EEG measurements from N electrodes placed on the head, measurements from nearby electrodes may be correlated or there may be underlying rhythms that appear across multiple electrodes. Such redundancies can be exploited by PCA, which attempts to find the dominant directions of variability in the data. Once these dominant directions corresponding to a low-dimensional "subspace" of the original L-dimensional space have been found, new data points can be projected along these "principal" directions. Each projection is called a "principal component,"[1]

---

[1] Sometimes incorrectly called "principle component."

and the resulting M-dimensional vector can be used as a feature vector for classification or other purposes in BCI applications.

How does one go about finding the low-dimensional subspace corresponding to the directions of maximum variance in the data? Let us use the vector $\mathbf{x}_i$ to denote the ith data point and let $\overline{\mathbf{x}}$ be the mean of the vectors $\mathbf{x}_i$. Consider the variance of the mean-subtracted data points along the direction given by a unit vector $\mathbf{v}$ (see Appendix for a review of vectors and other linear algebra concepts):

$$\text{var}(\mathbf{v}) = \frac{1}{N} \sum_{i=1}^{N} \| (\mathbf{x}_i - \overline{\mathbf{x}})^T \mathbf{v} \|^2 \tag{4.31}$$

where $\|\mathbf{z}\|$ denotes the length (L_2 norm) of the vector $\mathbf{z}$.

We would like to find a vector $\mathbf{v}_1$ that maximizes this variance: $\mathbf{v}_1 = \arg\max_{\mathbf{v}} \text{var}(\mathbf{v})$. This can be done by some mathematical maneuvering:

$$\begin{aligned}
\text{var}(\mathbf{v}) &= \frac{1}{N} \sum_{i=1}^{N} \| (\mathbf{x}_i - \overline{\mathbf{x}})^T \mathbf{v} \|^2 \\
&= \frac{1}{N} \sum_{i=1}^{N} \mathbf{v}^T (\mathbf{x}_i - \overline{\mathbf{x}})(\mathbf{x}_i - \overline{\mathbf{x}})^T \mathbf{v} \\
&= \mathbf{v}^T \left(\frac{1}{N} \sum_{i=1}^{N} (\mathbf{x}_i - \overline{\mathbf{x}})(\mathbf{x}_i - \overline{\mathbf{x}})^T \right) \mathbf{v} \\
&= \mathbf{v}^T A \mathbf{v}
\end{aligned} \tag{4.32}$$

where A is the $L \times L$ sample covariance matrix of the input data. We can thus maximize $\text{var}(\mathbf{v})$ by maximizing $\mathbf{v}^T A \mathbf{v}$ subject to the constraint that $\mathbf{v}$ is a unit length vector, i.e., $\mathbf{v}^T \mathbf{v} = 1$. One can use the Lagrange multiplier method to do this: we find the vector $\mathbf{v}_1$ that maximizes $\mathbf{v}^T A \mathbf{v} - \lambda (\mathbf{v}^T \mathbf{v} - 1)$, where λ is the Lagrange multiplier whose value is determined by the optimization process. Setting the derivative of this expression with respect to $\mathbf{v}$ to 0, we get:

$$A\mathbf{v} = \lambda \mathbf{v} \tag{4.33}$$

which is the classic eigenvector-eigenvalue equation from linear algebra for the matrix A (see Appendix for a review of eigenvectors and eigenvalues).

Thus, to find the directions of maximal variance in the data, we need to compute the eigenvectors of the data covariance matrix A. The eigenvectors and eigenvalues can be obtained by solving Equation 4.33 using standard linear algebra techniques, or directly via any of a number of efficient algorithms for eigenvalue decomposition of a matrix. The resulting eigenvectors are orthonormal – that is, they are of unit length and orthogonal to each other.

An L-dimensional input data set can have up to L distinct eigenvectors. These eigenvectors can be ordered according to their eigenvalues: the eigenvector v_1 with the largest eigenvalue λ_1 captures the most variation in the data whereas the eigenvector with the smallest eigenvalue captures the least. For natural datasets, which contain regularities and redundancy, it is common to have a small number of eigen-values $\lambda_1, \ldots, \lambda_M$ that are large, with the rest being close to zero. The corresponding eigenvectors $\mathbf{v}_1, \ldots, \mathbf{v}_M$ are called *principal component vectors* and define a low-dimensional subspace of the input space. Given an input $\mathbf{x}$, one can thus perform dimensionality reduction by computing an M-dimensional representation of the L-dimensional input. This can be done by projecting the input along the M-dominant principal component vectors:

$$\mathbf{a} = \begin{bmatrix} (\mathbf{x} - \overline{\mathbf{x}})^T \mathbf{v}_1 \\ \vdots \\ (\mathbf{x} - \overline{\mathbf{x}})^T \mathbf{v}_M \end{bmatrix} \tag{4.34}$$

It is interesting to note that this transformation is invertible in the sense that one can reconstruct the original input x as a linear combination of the eigenvectors:

$$\hat{\mathbf{x}} = \sum_{i=1}^{M} a_i \mathbf{v}_i \tag{4.35}$$

where a_i are the elements of the vector $\mathbf{a}$. The reconstruction is not a perfect copy of $\mathbf{x}$ unless all L eigenvectors are used, but good reconstructions can be obtained by using all eigenvectors associated with large eigenvalues.

In addition to dimensionality reduction, PCA also *decorrelates* the input: correlations between the components of the vector $\mathbf{x}$ are no longer present in the transformed vector $\mathbf{a}$. To see this, note that the equation for $\mathbf{a}$ can be written in matrix-vector form as:

$$\mathbf{a} = V^T (\mathbf{x} - \overline{\mathbf{x}}) \tag{4.36}$$

where V is a matrix whose columns are the eigenvectors $\mathbf{v}_1, \ldots, \mathbf{v}_M$. Then, the covariance of $\mathbf{a}$ is given by:

$$\begin{aligned} C = \mathrm{cov}(\mathbf{a}) = E(\mathbf{a}\mathbf{a}^T) &= E\left(V^T (\mathbf{x} - \overline{\mathbf{x}})(\mathbf{x} - \overline{\mathbf{x}})^T V \right) \\ &= V^T A V \\ &= D \end{aligned}$$

where D is a diagonal matrix (all entries zero except the diagonal) whose diagonal entries are the eigenvalues $\lambda_1, \ldots, \lambda_M$. The last equality follows by noting that $A\mathbf{v}_i = \lambda_i \mathbf{v}_i$ (Equation 4.33) for each $\mathbf{v}_i$ in V and the eigenvectors $\mathbf{v}_i$ are all orthonormal to each other. Thus, since the covariance matrix of $\mathbf{a}$ is diagonal, there are no correlations between a_i and a_j for $i \neq j$. PCA therefore decorrelates the input signal $\mathbf{x}$.

In summary, PCA produces a vector $\mathbf{a}$ that is both *low-dimensional* and *decorrelated*. Such a representation can be a useful "feature vector" for classification and other types of analysis in BCI applications. Figure 4.10 illustrates the result of applying PCA to data collected using EEG.

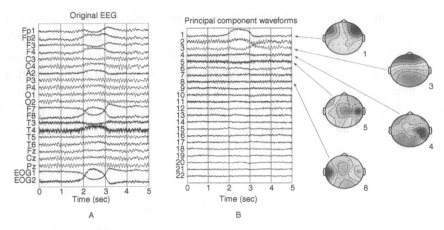

Figure 4.10. **PCA applied to EEG data.** (See color plates for the same figure in color) (A) Five seconds of EEG data recorded from 20 scalp locations labeled according to the 10–20 system (see Figure 3.7) and two EOG electrodes for detecting eye movements. Note how the data is corrupted by an eye movement artifact between 2 and 4 seconds. (B) Output of PCA when applied to the EEG data in (A). The principal component "waveforms" are the components $a_1, \ldots, a_{22}$ of the vector $\mathbf{a}$ at each time instant, obtained by projecting the input at each time instant along the 22 principal component vectors $\mathbf{v}_1, \ldots, \mathbf{v}_{22}$. Five of the principal component vectors ($\mathbf{v}_1, \mathbf{v}_3, \mathbf{v}_4, \mathbf{v}_5, \mathbf{v}_8$) are shown on the right as two-dimensional scalp maps (obtained by interpolating across the 22 values in each $\mathbf{v}_i$). Red denotes positive values while blue denotes negative values. Note how the first three PCA components (channels 1–3) have captured the eye movement; this is achieved by the large positive and negative weights for the corresponding principal component vectors in the vicinity of the forehead and eyes (see scalp map 1 and 3) (adapted from Jung et al., 1998).

4.5.3 Independent Component Analysis (ICA)

PCA finds a matrix V that decorrelates the inputs but the resulting feature vector $\mathbf{a}$ may still retain higher order statistical dependencies (beyond correlation). In particular, for any two distinct random variables a_1 and a_2, PCA ensures that their covariance is zero, i.e., $E(a_1 a_2) - E(a_1)E(a_2) = 0$, but this does not imply higher order independence, i.e., it is possible $E(a_1^2 a_2^2) - E(a_1^2)E(a_2^2) \neq 0$ (see Appendix for a review of independence in probability theory).

Why is achieving independence important? In the case of brain signals such as EEG, a reasonable starting point is a simple model where the input vectors $\mathbf{x}$ measured over the scalp are the result of linearly mixing a set of *statistically independent sources* inside the brain:

$$\mathbf{x} = M\mathbf{y} \tag{4.37}$$

where M is an unknown *mixing matrix* and $\mathbf{y}$ represents the vector of hidden independent sources.

Independent Component Analysis (ICA) attempts to recover the hidden sources by finding a matrix W such that:

$$\mathbf{a} = W\mathbf{x} \tag{4.38}$$

and the components of the feature vector $\mathbf{a}$ are maximally statistically independent, i.e.,

$$P(\mathbf{a}) \approx \prod_{i=1}^{M} P(a_i) \tag{4.39}$$

The matrix W is sometimes called the *unmixing* matrix because it attempts to invert the mixing of the sources. Indeed, in the case where $\mathbf{a}$ and $\mathbf{x}$ are of the same size, the optimal $W = M^{-1}$.

There exist a number of algorithms for computing the matrix W, the most commonly used ones being the Bell-Sejnowski "infomax" algorithm (Bell & Sejnowski, 1995) and FastICA (Hyvärinen, 1999). The Bell-Sejnowski algorithm estimates the matrix W by minimizing the mutual information between the a_i. Alternately, one could exploit the fact that linear mixtures of independent source signals are almost always Gaussian (from the Central Limit Theorem). This leads to the reasonable assumption that the source distributions are non-Gaussian, e.g., highly kurtotic distributions that are spiky at zero with large tails. Thus, algorithms for ICA have been proposed that utilize a suitable non-Gaussian distribution as the desired $P(a_i)$ and derive an estimation rule for W from the resulting optimization function. The reader is referred to Hyvärinen & Oja (2000) for derivations and more details of these algorithms.

Note that unlike PCA, where the dimensionality of the vector $\mathbf{a}$ is smaller than (or at most equal to) the dimensionality of the input $\mathbf{x}$, the feature vector dimension in ICA can be lesser than, equal to, or greater than the number of input dimensions. Additionally, the vectors that form the rows of the matrix W are no longer constrained to be orthogonal. Thus, ICA has proved useful in a variety of settings in BCI applications, ranging from the use of the output vector $\mathbf{a}$ as a feature vector in classification to isolation of interesting brain rhythms and elimination of muscle artifacts in EEG.

Figure 4.11 illustrates the application of ICA to EEG data for isolating electro-oculographic (EOG) (eye-related), electromyographic (EMG) (muscle-related) and electrocardiographic (ECG) (heart-related) artifacts, and unmixing putative source signals in the brain.

4.5.4 Common Spatial Patterns (CSP)

The method of *common spatial patterns* (CSP) differs from PCA and ICA in that it is a supervised technique – that is, the training dataset is labeled; we are given the class

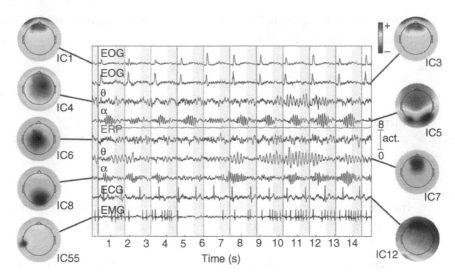

Figure 4.11. **ICA applied to EEG data.** (See color plates for the same figure in color) The figure shows 9 different components (ICA outputs) a_i obtained by projecting the input EEG data vector for each time instant along nine different ICA vectors (rows of the unmixing matrix W). These nine ICA vectors are depicted as scalp maps on the left and right side of the plot. The scalp maps follow the convention in Figure 4.10. Note how some of the independent components are artifacts (e.g., eye movements – EOG) while others appear to be brain rhythms, such as α and θ, or event related potentials (ERPs) (adapted from Onton and Makeig, 2006).

to which each data vector belongs. As an example, suppose we have collected brain data when the subject is performing two different tasks (e.g., hand versus foot motor imagery). CSP finds spatial filters such that the variance of the filtered data from one class is maximized while the variance of the filtered data from the other class is minimized. The resulting feature vectors thus enhance the discriminability between the two classes. CSP has emerged as a popular filtering method for EEG BCIs (see Section 9.1) because these BCIs rely on the power in a frequency band for control. Since the variance of EEG signals filtered in a given frequency band corresponds to the power in this band, CSP essentially maximizes the discriminability of the features used in the BCI (Ramoser et al., 2000).

We are given input data $\left\{X_c^i\right\}_{i=1}^{K}$ from trial i for class $c\in\{1,2\}$. Each X_c^i is an $N\times T$ matrix, where N is the number of channels and T the number of samples in time per channel. We assume that the X_c^i are centered and scaled.

The goal of CSP is to find M spatial filters, given by an $N\times M$ matrix W (each column is a spatial filter), that linearly transforms the input signals according to:

$$\mathbf{x}_{CSP}(t) = W^T \mathbf{x}(t) \tag{4.40}$$

where $\mathbf{x}(t)$ is the vector of input signals at time t from all the channels. In order to find the filters, the two class-conditional covariance matrices are first estimated as:

$$R_c = \frac{1}{K} \sum_i X_c^i (X_c^i)^T \tag{4.41}$$

for $c \in \{1,2\}$. The CSP technique involves determining a matrix W such that:

$$W^T R_1 W = \Lambda_1$$
$$W^T R_2 W = \Lambda_2 \tag{4.42}$$

where the Λ_i are diagonal matrices and $\Lambda_1 + \Lambda_2 = I$, where I is the identity matrix (see Appendix for a review of diagonal and identity matrices). This can be done by solving a generalized eigenvalue problem given by:

$$R_1 \mathbf{w} = \lambda R_2 \mathbf{w} \tag{4.43}$$

The generalized eigenvectors $\mathbf{w} = \mathbf{w}_j$ that satisfy the above equation form the columns of W and represent the CSP spatial filters. The generalized eigenvalues $\lambda_1^j = \mathbf{w}_j^T R_1 \mathbf{w}_j$ and $\lambda_2^j = \mathbf{w}_j^T R_2 \mathbf{w}_j$ form the diagonal elements of Λ_1 and Λ_2 respectively. Since $\lambda_1^j + \lambda_2^j = 1$, a high value for λ_1^j means that the filter output based on filter $\mathbf{w}_j$ produces a high variance for input signals in class 1 and a low variance for signals in class 2 (and vice versa). Figure 4.12 illustrates this property of CSP filters for EEG data. Spatial filtering with such filters can significantly enhance discrimination ability. Typically, a small number of eigenvectors (e.g., 6) are used as CSP filters in BCI applications. A more detailed overview of the CSP method can be found in Blankertz et al. (2008).

4.6 Artifact Reduction Techniques

Artifacts in BCIs are any undesirable signals that originate from outside the brain. For example, in EEG BCIs, one often encounters 50/60Hz power-line noise and artifacts caused by muscle or eye movements. Some of these artifacts may be permissible or even exploited as control signals for certain applications such as gaming or novel modes of human-computer interaction. However, a true brain-computer interface should possess the ability to eliminate or reduce such artifacts so that the signals being used to control a device originate solely from the brain. Signal-processing techniques can be used to achieve this goal.

Artifacts that originate from outside the body such as 50/60Hz power-line noise can often be reduced by using a *Faraday cage*, a physical enclosure made of conducting material, to block external electrical interference. When this is not possible, one can remove such noise in software using filtering techniques as described below.

Artifacts originating from within the subject's body may include: (1) rhythmic artifacts due to respiration and heartbeat (the latter are called electrocardiographic or ECG artifacts), (2) signal distortion or attenuation due to skin conductance changes

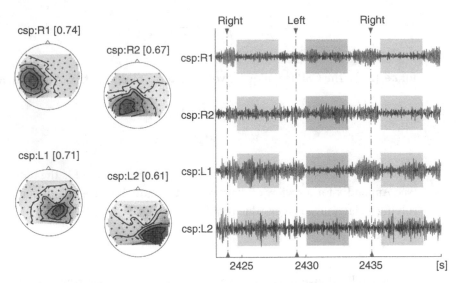

Figure 4.12. **CSP applied to EEG data.** The scalp maps on the left depict four spatial filters obtained by applying CSP to EEG data recorded while the subject performed left- and right-hand imagery. The two CSP filters at the top left (R1, R2) are tuned for right-hand imagery; the bottom left filters (L1, L2) are tuned for left-hand imagery. The result of spatial filtering using these filters is shown in the panel on the right. Note how the variance of the R1 and R2 channels is low for right-hand imagery and high for left-hand imagery (and vice versa for L1 and L2) (from Müller et al., 2008).

(as a result of sweating, etc.), (3) eye movement and eye blink artifacts (also called electro-oculographic or EOG artifacts), which appear as high-amplitude deflections in brain signals such as EEG with frequencies in the range 3–4Hz, and (4) muscle artifacts (electromyographic or EMG artifacts) caused by movements of the head, face, jaw, tongue, neck, and other parts of the body; EMG artifacts tend to occur maximally in the 30Hz or higher frequency range.

In this section, we review some of the most common methods for handling artifacts. For a more detailed discussion, see Fatourechi et al. (2007).

4.6.1 Thresholding

One approach to handling artifacts is to reject any data that is contaminated. The simplest method for such automatic artifact rejection is *thresholding*: if the magnitude or some other characteristic of a recorded EOG or EMG signal exceeds a pre-determined threshold, the brain signals recorded during that epoch are deemed to be contaminated and rejected. A similar thresholding technique can be applied directly to brain signals, provided a suitable threshold has been determined a priori by, for example, asking the subject to make various kinds of eye or body movements to calibrate the threshold. A major drawback of the thresholding method is that not all artifact-contaminated data may be rejected by this method, given the wide variety of possible artifacts and the nonstationarity of biological signals over time.

A complementary approach to handling artifacts is to not throw away all collected data when artifacts are detected but to attempt to remove them while retaining useful neural data. The goal of such *artifact removal* methods is to identify and excise artifacts from data while preserving neurological phenomena useful for BCI. Some important artifact removal methods are discussed below.

4.6.2 Band-Stop and Notch Filtering

Band-stop filtering is a useful artifact reduction technique that attenuates the components of a signal in a specific frequency band and passes the rest of the components of the signal. Band-stop filtering can be performed by first transforming the signal to the frequency domain (e.g., using FFT), filtering out the desired frequency band, and using the inverse FFT to transform back to the time domain. A commonly used band-stop filter is a notch filter set to the 59–61 Hz band (in the United States) for filtering out the 60 Hz power-line noise artifact. Another band-stop filter set to a low frequency band (e.g., 1–4 Hz) is sometimes used in EEG recordings to reduce EOG artifacts. Low-pass filtering is sometimes used to exclude EMG artifacts. However, filtering approaches work only when the brain signal of interest does not fall within the frequency range of artifacts. For example, low-pass filtering may remove EMG artifacts, but if the BCI utilizes high-frequency components of the brain signal, such filtering may eliminate these useful components as well.

4.6.3 Linear Modeling

A simple way of modeling the effect of artifacts on a recorded brain signal is to assume that the effect is additive. For example, if $EEG_i(t)$ is the EEG signal recorded from electrode i at time t, then a model of how the signal has been contaminated could be:

$$EEG_i(t) = EEG_i^{true}(t) + K \cdot EOG(t) \tag{4.44}$$

where $EEG_i^{true}(t)$ is the uncontaminated ("true") EEG signal from electrode i at time t, $EOG(t)$ is the recorded EOG signal at time t and K is a constant that can be estimated from data using a least-squares approach (see, for example, Croft et al., 2005). Given an estimated value for K, one can obtain an estimate of the true EEG signal using:

$$EEG_i^{true}(t) = EEG_i(t) - K \cdot EOG(t) \tag{4.45}$$

Figure 4.13 illustrates the use of linear modeling for correcting EEG data corrupted by eye movement artifacts.

Applying linear modeling for removing EMG artifacts is more difficult because EMG artifacts arise from multiple muscle groups, and an additive model with a single $EMG(t)$ signal as for EOG may not be appropriate.

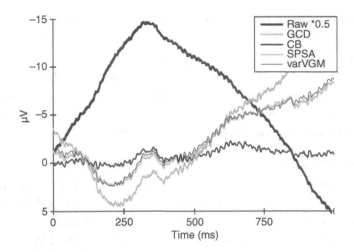

Figure 4.13. **Artifact reduction using linear modeling.** The plot shows an averaged raw EEG wave-form from scalp location Fp1 during a downward eye movement and corrected waveforms obtained using four linear modeling methods. These methods differed in how the constant K was determined for horizontal/vertical eye movement in the linear modeling equation; (see Croft et al., 2005) for details. The raw waveform was halved ("Raw × 0.5") to allow compar-ison with the corrected waveforms (from Croft et al., 2005).

4.6.4 Principal Component Analysis (PCA)

One can use PCA to find the directions of maximum variance in the recorded brain data (the eigenvectors of the data covariance matrix as discussed in Section 4.5.2). By projecting new data onto the eigenvectors, one can find a set of orthogonal "com-ponents" of the brain signals recorded from a set of electrodes. PCA has been shown to be useful for removing EOG artifacts from EEG signals (Lins et al., 1993) (see also Figure 4.10). However, the assumption that artifacts are uncorrelated with the brain signal may not be appropriate in certain cases, and PCA may be unable to separate these artifacts from the true brain signals.

4.6.5 Independent Component Analysis (ICA)

We already encountered ICA above in our discussion of spatial filtering techniques. ICA overcomes some of the shortcomings of PCA by seeking statistical indepen-dence rather than decorrelation. ICA decomposes brain signals (e.g., EEG) from a set of electrodes into a set of "components" that are as statistically independent as possible. By visually inspecting the components or automatic detection using a learned model for artifacts, one can often identify components due to EOG, EMG, or other artifacts (as in Figure 4.11), and reconstitute the brain signal without these components (see, for example, Jung et al., 1998; Makeig et al., 2000).

Figure 4.14 shows an example of how ICA can be used to remove components corresponding to artifacts and reconstitute a set of "corrected" EEG signals.

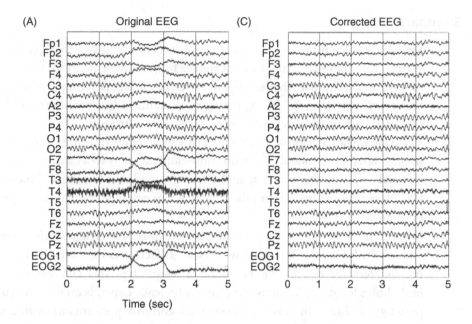

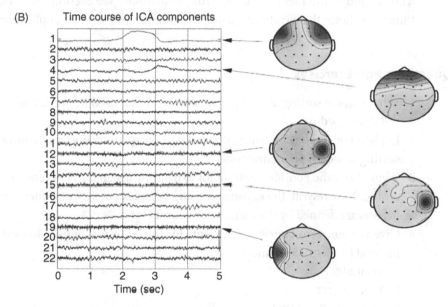

Figure 4.14. **Artifact reduction using ICA.** (A) Five seconds of EEG data (same as Figure 4.10A). (B) Output of ICA when applied to the data in (A). The time courses of 22 ICA components are shown along with five of the ICA "unmixing" vectors rendered as interpolated scalp maps. These five components account for horizontal and vertical eye movements (top two) and muscle artifacts in the right/left temporal regions (bottom three). (C) Corrected EEG signals obtained by zeroing out the ICA outputs corresponding to eye movements and muscle artifacts (the five components in (B): 1, 4, 12, 15, and 19) and projecting the rest of the components back to the scalp electrode space using the inverse of the ICA unmixing matrix (from Jung et al., 1998).

4.7 Summary

Signals recorded from the brain, either invasively or noninvasively, typically contain various types of noise or mixtures of signals from multiple neurons. In this chapter, we reviewed techniques that attempt to extract useful signals from raw brain signals. Spike sorting isolates spikes originating from an individual neuron from the multi-neuronal hash typically recorded by extracellular electrodes.

For noninvasive approaches, there exist a wide range of feature extraction techniques based on frequency-domain, time-domain, or wavelet analysis, which can be used in conjunction with spatial filtering techniques to reduce dimensionality (PCA), separate sources from mixtures (ICA), or enhance discriminability between output classes (CSP).

Some of these techniques can also be used to reduce artifacts originating from outside the brain (e.g., line noise or muscle artifacts). As we shall see in the following chapters, there is no one technique or feature type that emerges as the single best choice for all applications – the choice typically depends on the particular BCI paradigm and task. In most cases, one must compare performance with a range of features and techniques (e.g., using cross validation – see Section 5.1.4) before settling on a choice that yields adequate performance for the given application.

4.8 Questions and Exercises

1. What is spike sorting and why is it necessary? Is it used in intracellular or extracellular recording?
2. Explain the window discriminator method for spike sorting, and contrast it with sorting based on peak amplitude.
3. Write down the Fourier equation for expanding a signal $s(t)$ in terms of sine and cosine. Now rewrite the expansion using complex coefficients where these coefficients are defined by the Fourier transform.
4. Give the non-zero Fourier coefficients for the following signals defined over the interval $t = -5$ to $+5$ seconds:
   a. $3\sin(20\pi t)$
   b. $1 - \cos(2\pi t)$
   c. $\cos(4\pi t) + 2\sin(4\pi t)$
   d. $2\sin(5\pi t)\cos(\pi t)$ [Hint: Use the trigonometric identity for expressing $\sin(x)\cos(y)$ as the sum of two sines]
5. Define the amplitude, phase, and power spectrum of a time-varying signal sampled at discrete time intervals.
6. Why is the fast Fourier transform (FFT) called "fast?"
7. What is a mother wavelet, and how is it used in the wavelet transform? Explain how the wavelet transform differs from the Fourier transform in terms of the basis functions they use.

8. What do the Hjorth parameters measure, and how are they computed?

9. What property of a signal does the fractal dimension measure? Describe how it can be empirically estimated.

10. Write the equation for an autoregressive (AR) model of order 3. How can it be used for characterizing the statistical properties of a time-varying signal?

11. Derive Bayes' rule from the definition of conditional probability.

12. Suppose a BCI user can select one of two commands, A or B. In prior trials, 30% of the commands selected by the user were the command A. If the likelihood of the current brain signal given command A is 0.6 and given command B is 0.5, what is the posterior probability that the command is A? Which command should the BCI execute and why?

13. Explain how the general Bayesian filtering equation implements a prediction-correction cycle that is recursive in nature.

14. What assumptions does the Kalman filter make about the dynamics and measurement processes of a signal being estimated? Explain using the equations used to describe the dynamics and measurement.

15. Derive the equation for computing the running average from the Kalman filter equations. What assumptions do you have to make about the dynamics and measurement processes? (Hint: See Rao (1999) for a derivation.)

16. In what way is a particle filter more powerful than a Kalman filter for estimating an arbitrary time-varying signal?

17. Explain how the prediction-correction cycle is implemented in a particle filter, and compare it with the way it is implemented in a Kalman filter.

18. (★ Expedition) Read about Bayesian networks and graphical models, and draw the graphical model that is assumed by both the Kalman filter and the particle filter.

19. (★ Expedition) Read about Hidden Markov Models (HMMs), a special type of Bayesian network model used frequently in speech recognition. Discuss the relationship between HMMs and Kalman filters, especially the assumptions made regarding the dynamics and measurement processes, and inference of hidden state from input data.

20. (★ Expedition) The Kalman filter and the particle filter are examples of Bayesian inference algorithms. Read about and explain the following more general inference algorithms:
    a. Belief propagation
    b. Gibbs sampling
    c. Variational inference

21. What is underlying motivation behind using simple spatial filtering techniques such as bipolar, Laplacian, and common average referencing?

22. Explain how PCA achieves:
    a. Dimensionality reduction
    b. Decorrelation

    c. Reconstruction of an input

23. How does ICA differ from PCA in terms of the statistical properties and dimensionality of the output vector?

24. If you are given the choice between using PCA and ICA for analyzing brain data, when would you opt for one versus the other? Explain the underlying assumptions that motivate your choice.

25. CSP is a supervised learning technique whereas PCA and ICA are unsupervised. Explain what this means and the circumstances under which it would make sense to use CSP.

26. How does CSP transform its inputs so as to aid classification? Why is CSP especially useful in EEG BCIs where power in a particular frequency band is used as a feature?

27. Enumerate some of the most common types of artifacts in EEG BCIs and discuss which of the following techniques can be useful in reducing each type of artifact:

    a. Faraday cage

    b. Thresholding

    c. Band-stop and notch filtering

    d. Linear modeling

    e. Principal component analysis (PCA)

    f. Independent component analysis (ICA)

5

Machine Learning

The field of machine learning has played an important role in the development of brain-computer interfaces by providing techniques that can learn to map neural activity to appropriate control commands. Algorithms for machine learning can be broadly divided into two classes: *supervised learning* and *unsupervised learning*. In supervised learning, we are given training data that consists of a set of inputs and corresponding outputs. The goal is to learn the underlying function from the training data such that new test inputs are mapped to the correct outputs. If the outputs are discrete classes, the problem is called *classification*. If the outputs are continuous, the problem is equivalent to *regression*. Given the emphasis on discovering an underlying function, supervised learning is sometimes also called *function approximation*. Unsupervised learning, on the other hand, emphasizes discovery of hidden statistical structure in unlabeled data: the training data consists of inputs, which are typically high-dimensional vectors, and the goal is to learn a statistical model that may be compact or useful for subsequent analysis. We have already discussed two prominent unsupervised learning techniques (PCA and ICA) in the previous chapter.

In this chapter, we focus on the two major types of supervised learning techniques: classification and regression. Classification is the problem of assigning one of N labels to a new input signal, given labeled training data consisting of known inputs and their corresponding output labels. Regression is the problem of mapping input signals to a continuous output signal. Many BCIs based on EEG, ECoG, fMRI, and fNIR have relied on classification to generate discrete control outputs (e.g., move a cursor up or down by a small amount). BCIs based on neuronal recordings, on the other hand, have predominantly utilized regression to generate continuous output signals, such as position or velocity signals for a prosthetic device. In general, the choice of whether to use classification or regression when designing a BCI will depend on both the type of brain signal being recorded and the type of application being controlled.

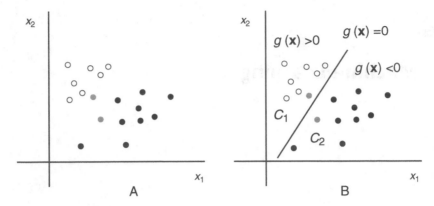

Figure 5.1. **Binary classification.** (A) The plot illustrates the binary classification problem for a two-dimensional dataset. The white circles represent two-dimensional data points (x_1, x_2) from class +1 and the black circles represent data from class −1. The goal is to determine whether new data points (represented by the two gray circles) belong to class +1 or −1. (B) Linear binary classifiers such as LDA estimate a hyperplane (in the two-dimensional case, a line such as the one shown) which separates the training data points into two classes. This separating hyperplane is determined by the equation $g(\mathbf{x}) = 0$. Data points are classified according to the side of the hyperplane they fall on.

5.1 Classification Techniques

5.1.1 Binary Classification

The task of a classifier is to assign class labels $y \in Y$ to a p-dimensional feature vector $\mathbf{x}$. The most simple case is when $Y = [−1, +1]$, i.e., discriminating between two classes (labeled -1 and +1). This case is known as *binary classification*. We focus first on binary classification methods, before discussing how these methods can be applied to multi-class classification (see Section 5.1.3 below).

The binary classification problem reduces to finding a boundary between the two classes based on the labeled training data – the goal is to find a boundary such that new data can be classified accurately (Figure 5.1A). The methods differ on how this boundary is computed from training data.

Linear Discriminant Analysis (LDA)

Linear discriminant analysis (LDA; sometimes also called *Fisher's linear discriminant*) is a simple and popular classification technique for classifying BCI data. LDA is a linear binary classifier that projects a p-dimensional input vector $\mathbf{x}$ onto a hyperplane that divides the input space into two halfspaces: each halfspace represents a class (+1 or -1). The decision boundary is given by the hyperplane equation (see Appendix, Equation A.8):

$$g(\mathbf{x}) = \mathbf{w}^T \mathbf{x} + w_0 = 0 \qquad (5.1)$$

The boundary between the two classes is thus characterized by the hyperplane's normal vector $\mathbf{w}$ and the threshold w_0, which are determined from the labeled training data.

Given a new input vector $\mathbf{x} \in X^p$, classification is achieved by computing:

$$y = sign(\mathbf{w}^T \mathbf{x} + w_0) \tag{5.2}$$

which assigns $y = -1$ if $\mathbf{w}^T \mathbf{x} + w_0$ is negative and $y = +1$ if $\mathbf{w}^T \mathbf{x} + w_0$ is positive (or zero) (see Figure 5.1B). During online BCI experiments, the (signed) distance to the hyperplane, given by $d(\mathbf{x}) = \mathbf{w}^T \mathbf{x} + w_0$ (assuming $\|\mathbf{w}\| = 1$), is sometimes also used to provide feedback to the user about how close to the boundary a point is.

To compute $\mathbf{w}$, LDA assumes that the class conditional distributions $P(\mathbf{x}|c = 1)$ and $P(\mathbf{x}|c = 2)$ are normal distributions with mean μ_c and covariance Σ_c for $c \in \{1,2\}$ (see Appendix for a review of mean, covariance, and multivariate normal (or Gaussian) distribution). It can be shown that the optimal classification strategy is to assign inputs to the first class if the log likelihood ratio $\log[P(\mathbf{x}|c=1)/P(\mathbf{x}|c=2)]$ is above a threshold (and to the second class if below or equal to the threshold). Because the two distributions are Gaussian, this reduces to the comparison:

$$(\mathbf{x} - \mu_1)^T \Sigma_1^{-1} (\mathbf{x} - \mu_1) - (\mathbf{x} - \mu_2)^T \Sigma_2^{-1} (\mathbf{x} - \mu_2) > K \tag{5.3}$$

where K is the threshold. If we now make the assumption that the class covariances are equal, i.e., $\Sigma_1 = \Sigma_2 = \Sigma$ and have full rank, we obtain the classification criterion:

$$\mathbf{w}^T \mathbf{x} > k \text{ where } \mathbf{w} = \Sigma^{-1} (\mu_1 - \mu_2) \tag{5.4}$$

The threshold k is often defined to be in the middle of the projection of the two class means; that is,

$$k = \mathbf{w}^T (\mu_1 + \mu_2) / 2 \tag{5.5}$$

It can be shown that the above choice for $\mathbf{w}$ defines a decision boundary that maximizes the distance between the means m_1 and m_2 of the projected data $\tilde{y} = \mathbf{w}^T \mathbf{x}$ from each class while minimizing the within-class variance of the projected data (see Figure 5.2). Further details can be found in Duda et al. (2000).

LDA has been a popular classifier in BCI research because it is simple to implement and can be computed fast enough for online use. In general, LDA has been found to produce good results, although due to the strong assumptions made in its derivation, factors such as non-Gaussian data distributions, outliers, and noise can adversely affect performance (Müller et al., 2003).

Regularized Linear Discriminant Analysis (RDA)

Regularization techniques are typically used to promote generalization and avoid overfitting, especially when the number of parameters to be estimated is large and

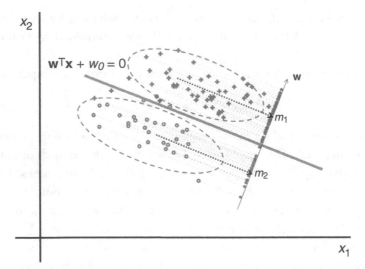

Figure 5.2.   **Linear discriminant analysis (LDA).** In LDA, the data points for the two classes are modeled as being generated by two Gaussians, each with its own mean and covariance. The plot
depicts these two Gaussians as dashed ovals around a set of two-dimensional data points.
The crosses represent class 1 while the circles represent class 2. The projections of these data
points onto a vector **w** are shown as smaller crosses and circles. LDA finds a vector **w** that
maximizes the distance between the means m_1 and m_2 of the projected data while minimizing the within-class variance. This **w** is normal to the separating hyperplane (here, the line
between the dashed ovals) (adapted from Barber, 2012).

the number of available observations small. For example, in the case of LDA, we
might have insufficient data to accurately estimate the class mean μ_c and class
covariance Σ_c. In particular, the Σ_c could become singular. Regularized linear discriminant analysis (RDA) (Friedman, 1989) is a simple variant of LDA where the
common covariance Σ is replaced by its regularized form:

$$\Sigma_\lambda = (1-\lambda)\Sigma + \lambda I \qquad (5.6)$$

where $\lambda \in (0,1)$ denotes the regularization parameter and I is the identity matrix. By
adding small constant values to the diagonal elements of Σ, one can ensure nonsin-
gularity and the existence of Σ_λ^{-1} which is needed to compute **w** as in Equation 5.4.
The regularization parameter λ can be chosen via model selection techniques (see
below) to allow better generalization.

   RDA has been used in applications such as classifying motor imagery in ECoG BCIs
(see Section 8.1.2). Comparisons suggest that the classification results obtained using
RDA are, in some cases, similar to those achieved using LDA (Vidaurre, 2007).

Quadratic Discriminant Analysis (QDA)

Quadratic discriminant analysis (QDA) begins with the same assumptions as LDA,
that is, that the class conditional distributions $P(\mathbf{x}|c=1)$ and $P(\mathbf{x}|c=2)$ are normal with

mean μ_c and covariance Σ_c for $c \in \{1,2\}$. It differs from LDA in allowing different covariance matrices (Σ_1 and Σ_2) for the two classes. This results in a quadratic decision boundary based on (the square of) the Mahalanobis distance (see Appendix) between the new observation $\mathbf{x}$ and the class mean μ_c:

$$m_c(\mathbf{x}) = (\mathbf{x} - \mu_c)^T \Sigma_c^{-1} (\mathbf{x} - \mu_c). \tag{5.7}$$

Classification is performed as in Equation 5.3 by comparing the difference between the two distances with a pre-determined threshold K:

$$y = sign(m_1(\mathbf{x}) - m_2(\mathbf{x}) - K). \tag{5.8}$$

Neural Networks and Perceptrons

Neural networks (also called artificial neural networks or ANNs) are inspired by their counterparts in biology and seek to reproduce the adaptive capabilities of networks in the brain in classifying input data in a robust manner. A prominent example is the *perceptron* and its generalization, the multilayered perceptron. The single-layer perceptron computes a hyperplane similar to LDA:

$$\mathbf{w}^T \mathbf{x} + w_0 = 0 \tag{5.9}$$

where the vector $\mathbf{w}$ represents the "synaptic weights" connecting the inputs to the neuron and $-w_0$ represents the threshold of firing for the neuron. The output of the perceptron is likewise identical to the output of the LDA:

$$y = sign(\mathbf{w}^T \mathbf{x} + w_0) \tag{5.10}$$

Equation 5.10 has a "neural" interpretation: the output of the neuron is based on computing a weighted sum of its inputs ($\mathbf{w}^T \mathbf{x} = \sum_i w_i x_i$) and comparing this sum to a threshold $-w_0$; if the weighted sum is greater than (or equal to) the threshold $-w_0$, the neuron's output is 1 (a "spike"), otherwise the output is 0. Note that this can be viewed as a simplified form of the threshold model for spike generation (Section 2.5).

The perceptron differs from the LDA in how the weights and the threshold parameter are adapted in response to inputs. Drawing inspiration from biology, the perceptron adapts its parameters in an online manner: given an input $\mathbf{x}$ and a desired output y^d, if the output error ($y - y^d$) is positive, the weights for positive inputs are decreased, the weights for negative inputs are increased, and the threshold is increased, all by a small amount. The net effect of this "learning" rule is to reduce the output error for similar inputs in the future. If the output error is negative, the weights for positive inputs are increased, the weights for negative inputs are decreased, and the threshold is decreased. Although this neurally inspired adaptive algorithm is simple and elegant, it is applicable only to classification problems where the data are linearly separable.

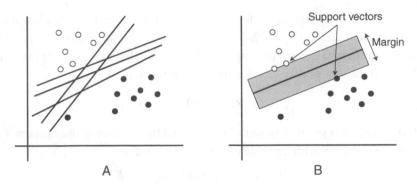

Figure 5.3.   **Support vector machine (SVM).** (A) The open and filled circles depict data points from two different classes. There are an infinite number of lines that can separate this set of data points (five possible lines are shown in blue). Which of these is "optimal" in terms of generalizing the best to new data? (B) The SVM finds the separating line with the maximum "margin" (here, the line at the center of the shaded rectangle); such a line (or hyperplane in higher dimensions) can be shown to provide the best generalization performance. The points from the training data set that define this maximum margin are called support vectors.

Multilayer perceptrons have been proposed as a nonlinear generalization of perceptrons to tackle harder classification problems. Multilayer perceptrons use a sigmoid ("soft threshold") nonlinearity (Section 5.2.2) rather than a hard threshold nonlinearity for their neuronal units:

$$y = sigmoid(\mathbf{w}^T \mathbf{x} + w_0) \tag{5.11}$$

The output of the sigmoid function (see Figure 5.10) is a number between 0 and 1, with values close to 0 indicating membership in class 1 and values close to 1 indicating membership in class 2. The reason for using the sigmoid is that it is differentiable, allowing a learning rule known as *backpropagation* (Section 5.2.2) to be derived for propagating the information about output error down from the outermost output layer of the network to inner "hidden" layers. Backpropagation-based neural networks have proved successful in a range of classification tasks, including classification of BCI data, and are widely available in software packages for classification. Although powerful, such neural networks often suffer from the problem of overfitting to the training data, resulting in poor generalization. As a result, the more recent technique of support vector machines (SVMs) are typically favored over neural networks as the classification algorithm of choice in many BCIs.

Support Vector Machine (SVM)

LDA and perceptrons select a hyperplane $\mathbf{w}^T \mathbf{x} + w_0 = 0$ to separate two classes. This hyperplane is only one among a potentially infinite number of hyperplanes separating the two input classes (Figure 5.3A). It can be shown (Vapnik, 1995) that among such hyperplanes, the best generalization is achieved by

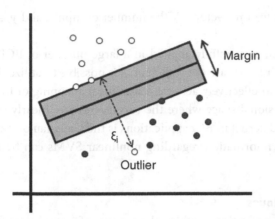

Figure 5.4.   **Soft-margin SVM.** In many cases, the training data may contain outliers due to noise or may simply not be linearly separable. In these cases, a *soft margin* SVM can be used to find the maximum margin separating line (line at the center of the shaded rectangle) that separates the training data with a minimal number of misclassifications. The soft-margin SVM uses slack variables ξ_i to measure the degree of misclassification in terms of how far a data point is from the correct side of the margin for its class.

selecting the hyperplane with the largest separation ("margin") between the two separable classes (Figure 5.3B).

The support vector machine (SVM) is a classifier that finds the separating hyperplane for which the margin between the samples of the two classes is maximized. Since the width of the margin is inversely proportional to $\|\mathbf{w}\|_2^2$ (Duda et al., 2000),[1] the search for the optimal $\mathbf{w}$ can be framed as a quadratic optimization problem, subject to the constraints that each training data point is correctly classified. However, due to the nature of EEG and ECoG data, one cannot assume that the data will be linearly separable. In this case, one could seek to separate the training data with a minimal number of errors. To allow for misclassifications and outliers, the *soft margin* SVM (Cortes and Vapnik, 1995) uses slack variables ξ_i to measure the degree of misclassification of an input i (Figure 5.4). The resulting optimization problem for the linear soft margin SVM is given by:

$$\underset{\mathbf{w}, \xi, w_0}{min} \left\{ \frac{1}{2}\|\mathbf{w}\|_2^2 + \frac{C}{K}\|\xi\|_1 \right\} \tag{5.12}$$

subject to:

$$y_i(\mathbf{w}^T\mathbf{x}_i + w_0) \geq 1 - \xi_i$$

with $\xi_i \geq 0$ for $i = 1, \ldots, K$.

---

[1] We use $\|\cdot\|_2$ to represent the Euclidean (or L2) norm and $\|\cdot\|_1$ the L1-norm, e.g., $\|\mathbf{w}\|_1 = \sum_i |w_i|$.

Here, $\mathbf{x}_i$ denotes input feature vector i, K the number of inputs, and $y_i \in \{-1, +1\}$ the class membership.

Linear SVMs have been successfully applied in a large number of BCI applications. In cases where linear SVMs are not sufficient, it is possible to utilize the *kernel trick* (Boser et al., 1992) to effectively achieve a nonlinear mapping of the data to a sufficiently high dimensional space where the two classes are linearly separable. The most commonly used kernel in BCI applications is the Gaussian or radial basis function kernel. Further information regarding nonlinear SVMs can be found in Burges (1998).

5.1.2 Ensemble Classification Techniques

Ensemble methods for classification combine the outputs of several classifiers (that disagree with each other on some training inputs) to produce an overall classifier with better generalization performance than any of the individual classifiers. The most popular ensemble methods, *bagging* and *boosting*, work by selecting different subsets of the training data to generate different classifiers and then combining their outputs using some form of voting.

Bagging

Bagging is the simplest of the ensemble learning methods. The method can be summarized as follows: (1) generate m new training datasets by sampling with replacement from the given dataset, (2) train m classifiers (e.g., neural networks), one for each newly generated dataset, and (3) classify a new input by running it through the m classifiers and choosing the class that receives the most "votes" (i.e., the class chosen by a majority of the classifiers).

Specifically, given a training dataset D of size N, bagging generates m new training sets D_i by sampling N' examples from D uniformly and with replacement (where $N' \leq N$). Sampling with replacement means that some examples may be repeated in each D_i. In the typical case where $N' = N$, D_i can be expected to have about 63% unique examples from D, the rest being duplicates (such a sample dataset is known as a *bootstrap* sample). One classifier is trained for each of the m bootstrap sample datasets. The outputs of the classifiers are combined by voting to generate the output of the ensemble classifier.

Random Forests

Perhaps the most popular bagging technique in use today is the technique known as random forests (Breiman, 2001). Random forests derive their name from the fact that they are comprised of a collection of decision-tree classifiers. A decision tree (Russell and Norvig, 2009) is a simple type of classifier that takes the form of a tree. Each node in the tree represents a test of one of the input variables; depending on the outcome of the test, we take one of the sub-branches of the tree. In this way, we follow a path all the way down to a leaf, which predicts an output class for the tree. In the case of random forests, an input vector is first run through each of the trees in the forest. Each tree predicts an output class, i.e., the tree "votes" for that class. The forest chooses as its output the class receiving the most votes from all the trees in the forest.

During training, each tree in the random forest is obtained in the following manner: (1) as in other bagging techniques, a bootstrap sample is obtained by sampling with replacement N times from the original training dataset, N being the size of the training dataset; (2) this sample dataset is used to grow a decision tree: starting from the root node and at each subsequent node, a subset of m input variables (e.g., features) is selected at random, and a test of these m input variables that best splits the sample into two separate classes is used as the test for the node (the value of m is kept constant for all trees). Random forests have become popular in recent years because they perform well and run efficiently on large datasets with large numbers of input variables. Their use in BCIs remains relatively unexplored.

Boosting

Boosting is an ensemble technique that finds a series of classifiers such that input data points for which the current set of classifiers predict incorrectly are given more weight than points that are correctly predicted. This leads to finding a new classifier that performs better on data points for which the current set of classifiers performs poorly. The final output of the ensemble classifier is based on a weighted sum of the outputs of all the classifiers. Boosting differs from bagging in that each new classifier is selected based on the performance of previous classifiers, whereas in bagging, the resampling of the training set at any given stage does not depend on the performance of earlier classifiers. Boosting is especially useful when the classifiers available for a problem are "weak" – they perform only slightly better than chance, and the goal is to boost accuracy by building a "strong" classifier based on the outputs of the weak classifiers.

Perhaps the best known boosting algorithm is AdaBoost (Freund and Schapire, 1997). AdaBoost creates an ensemble classifier in a series of rounds $t = 1, \ldots, T$. In each round, a set of weights $W_t(i)$ is updated, representing the weight for the ith data point in the training set. In each round, the weight of each incorrectly classified data point is increased while the weight of each correctly classified data point is decreased, thereby ensuring that the classifier selected in the next round does well on the incorrectly classified examples.

The AdaBoost algorithm can be summarized as follows. We are given a training set of m data points (x_i, y_i), where x_i is the input and y_i is the label of the output class $(+1$ or $-1)$. The weight for ith data point is initialized as $W_1(i) = \dfrac{1}{m}$. In each round $t, t = 1, \ldots, T$:

1. Find the classifier f_t from the given set of weak classifiers that minimizes the total classification error weighted by W_t:

$$f_t^* = \arg\min_{f_t} E_t \text{ where } E_t = \sum_{i=1}^{m} W_t(i)\left[f_t(x_i) \neq y_i\right]$$

where the expression inside [.] evaluates to 1 if true and 0 otherwise.
2. If $E_t \geq 0.5$ then stop.

3. Otherwise, choose $\alpha_t = \dfrac{1}{2}\ln\dfrac{1-E_t}{E_t}$.

4. Update the weights for the next round:

$$W_{t+1}(i) = \frac{W_t(i)e^{-\alpha_t y_i f_t(x_i)}}{Z_t}$$

where Z_t is a normalization factor chosen so that W_{t+1} sums to one.

The final AdaBoost classifier is given by:

$$F(x) = \text{sign}(\sum_{t=1}^{T} \alpha_t f_t(x))$$

where $\text{sign}(x) = +1$ if $x \geq 0$ and -1 if $x < 0$. The final output is thus a weighted majority vote of all the individual classifiers.

The key step that makes AdaBoost a powerful ensemble classifier is step 1 where the classifier f_t is chosen based on the weights W_t: these weights on the errors ensure the selection of a classifier that performs better on those examples that a previous classifier may have erred on.

5.1.3 Multi-Class Classification

The classifiers discussed thus far were designed for classifying data into one of two classes. In BCI applications, the number of desired output signals is frequently greater than two, requiring methods for multi-class classification. There are several strategies for applying binary classifiers to the multi-class problem.

Combining Binary Classifiers

One strategy for multi-class classification is to train several binary classifiers and use majority voting. Given N_Y classes, a total of $N_Y(N_Y-1)/2$ binary classifiers are trained, one for each binary combination of classes. For classification, a given input is fed to each of these classifiers, and the class with the most votes – the class selected by the largest number of classifiers – is selected as the output. A disadvantage of this approach is the relatively large number of classifiers that need to be trained and used during classification.

An alternate strategy for multi-class classification using binary classifiers is the one-versus-the-rest approach: for each class, an individual classifier is trained to separate the data belonging to this class from the rest of the classes. Classification is achieved by running each of these N_Y classifiers on the given input and picking the class with the highest output value.

Nearest Neighbor and k-Nearest Neighbors

Perhaps the simplest multi-class classification technique is nearest neighbor (NN) classification. As the name implies, an input is simply assigned to the class of its

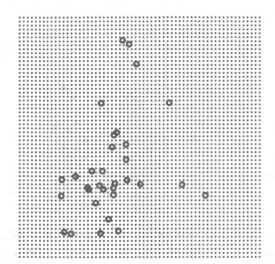

Figure 5.5. **Nearest-neighbor (NN) classification.** (See color plates for the same figure in color) The figure illustrates NN classification applied to a training data set containing two-dimensional points belonging to three different classes (represented by the open red, green, and blue circles respectively). The small dots represent new data points that have been classified according to the label of their nearest neighbor in the training data set (color of a dot represents the class it was assigned to). Note that the boundary between the different classes is not linear (compare with Figures 5.1–5.3) but is piecewise linear, and the region for any class can be discontinuous (e.g., the "red" and "green" classes) (from Barber, 2012).

nearest neighbor. The nearest neighbor is determined by a metric such as the *Euclidean distance* between vectors (denoted here by **x** and **y**):

$$d_{\mathbf{x},\mathbf{y}} = \sqrt{\sum_{n=1}^{M}\left(x_n - y_n\right)^2} \qquad (5.13)$$

Figure 5.5 illustrates how NN classification works for two-dimensional data points from three classes. The technique implicitly defines a decision boundary that is piecewise linear, with each segment corresponding to the perpendicular bisector between two data points belonging to different classes. The input space is thus partitioned into different regions belonging to different classes (colored regions in Figure 5.5). Note that the regions can be discontinuous and the boundaries highly nonlinear (even if piecewise linear).

One problem with NN classification is that it can be quite sensitive to noise and outliers (see Figure 5.6A). The technique can be generalized to be more robust using *k-nearest neighbors* (*k*-NN): an input is assigned to the class that is most common among its *k* nearest neighbors, where *k* is a small positive integer. Figure 5.6B illustrates how *k*-NN can overcome the problem of outliers and make classification more robust.

One potential problem with the *k*-NN technique is that it is biased toward classes that have the most examples in the training data. A variant of the technique addresses this problem by taking into account the distance from the input to each of

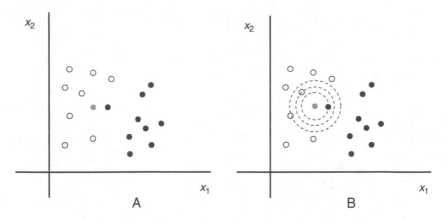

Figure 5.6. **_k_-nearest neighbors(_k_-NN)**. (A) Two-dimensional data set showing points belonging to two classes (class 1: white points; class 2: black points). The gray point is a new data point to be classified. (B) The simple nearest-neighbor technique ($k = 1$) classifies the gray point as class 2 because it is closest to a black point (innermost dashed circle). However, as can be seen, this black point is an outlier in the training data set. A 3-NN classifier is able to correctly classify the gray point as class 1 because the majority of the nearest neighbors are from class 1 (for $k = 3$, 2 white points versus 1 black point).

the k-nearest neighbors and using an inverse-distance weighted average of the class predicted by the k-nearest neighbors.

Learning Vector Quantization (LVQ) and DSLVQ

In learning vector quantization (LVQ), classification is based on a small set of labeled feature vectors $\{\mathbf{m}_i, Y_i\}_{i=1}^{N}$ (also known as *codebook vectors*) with labels $Y_i \in [1, \dots N_Y]$. Classification of a new sample is achieved by assigning to it the label Y_k of its closest codebook vector $\mathbf{m}_k$. How close an input sample $\mathbf{x}$ is to a codebook vector $\mathbf{m}$ is determined using, for instance, the Euclidean distance between vectors (Equation 5.13).

The codebook (or feature) vectors $\mathbf{m}_i$ and their labels are initialized randomly. Learning proceeds by changing the codebook vectors according to the training data as follows. The closest codebook vector is selected for each training sample. If it correctly classifies the sample, the vector is changed to be more similar to the sample, otherwise it is moved away to make it less similar to the sample.

Note that in LVQ, each codebook or feature vector contributes equally. A more common scenario in BCI is the case where we are given a fixed set of features $\mathbf{f}_i$ (e.g., power spectral features) but would like to weight them differently in terms of their discriminative ability. A variant of the LVQ algorithm, called distinction sensitive LVQ (DSLVQ), can be used in this case. DSLVQ employs a weighted distance function

$$d_{w,x,m} = \sqrt{\sum_{n=1}^{M} \left(w_n \cdot (x_n - m_n) \right)^2}$$ (5.14)

to differentially weight features in classification. The weights vectors **w** are adapted in a manner similar to how codebook vectors are adapted in LVQ (see Pregenzer (1997) for details).

Naïve Bayes Classifier

A naïve Bayes classifier is a probabilistic classifier based on Bayes' rule with strong independence ("naïve") assumptions (it is sometimes also called the "independent feature model"). Suppose the goal is to find out which class (out of N possible classes) a specific input belongs to, based on a large number of features $F_1, F_2,\ldots, F_n$ computed from the input. One way of doing this is by picking the class i with the maximum posterior probability:

$$P(C = i \mid F_1,\ldots, F_n)$$

Using Bayes' rule, this probability can be computed as:

$$P(C = i \mid F_1,\ldots, F_n) = \frac{P(C = i)P(F_1,\ldots, F_n \mid C = i)}{P(F_1,\ldots, F_n)}$$

where the two terms in the numerator are the prior probability of class i and the joint likelihood of the input features given class i. Without further assumptions, it is computationally impractical to estimate and store the joint likelihood of every possible combination of features, especially when the number of features is large.

The naïve Bayes model makes the assumption that the features are independent of each other given the class:

$$P(F_1,\ldots, F_n \mid C = i) = P(F_1 \mid C = i)P(F_2 \mid C = i)\ldots P(F_n \mid C = i)$$

In this case, rather than estimating the joint likelihood for every combination of features, we need to estimate only the individual likelihood functions for each feature and multiply them together, resulting in the following expression for the posterior probability:

$$P(C = i \mid F_1,\ldots, F_n) = \frac{P(C = i)P(F_1 \mid C = i)P(F_2 \mid C = i)\ldots P(F_n \mid C = i)}{P(F_1,\ldots, F_n)}$$
$$\propto P(C = i)P(F_1 \mid C = i)P(F_2 \mid C = i)\ldots P(F_n \mid C = i)$$

Classification in this simplified and more tractable model reduces to computing the expression on the right-hand side for each class and picking the class with the maximum value (the *maximum a posteriori*, or MAP, class).

Table 5.1. Confusion matrix for 2-class problems.

True class	Classification	
	Positive	Negative
Positive	true positives (TP)	false negatives (FN)
Negative	false positives (FP)	true negatives (TN)

5.1.4 Evaluation of Classification Performance

In BCI applications, as in other applications of classifiers, it is important to evaluate the accuracy and generalization performance of a chosen classifier. We briefly review some of the major evaluation techniques.

Confusion Matrix and ROC Curve

When evaluating performance, it is useful to compute the $N_Y \times N_Y$ "confusion" matrix M, where N_Y denotes the number of classes. The rows of M represent the true class labels and the columns represent the classifier's output. The case of binary classification ($N_Y = 2$) is shown in Table 5.1. The four entries in the matrix correspond to: the number of *true positives* (TP) or correct positive classifications, the number of *false negatives* (FN) or missed positive classifications (sometimes called Type II errors), the number of *false positives* (FP) or incorrect positive classifications (sometimes called Type I errors), and the number of *true negatives* (TN) or correct rejections. The diagonal elements M_{ii} of the matrix represent the number of correctly classified samples. The off-diagonal elements M_{ij} show how many samples of class i have been misclassified as class j.

When we vary some parameter of the classifier (e.g., a threshold), we obtain different numbers of true positives and false positives. A plot of the proportion of true positives versus the proportion of false positives, when some parameter of the classifier is varied, is known as a *ROC curve* ("receiver operating characteristic" curve, a term with origins in signal-detection theory). Figure 5.7 illustrates where different kinds of classifiers fall in the ROC space, including classifiers that perform better than, worse than, or at chance levels (random guessing) as well as the seldom attained perfect classifier (see Figure 9.13 for actual ROC curves for a noninvasive BCI).

Classification Accuracy

The *classification accuracy ACC* is defined as the ratio between correctly classified samples and the total number of samples. It can be derived from the confusion matrix M as follows:

$$ACC = \frac{TP + TN}{TP + FN + FP + TN} \tag{5.15}$$

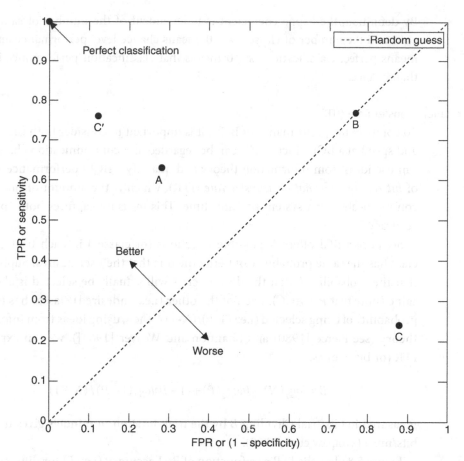

Figure 5.7.   **The ROC space.** TPR stands for true positive rate, or the fraction of positives correctly identified as positives (this is sometimes also called "sensitivity" or "recall rate"). FPR stands for
false positive rate (which is also equal to one minus "specificity," which is the fraction of
negatives correctly classified as negatives). A and C' are classifiers that perform better than
chance (random guessing) whereas B performs at chance levels. C performs significantly
worse than chance. The perfect classifier occupies the top left corner and has a TPR of 1 and
FPR of 0. Ideally, we would like our classifier to be as close to the top left corner as possible.
(Image: Adapted from Wikimedia Commons).

We can then define the *error rate* as $err = 1 - ACC$. When the number of examples for
each class is the same, the *chance level* is $ACC_0 = 1 / N_Y$ where N_Y denotes the number
of classes.

Kappa Coefficient

Another useful performance measure is the *kappa coefficient* (Cohen's κ):

$$\kappa = \frac{ACC - ACC_0}{1 - ACC_0} \qquad (5.16)$$

By definition, the kappa coefficient is independent of the number of samples per class and the number of classes. $\kappa = 0$ means chance level performance and $\kappa = 1$ means perfect classification. $\kappa < 0$ means that classification performance is worse than chance.

Information Transfer Rate (ITR)

To compare the performance of BCIs, it is important to consider both the accuracy and speed of a BCI. Since a BCI can be regarded as a communication channel, one can use ideas from information theory and quantify a BCI's performance in terms of *bit rate* or *information transfer rate* (ITR), which is the amount of information communicated by a system per unit time. This measure captures both speed and accuracy.

Suppose a BCI offers N possible selections (or classes) in each trial and each class has the same probability of being the one that the user desires. Suppose also that the probability P that the desired class will actually be selected is always the same (note that $P = ACC$). Each of the other (i.e., undesired) classes has the same probability of being selected (i.e., $(1-P)/(N-1)$). Then, using ideas from information theory (see Pierce [1980] and Shannon and Weaver [1964]), we can express the ITR (or bit rate) as:

$$B = log_2(N) + Plog_2(P) + (1-P)log_2(1-P)/(N-1) \qquad (5.17)$$

measured in bits/trial (dividing B by the trial duration in minutes gives the rate in bits/min) (Wolpaw et al., 2000).

Figure 5.8 plots the ITR as a function of BCI accuracy (i.e., P) for different values of N. The assumptions made to derive B above may not always be fulfilled, but B provides a useful upper limit on the performance that can be achieved.

Cross-Validation

A final but important issue that we briefly discuss here is the estimation of the error rate *err*. To get a true estimate of the error rate, classifiers are typically tested on "test data" that are different from the data used to train the classifier. One approach is to simply partition a given input dataset into two subsets, one for training and one for testing (the *hold out method*), but this strategy is sensitive to how the data is split. A more sophisticated strategy is *K-fold cross-validation*: the dataset is split into K subsets of approximately equal size, of which K-1 are used to train the classifier and the remaining subset is used for testing. The classifier is trained and tested K times, resulting in K different error rates err_k. The overall error rate is computed by averaging the individual err_k:

$$err = \frac{1}{K} \sum_{k=1}^{K} err_k. \qquad (5.18)$$

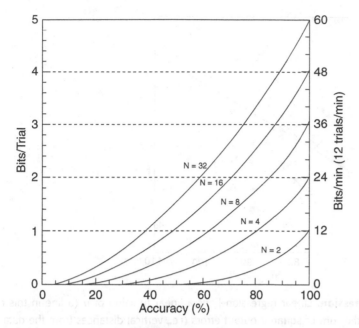

Figure 5.8. **Information transfer rate (ITR).** ITR is shown in bits/trial and in bits/min (data shown for 12 trials/min) when the number of possible classes (i.e., N) is 2, 4, 8, 16, or 32 (from Wolpaw et al., 2000).

Different variations of the above procedure exist. For example, *leave-one-out cross-validation* is an extreme form of K-fold cross-validation where K is set equal to the number of training samples. In another variation that seeks to minimize the effects of specific partitions of the data, K-fold cross-validation is repeated N times, yielding $N \cdot K$ individual error rates err_i, with the final error rate being the average over these $N \cdot K$ values.

In many applications, it is common to split the training dataset into three subsets: a training subset to find the parameters of the classifier, a validation subset to tune these or other parameters of the classifier, and a test subset to report the performance of the optimized classifier. Although these procedures are computationally costly, they play an important role in improving the generalization ability of the classifier.

5.2 Regression

We saw in Section 5.1 that classification involves mapping inputs to one of a finite number of classes. This can be regarded as a special case of the function approximation problem where the output is discrete. When the output is continuous, that is, a real-valued scalar or vector, the problem is equivalent to *regression*. As was the case with classification, we are given a training set of N example input-output pairs of vectors $(\mathbf{u}^m, \mathbf{d}^m)$, where $m = 1, \ldots, N$, and we wish to learn a function that maps arbitrary input vectors to appropriate outputs. We discuss the simplest form

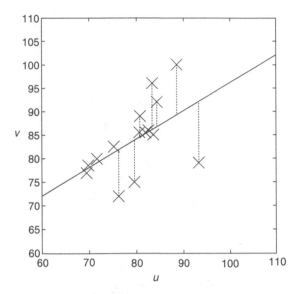

Figure 5.9. **Linear regression.** Linear regression finds a linear function of u (a line in this case) that minimizes the sum of squared output errors (i.e., vertical distances from the data points to the line) (adapted from Barber, 2012).

of regression, *linear regression*, before proceeding to nonlinear and probabilistic regression methods.

5.2.1 Linear Regression

Linear regression assumes that the underlying function generating the data is linear, i.e., the output vector is a linear function of the input vector. For the purposes of illustration, we consider here the special case where the input $\mathbf{u}$ is a K-dimensional vector (e.g., firing rates of K neurons) and the output v is a scalar value (e.g., end effector position). The output is then given by the linear function:

$$v = \sum_{i=1}^{K} w_i u_i = \mathbf{w}^T \mathbf{u} \tag{5.19}$$

where $\mathbf{w}$ is a "weight" vector or *linear filter* which we need to determine from the training data.[2] Linear least squares regression finds the weight vector $\mathbf{w}$ that minimizes the sum of squared output errors (see Figure 5.9) over all the training examples:

$$E(\mathbf{w}) = \sum_m \left(d^m - v^m \right)^2$$
$$= \| \mathbf{d} - U\mathbf{w} \|^2 \tag{5.20}$$

---

[2] We can model a constant offset, i.e., $v = \mathbf{w}^T \mathbf{u} + c$, using Equation 5.19 by replacing $\mathbf{u}$ with $\begin{bmatrix} \mathbf{u} \\ 1 \end{bmatrix}$ and estimating c as part of $\mathbf{w}$.

where $\mathbf{d}$ is the vector of training outputs, U is the input matrix whose rows are the input vectors $\mathbf{u}$ from the training set, and $\| \ \|$ is the square root of the sum of squares of each component of a vector. We can minimize the error by taking the derivative of E with respect to $\mathbf{w}$ and setting the result to zero, obtaining:

$$2 \cdot U^T (\mathbf{d} - U\mathbf{w}) = 0, \text{ i.e.,}$$
$$U^T U \mathbf{w} = U^T \mathbf{d}, \text{ i.e.,} \tag{5.21}$$
$$\mathbf{w} = \left(U^T U \right)^{-1} U^T \mathbf{d}$$

The last step assumes $(U^T U)^{-1}$ exists. The weight vector that minimizes output error is thus a function of both the inputs and the desired outputs as specified by the training data. The above method for estimating the weight vector is sometimes called the *Moore-Penrose pseudoinverse* method (the matrix $(U^T U)^{-1} U^T$ is the "pseudoinverse").

Linear regression has proved to be surprisingly effective in many invasive brain-computer interfaces as we shall see later in the book. It is also fast and easy to compute. Its main drawback is that it is too simplistic a model for some settings such as noninvasive BCIs where the mapping from brain signals to control is typically non-linear. Additionally, it does not provide any estimates of uncertainty in its output.

5.2.2 Neural Networks and Backpropagation

Neural networks have been popular algorithms for nonlinear function approximation since the discovery of the backpropagation learning algorithm in the 1980s. In this section, we briefly review multilayered sigmoid neural networks for nonlinear regression and derive the backpropagation algorithm from first principles.

When discussing classification techniques (Section 5.1), we encountered the perceptron, a type of neural network where each "neuron" utilizes a threshold output function on a weighted sum of its inputs. The threshold function is useful for classification but for nonlinear regression, a popular choice is the *sigmoid* (or *logistic*) output function:

$$v = g(\mathbf{w}^T \mathbf{u}) \tag{5.22}$$

where

$$g(x) = \frac{1}{1 + e^{-\beta x}} \tag{5.23}$$

As shown in Figure 5.10, the sigmoid function can be seen as a smoother version of the threshold function: it squashes its inputs to lie between 0 and 1, with the parameter β controlling the slope of the function (higher values of β push the sigmoid closer to a threshold function). The sigmoid is also easily differentiable, which will become important when we derive the backpropagation learning rule below.

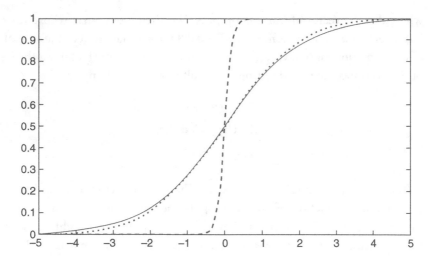

Figure 5.10. **The sigmoid function.** The solid curve is the sigmoid function for $\beta = 1$ while the dashed curve is the sigmoid for $\beta = 10$. As β gets larger, the sigmoid approaches the threshold (or step) function with the threshold at 0. For comparison, the cumulative distribution of the standard normal distribution is shown as a dotted curve (close to the solid sigmoid) (from Barber, 2012).

For nonlinear regression, we are interested in networks containing multiple layers of neurons, where the output of one layer is fed as input to the next layer of neurons. The most common type of multi-layered network is a three-layer network containing an input layer, a "hidden" layer, and an output layer. It has been shown that at least theoretically, such networks can approximate arbitrary nonlinear functions, given enough neurons in the hidden layer. We will focus on such networks (with a single hidden layer) below.

Suppose we have a three-layered network of sigmoid neurons (Figure 5.11), with matrix V representing the weights from input layer to the hidden layer and the matrix W representing the weights from the hidden to the output layer. The output of the ith neuron in the output layer can then be described as:

$$v_i = g(\sum_j W_{ji} g(\sum_k V_{kj} u_k)) \tag{5.24}$$

As in the case of linear regression above, the goal is once again to minimize the error between the desired output vector in the training data and the actual output vector produced by the network. For each input in the training data, this error is given by:

$$E(W,V) = \frac{1}{2}\sum_i (d_i - v_i)^2 \tag{5.25}$$

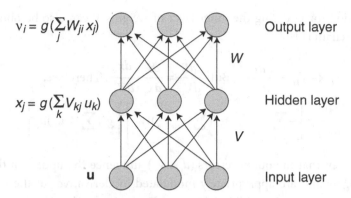

Figure 5.11. **Three-layer neural network.** Each neuron in the hidden layer takes a weighted sum of its inputs and passes this sum through the nonlinearity g to produce an output x_j. Output-layer neurons take a weighted sum of these x_j and pass this sum through g to yield the output of the network.

Two points should be noted here: (1) due to the presence of the sigmoid nonlinearities, we can no longer derive an analytical expression for the weights by setting the derivative of E to zero as we did above for linear regression, and (2) we know only the error for the output layer (the expression for E above); we therefore need to "backpropagate" this error information down to the lower layers of the network so that we can correct the weights there in proportion to their contribution to the output error (this is sometimes called the "credit assignment" problem). The backpropagation algorithm was proposed as a solution to these two problems.

The backpropagation algorithm attempts to minimize the output error function $E(W,V)$ by performing *gradient descent* on E with respect to the weights W and V. This means updating the weights in proportion to $-\dfrac{\partial E}{\partial W}$ and $-\dfrac{\partial E}{\partial V}$ until the changes in weights become small, indicating we have reached a local minimum of the error function. The expression for updating the outer layer of weights W can be derived easily using the chain rule of calculus as follows:

$$W_{ji} \leftarrow W_{ji} - \varepsilon \frac{dE}{dW_{ji}}$$

$$\frac{dE}{dW_{ji}} = -(d_i - v_i)g'(\sum_m W_{mi}x_m)x_j$$

(5.26)

where $\leftarrow$ means the left-hand-side expression is replaced by the one on the right-hand side, ε is the "learning rate" (a small positive number between 0 and 1), g' is the derivative of the sigmoid function g, and x_j is the output of hidden layer neuron j:
$$x_j = g(\sum_k V_{kj}u_k).$$

The equation for updating the inner layer of weights V can also be obtained by applying the chain rule:

$$V_{kj} \leftarrow V_{kj} - \varepsilon \frac{dE}{dV_{kj}} \quad \text{But:} \quad \frac{dE}{dV_{kj}} = \frac{dE}{dx_j} \cdot \frac{dx_j}{dV_{kj}}. \text{ Therefore,}$$

$$\frac{dE}{dV_{kj}} = \left[-\sum_i (d_i - v_i) g'(\sum_m W_{mi} x_m) W_{ji} \right] \cdot \left[g'(\sum_n V_{nj} u_n) u_k \right] \tag{5.27}$$

It can be seen that the output errors $(d_i - v_i)$ influence the update of the inner layer of weights and are appropriately modulated by derivatives of the nonlinear activation function (the sigmoid) in each layer. The errors are thus "backpropagated" down to the lower layer, giving the algorithm its name. This learning procedure can be generalized to an arbitrary number of layers, including "deep" networks containing a large number of hidden layers, although such networks can be prone to overfitting the training data, resulting in poor generalization. Most BCI applications tend to use three-layer networks such as the one described, with the number of neurons in the hidden layer determined using cross-validation (see Section 5.1.4).

5.2.3 Radial Basis Function (RBF) Networks

Consider the linear regression model we have discussed above:

$$v = \mathbf{w}^T \mathbf{u} \tag{5.28}$$

One way of increasing the power of this linear model is to use a set of M fixed *non-linear basis functions* (or *"features"*) φ_i defined on the input vector $\mathbf{u}$ such that:

$$v = \mathbf{w}^T \boldsymbol{\varphi}(\mathbf{u}) \tag{5.29}$$

where $\boldsymbol{\varphi}(\mathbf{u})$ is the M-dimensional vector $\left[\varphi_1(\mathbf{u}) \quad \cdots \quad \varphi_M(\mathbf{u}) \right]^T$.

One can then follow the approach we described above for linear regression to estimate the weight vector $\mathbf{w}$ for the given set of basis functions. If each basis function φ_i depends only on the radial distance (e.g., Euclidean distance) from a "center" $\boldsymbol{\mu}_i$ such that $\varphi_i(\mathbf{u}) = f(\|\mathbf{u} - \boldsymbol{\mu}_i\|)$, the resulting model is called a *radial basis function* (RBF) network. RBF networks can be regarded as three-layer neural networks where the input to hidden layer connections store the means $\boldsymbol{\mu}_i$, the output of the hidden layer neurons is $\varphi_i(\mathbf{u})$, and the output of the network v is a linear weighted combination of these hidden neuron outputs (see Figure 5.12A):

$$v = \sum_{i=1}^{M} w_i \varphi_i(\mathbf{u}) = \mathbf{w}^T \boldsymbol{\varphi}(\mathbf{u}) \tag{5.30}$$

A commonly used basis function is the "Gaussian kernel" (Figure 5.12B):

$$\varphi_i(\mathbf{u}) = \exp(-\|\mathbf{u} - \mathbf{u}_i\|^2 / 2\sigma^2) \tag{5.31}$$

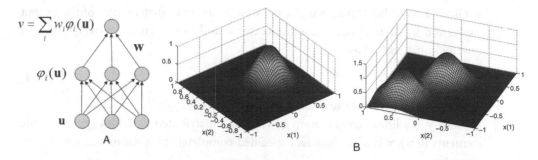

$v = \sum_i w_i \varphi_i(\mathbf{u})$

$\varphi_i(\mathbf{u})$

$\mathbf{w}$

$\mathbf{u}$

A

B

Figure 5.12. **Radial basis function (RBF) networks.** (A) Three-layer neural network implementing a radial basis function (RBF) network. The hidden layer neurons represent the basis functions whereas the output neuron computes a linear weighted sum of the hidden layer outputs. (B) (Left) Output of a Gaussian basis function with $\mu = [0\ 0.3]^T$ and $\sigma = 0.25$. (Right) Combined output of 2 Gaussian basis functions with $\mu_1 = [0\ 0.3]^T$ and $\mu_2 = [0.5{-}0.5]^T$. (Part B adapted from Barber, 2012).

which results in a *mixture-of-Gaussians* representation for mapping inputs to outputs.

5.2.4 Gaussian Processes

One major drawback of the regression methods described above is that they do not give us an estimate of the confidence in their prediction of the output. For example, one would expect an algorithm to be more certain in regions of input space where the training examples are plentiful and less certain in regions where the training examples are scant or nonexistent. *Gaussian process regression* provides such a measure of uncertainty regarding its outputs. It also has the advantage that it is non-parametric, that is, the model structure changes with the data to accommodate the complexity of the data rather than being fixed a priori.

Suppose we start with the same model as the one used in RBF networks in the previous section:

$$v = \mathbf{w}^T \boldsymbol{\varphi}(\mathbf{u}) \tag{5.32}$$

However, we now adopt a probabilistic approach by assuming $\mathbf{w}$ follows the distribution:

$$p(\mathbf{w}) = G(\mathbf{w} \,|\, \mathbf{0}, \sigma^2 I) \tag{5.33}$$

where G denotes the multivariate Gaussian (or normal) distribution with mean $\mathbf{0}$ and a covariance $\sigma^2 I$ (see Appendix for a review of multivariate Gaussians). In Bayesian parlance, the distribution in Equation 5.33 is known as the prior distribution over $\mathbf{w}$. Note that the probability distribution over $\mathbf{w}$ in Equation 5.33 defines a probability distribution over functions $v(\mathbf{u})$ via Equation 5.32.

Given a set of input points $\mathbf{u}_1,\ldots,\mathbf{u}_N$, what is the joint distribution of the output values $v(\mathbf{u}_1),\ldots,v(\mathbf{u}_N)$? Let us use the vector $\mathbf{v}$ to denote $[v(\mathbf{u}_1),\ldots,v(\mathbf{u}_N)]^T$. We can rewrite Equation 5.32 as:

$$\mathbf{v} = \boldsymbol{\Phi}\mathbf{w} \tag{5.34}$$

where $\boldsymbol{\Phi}$ is a matrix whose elements are $\Phi_{ji} = \varphi_i(\mathbf{u}_j)$.

Since $\mathbf{v}$ is a linear combination of Gaussian distributed variables (given by the elements of $\mathbf{w}$), $\mathbf{v}$ is also Gaussian, specified completely by a mean and covariance given by:

$$\text{mean}(\mathbf{v})=E(\boldsymbol{\Phi}\mathbf{w})=\boldsymbol{\Phi}E(\mathbf{w})=\mathbf{0} \tag{5.35}$$

$$\text{cov}(\mathbf{v}) = E(\mathbf{v}\mathbf{v}^T) = \boldsymbol{\Phi}E(\mathbf{w}\mathbf{w}^T)\boldsymbol{\Phi}^T = \sigma^2\boldsymbol{\Phi}\boldsymbol{\Phi}^T = K \tag{5.36}$$

where K is known as the *Gram matrix* whose elements are given by:

$$K_{ij} = k(\mathbf{u}_i,\mathbf{u}_j) = \sigma^2\varphi(\mathbf{u}_i)^T\varphi(\mathbf{u}_j) \tag{5.37}$$

The function $k(\mathbf{u}_i,\mathbf{u}_j)$ is known as the *kernel function*.

The above model for $\mathbf{v}$ is one example of a *Gaussian process*, which can be defined as a probability distribution over functions $v(\mathbf{u})$ such that the joint distribution over $v(\mathbf{u}_1),\ldots,v(\mathbf{u}_N)$ for arbitrary N is Gaussian.

Without any prior knowledge about the function $v(\mathbf{u})$, the mean is assumed to be $\mathbf{0}$, which implies that the Gaussian process is completely specified by the covariance function K, or equivalently, the kernel function $k(\mathbf{u}_i,\mathbf{u}_j)$. The kernel function in the example above was obtained by assuming basis functions φ_i defined on an input $\mathbf{u}$ but a kernel function can also be defined directly. For example, one can use a Gaussian kernel function given by:

$$k(\mathbf{u}_i,\mathbf{u}_j) = \exp(-\|\mathbf{u}_i - \mathbf{u}_j\|^2 / 2\sigma^2) \tag{5.38}$$

The kernel function can be regarded as providing a measure of the similarity between two inputs. It affects attributes such as the smoothness of the function. Figures 5.13A and 5.13C illustrate sampled functions $v(\mathbf{u})$ for two different kernel (or covariance) functions.

In general, any function can be used as the kernel function as long as the corresponding matrix K is positive semidefinite for any set of inputs. The choice of which kernel to use depends on the application, with the Gaussian kernel being a popular choice.

To use a Gaussian process for regression, we need to predict an output v_{N+1} for a new input $\mathbf{u}_{N+1}$, given training data consisting of outputs, denoted by the vector $\mathbf{v}_N = [v_1\ldots v_N]^T$ and corresponding inputs $\mathbf{u}_{1,\ldots,}\mathbf{u}_N$. It can be shown (see Bishop, 2006) that the desired posterior distribution $p(v_{N+1}|\mathbf{v}_N, \mathbf{u}_{1,\ldots,}\mathbf{u}_{N+1})$ is again a Gaussian distribution with mean and variance as follows:

$$\text{mean} = \mathbf{k}^T C_N^{-1}\mathbf{v}_N \tag{5.39}$$

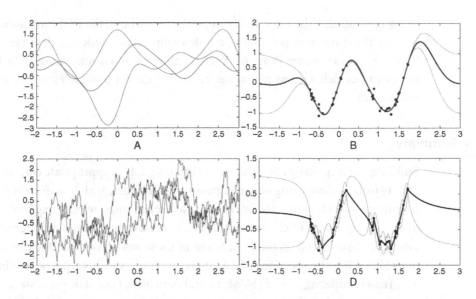

Figure 5.13. **Gaussian processes (GPs).** (A) shows three sampled functions from a prior probability distribution over functions based on a Gaussian kernel (or covariance) function ($\sigma^2 = 1/2$). (B) Posterior predicted function based on a set of training points (black dots) and the Gaussian covariance function in (A). The dark curve at the center is the mean prediction, and the gray curves represent standard error bars on either side. (C) and (D) show samples and the posterior prediction respectively when using a Ornstein-Uhlenbeck prior (see Barber, 2012 for details). The samples and predicted function are not as smooth as in (A) and (B). Note that both (B) and (D) exhibit one of the favorable properties of GP regression: the functions exhibit greater uncertainty in regions of the input space where there is less training data (from Barber, 2012).

$$\text{variance} = c - \mathbf{k}^T C_N^{-1} \mathbf{k} \qquad (5.40)$$

where $\mathbf{k}$ is the vector containing the elements $k(\mathbf{u}_i, \mathbf{u}_{N+1})$, $i = 1, \ldots,$ N, (k essentially measures the similarity between each training input and the new input) and C_N is the covariance matrix whose elements are given by $C_N(\mathbf{u}_i, \mathbf{u}_j) = k(\mathbf{u}_i, \mathbf{u}_j)$ for $i \neq j$, and $k(\mathbf{u}_i, \mathbf{u}_j) + \lambda$ for $i = j$, with $i, j = 1, \ldots, N$ (here, λ is a parameter associated with the noise on the outputs). The scalar value c is defined as $c - k(\mathbf{u}_{N+1}, \mathbf{u}_{N+1}) + \lambda$.

It can be seen from these equations that the posterior distribution for the output v_{N+1} depends both on the past training inputs and outputs (via C_N and $\mathbf{v}_N$) as well as the new input (via $\mathbf{k}$ and c). Note that the method is nonparametric: the terms above defining the mean and variance grow as a function of the size N of the training data. The model exhibits the favorable property alluded to earlier in this section: in the regions where training data is sparse or nonexistent, the output prediction has a larger variance, reflecting greater uncertainty, compared to regions where the training data is dense (Figures 5.13B and 5.13D). This is especially useful in BCI applications where robotic devices such as prosthetics, wheelchairs, or assistive robots are being controlled: if the uncertainty in prediction is high, the BCI can choose not to execute the command, preventing a potentially catastrophic accident (see Section 9.1.8 for an example application). Such an ability is often missing in BCIs that use regression models such as neural networks that do not provide estimates of output uncertainty.

5.3 Summary

Building a BCI typically entails mapping brain signals to appropriate control signals. This is usually done using either regression techniques, which map neural activity to continuous output signals, or classification techniques, which map brain activity to one of a given set of classes. In this chapter, we delved into a number of regression and classification techniques. Some of these were based on linearity assumptions (LDA, linear regression) while others employed various types of nonlinearities for greater modeling power (SVM, neural networks, Gaussian processes). We also examined how classifiers can be combined to create more powerful classifiers (bagging, random forests, boosting). We learned about performance metrics such as the kappa coefficient and ITR, as well as evaluating generalization ability via cross-validation. We will encounter these techniques again in subsequent chapters where we will see them applied to specific BCI tasks.

5.4 Questions and Exercises

1. Describe the goals of classification and regression, and provide an example of how each may be used in a BCI.
2. Write down the equation for the decision boundary in linear binary classification and explain how it can be used to classify an input.
3. Explain how the weight vector $\mathbf{w}$ and the threshold c in the technique of LDA are related to the class conditional normal distributions for the inputs.
4. What are the main differences between LDA, RDA, and QDA?
5. Describe how the perceptron differs from LDA in the way the weight vector and threshold parameters are "learned" from input data.
6. What can multilayer perceptrons do that a single-layer perceptron cannot?
7. SVMs and perceptrons both use linear hyperplanes to separate data into two classes. Why then does the SVM typically outperform the perceptron when it comes to generalization to new data?
8. Explain the difference between a standard SVM and a soft-margin SVM. Which one is potentially more applicable to classification of brain data and why?
9. (♄ Expedition) What is the "kernel trick?" Describe how it allows one to use SVMs for nonlinear classification while retaining tractability.
10. Explain the general idea behind the ensemble classification technique of bagging. How does bagging generate and use bootstrap samples?

11. (✵ Expedition) Random forests is an example of a bagging technique based on decision trees. Each node in a decision tree performs a test on one or more input variables, and the outcome of the test dictates which branch to take. Describe how a decision tree can be constructed from a labeled bootstrap sample. In particular, at each node, given a subset of m randomly selected input variables, how do we find a test of these m input variables that best splits the sample into two separate classes?

12. How does the ensemble technique of boosting differ from bagging? Under what circumstances is boosting the preferred method of choice compared to bagging?

13. Answer the following questions about AdaBoost:
    a. How is a classifier chosen in each round?
    b. Write the expression for the weight assigned to the chosen classifier.
    c. Write the expression for the final output of the ensemble classifier.

14. Describe the two main methods for combining binary classifiers to achieve multi-class classification.

15. Compare and contrast the k-NN and LVQ methods for multi-class classification.

16. What "naïve" assumption does the naïve Bayes classifier make? What is the motivation behind making such an assumption? Discuss potential examples, if any, of brain data where the naïve Bayes assumption may fail.

17. Draw the confusion matrix for a 3-class classifier and write down the expression for its accuracy in terms of entries of the matrix.

18. Plot the ROC curve and write down the accuracies (ACC) for a classifier that exhibits the following performance as you vary one of its parameters. Assume that the number of positives in the training data set is 50 and the number of negatives 30.
    a. 5 false positives, 25 false negatives
    b. 10 false positives, 5 false negatives
    c. 20 false positives, 0 false negatives

19. Calculate the kappa coefficients for (a), (b), and (c) in Question 18, assuming binary classification.

20. Explain how the information transfer rate (ITR) captures both the speed and accuracy of a system such as a BCI by analyzing its definition (Equation 5.17).

21. Why is cross-validation a useful procedure for evaluating the performance of a classifier, compared to just using the error rate on training data?

22. Compare and contrast the following methods for cross-validation:
    a. Hold out method
    b. K-fold cross-validation
    c. Leave-one-out cross-validation

23. In Section 5.2.1, we derived the Moore-Penrose pseudoinverse method for obtaining the weights **w** for linear regression. Under what condition does this

pseudoinverse exist? (Hint: Think about the linear independence of the columns of U). If this condition is not satisfied, can you think of a way of ensuring an approximate pseudoinverse exists?

24. Consider neural networks whose neurons have *linear activation functions*, i.e., each neuron's output function is $g(x) = bx+c$, where x is the weighted sum of inputs to the neuron, and b and c are two fixed real numbers.

    a. Suppose you have a single neuron with a linear activation function g as above with input $u_0, \ldots, u_n$ and weights $W_0, \ldots, W_n$. Write down the squared error function in terms of the input and weights if the true output is d.

    b. Write down the weight update rule for the neuron based on gradient descent on the error function in (a).

    c. Now consider a network of linear neurons with one hidden layer of m units, n input units, and one output unit. For a given set of weights w_{kj} in the input-hidden layer and W_j in the hidden-output layer, write down the equation for the output unit as a function of w_{kj}, W_j, and input $\mathbf{x}$. Show that there is a single-layer linear network with no hidden units that computes the same function.

    d. Given your result in (c), what can you conclude about the computational power of N-hidden-layer linear networks for $N = 1, 2, 3, \ldots$?

25. What are some of the advantages and disadvantages of using a Gaussian process for regression compared to a radial basis function (RBF) network?

Part II

Putting It All Together

Building a BCI

The preceding chapters introduced you to the basic concepts in neuroscience, record-ing and stimulation technologies, signal processing, and machine learning. We are now ready to put it all together to consider the process of building an actual BCI.

6.1 Major Types of BCIs

BCIs today can be broadly divided into three major types:

- **Invasive BCIs**: These involve recording from or stimulating neurons inside the brain.
- **Semi-invasive BCIs**: These involve recording from or stimulating the brain sur-face or nerves.
- **Noninvasive BCIs**: These employ techniques for recording from or stimulating the brain without penetrating the skin or skull.

Within each of these types, we can have BCIs that:

- Only record from the brain (and translate the neural data into control signals for output devices).
- Only stimulate the brain (and cause certain desired patterns of neural activity in the brain).
- Both record and stimulate the brain.

In the next five chapters, we will encounter concrete examples of the major types of BCIs defined above. Before we proceed to these concrete BCI examples, it is use-ful to first discuss some of the major types of brain responses that researchers have exploited for building BCIs.

6.2 Brain Responses Useful for Building BCIs

6.2.1 Conditioned Responses

One of the most important properties of neural circuits is their plasticity, allow-ing responses of neurons to be adapted as a function of inputs. In many cases, this plasticity is modulated by the rewards received by the animal. One well-known behavioral example of this plasticity is *Pavlovian (or classical) conditioning*, first demonstrated by the Russian scientist I. Pavlov: a dog that originally salivates in response to food starts salivating in response to a bell after the bell is consistently paired with the food stimulus. In this example, the bell is called the conditioned stimulus and the salivation the conditioned response. In contrast, in *instrumental (or operant) conditioning*, the animal receives a reward only upon completion of an appropriate action, e.g., pressing a lever. In this case, after the reward has been paired with the action of pressing the lever, the action of pressing the lever becomes the conditioned response.

Conditioned responses are also seen in single neurons and networks. In one of the earliest demonstrations of brain-computer interfacing (see Section 7.1.1), Eberhard Fetz at the University of Washington utilized the idea of conditioning to demonstrate that the activity of a single neuron in primate motor cortex can be conditioned to control the needle of an analog meter. The movement of the needle was directly coupled to the firing rate of the neuron; when the needle crossed a threshold, the monkey was rewarded. After several trials, the monkey learned to consistently move the needle past the threshold by increasing the firing rate of the recorded neuron. This is an example of operant conditioning where the action (needle movement) that produces reward is coupled to increased activity in the recorded neuron (the conditioned response).

Conditioned responses can also be obtained in large populations of neurons. For example, after several sessions of training, human subjects can control the power in particular frequency bands in EEG signals recorded from the scalp (Section 9.1.1). In these experiments, the power is coupled to the movement of a cursor on a computer screen using a fixed mapping function, and the goal is to move the cursor in a desired direction to hit a target. The subject gradually learns to control the movement of the cursor by modulating the power in the frequency band(s) used in the mapping function. In this case, conditioning occurs at the neural population level, and the conditioned response involves the activities of large numbers of neurons being modulated in concert to generate the appropriate increase or decrease in power in the desired frequency band.

In summary, the responses of both single neurons as well as networks of neurons can be modulated as a consequence of coupling neural activity with external actions (such as cursor movement) and rewards that are contingent on execution of appropriate actions (hitting a target).

6.2.2 Population Activity

Neurons in the primary motor cortex code for various attributes of movement such as direction of motion of a limb, velocities, forces, etc. In a seminal series of experiments, Georgopoulos and colleagues showed that movement is represented using a population code (Georgopoulos et al., 1988). For example, in the case of movement direction, neurons in the population fire according to how close their preferred direction of movement is to the actual direction of movement. The actual direction of movement can be predicted, for instance, by a weighted combination of the preferred directions of the neurons, the weight for each neuron being the neuron's firing rate (see Equation 7.1 and Figure 7.3 for more details). This method of decoding movement direction is sometimes called *population vector* decoding.

The fact that movement-related variables can be extracted from the activities of populations of neurons was an important finding for brain-computer interfacing because it led to the realization that the same population motor activity could be used to control the movement of artificial limbs and other devices. As we shall discuss in Chapter 7, some of the most impressive demonstrations of brain-computer interfacing in animals have relied on using regression techniques to map population motor activity to appropriate control signals for prosthetic devices.

6.2.3 Imagined Motor and Cognitive Activity

A third type of brain response that is widely used for brain-computer interfacing in humans is neural activity produced when a subject voluntarily imagines making particular movement (this is called *motor imagery*). Imagining a movement typically produces neural activity that is spatiotemporally similar to the activity generated during actual movement, but smaller in magnitude (see, e.g., Miller et al., 2010). A variety of machine learning algorithms (typically, classifiers) can be applied to discriminate between two or more types of imagined movements, allowing each imagined activity to be mapped to a particular control signal (e.g., moving a cursor up). It has been noted that the initially weak response due to imagined movement becomes more robust as the subject receives feedback while learning to control the cursor. Eventually, in some subjects, the imagined activity during cursor control can even exceed the activity observed during actual movement (Miller et al., 2010).

Similar to imagining movements, one can also ask a human subject to perform a cognitive task such as mental arithmetic or visualizing a face. If the cognitive tasks are sufficiently distinct, the brain areas that are activated will also be different, and the resulting brain activation, measured for example using EEG, can be discriminated using a classifier trained on an initial data set collected from the subject. Each cognitive task is mapped to one control signal (e.g., performing mental arithmetic is mapped to moving the cursor up, etc.). The approach thus relies strongly on being able to reliably discriminate the activity patterns for different cognitive tasks, making the choice of the cognitive tasks an important and tricky experimental design decision.

6.2.4 Stimulus-Evoked Activity

A final class of brain signals useful for BCI is based on stereotyped activity generated by the brain in response to special types of stimuli. One particularly important example is the P300 (or P3) signal observed in EEG recordings, so named because it is a positive deflection in the EEG signal that occurs approximately 300 milliseconds after a stimulus. The P300 is an example of an "event-related potential" (ERP) or "evoked potential" (EP) – it is evoked by the occurrence of a rare or unpredictable stimulus such as a flashing bar at a location being attended to by the subject. It is generally observed most strongly over the parietal lobe, although some components also originate in the temporal and frontal lobes. The exact neural mechanisms responsible for the P300 are as yet unclear: various brain structures such as the parietal cortex, cingulate gyrus, and the temporoparietal cortex as well as limbic structures (hippocampus, amygdala) have been implicated as substrates for the P300.

Other common types of evoked potentials include the steady state visually evoked potential (SSVEP), the N100, and the N400. SSVEP is the response elicited in populations of neurons in the visual cortex when the subject is fixating on a visual stimulus (e.g., a checkerboard pattern) flickering at a particular frequency (e.g., 15 Hz). The associated brain signal, recorded for example using EEG, exhibits peaks in the power spectrum at the stimulus frequency and its harmonics. If different frequencies are associated with different choices, a BCI can decode the subject's choice by detecting where the peaks are.

The N100 (or N1) is a negative going potential that occurs approximately 100 ms after an unpredictable stimulus and is typically distributed over the frontal and central regions of the head. It is usually followed by a positive wave (known as the P200), resulting in the "N100-P200 complex." The N100 occurs for example in response to a sudden, loud noise, but not if the sound is created by the subject.

The N400 is another example of a negative deflection in potential that peaks about 400 milliseconds after particular types of incongruent but potentially meaningful inputs, such as semantically inappropriate words uttered in a sentence during speech. It is typically distributed over central and parietal sites on the scalp. The N400 is similar to another type of potential called an *error potential* (ErrP) evoked when an error is observed after performing an action (see Section 9.1.6).

6.3 Summary

After having reviewed the basic techniques for brain signal acquisition, signal processing, and machine learning in the previous chapters, we began in this chapter the journey toward building full-fledged BCI systems. We became familiar with the major types of BCIs. We discussed the brain responses that researchers have exploited to construct BCIs, ranging from conditioned responses and motor population activity to motor or cognitive imagery and stimulus-evoked responses. The first two types tend to be used in invasive BCIs whereas the second two types have been used in noninvasive BCIs. We begin our in-depth treatment of BCIs by journeying into the world of invasive BCIs in the next chapter.

6.4 Questions and Exercises

1. List the three major types of BCIs. Describe how they differ from one another, and compare their advantages and disadvantages.
2. Explain the difference between classical conditioning and operant conditioning. Which one has been used to construct BCIs and how?
3. Describe the population vector method for decoding motor cortical activity. Discuss how it could be used in a BCI for controlling a prosthetic arm.
4. Discuss how imagined motor or cognitive activity could be used in conjunction with an appropriate machine-learning technique to control a cursor on a computer screen. Based on your design, comment on whether motor or cognitive activity-based control is more natural.
5. Describe the defining characteristics of the following evoked potentials (EPs):
   a. P300
   b. SSVEP
   c. N100
   d. N400
6. (✻ Expedition) Brainstorm about possible ways the EPs in (a) through (d) in Question 5 could be used to build a BCI for selecting an item from a menu.

Part III

Major Types of BCIs

Invasive BCIs

Some of the most important developments in brain-computer interfacing have come from BCIs based on invasive recordings. As reviewed in Chapter 3, invasive recording techniques allow the activities of single neurons or populations of neurons to be recorded. This chapter describes some of the achievements of invasive BCIs in animals and humans.

7.1 Two Major Paradigms in Invasive Brain-Computer Interfacing

7.1.1 BCIs Based on Operant Conditioning

A number of BCIs in animals have been based on operant conditioning, a phenomenon discussed in Section 6.2.1. In operant conditioning, an animal receives a reward upon selection of an appropriate action, e.g., pressing a lever. After repetitive pairing, the animal learns to execute the action in anticipation of the reward. In a BCI paradigm, the animal is rewarded if it selectively activates a neuron or population of neurons to move a cursor or prosthetic device in an appropriate manner.

Early BCI Studies

In the late 1960s, in one of the earliest demonstrations of brain-computer interfacing, Eberhard Fetz at the University of Washington in Seattle utilized the idea of operant conditioning to demonstrate that the activity of a single neuron in a primate's motor cortex can be conditioned to control the needle of an analog meter (Fetz, 1969). The movement of the needle was directly coupled to the firing rate of the neuron: when the needle crossed a threshold, the monkey was rewarded. After several trials, the monkey learned to consistently move the needle past the threshold by increasing the firing rate of the recorded neuron (Figure 7.1). In this example of operant conditioning, the action (needle movement) that produces reward is coupled to increased activity in the recorded neuron (the conditioned response).

Operant conditioning remains an important technique for brain-computer interfacing since it does not require complex machine-learning algorithms and relies on

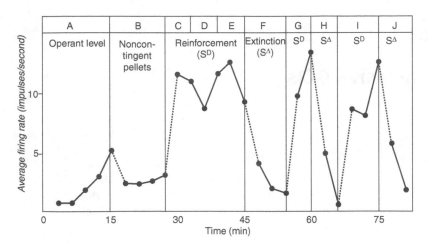

Figure 7.1. **Early BCI study demonstrating control of a meter via motor cortical activity.** The plot shows the average firing rate of a motor cortical neuron used to control the needle of a meter at different times – initially (operant level), noncontingent period (reward of banana-flavored pellets uncorrelated with neuron's firing rate), reinforcement (S^D) periods (reward correlated with high firing rate and deflection of the meter's needle past a threshold), and extinction (S^Δ) periods (no reward or visual feedback from the meter). As observed in the plot (S^D periods), the monkey learned to increase the firing rate of the recorded cortical neuron to sufficiently high levels to deflect the needle of the meter past the preset threshold and obtain the reward (figure adapted from Fetz, 1969).

the brain's remarkable ability to adapt to achieve control over devices. A potential drawback of relying only on conditioning is that the training time required to achieve control over complex devices may be long. This has sparked efforts to develop "coadaptive" BCIs in which both the brain and the BCI system adapt to speed up acquisition of control (see Section 9.1.7).

Recent Developments

Fetz and colleagues have continued to demonstrate the utility of operant conditioning for BCI (Fetz, 2007; Moritz & Fetz, 2011). In one set of experiments, Moritz and Fetz explored whether monkeys could control the firing rates of single cortical cells by providing visual feedback of neural activity and rewarding changes in firing rates. Neurons were recorded from the pre-central (motor) cortex as well as post-central (somatosensory) cortex. In BCI mode, the monkeys modulated the activity of each of up to 250 different neurons to move a cursor along one dimension to targets requiring high or low firing rates (Figure 7.2). Specifically, the recorded neuron's inter-spike intervals were averaged over a 0.5 ms sliding window, and this was continuously mapped to cursor position.

There was more than two-fold improvement in target acquisition rate from the beginning of practice to peak performance: after an average of 24 ± 17 minutes of

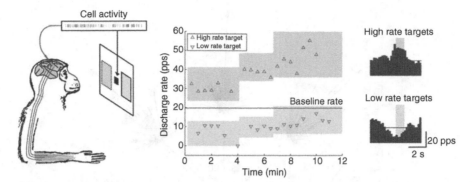

Figure 7.2.   **BCI control of a cursor via single-cell operant conditioning.** The position of the cursor (small black square) was plotted based on the firing rate of the cell. Either the high firing rate target (dotted rectangle on the left) or the low firing rate target (solid rectangle on the right) was shown, and the monkey had to increase or decrease the cell's firing rate to move to the target shown. The middle panel shows the average firing (or discharge) rate (in pulses per second, pps) while holding each randomly presented target for 1 second. The histograms on the right show average cell activity around acquisition of each target. The shaded region on each histogram denotes the target hold period, and the horizontal line denotes the baseline firing rate (adapted from Moritz & Fetz, 2011).

practice with each cell, the monkeys' performance climbed from 6.4 ± 4.5 targets per minute to 13.3 ± 5.6 targets per minute. The monkeys maintained firing rates within each target for 1 second, but could maintain rates for up to 3 seconds for some cells. Based on these results, Fetz and Moritz suggest that direct conversion of activity from single cortical cells to a control signal may be a useful BCI design strategy that is complementary to strategies based on population decoding of intended movement direction (see next section).

7.1.2 BCIs Based on Population Decoding

Operant conditioning relies completely on the user's ability to robustly and reliably modulate brain activity to perform a BCI task. This may however require a considerable amount of practice and may be difficult or impossible to achieve for some subjects and some tasks.

A different strategy relies on using mathematical techniques to decode BCI control signals from neurons activated during movement such as the movement of an arm. As discussed in Section 6.2.2, neurons in the primary motor cortex use a population code to represent various attributes of movement such as direction of motion of a limb, velocities, forces, etc. For example, in the case of movement direction, neurons in the population fire according to how close their preferred direction of movement is to the actual direction of movement. The actual direction of movement $\mathbf{d}$ can be predicted to a reasonable degree using a weighted sum of the preferred directions $\mathbf{p}_i$ of the neurons:

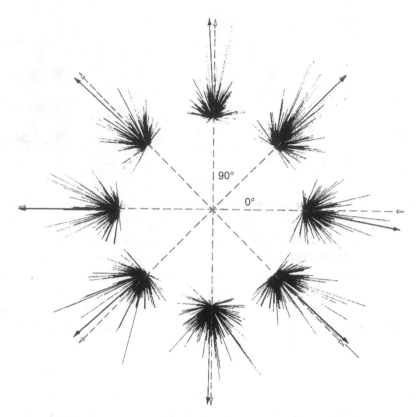

Figure 7.3.   **Comparison of motor cortex population vectors with actual arm movement directions.**
Actual arm movements were along the 8 radially outward directions shown as dashed arrows
that are multiples of 45 degrees. The 8 groups of lines without arrows represent the preferred
directions of neurons multiplied by their firing rates. The sum of each group of vectors is indicated
by a solid arrow. Note that these arrows, representing the population vector, approximately point
in the direction of actual movement for each of the 8 directions. (From Kandel et al., 1991).

$$\hat{\mathbf{d}} = \sum_i \mathbf{p}_i \left(\frac{r - r_0}{r_{\max}} \right)_i \tag{7.1}$$

where r is each neuron's current firing rate, r_0 is its baseline firing rate, and r_{max} is
its maximum average firing rate. Figure 7.3 shows that the prediction made by this
population vector method is quite close to the actual direction of movement made
by the monkey.

The fact that movement-related variables can be extracted from the activities of
populations of neurons was an important finding for brain-computer interfacing
because it led to the realization that the same population motor activity could be
used to control the movement of artificial limbs and other devices. As discussed
below, some of the most impressive demonstrations of brain-computer interfacing
in animals have relied on using regression techniques to map population motor
activity to appropriate control signals for prosthetic devices.

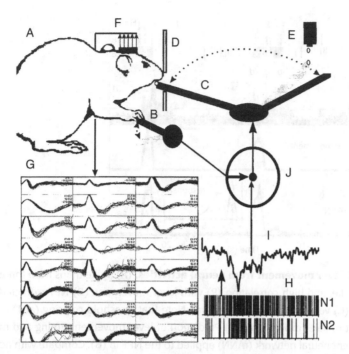

Figure 7.4.   **Invasive BCI in rats.** (A) Rats were trained to press a lever (B) to proportionally move a robot arm (C) from rest position through a slot in a barrier (D) to a water dropper (E) to obtain water. (F) Multielectrode arrays were implanted in the primary motor cortex and VL thalamus for recording up to 46 different neurons. (G) Spike waveforms (superimposed) of 24 such neurons. (H) Spike trains from 2 neurons over 2 seconds. (I) Neuronal population function (NPF) representing the first principal component of a 32-neuron population. (J) Switch that determines whether robot arm is controlled by lever movement or the NPF (adapted from Chapin et al., 1999).

7.2 Invasive BCIs in Animals

7.2.1 BCIs for Prosthetic Arm and Hand Control

An early example of a population activity-based BCI was demonstrated in the laboratory of Nicolelis in 1999 (Chapin et al., 1999). In this BCI, rats were trained to press a spring-loaded lever to proportionally move a robotic arm to a water dropper to obtain a reward of water (Figure 7.4). As the rat was performing this action, the activities of up to 46 neurons in the rat's primary motor cortex and ventrolateral thalamus (VL) were recorded using a multielectrode array (Section 3.1.1).

Principal component analysis (PCA; see Section 4.5.2) was applied to the (up-to-46-dimensional) vectors of firing rates recorded over time across many trials. The principal component corresponding to the largest eigenvalue was used as a neural population function (NPF) (Figure 7.4I). It was found that simple thresholding of this NPF predicted the onset of lever movements with a high degree of accuracy (compare Figures 7.5B and 7.5C; T represents the threshold). To predict the full trajectory of the lever movements, the NPF and corresponding lever position were

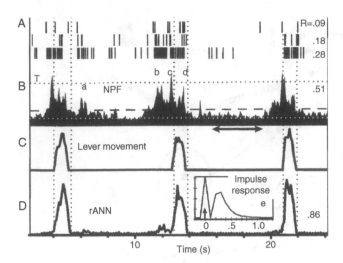

Figure 7.5.   **Prediction of lever movement from neural activities.** (A) Spike trains from three neurons with low, middle, and high correlation (R) with lever movement. (B) NPF extracted from 32 neurons and (C) vertical position of the lever. Note that threshold crossing (at T) of the NPF predicts onset of lever movement. (D) Prediction of lever movement timing and magnitude using a recurrent neural network (rANN) applied to the NPF in (B). Compare with actual lever movement in (C) and note the high correlation value (0.86) with lever position (adapted from Chapin et al., 1999).

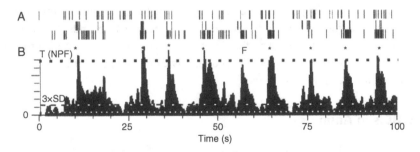

Figure 7.6.   **Neural control of a robotic arm by a rat.** (A) Spike trains from three neurons over a period of 100 seconds after switching to NPF (i.e., neural activity-based) mode of control of a robotic arm. (B) NPF for the same period. Asterisks denote pre-movement peaks of the NPF in trials in which the robot arm was successfully moved to the water dropper using the NPF signal in real time (see text for details) (adapted from Chapin et al., 1999).

fed as input and output respectively to a neural network with recurrent connections, and the network was trained using backpropagation (Section 5.2.2). After training, it was found that the network could accurately predict the lever movements from a test dataset (Figure 7.5D). The final demonstration involved using the NPF to directly control the robotic arm: after a five-minute session during which the rats physically moved the lever to get reward, the control of the robotic arm was suddenly switched to NPF control mode. As shown in the example in Figure 7.6, in 8

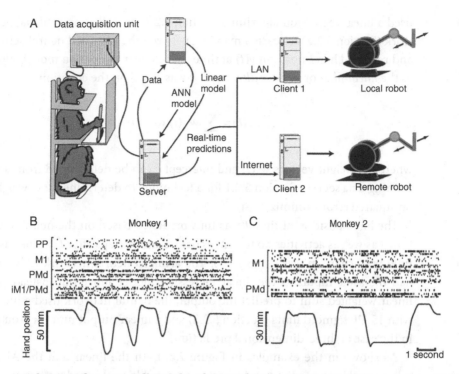

Figure 7.7.   **Monkey BCI for a one-dimensional control task.** (A) Experimental setup for a BCI that uses simultaneously recorded cortical neuronal data from a monkey making one-dimensional hand movements and uses this data to control local and remote robotic arms. Linear and ANN models were used to predict hand position from neural data. (B) and (C) Examples of spike trains recorded from two monkeys in 5 and 2 cortical areas respectively during the execution of one-dimensional hand movements (hand position data is shown in the trace below). PP, posterior parietal cortex; M1, primary motor cortex; PMd, dorsal premotor cortex; iM1/PMd, ipsilateral M1 and PMd (adapted from Wessberg et al., 2000).

out of 9 cases where the rat moved the lever, the NPF successfully moved the robot arm to obtain the water reward. In 15 trials, this particular animal was 100 percent successful in using its neural activity to obtain reward, provided appropriately large lever movements were made. Interestingly, the researchers found that after a certain number of trials, many of the rats no longer pressed the lever but retrieved reward directly using neural activity.

Following their experiments with rats, Nicolelis, Wessberg, and, colleagues demonstrated the control of a robotic arm by two monkeys based on spikes recorded simultaneously from three cortical areas in both hemispheres: primary motor cortex, dorsal premotor cortex, and posterior parietal cortex (Wessberg et al., 2000). They trained the monkeys to perform two motor tasks, one involving one-dimensional hand movements and the other involving three-dimensional hand movements. In the first task, the monkey made one-dimensional hand movements to the left or right to move a manipulandum in response to a visual cue (Figure 7.7). The researchers used a linear regression algorithm (Section 5.2.1) as well as an artificial neural network (Section 5.2.2) to learn a mapping between the recorded neural activities $\mathbf{u}(t)$ and recorded hand position $v(t)$ at time t. The linear regression model (also known as the *linear filter* or *Weiner filter* model) was based on the equation:

$$v(t) = \sum_{i=-m}^{n} \mathbf{w}^T(i)\mathbf{u}(t-i) + c \qquad (7.2)$$

where the weight vectors $\mathbf{w}^T(i)$ and intercept c can be determined from a recorded training data set (see Section 5.2.1 for a technique to determine these weights based on squared error minimization).

The hand position at time t was thus predicted based on the neural activities at time t as well as activities up to n steps before and m steps after t (in the case of real-time prediction, m was set to zero). The artificial neural network (ANN) method had the same inputs as the linear regression model above but instead of using a linear weighted sum to predict the output, the neural network used a hidden layer with 15–20 sigmoid units (Section 5.2.2) and a linear output unit (or 3 output units in the case of three-dimensional prediction).

As shown in the examples in Figure 7.8, both the linear and the ANN methods were able to predict hand position reasonably well based on neural activities. No significant difference in accuracy was observed between the two methods. The performance of both methods, as captured by the correlation coefficient r between predicted and actual hand position, improved within the first few minutes of the experiment and remained stable at average values between 0.6 and 0.7 throughout the period of the experiment (Figure 7.8C and 7.8D). To guard against non-stationarity in the neural activities over time, the models were continuously updated throughout the experiment using the most recently recorded 10 minutes of data. The predicted hand position signal was in turn used to control a local and remote robotic arm to mimic the one-dimensional hand movements of the monkey (Figure 7.8E).

In a second task, the monkeys made three-dimensional hand movements to reach for pieces of food placed randomly at one of four different positions on a tray (Figure 7.9C). The sequence of movements made by the monkeys are shown in Figures 7.9A and 7.9B. Both the linear and ANN models discussed above performed well in predicting these three-dimensional hand movements. Figures 7.9D and 7.9E show examples of the actual and predicted hand trajectories for the two monkeys. The predicted trajectories are roughly similar to the actual ones, though with some noticeable deviations such as for the endpoints in the panels on the right in Figures 7.9D and 7.9E. The correlation coefficients along the X, Y, and Z dimensions are shown in Figures 7.9F and 7.9G. These reflect the improvement in prediction accuracy over time, especially in the early trials, followed by a plateau (or even a slight decrease in performance as in the case of monkey 2 for X and Y directions).

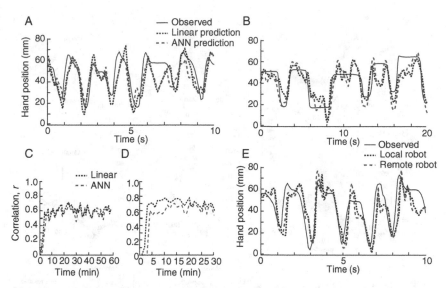

Figure 7.8.   **BCI control of one-dimensional hand movements.** (A) and (B) Example of observed (line) and real-time predicted one-dimensional hand position using linear (dotted line) and ANN (gray dashed line) models in monkey 1 (A) and 2 (B). (C) and (D) Correlation coefficient *r* between predicted and actual hand movements, using linear (dotted line) and ANN (gray dashed line) models, in one experimental session in monkey 1 (C) and 2 (D). (E) Comparison of actual movements and movements made by a local (dotted line) and remote (gray dashed line) robot arm using neural data from monkey 1 and the linear model (adapted from Wessberg et al., 2000).

The researchers further found that model parameters learned from data for one set of directions (e.g., targets on the right) could be used to predict hand trajectories in another direction (e.g., targets on the left).

Other experiments by Schwartz, Velliste, and colleagues have demonstrated the use of cortical signals to control a multi-jointed prosthetic device for direct real-time interaction with the physical environment (Velliste et al., 2008). In their experiments, monkeys used responses from primary motor cortex neurons to control a prosthetic arm and gripper in a continuous self-feeding task (Figure 7.10). The monkey had to move the prosthetic arm to arbitrary locations in the three-dimensional workspace in front of it where food was presented. The animal then had to close the gripper to grab the piece of food, move the arm to its mouth, and open the gripper to retrieve the food.

In this task, in addition to the three dimensions of movement, the BCI also proportionally controlled the distance between the two "fingers" on the gripper to open or close it. The algorithm used to control the arm and gripper was the *population vector* method discussed above in Section 7.1.2. The output vector was four-dimensional, comprising the velocity of the endpoint of the robotic arm along X, Y, and Z directions in an extrinsic three-dimensional Cartesian coordinate frame, along with the aperture velocity between the gripper fingers (fourth dimension). This output vector

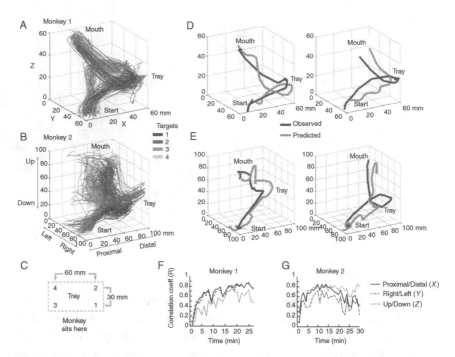

Figure 7.9.   **Prediction of three-dimensional hand movements from neural activity**. (A) and (B) Three-dimensional hand movement trajectories produced by monkey 1 (A) and 2 (B) during an experimental session. (C) Schematic diagram of the four possible target locations in the reaching task. (D) and (E) Examples of observed (black) and predicted (gray) three-dimensional hand trajectories for monkey 1 (D) and 2 (E). (F) and (G) Correlation coefficient for X (line), Y (dashed line), and Z (dotted line) directions between actual and predicted three-dimensional hand movements using the linear model (adapted from Wessberg et al., 2000).

was computed as a weighted sum of the four-dimensional preferred directions of the neurons (the dimensions being X, Y, Z, and gripper aperture). The weights were the instantaneous firing rates of the units, similar to Equation 7.1. The predicted four-dimensional endpoint velocity was integrated to obtain endpoint position, which was then converted (via inverse kinematics) to joint-angle commands for each of the robot's four degrees of freedom.

One monkey performed 2 days of this continuous self-feeding task with a combined success rate of 61% using 116 primary motor cortex neurons. For just the positioning portion of the task (move arm to feeder position), the success rate was 98%. Figure 7.11 illustrates the spike trains from the 116 neurons and the resulting arm and gripper movement for four successful trials. The four-dimensional preferred directions of the neurons are depicted in Figure 7.11G and can be seen to span the range of X, Y, and Z directions and gripper opening.

One can also use more sophisticated decoding techniques such as Kalman filtering (Section 4.4.5) to estimate hand kinematics (position, velocity, acceleration) from

Figure 7.10. **BCI control of a prosthetic arm and gripper for self-feeding.** The monkey's arms were restrained (inserted up to the elbow in horizontal tubes as shown in the image), and a prosthetic arm was positioned next to the monkey's shoulder. Spikes recorded from multi-electrode arrays implanted in primary motor cortex were processed (boxes at top right) and used to control the three-dimensional arm velocity and the gripper aperture velocity in real time. Food targets were presented (top left) at arbitrary positions in the three-dimensional workspace in front of the animal (adapted from Velliste et al., 2008).

the firing rates of motor cortex neurons. The advantage of using a technique such as the Kalman filter is that one can model the measurement and temporal dynamics of the signals using a probabilistic model, allowing a principled approach to estimating variables such as position and velocity over time. We discuss here the approach of Wu, Black, and colleagues (2006), who used a Kalman filter to estimate the posterior probability distribution over hand kinematics given a sequence of observed firing rates. The experiments utilized multielectrode neural recordings from the arm area of primary motor cortex in two monkeys. Monkeys performed two tasks: a pinball task (using a manipulandum on a 30 cm × 30 cm tablet to move the cursor to a target placed at random locations on the screen) and a pursuit tracking task (making the cursor follow a moving target within a fixed distance range).

The state vector for the Kalman filter was chosen to be $\mathbf{x}_t = [px, py, vx, vy, ax, ay]^T$, representing hand position, velocity, and acceleration along x, y, and z directions respectively. The sampling interval between t and $t + 1$ was chosen to be 70 ms for the pinball task and 50 ms for the pursuit task. The likelihood (or measurement) model for the Kalman filter specifies how the hand kinematics vector $\mathbf{x}_t$ relates to the observed firing rates $\mathbf{y}_t$:

$$\mathbf{y}_t = B\mathbf{x}_t + \mathbf{m}_t \tag{7.3}$$

and the dynamics model specifies how the hand kinematics vector changes over time:

$$\mathbf{x}_t = A\mathbf{x}_{t-1} + \mathbf{n}_t \tag{7.4}$$

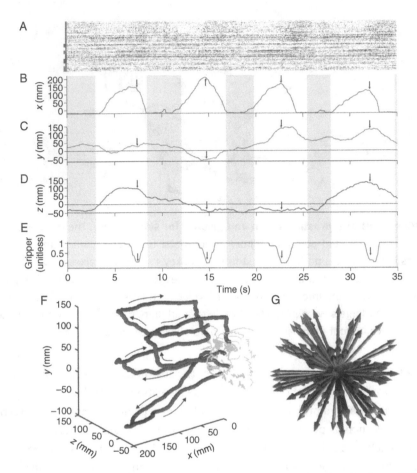

Figure 7.11. **Neural responses and prosthetic arm/gripper trajectories in the self-feeding task.**
(See color plates for the same figure in color) (A) Spike trains from 116 neurons used for
controlling the arm and gripper in 4 successful trials. Each row represents spikes from one
neuron, rows being grouped by major tuning preference (red, X; green, Y; blue, Z; purple,
gripper; thin bar: negative major tuning; thick bar: positive). (B) through (D) show X, Y, and
Z components of arm endpoint position (gray regions: inter-trial intervals; arrows: gripper
closing at target). (E) Gripper aperture (0: closed; 1: open). (F) Arm trajectories for the same
4 trials, with color indicating gripper aperture (blue: closed; purple: half-closed; red: open).
(G) Four-dimensional preferred directions of the 116 neurons. Arrow direction represents X,
Y, Z direction preference, color indicates gripper aperture opening preference (blue, negative
value; purple, zero; red, positive value) (adapted from Velliste et al., 2008).

In these equations, $\mathbf{n}_t$ and $\mathbf{m}_t$ are zero-mean Gaussian noise processes with covariance matrices Q and R respectively. A training dataset was collected for the two
tasks containing both the monkey's hand position data and the neural data over
time for several trials. Hand velocity and acceleration for each time point were calculated from the position data by approximating the derivative with the difference
between consecutive data points divided by the sampling interval. This training

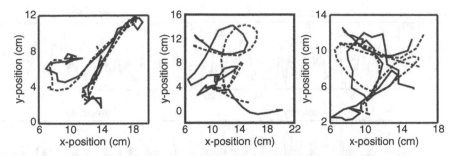

Figure 7.12. **Predicting hand trajectories from neural activities using a Kalman filter.** The dashed line shows the true hand trajectory for the pinball task (see text). The solid line is the Kalman filter's predicted trajectory from neural activity. The trajectories span 50 time-steps (3.5 seconds) (adapted from Wu et al., 2006).

dataset, which contains both $\mathbf{x}_t$ and $\mathbf{y}_t$, can be used to learn the matrices A, B, Q, R by, for example, maximizing the joint probability $P(\mathbf{x}_1,\ldots,\mathbf{x}_T,\mathbf{y}_1,\ldots,\mathbf{y}_T)$ of the training data. Since there is a delay between neural activity and the resulting hand motion, the researchers also incorporated a time lag in their Kalman filter likelihood model so that $\mathbf{x}$ at any time instant is related to firing rates from some time in the past. They found that while a uniform time lag of 140–150 ms for all neurons worked better than no lag, the best performance was achieved by choosing different lags (between 0 and 280 ms) for the different neurons.

Once the Kalman filter parameters A, B, Q, and R have been learned from training data, the Kalman filter can be used to compute the Gaussian posterior probability of hand kinematics given observed firing rates. As described in Section 4.4.5, this involves using the Kalman filter equations to compute the mean $\hat{\mathbf{x}}_t$ and covariance S_t of the Gaussian representing the posterior $P(\mathbf{x}_t \mid \mathbf{y}_1,\ldots, \mathbf{y}_t)$.

As seen in the examples in Figure 7.12 for the pinball task, the estimated hand trajectories using the Kalman filter (given by the mean $\hat{\mathbf{x}}_t$) are close to the actual hand trajectories. This is further illustrated by Figure 7.13 which shows the 6 different components of the state vector as estimated by the Kalman filter for a 20-second test sequence.

The performance of the Kalman filter method was measured using two similarity metrics: mean squared error (MSE) and correlation coefficient (CC) between predicted and actual hand positions for x and y coordinates:

$$MSE = \frac{1}{T}\sum_{t=1}^{T}\left((p_{x,t} - \hat{p}_{x,t})^2 + (p_{y,t} - \hat{p}_{y,t})^2\right) \tag{7.5}$$

$$CC = \left(\frac{\sum_t (p_{x,t} - \overline{p}_x)(\hat{p}_{x,t} - \overline{\hat{p}}_x)}{\sqrt{\sum_t (p_{x,t} - \overline{p}_x)^2 \sum_t (\hat{p}_{x,t} - \overline{\hat{p}}_x)^2}}, \frac{\sum_t (p_{y,t} - \overline{p}_y)(\hat{p}_{y,t} - \overline{\hat{p}}_y)}{\sqrt{\sum_t (p_{y,t} - \overline{p}_y)^2 \sum_t (\hat{p}_{y,t} - \overline{\hat{p}}_y)^2}}\right) \tag{7.6}$$

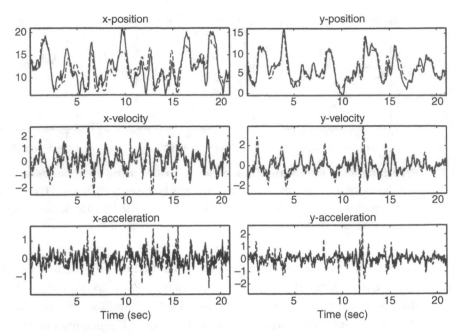

Figure 7.13. **Hand kinematics estimated using a Kalman filter.** The plots show the 6 components of the hand kinematics state vector for a 20-second test sequence for the pinball task (true values: dashed; estimated values: solid) (adapted from Wu et al., 2006).

As shown in Table 7.1, the Kalman filter method outperformed both the population vector method (Equation 7.1) and the linear-filter method (Equation 7.2) discussed earlier in this chapter.

A different approach to using a linear model (as in the Kalman filter) for decoding movements is to use an unknown time-varying hidden state vector $\mathbf{x}_t$ to mediate the mapping from firing rates $\mathbf{f}_t$ to kinematic outputs $\mathbf{y}_t$. This leads to the equations:

$$\mathbf{x}_t = A\mathbf{x}_{t-1} + C\mathbf{f}_t + \mathbf{n}_t \tag{7.7}$$

$$\mathbf{y}_t = B\mathbf{x}_t + \mathbf{m}_t \tag{7.8}$$

where once again $\mathbf{n}_t$ and $\mathbf{m}_t$ are zero-mean Gaussian noise processes. Such an approach was explored by Donoghue, Vargas-Irwin, and colleagues (Vargas-Irwin et al., 2010) to map neural activity in primary motor cortex of monkeys to arm, wrist, and hand postures during a dynamic reaching and grasping task (Figure 7.14A). In particular, the linear model was used to predict 25 joint angles of a model of the monkey's arm, wrist, and hand (Figure 7.14B). The training data consisted of neural firing rates from 30 to122 neurons (recorded using microelectrode arrays implanted in the primary motor cortex upper-limb area) and the 25 joint angles estimated using a motion-capture system based on reflective markers placed on the monkey's body (Figure 7.14A). For each joint angle y_t, an unknown

Table 7.1. Comparison of the Kalman filter-based method with other methods for predicting hand position from neural activity in the Pinball and Pursuit tasks. The variable N is the number of time steps before the current time step for which the firing rate is used in the linear model (same as n in Equation 7.2, with $m = 0$) (from Wu et al., 2006).

	$CC\ (x, y)$	$MSE\ (cm^2)$
Pinball task		
Method	$CC\ (x, y)$	$MSE\ (cm^2)$
Population vector	(0.26, 0.21)	75.0
Linear filter $(N = 14)$	(0.79, 0.93)	6.48
Kalman $\Delta t = 140$ ms, nonuniform lag	**(0.84, 0.93)**	**4.55**
Pursuit Tracking task		
Method		
Population vector	(0.57, 0.43)	13.2
Linear filter $(N = 30)$	(0.73, 0.67)	4.74
Kalman $\Delta t = 300$ ms, 150 ms uniform lag	**(0.81, 0.70)**	**4.66**

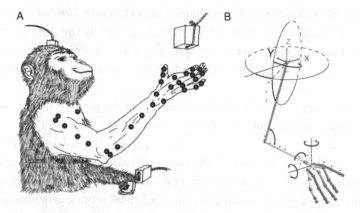

Figure 7.14. Monkey BCI for dynamic reaching and grasping. (A) Neural activities are recorded from the upper-limb area of the primary motor cortex while the monkey performed a task involving intercepting and holding objects swinging toward the animal from the end of a string. The monkey's movements were recorded using a motion-capture system based on tracking 29 reflective markers attached to the monkey's arm, wrist, and hand. (B) Joint angles for a model of the monkey's hand, wrist, and arm were calculated from the three-dimensional position of the markers for each frame (adapted from Vargas-Irwin et al., 2010).

three-dimensional state vector $\mathbf{x}_t$ was assumed, and the corresponding matrices A, B, and C were learned from training data by iterating between re-estimating the most likely values of the hidden states and minimizing, via gradient descent (Section 5.2.2), the output prediction error under these values. In addition to the joint angles, linear models for the grip aperture and (x, y, z) position of the arm endpoint were also learned in a similar manner. After learning, given firing rates as input, each kinematic variable y_t was predicted by first predicting the state using

Equation 7.7 and then predicting the kinematic value using Equation 7.8. Each kinematic prediction was based on the firing rates of 30 neurons, selected to optimize accuracy for that parameter.

Figure 7.15A shows examples of actual arm postures (shown in lighter color) from a single reach-and-grasp trial and the arm postures predicted from neural activity. There appears to be a close correspondence between the two. This is further illustrated in the plots in Figure 7.15B showing the actual and predicted grip aperture and one of the joint angles (shoulder azimuth). A summary of the performance of the method (in terms of correlation coefficient between actual and predicted values) for all 25 joint angles as well as grip aperture and arm endpoint position is shown Figure 7.15C. The mean correlation coefficient across sessions of all decoded joint angles was quite high (0.72 ± 0.094) suggesting that there is enough information in populations of several tens of motor cortical neurons to reconstruct naturalistic reaching and grasping movements, at least for the task studied.

Estimating Kinetic Parameters from Neural Activity

The invasive BCIs described above focused on extracting *kinematic* parameters such as position and joint angles from neural activity. If the goal is to control robotic prostheses, which have their own physical dynamics, it may be more desirable to extract *kinetic* parameters such as force and joint torque from neural activity.

Hatsopoulos, Fagg, and colleagues have shown that it is possible to reconstruct the torque trajectories of the shoulder and elbow joints from the activity of neurons in the primary motor cortex of monkeys (Fagg et al., 2009). The task involved the monkeys making reaching movements in the horizontal plane. The activities of between 31 and 99 neurons were recorded across different sessions using an electrode array while kinematic data was recorded using an exoskeletal robotic arm attached to the monkey's upper arm. Using standard physics-based equations of motion for the monkey-and-robot-arm system, the recorded kinematic data was used to compute net torque applied to the shoulder and elbow in order to account for the observed motion. A linear filter approach (Equation 7.2) was used to predict torque based on neural activity up to one second in the past.

The researchers found that torque reconstruction performance was nearly equal to that of hand position and velocity. Furthermore, the addition of delayed position and velocity feedback to the torque prediction algorithm substantially improved torque reconstructions. This suggests that a combination of kinematic and kinetic information may prove to be a useful strategy for future BCI applications involving control of robotic prosthetics and other physical devices.

Using Local Field Potentials (LFPs) Instead of Spikes

We have thus far learned about BCIs that rely on spikes from individual neurons (isolated using spike-sorting algorithms – see Section 4.1). However, if the goal is to

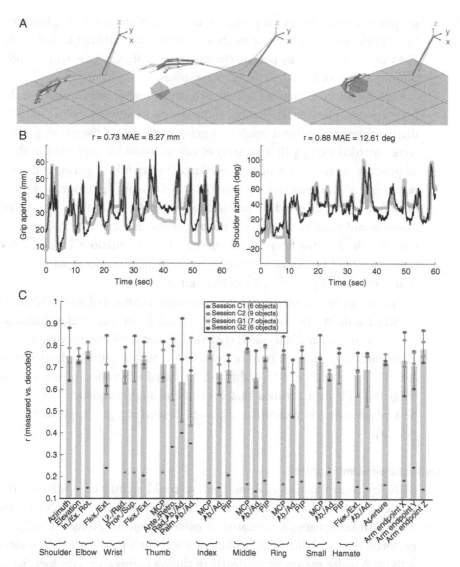

Figure 7.15. **Comparison of actual and predicted movements in the dynamic grasping task.** (A) Examples of actual (lighter color) and predicted (solid) arm postures from a reach-and-grasp trial (each of the 25 joint angles were decoded independently based on Equations 7.7 and 7.8). (B) Comparison of actual (gray) and predicted (black) grip aperture and shoulder azimuth values over time. (C) Correlation coefficients between actual and predicted kinematic variables. Shaded dots represent the values for each experimental session, and the bars mark the mean of all sessions. Black asterisks represent chance levels of performance. MAE, mean absolute error; In./Ex. Rot., internal/external rotation; Flex./Ext., flexion/extension; Ul./Rad., ulnar/radial deviation; Pron./Sup., pronation/supination; MCP, metacarpophalangeal; Ante./Retro., anteposition/retroposition; Rad. Ab./Ad., radial abduction/adduction; Palm. Ab./Ad., palmar abduction/adduction; PIP, proximal interphalangeal (adapted from Vargas-Irwin et al., 2010).

control a communication or prosthetic device, can one simply use local field potentials (LFPs) recorded by these electrodes rather than attempt to isolate the spikes? LFPs can be obtained by placing electrodes far from any one neuron and low-pass filtering the recorded signal to eliminate spikes.

LFPs reflect the combined activity of a large number of neurons near the recording electrode. Donoghue, Zhuang, and colleagues explored the use of LFPs for predicting three-dimensional reach-and-grasp kinematics (Zhuang et al., 2010). LFPs were recorded using a 10 × 10 array of microelectrodes implanted in the arm area of primary motor cortex of two monkeys. The monkeys performed the dynamic reaching-and-grasping task in Figure 7.14. A Kalman filter model was trained based on the recorded LFP and corresponding kinematic data (three-dimensional hand position and velocity, along with grasp aperture and aperture velocity). The equations for the Kalman filter model are the same as Equations 7.3 and 7.4, except y_t represents the LFP power in a particular frequency band computed in a time window immediately preceding the current kinematic state.

The researchers characterized the information content of seven different LFP frequency bands in the range of 0.3–400 Hz and found that higher frequency bands (e.g., 100–200 Hz and 200–400 Hz) carried the most information about the recorded kinematics (similar results have been obtained for human electrocorticography [ECoG] – see Section 8.1). Kalman-filter-based estimation of the kinematic data from the LFP data revealed that broad-band high frequency LFPs provided the best performance in reconstructing reach kinematics, grasp aperture, and aperture velocity.

7.2.2 BCIs for Lower-Limb Control

BCIs for controlling bipedal locomotion could significantly improve the quality of life of individuals who have lost control of their lower limbs due to spinal cord injury, stroke, or neurodegenerative diseases. To date, relatively few BCI studies have explored the feasibility of controlling a lower-limb prosthetic device using neural activity. A major reason for the dearth of studies in this area is the logistical difficulty in recording from the brain while the animal is walking or otherwise moving. An exception is the study by Nicolelis, Fitzsimmons, and colleagues (2009) who investigated whether kinematics of bipedal walking (on a treadmill) can be predicted using the ensemble activity of cortical neurons in rhesus monkeys. Their approach is based on decoding the major parameters of walking such as step time, step length, foot location, and leg orientation, while relying on existing lower-level systems for automatic controls such as foot orientation, load placement, balance, and other safety concerns. The result is a BCI that follows the general commands of the user while enforcing stability and overriding commands likely to result in falls.

Figure 7.16A illustrates the experimental setup used to study whether the kinematic parameters of walking can be predicted from neural activity. Two rhesus monkeys were trained to walk on a treadmill while the activities of about 200

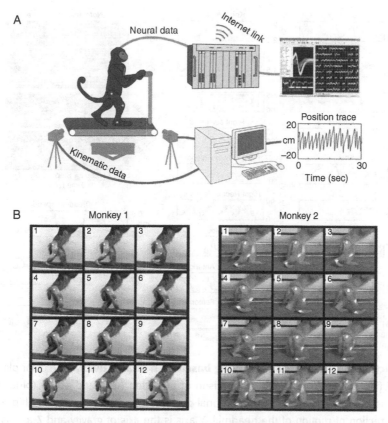

Figure 7.16. **Predicting lower-limb kinematics using neural activity.** (A) A monkey walked on a custom-built hydraulically driven treadmill while neural activity in its primary motor cortex and primary somatosensory cortex was recorded. Simultaneously, two wireless cameras tracked the position of the monkey's right leg. (B) Images captured by one of the cameras showing the typical bipedal walk cycle of the two monkeys (adapted from Fitzsimmons et al., 2009).

neurons in the lower-limb areas of their primary motor and somatosensory cortices were recorded. The three-dimensional coordinates of fluorescent markers on the right hip, knee, and ankle (Figure 7.16A and 7.16B) were tracked using two cameras, and this information was used to extract the following additional kinematic parameters: hip and knee joint angles, foot contact with the treadmill, walking speed, step frequency, and step length. The recorded neural and kinematic data were used to learn a linear (Weiner filter) model (see Equation 7.2) using the Moore-Penrose pseudoinverse method (Section 5.2.1) to estimate the weights.

Figure 7.17 demonstrates that the kinematics of walking can be predicted reasonably well from the activities of neurons in primary motor and somatosensory cortices. Additionally, the trained model was also able to predict muscle activations during walking recorded via EMG (Figure 7.17D) as well as slowly changing variables such as walking speed, step frequency, and step length (Figure 7.17F). The researchers found that overall, for the two monkeys studied, the correlation coefficients (CCs;

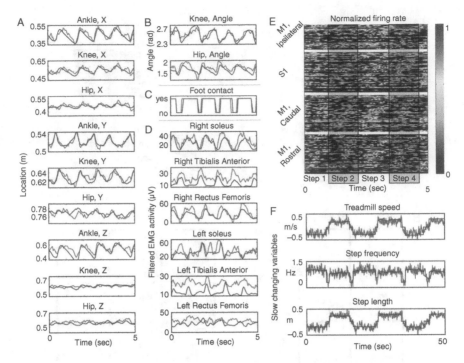

Figure 7.17. **Predicting the kinematics of walking based on neural activity.** (See color plates for the same figure in color). (A)–(C) Comparison of predicted (red) and actual (blue) kinematic variables. (A) shows the three-dimensional position of the ankle, knee, and hip. X-axis is in the direction of motion of the treadmill, Y axis is the axis of gravity and Z axis is lateral to the surface of the treadmill and orthogonal to the direction of motion. (B) shows hip and knee joint angle variables and (C) depicts foot contact (binary variable defining swing versus stance phase of walking). (D) Predicted versus actual muscle signals (EMG). (E) Normalized firing rates of 220 neurons, sorted by cortical area and by phase within the step cycle. M1: primary motor cortex; S1: primary somatosensory cortex. (F) Prediction of slowly changing variables (walking speed, step frequency, and step length) over a 50 second time window (adapted from Fitzsimmons et al., 2009).

Equation 7.6) were in the range 0.2 to 0.9, with the best predictions being the X, Y coordinates of the ankle and the knee (CC in the range 0.61–0.86). The hip angle and foot contact were predicted with CCs in the range 0.58–0.73 and 0.58–0.61 respectively. Prediction accuracy for the slowly changing variables was generally lower, though still potentially useful for prosthetic control, with CCs in the range 0.24–0.42 for walking speed, 0.48–0.57 for step frequency, and 0.30–0.40 for step length.

While the study suggests that kinematic parameters of walking can be predicted from neural activity, there has yet to be a convincing demonstration of closed-loop cortical control of walking. An alternate approach to restoring locomotion, for example, after spinal injury, is to rely on neuroplasticity: Courtine, van den Brand, and colleagues (2012) have shown that combining electrical stimulation of the spinal cord with a chemical injection of monoamine agonists allows rats with paralyzing lesions to regain the capacity for refined locomotion by causing new cortical connections to grow. These results offer a promising direction for movement restoration in spinal cord injury patients. These results are however less applicable to lower-limb amputees, for whom BCIs that directly control prosthetic legs offer the most viable path toward restoration of movement.

7.2.3 BCIs for Cursor Control

A large group of invasive BCI studies in monkeys have focused on the control of computer cursors using motor neuron activity. One reason for the popularity of the cursor control paradigm is that it provides a simple framework for studying closed-loop visual-feedback-based control of a device (in this case, the cursor). Additionally, BCI control of a cursor also has an immediate biomedical application in that it would allow locked-in patients to communicate via selection of items on a menu.

Cursor Control Using a Linear Model

In one of the first invasive BCI demonstrations of cursor control, Serruya, Donoghue, and colleagues (2002) showed that the activity of 7–30 primary motor cortical neurons can be used by a monkey to move a computer cursor to any new position on a computer screen (size 14 degrees × 14 degrees of visual angle). The monkeys in the experiment first used their hand to move a manipulandum that controlled the position of a cursor and tracked a continuously moving target that began at an arbitrary location and followed a pseudorandom trajectory. The linear filter method (Equation 7.2 above) was used to predict cursor position from neural activity recorded over the previous one second. The filter was then used in a closed-loop visual feedback task that required the cursor to be moved to stationary targets of size 0.6 degrees, which were displayed one at a time at random locations on the screen. Hand control of the cursor position was substituted with neural control. The linear filter was also updated using data from 2 minutes of neural control to relate firing rates to target position.

The plots in Figure 7.18A and 7.18B show two examples of cursor trajectory under neural control (dark gray). In some cases, the monkey used its hand to move the manipulandum (light gray trajectory in Figure 7.18A) at the same time that it was using neural control to move the cursor, whereas in other cases, it did not move its hand (Figure 7.18B). The researchers found that cursor control was nearly as good as hand-based control, with time required to acquire targets using the neural signal not statistically different from that required for hand motions (Figure 7.18C and 7.18D).

Cursor Control Using a Nonlinear Kalman Filter Model

A different approach to controlling cursors using neural activity is to use the Kalman filter (Section 4.4.5). One such approach was investigated by Li, Nicolelis and colleagues (2009). Two monkeys were trained to manipulate a handheld joystick to

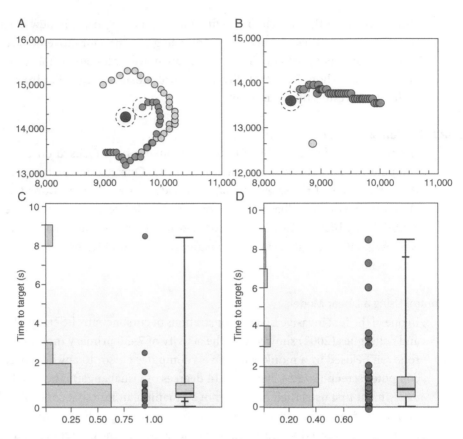

Figure 7.18. **Cursor control using an invasive BCI.** (A) and (B) Examples showing neural control of cursor movement (dark gray) toward a target (black). Movement of the hand during neural control in these 2 examples is shown in light gray. Each circle represents an estimate of position, updated at 50 ms intervals. Axes are in x, y screen coordinates (1,000 units corresponds to a visual angle of 3.57). (C) and (D) Time taken to reach the target under hand (C) and neural (D) control. Histogram shows the data frequency distribution and spheres represent trial times. The summary statistic at the right shows the range of the data (vertical lines), the median time taken to reach the target (thick horizontal line within shaded box), and the 25th and 75th percentiles (bottom and top of box) (from Serruya et al., 2002)

perform two tasks (Figure 7.19): a "center-out" task, where the cursor was to be moved from the screen center to targets randomly placed at a fixed distance from the center, and a "pursuit" task where the monkeys tracked a continuously moving target. The activity of between 94 and 240 neurons were recorded using multielectrode arrays implanted in several cortical areas: the primary motor cortex (M1), the primary somatosensory cortex (S1), the dorsal premotor cortex (PMd), the posterior parietal cortex (PP), and the supplementary motor area (SMA).

The neural data and the corresponding cursor movement data were used to train a nonlinear version of the Kalman filter known as the *unscented Kalman filter* (UKF). Figure 7.20 compares the standard Kalman filter model with the UKF. The UKF

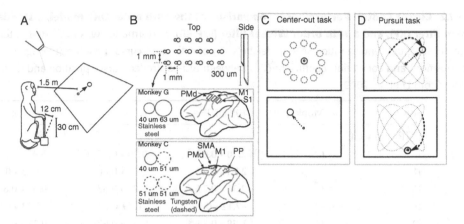

Figure 7.19. **Experimental setup for demonstrating BCI control of a cursor.** (A) A cursor and a target were projected onto a screen in front of a monkey. The monkey was trained to move the cursor using a handheld joystick. The monkey was rewarded with fruit juice when the cursor was placed inside the target. (B) Schematic diagram showing the microelectrode array (top) and implanted locations of the arrays in the cortex of two monkeys (bottom two panels). (C) Center-out task. Monkeys moved the cursor from the center to a peripheral target at a random angle and fixed radius from the center. (D) Pursuit task. Monkeys moved the cursor to track a continuously moving target following a Lissajous curve (adapted from Li et al., 2009).

allows both the measurement and dynamics models to be nonlinear. In our case, if the hidden state vector consists of cursor position and velocity, the UKF allows us to use, for example, a potentially more accurate *quadratic* function to relate cursor position and velocity to neuronal firing rates (Figure 7.20D). Additionally, rather than using a state vector with just the current position and velocity values (Figure 7.20A and 7.20E), the researchers used a state vector consisting of position and velocity values from 10 consecutive time steps, resulting in a 10th order autoregressive (AR) model for the evolution of state (Figure 7.20B and 7.20E).

Figure 7.21 provides an example of online cursor control using the 10th order UKF compared to the standard Kalman filter and a 10th order Weiner filter (Equation 7.2). The dashed curves in the plots represent target positions. Table 7.2 summarizes the results. The 10th order UKF outperformed a slew of other methods for online cursor control, including a 1st order UKF, the standard Kalman filter, the 10th order Weiner filter, and the population vector method (Equation 7.1).

Enhancing BCI Control by Combining Proprioceptive and Visual Feedback

The BCIs described above rely only on visual feedback for closed-loop BCI control. However, when controlling the body, the brain relies on feedback from additional modalities such as *kinesthetic* (or *proprioceptive*) *feedback* from muscles, tendons, and joints to guide and correct movement. Suminski, Hatsopoulos, and colleagues (2010) have demonstrated that kinesthetic feedback can be used together with vision

Table 7.2. Cursor Control Performance. Comparison of the 10th order UKF model, a standard Kalman filter (KF), and a 10th order Wiener filter (WF RR). Performance was evaluated in terms of two metrics: signal-to-noise-ratio (SNR, in decibels dB) of estimated cursor position (the signal was the target position) and correlation coefficient (CC) between BCI-controlled cursor position and target cursor position (from Li et al., 2009)

Session	Monkey	10th UKF	KF	WF RR
SNR, dB • CC				
17	C	**2.70 • 0.69**	0.70 • 0.47	NA
18	C	**2.73 • 0.72**	2.42 • 0.60	−1.13 • 0.54
19	C	**2.51 • 0.71**	0.80 • 0.53	0.07 • 0.68
20	G	−2.12 • 0.10	**-1.49 • 0.15**	−3.23 • 0.07
21	G	**1.58 • 0.56**	1.55 • 0.57	0.77 • **0.58**
22	G	**3.23 • 0.71**	0.39 • 0.48	−0.06 • 0.47
Mean difference from KF		**1.04 • 0.12**	0.00 • 0.00	−1.45 • 0.00

to significantly improve control of a cursor controlled by neural activity of the primary motor cortex of a monkey. In their experiment, an exoskeletal robot was used to make the monkey's arm passively follow a cortically controlled visual cursor. This coupling provided the monkey with kinesthetic information about the motion of the cursor in addition to visual information. The researchers found that when visual feedback and kinesthetic feedback were congruent, targets were reached faster and cursor paths became straighter, compared to incongruent feedback conditions. These early results suggest that future BCIs may benefit from combining proprioceptive and other types of sensory feedback in addition to the more commonly used visual feedback for closed-loop control.

7.2.4 Cognitive BCIs

The BCIs described above were based on decoding continuous movement trajectories for prosthetic limbs or computer cursors from the activities of neurons in the motor cortex. An alternate approach is to directly decode the *target* of the intended movement from brain areas farther upstream from motor cortex and then guide the prosthetic device autonomously to the target or place the cursor directly on the decoded target. Such BCIs are known as *cognitive BCIs* because they rely on higher-level cognitive signals rather than signals from the primary motor cortex for moment-by-moment control.

Cognitive BCI for Reaching Movements

One way of building a cognitive BCI for controlling a prosthetic arm is to use the neural activity in the parietal reach region (PRR) of the cerebral cortex to decode the target location of an intended reaching movement. Musallam et al. (2004) and Andersen et al. (2010) explored this idea in experiments where monkeys were first

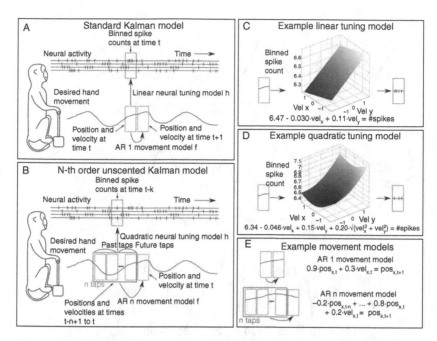

Figure 7.20. **The standard Kalman filter and the nth order unscented Kalman filter (UKF) for esti-mating cursor position and velocity from neural activity**. (A) In the standard Kalman filter model, a linear model relates the current state (here, cursor position and velocity) to current neural activity. Additionally, the position and velocity at the next time step is linearly related only to the current (and not past) position and velocity. (B) In an nth order UKF, a nonlinear model (here, quadratic) relates position and velocity from n consecutive time steps to neural activity at a particular time step. The same n position and velocity values are used to predict the position and velocity at the next time-step (here, using a linear autoregressive (AR) model). (C) Example of a linear measurement model ("linear tuning" model) used in a standard Kalman. (D) Example of a nonlinear measurement model ("quadratic tuning" model) used in the UKF model. (E) Example of 1st order and nth order AR models for dynamics of position (adapted from Li et al., 2009).

trained to reach to a target flashed at one of a set of fixed locations on a computer screen (Figure 7.22A, left panel). The monkeys were trained to reach to the flashed location only after a variable delay period, whose beginning is marked by the offset of the target on the screen. The neural activity during the memory period before the reaching movement (Figure 7.22B) and the reach target location were stored for training a classifier for decoding target location.

During "brain control" trials (Figure 7.22A, right panel), the target location was decoded from 900 ms of neural data during the memory period, starting 200 ms after the beginning of the memory period. Only data during the memory period was used for decoding so that the monkeys' intentions and not signals related to motor or visual events were used for decoding.

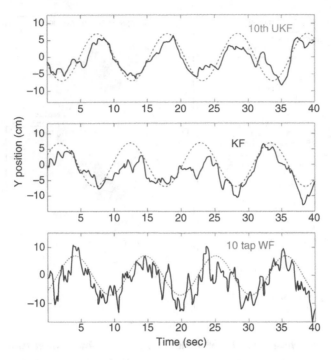

Figure 7.21. **Example cursor trajectories during closed-loop BCI control.** Motion along the Y-coordinate is shown for three different estimation methods: a 10th order UKF, a standard KF, and a 10th order Weiner filter (WF). The dashed sinusoidal curves denote target position (adapted from Li et al., 2009).

A Bayesian method was used for decoding target location. As a preprocessing step, spike trains from the 900 ms memory period were first projected onto a family of wavelets known as *Haar wavelets* – these are essentially a sequence of scaled and shifted square-shaped functions. As discussed in Section 4.3, the wavelet basis functions allow a signal over an interval to be represented using a set of coefficients. For decoding target location, a set of 100 wavelet coefficients were used. The choice of Haar wavelets was motivated by the need to capture the temporal features of a spike train, rather than simply the spike count or firing rate in the memory period.

A probabilistic model $P(\mathbf{r}|t)$ can then be learned from the training data, where $\mathbf{r}$ represents the neural response (in terms of wavelet coefficients) and t represents the target location. For example, if there are six possible target locations, one can learn a Gaussian model for each target location, where the mean and covariance of the Gaussian for a given target location is estimated from the responses observed for that target location. Given such a model, one can estimate the posterior probability of a target location $P(t|\mathbf{r})$ using Bayes' rule (Section 4.4.4). The decoded target location was taken to be the maximum of all $P(t|\mathbf{r})$. If the correct target location was decoded, a cursor was placed at the target location (Figure 7.22A, right panel) and the monkey was rewarded.

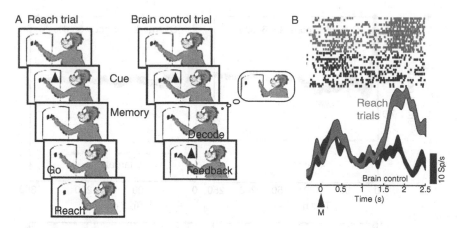

Figure 7.22. **Cognitive BCI for a reaching task.** (A) Reaching and brain control tasks. The monkey was required to fixate on the square spot on the left and touch a central cue to initiate the trail. After 500 ms, a peripheral target (here, the triangle on the right) was flashed for 300 ms, followed by a 1500 ± 300 ms variable memory period. For reach trials, the monkey was rewarded if it reached the target at the end of a memory period. For brain control trials, 900 ms of data (starting after 200 ms of the memory period) was used to decode the intended reach location using a Bayesian algorithm (see text). The monkey was rewarded if the correct target location was decoded. (B) Neural activity during reach and brain control trials. (Top panel) Each row of spikes is a single trial aligned to the beginning of the memory period. Top half of rows correspond to reach trials while bottom half of rows correspond to brain control trials. (Bottom panel) Poststimulus-time histogram (PSTH) of spikes. Thickness of PSTH represents standard error. M: start of memory period; Sp: spikes (from Musallam et al., 2004).

Based on the memory period activity of 8 PRR neurons in a monkey, 4 targets could be correctly decoded with 64.4% accuracy (chance level is 25%) in 250 brain control trials, and 6 targets with 63.6% accuracy (chance 17%) in 275 brain control trials (Figure 7.23A). When the responses of 16 neurons in the dorsal premotor cortex (PMd) were used, 8 targets could be decoded with 67.5% accuracy (chance 12.5%) in 310 trials (Figure 7.23B). The average accuracy across all sessions using PRR neurons for 3 monkeys ranged from 34.2% to 45% for the 4-target case and 25.6% to 37.1% for the 6-target case, while the rates for PMd neurons were significantly higher (Figure 7.23C). These results suggest that PMd might be a suitable target for high-performance decoding of target locations (see next section).

More recent work (Hwang and Andersen, 2010) has established the utility of using both spikes as well as local field potentials (LFPs) from PRR to jointly decode target location. The decoding accuracy in one monkey was found to be 86% for 6 target locations using spikes and LFPs from 16 electrodes, improving upon the 63.6% rate (which was obtained using spikes alone).

Enhancing the Performance of Cognitive BCIs

In the previous section, we saw how target locations for a reaching movement can be predicted from parietal cortex and dorsal premotor (PMd) cortex neurons, but

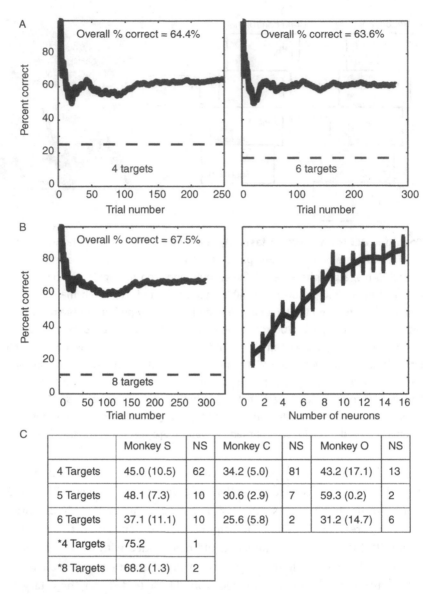

Figure 7.23. **Performance of the cognitive BCI.** (A) Cumulative percent accuracy (percentage of successfully decoded trials) for a monkey during brain control trials for 4 targets and 6 targets using 8 PRR neurons (dashed line: chance performance). (B) (Left) Cumulative percent accuracy in a brain control session using 16 PMd neurons. (Right) Offline performance based on the same data as a function of the number of neurons used for decoding. (C) Mean percent accuracy across all sessions for three monkeys (number in parentheses: standard deviation of the distribution of accuracies). NS: number of sessions; *: recordings from PMd; all other recordings from PRR (from Musallam et al., 2004).

how rapidly can such target locations be decoded? Santhanam, Shenoy, and colleagues (2006) addressed this question using a reach task similar to the task in the previous section, with 2, 4, 8, or 16 possible target locations (Figure 7.24A). Target location was predicted using the responses of 100–200 PMd neurons recorded with a 96-electrode array. The prediction was based on the spike counts from these neurons during an integration interval (Tint) within the memory period (this interval was fixed at 900 ms in the previous section but was varied here to optimize performance). Decoding followed a similar model as the probabilistic model in the previous section, with the likelihood $P(\mathbf{r}|t)$ given by a Gaussian or Poisson model and with uniform prior probability $P(t)$ over targets (this non-informative prior reduces the Bayesian decoding method to a *maximum likelihood* [ML] method).

The researchers divided the delay period (between appearance of target and "go" cue) into a time interval to skip (Tskip) during which target information was not yet reliable and the integration interval (Tint) used to predict the target. Based on data from control experiments involving actual reaching (Figure 7.24A), Tskip was fixed to be 150 ms. Tint was varied and the accuracy with which the reach target could be predicted was determined from data from the control experiments. As shown in Figure 7.25A, the accuracy continues to increase as Tint is increased because a longer interval can be expected to average out more noise from the neural response.

More interestingly, overall performance, when quantified in terms of *information transfer rate or ITR* (see Section 5.1.4) peaked at 7.7 bits per second (bps) for the control data for Tint = 70 ms (Figure 7.25A). To measure ITR during actual cursor control experiments, a sequence of rapid BCI cursor trials was used. In these trials, a circular cursor was rendered on the screen at the target location predicted by neural activity; if the prediction was correct, the next target was displayed immediately (see Figure 7.24B). Task difficulty, which contributes to ITR, was varied by varying the number of possible target locations. The best overall performance of 6.5 bps was achieved with the 8-target task (Figure 7.25B). This performance corresponds to typing approximately 15 words per minute with a basic alphanumeric keyboard, which compares favorably with physical typing speeds of about 20 words per minute by novice computer users on a keyboard.

7.3 Invasive BCIs in Humans

Only a few studies have been conducted to date on brain-computer interfacing in humans using electrode arrays implanted *inside* the brain, the exceptions being BCIs such as cochlear implants (Section 10.1.1) and deep brain stimulators (Section 10.2.1) that stimulate (but do not record from) specific parts of the nervous system. Here we focus on experimental studies with tetraplegic humans who have consented to have an electrode array implanted in their brain to test BCI strategies for better communication and control.

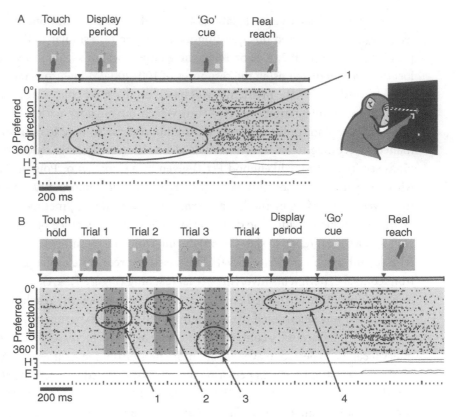

Figure 7.24. **Cognitive BCI for high-speed cursor control.** (A) Delayed reach task with spike trains from selected neurons shown below (shaded box). Neurons are ordered by angular tuning direction (preferred direction) during the delay period. Ellipse shows the increase in neural activity related to the peripheral reach target. Lines labeled H and E show the horizontal and vertical coordinates of hand (H) and eye (E) traces respectively. (B) Sequence of 3 rapid BCI cursor trials followed by an actual reach trial. Tint, the time interval used for predicting target location, is the shaded interval overlayed on the spike trains. After a short processing time, a circular cursor (here shown as a dotted circle on the screen) was briefly rendered and a new target was displayed (adapted from Santhanam et al., 2006).

7.3.1 Cursor and Robotic Control Using a Multielectrode Array Implant

In one of the first clinical trials aimed at translating BCI results from animals to humans, an electrode array called the *BrainGate* sensor (Figure 7.26A) with 100 silicon microelectrodes (Figure 7.26B) was implanted in the arm area of the primary motor cortex of a tetraplegic human (MN) (Figure 7.26C–D) (Hochberg et al., 2006; Donoghue et al., 2007). An important question being addressed in this trial was whether motor intention could still modulate cortical activity three years after spinal cord injury and in the absence of hand motion. In a first set of experiments involving imagining movements on cue, the researchers found that neurons in the primary motor cortex can be modulated by imagined limb motions: some neurons were

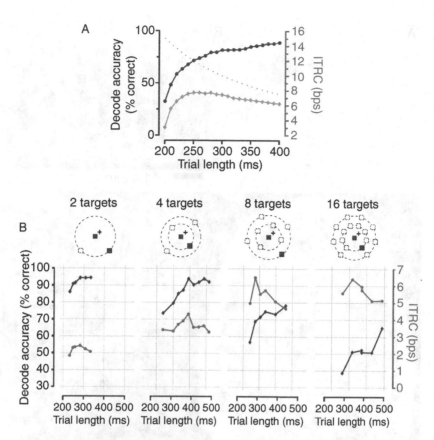

Figure 7.25. **Accuracy and information transfer rate of the cognitive BCI.** (A) Accuracy and information transfer rate (ITR, here labeled ITRC) as a function of trial length, calculated from a control experiment involving the reach task (8-target configuration). Trial length is given by Tskip+Tint+Tproc, where Tskip = 150ms and Tproc ~ 40ms. Tint was varied and prediction accuracy and ITR were computed for each value of Tint. A peak ITR of 7.7 bps was achieved at a trial length of 260 ms, corresponding to Tint = 70 ms. The dotted curve is the theoretical maximum ITR, assuming 100% accuracy regardless of Tint. (B) Performance during high-speed BCI cursor experiments for each target configuration and across varying total trial lengths. Performance was calculated from one experiment with many hundreds of trials. As the number of targets increases, prediction accuracy decreases, but ITR increases up to about 6.5 bps (adapted from Santhanam et al., 2006).

activated by one imagined action, for instance, imagining moving the hands together and apart, while others responded to a different imagined action, e.g., wrist or elbow flexion and extension (Figure 7.27A), or hand opening and closing (Figure 7.27C). Some neurons nonselectively responded to all imagined actions (Figure 7.27B).

Given the diversity of neural responses observed for imagined actions, a linear filter method (Equation 7.2) was used to translate neural activity into two-dimensional cursor positions. The subject was asked to imagine tracking a cursor on the screen which was controlled by a technician. During this training session, the firing rates of

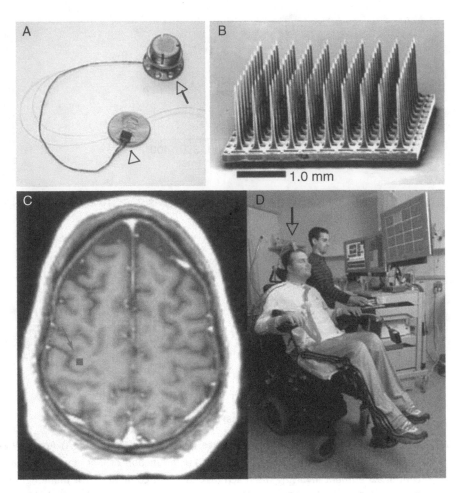

Figure 7.26. **Invasive BCI in a human.** (A) The electrode array (BrainGate sensor) shown on a U.S. penny with a ribbon cable to a percutaneous pedestal (arrow) that is secured to the skull via surgery. (B) Close-up view of the 10 × 10 electrode array. Electrodes are 1 mm long and spaced 0.4 mm apart. (C) MRI image of the brain of participant. Arrow shows the approximate location of the implant site in the arm/hand area of the primary motor cortex. The box that the arrow points to represents a scaled projection of the implanted array (actual size: 4 × 4 mm). (D) The subject MN sitting in a wheelchair looking at the computer screen and moving the neural cursor toward the shaded square in a 16-target "grid" task. The arrow points to a box containing the amplifier and signal processing hardware attached to the percutaneous pedestal. The cable from this box conveys the amplified neural responses to computers in the room (from Hochberg et al., 2006).

up to 73 discriminated neurons over the past second (twenty 50-ms bins) were linearly mapped onto technician-cursor position using a linear filter computed via the pseudoinverse technique (see Section 5.2.1). In subsequent sessions, the predicted cursor position was plotted to provide visual feedback. The filter continued to be updated after each session.

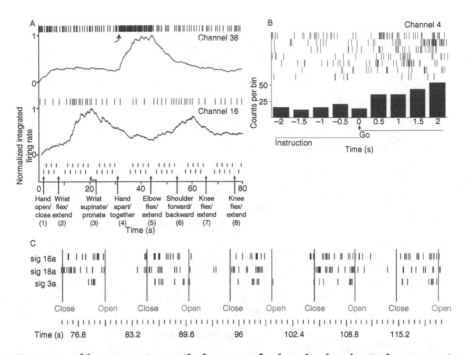

Figure 7.27. **Response of human motor cortical neurons for imagined and actual movements.** (A) Spikes and integrated firing rates from 2 simultaneously recorded neurons. The subject was asked to imagine performing a series of left limb movements (labeled on the x-axis), alternating between the two phases of movement (e.g., open and close) at the times marked by the small vertical bars above the x-axis (these times were conveyed to the subject using a "go" cue). The neuron at the top increases its firing rate (curved arrow) with the instruction to move both hands apart/together, while the neuron at the bottom responds the most to the instruction to flex/extend the wrist and to move the shoulder. All movements are imagined except for shoulder movement, which the subject was able to perform. (B) 7 spike trains from a neuron elicited for 7 different movements, along with histograms showing the total number of spikes in each 500-ms bin. The neuron increased its firing rate during imagined movements but was not selective for any particular instruction like the neurons in (A). (C) Spike trains from 3 neurons in response to a text instruction to open and close a hand. These neurons increase their firing rate for the "close hand" instruction, reflecting the paralyzed subject's intention to close the hand (from Hochberg et al., 2006).

Figure 7.28A provides an example of neural cursor control while the subject attempted to track the technician's cursor. The subject was able to move the cursor in the general direction of the technician's cursor movement as the cursor changed directions, but the tracking is only approximate. This is illustrated in Figure 7.28B, which compares the x- and y- coordinates of the two cursors. The correlation between the neural and technician-controlled cursor positions was found to be 0.56 ± 0.18 (x-coordinate) and 0.45 ± 0.15 (y-coordinate) over 6 sessions, which is comparable to the performance of monkey BCIs using linear filters.

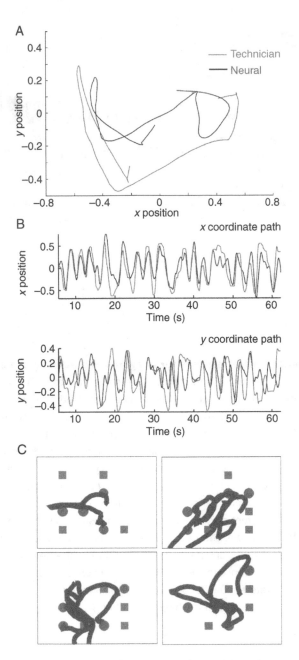

Figure 7.28. **Cursor control with a BCI implanted in a human.** (A) Trajectories of the technician-controlled cursor (gray) and neurally-controlled cursor (black) for a 5-second period in which the subject was asked to neurally track the technician's cursor. (B) Comparison of x- and y-coordinates of technician cursor (gray) and neural cursor (black) for a 1-minute period. (C) Four examples of neural cursor control in a target acquisition and obstacle avoidance task (circles: targets; squares: obstacles; thick line: cursor trajectory) (from Hochberg et al., 2006).

More interestingly, the subject was able to perform more challenging tasks such as moving the cursor neurally to randomly placed targets while avoiding obstacles (Figure 7.28C) and using the neural cursor to open simulated e-mail, draw using a paint program, adjust volume, channel, and power on a television, and play video games such as Pong. The subject was also able to open and close a prosthetic hand through neural activity (cf. Figure 7.27C), and control a multi-jointed robotic arm to grasp an object and transport it to a different location.

In follow-up experiments (Kim et al., 2008), the researchers investigated the role of design choices such as the kinematic representation for cursor movement, the decoding method used, and the task used during training to optimize decoding parameters. They found that two tetraplegic subjects were able to gain more accurate closed-loop control by controlling a cursor's velocity than by controlling its position directly. Additionally, cursor velocity control was achieved more rapidly than position control. The researchers also found an improvement in cursor control with a Kalman filter (Section 4.4.5) rather than a linear filter as in the previous study.

7.3.2 Cognitive BCIs in Humans

The previous section illustrated how neural activity from the human primary motor cortex can be used to control the trajectory of a cursor and move simple prosthetic devices. It is well known that areas in the frontal cortex beyond primary motor cortex exhibit neural activity related to planning and initiating movement direction, remembering movement instructions over delays, or mixtures of these features. We saw in Section 7.2.4 how cortical areas such as PMd and the PRR in monkeys can be used to build cognitive BCIs that directly predict intended target locations.

Can such BCIs also be designed in humans? Although the question has not yet been studied in depth, some early work by Ojakangas, Donoghue, and colleagues (2006) suggests an affirmative answer to this question. During the process of intra-operative mapping for deep brain stimulation (Section 10.2.1) in human patients, the researchers found that recordings from small groups of human prefrontal/premotor cortex neurons can be used to decode the planned direction of movement. It remains to be seen whether these neurons can be harnessed in a closed-loop setting to achieve true cognitive brain-computer interfacing.

7.4 Long-Term Use of Invasive BCIs

For invasive BCIs to be practical, they ought to be useful to the subject for long time periods ranging from months to years. Two important questions arise when BCIs are to be used on a long-term basis: (1) Can a BCI implanted with a fixed set of parameters be used over an extended period of time, or do the parameters need to be adjusted from day to day?, and (2) Do the electrodes continue to provide reliable recordings of neural activity after long periods of time, or do they succumb to biological phenomena (such as gliosis or scar-tissue formation)?

7.4.1 Long-Term BCI Use and Formation of a Stable Cortical Representation

The first question has been addressed in a study involving monkeys perform-ing a BCI cursor task using the same set of parameters over 19 days (Ganguly and Carmena, 2009). Two monkeys performed a center-out reaching task (see Figure 7.19C) using a robotic exoskeleton that limited movements to the horizontal plane. A 128-electrode array was used to record the activities of neurons in bilateral motor cortex while the monkey was performing this manual control (MC) task. A linear filter method (Equation 7.2, with 10 time lag values for i) was used to create a "decoder" for mapping the recorded motor cortex activity to recorded elbow and shoulder angular positions.

The linear decoder learned on day 1 was kept fixed and used in "brain con-trol" (BC) mode to control the cursor directly on all subsequent days. Fifteen of the first monkey's neurons were stably recorded from across 19 days and used in the fixed linear decoder, and 10 neurons were used from the second monkey. As shown in Figure 7.29A, the performance of both monkeys steadily improved over the first 10 days. Starting from day 10, the mean accuracy remained close to 100%, and the monkeys performed accurately right from the very beginning of each day (Figures 7.29B and 7.29C). With practice, cursor trajectories became more direct (Figure 7.29D) and stereotyped, as quantified by the increasing pairwise correla-tions between the mean paths for each day (color map in Figure 7.29D). By exam-ining the directional tuning and other properties of the neurons used in decoding, the researchers were able to show that stable task performance was associated with the formation of a stable neural representation for BCI control in response to a fixed decoder.

A surprising result was that the exact form of the decoder did not matter in the long run: when the weights $\mathbf{w}(i)$ (see Equation 7.2) were shuffled, prediction of previously collected shoulder and elbow position data was inaccurate as expected (Figure 7.30A), but accurate BCI control was restored after just a few days of prac-tice with the new shuffled decoder (Figure 7.30B). This result bears testimony to the remarkable plasticity of motor cortical neurons in gaining control over an external device even when given a randomized mapping, harking back to the early experi-ments of Fetz showing operant conditioning of single motor cortical neurons to gain control of an analog meter (Section 7.1.1).

7.4.2 Long-Term Use of a Human BCI Implant

In humans, important questions pertaining to the feasibility of implants such as the BrainGate neural interface system include how long implanted microelectrodes can record useful neural signals and how reliably these signals can be acquired and decoded on a long-term basis.

Not many studies have been conducted to date to answer these questions, but exper-iments by Simeral, Hochberg, and colleagues (2011) have produced some encourag-ing results. They examined neural point-and-click cursor control on 5 consecutive

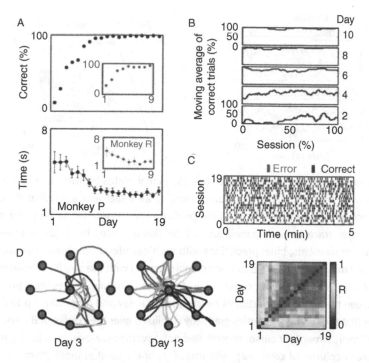

Figure 7.29. BCI performance over a period of 19 days. (See color plates for the same figure in color) (A) Cursor control performance over consecutive days using a BCI with a fixed linear decoder and a fixed set of neurons in two monkeys (red inset boxes are data for the second monkey). (Top) Mean accuracy per day. (Bottom) Mean time to reach target. Error bars: ±2 standard errors of the mean. (B) Performance trend on specific days for a single monkey, plotted as a moving average (% correct trials in a moving window of 20 trials). (C) Performance in the first 5 minutes of BCI cursor control in each daily session from day 1 to day 19. Bars denote correct (blue) or error (red) trials. (D) Left: Example cursor trajectories during an early stage (day 3) and later (day 13), showing that trajectories become more direct and stereotyped with daily practice. Right: Color map showing the pairwise correlation between the mean paths for each day from the center to a target (R = correlation coefficient) (from Ganguly and Carmena, 2009).

days for a human with tetraplegia who returned to the laboratory 1,000 days after implantation of an array of 100 microelectrodes in the motor cortex. On each of the 5 days, a Kalman filter (Section 4.4.5) based on spikes from a group of neurons was used to decode two-dimensional cursor velocity, and a linear discriminant classifier (Section 5.1.1) was used to classify the intention to click. Closed-loop point-and-click cursor control was tested in two tasks: an eight-target center-out task and a random target task adapted from a human-computer interaction standard test used to quantify performance of computer input devices. Successful trials required that the cursor be moved to the target and a click executed within an allotted time while the cursor hovered over the target. Electrode impedances, neural spike waveforms, and local field potentials were measured daily to quantify any changes in the neural interface.

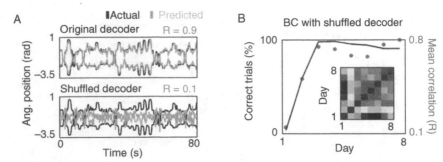

Figure 7.30. **BCI performance with a shuffled decoder.** (See color plates for the same figure in color) (A) Comparison of the "offline" predictive ability of an intact and a shuffled decoder. The shuffled decoder performs poorly in offline prediction of recorded data on positions of the shoulder (upper trace in each panel) and elbow (lower trace) from neural activity. Black traces: actual movements; blue: predictions with each decoder; R: correlation between actual and predicted movements. (B) Performance improvement with the shuffled decoder over the course of 8 days in terms of % of correct trials. The inset color map shows the pairwise correlation between the tuning properties of neurons for one day and other days up to day 8. The plot shows that the tuning properties gradually stabilized over the course of 8 days, resulting in a stable "cortical map" for cursor control. Red dots: average correlation in tuning properties (mean of each column of color map with exclusion of diagonal entries) (from Ganguly and Carmena, 2009).

Across the 5 days, spiking signals were obtained from 41 of the 96 electrodes available for neural measurements. These neural signals were found to be sufficient to yield an average target-acquisition-and-click rate of 94.9% for the center-out task and 91.9% for the random target task. By demonstrating that the electrode array maintained accuracy nearly 2.75 years after implantation, these results help alleviate concerns that tissue reaction from penetrating electrodes could diminish BCI performance in the long term. Although encouraging, the results need to be validated with a more extensive set of clinical trials with additional subjects.

7.5 Summary

Some of the most impressive achievements in brain-computer interfacing to date have come from invasive BCIs in animals and humans, with demonstrations ranging from highly accurate control of two-dimensional cursors to real-time control of prosthetic arms and grippers. The two dominant approaches adopted in these invasive BCIs have been using *operant conditioning*, where the BCI relies solely on adaptation by neurons to achieve control, and *population decoding* methods, which use statistical techniques to learn a mapping between neural activity and control parameters. The most successful decoding methods have been methods based on the population vector (Equation 7.1), the linear (Weiner) filter (Equation 7.2), and the Kalman filter (Section 4.4.5). The question of long-term use of BCIs is also beginning to be addressed, with studies in animals and humans showing that the brain can form a stable neural representation with daily BCI use much like other forms of motor skill acquisition, and electrodes used for recording neural activity can remain viable more than two-and-a-half years after implantation of the BCI inside the brain.

7.6 Questions and Exercises

1. Suppose the goal is to design a BCI for controlling a prosthetic arm that can reach different locations in three-dimensional space. How would you use operant conditioning to train a monkey to control the arm?

2. Write down the equation for population vector decoding of movement direction from cortical activity. Explain how the various quantities used in the equation can be estimated from experiments.

3. Compare the strengths and weaknesses of operant conditioning versus population decoding as a method for building a BCI for cursor and prosthetic control.

4. Describe how the neural population function (NPF) was computed in the experiment by Chapin and colleagues for BCI in a rat. How was the NPF used to control a robotic arm?

5. Write down the equation for the linear filter (or Weiner filter) method for decoding a variable (such as hand position) from neural activity (such as the firing rates of a population of neurons) over time. How can the filter weights be estimated from recently collected data?

6. Compare the performance of the following decoding methods based on the studies described in Section 7.2.1:

   a. Linear filter

   b. Artificial neural network with three layers and sigmoidal units

   c. Population vector method

7. What are the advantages of using a Kalman filter for decoding compared to the population-vector or linear filter methods?

8. In Section 7.2.1, we encountered two different ways of formulating the decoding problem using the Kalman filter. In one case, the firing rates recorded from neurons were the observations, whereas in the other the observations were kinematic outputs (joint angles). Write down the equations for each and discuss the advantages, if any, of one model over the other.

9. Enumerate some of the advantages and disadvantages of using LFPs versus spikes for brain-computer interfacing.

10. (⋔ Expedition) The results in Section 7.2.2 showed that lower-limb kinematics during walking can be predicted from the activity of neurons in primary motor and somatosensory cortices. However, this by itself is insufficient for restoring locomotion in a lower-limb amputee since it does not take into account the dynamics of the body and prosthetic. Find out the newest technology in

powered lower-limb prosthetic devices and discuss whether and how the technique in Section 7.2.2 could potentially be modified to control a powered prosthetic device for walking.

11. What are some of the brain areas (in the monkey) that have been successfully used for cursor control, either individually or in conjunction with other areas?

12. Explain the difference between an unscented Kalman filter (UKF) and a standard Kalman filter. What are the potential advantages of using the UKF in BCI applications?

13. What are cognitive BCIs and how do they differ from BCIs based on decoding movement trajectories from motor cortical activity?

14. (ℏ Expedition) Section 7.2.4 explored two different cognitive BCIs. Read the papers by Musallam et al. (2004) and Santhanam et al. (2006) that describe these BCIs, and provide a detailed description and comparison of the two Bayesian decoding methods used by them.

15. Compare the training paradigm and the results obtained using the BrainGate sensor in humans to the results obtained using electrode arrays in monkeys. Is the human performance on par with monkey performance in cursor and prosthetic-control tasks?

16. In Section 7.4.1, we discussed the surprising result that BCI control can be achieved even with a randomly shuffled decoder. What are the implications of this result for the endeavor of designing sophisticated decoders for BCI? Why would one need to employ sophisticated machine-learning and statistical algorithms for decoding if a random decoder might do the job?

17. What did the 1,000-days-after-implantation tests of the BrainGate system reveal about the performance of the BCI, and what are the implications for long-term use?

18. (ℏ Expedition) A major concern with implantable BCIs is their long-term viability given the likelihood of scar-tissue formation around the electrodes. One way to counter this problem is to make the electrodes biocompatible. Write a review of the most promising biocompatible electrode technologies that are currently being investigated or are available for use in BCIs.

8

Semi-Invasive BCIs

In the previous chapter, we learned about BCIs that required placing electrodes *inside* the brain. While such an approach provides a high-fidelity window into the spiking activity of neurons, it also comes with significant risks: (1) possible infections due to penetration of the blood-brain barrier, (2) encapsulation of electrodes by immunologically reactive tissue, which can degrade signal quality over time, and (3) the potential for damage to intact brain circuits during implantation.

To counter these risks, researchers have investigated the use of BCIs that do not penetrate the brain surface. Such BCIs can be regarded as *semi-invasive BCIs*. We will focus on two types of semi-invasive BCIs: electrocorticographic (ECoG) BCIs and BCIs based on recording from nerves outside the brain. As discussed in Chapter 3, ECoG requires surgical placement of electrodes underneath the skull, either under the dura mater (*subdural ECoG*) or outside the dura mater (*epidural ECoG*). The procedure is invasive but less so than the methods of the previous chapter. In this chapter, we explore the ability of ECoG BCIs to control cursors and prosthetic devices.

Even less invasive than ECoG are methods that tap into intact nerve endings in different parts of the body. We conclude the chapter with a discussion of such nerve-based BCIs.

8.1 Electrocorticographic (ECoG) BCIs

Much of ECoG BCI research has been conducted on consenting human patients who are being monitored in a hospital to locate the source of seizures in the days prior to surgery. BCI experiments are conducted in those patients who are willing and able. There has also been some recent work on ECoG in animals with the goal of characterizing the spatial and temporal resolution of ECoG signals for BCI. We examine these results next, before proceeding to ECoG BCIs in humans.

8.1.1 ECoG BCIs in Animals

We already know from the work of Fetz and others that monkeys can learn via operant conditioning to modulate the responses of neurons in the motor cortex to control an external device (Section 7.1.1). Can ECoG signals recorded from the surface of the brain also be modulated in a similar manner? Rouse and Moran (2009) explored this question with monkeys using two cursor-control tasks. The first task was the center-out reaching task frequently used in invasive BCIs (see Figure 7.19C in previous chapter). The monkeys were required to control the cursor so as to first hit a center target and then move to one of four targets displayed at the periphery. The second task was a drawing task that involved controlling the cursor to trace a circle in either the clockwise or counter-clockwise direction.

Two electrodes placed 1 cm apart at two arbitrary epidural locations over primary motor cortex were used to control the cursor. The signals from these electrodes were converted to the frequency domain using the Fourier transform (Section 4.2), and the power in the frequency band 65–100 Hz was used for cursor control. One electrode was selected to control the cursor's horizontal velocity where an increase in the 65–100 Hz amplitude (compared to the resting state) caused the cursor to move to the right while a decrease caused the cursor to move to the left. The other electrode was similarly used to control the cursor's vertical velocity. This mapping from neural activity to cursor velocity was kept fixed for a series of daily sessions over five days.

Over the course of one week, the monkeys learned to modulate the ECoG signals from the two electrodes to control the cursor in two dimensions to accomplish both the tasks. For the center-out task, one monkey was able to successfully perform forty movements in about six minutes. In the drawing task, the monkey was able to draw thirty circles in approximately seven minutes.

Figure 8.1A shows the average cursor trajectory for counter-clockwise and clockwise circles drawn using ECoG activity on the third day of recording. Note that rather than resembling a circle, the average trajectory is more of an ellipse along the upper-left to lower-right axis. This suggests that the ECoG signals from the two electrodes may have been correlated such that their amplitude in the 65–100 Hz band tended to be higher or lower together rather than one being high and low for certain parts of the trajectory as required for circular motion. To improve its cursor-control ability, the monkey needs to decorrelate the signals from the two electrodes as much as possible. Figure 8.1B shows that the monkey was indeed adapting its neural activity to reduce the correlation between the two electrodes. The plot shows that the correlation between the powers at most frequencies decreased over the course of the five days of recording, with the largest decrease in correlation occurring in the 65–100 Hz frequency band used for controlling the cursor. These results suggest that as in the case of invasive BCIs based on operant conditioning of individual spiking neurons, animals can also adapt population-level activity, as measured using ECoG, to obtain control over external devices.

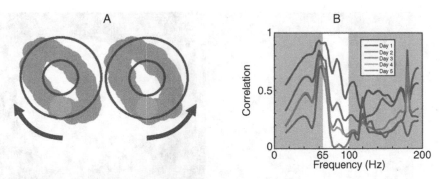

Figure 8.1.   **Cursor control using an ECoG BCI in a monkey.** (See color plates for the same figure in color) (A) Average cursor trajectory for a monkey drawing clockwise (left) and counterclockwise (right) circles using ECoG. The large green circle represents the cursor at the start/end location for the trial. (B) Correlation between the powers for the two electrodes used for horizontal and vertical cursor control at various frequencies across five days of recording (power spectrum was computed using 300 ms time bins and 3 Hz frequency bins). Note the dramatic decrease in correlation between the two electrodes, especially in the 65–100 Hz band used for cursor control, over the course of five days (adapted from Rouse and Moran, 2009).

8.1.2 ECoG BCIs in Humans

ECoG Cursor Control Based on Motor Imagery

As mentioned earlier, ECoG BCI experiments in humans have been conducted in patients in whom subdural or epidural electrodes have been implanted for about a week in preparation for surgery to remove an epileptic focus. If the patient consents to participate in BCI experiments, the BCI protocol typically employed involves asking the patient to perform various types of movements and motor imagery (e.g., hand, tongue, or foot movements). The recorded ECoG data is then screened to identify the electrodes and frequency bands that exhibit the highest correlation with the executed movements or imagery. These channels and frequency bands are then used for closed-loop BCI tasks such as cursor control.

One-Dimensional Cursor Control

In an early set of 1D cursor-control experiments by Leuthardt and colleagues (2004), ECoG signals were recorded from four patients using 32 subdural electrodes placed over the left frontal-parietal-temporal cortex (Figure 8.2A and 8.2B). Patients were asked to perform six tasks: three motor actions (opening/closing right or left hand, protruding the tongue, and saying the word "move") and imagining each of these actions. For each electrode location, the power spectrum from 0–200 Hz was computed (the researchers used an autoregressive method [Section 4.4.3] instead of a Fourier transform for efficiency reasons).

For each patient, one or two electrodes and up to four frequency bands were selected based on having the highest correlations with one of the three actions or

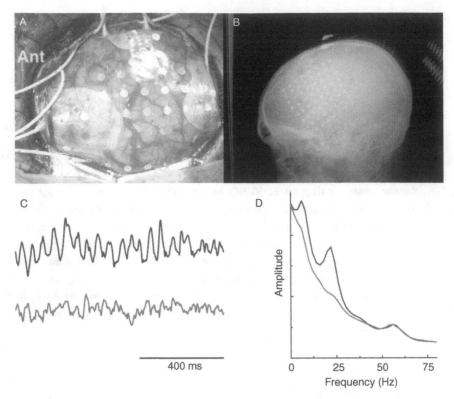

Figure 8.2.   **ECoG BCI in humans.** (A) An 8×8-electrode array placed under the dura of a patient. The electrodes are 2 mm in diameter and separated from each other by 1 cm. Ant: anterior. (B) X-ray image of the skull showing the location of the electrode array. (C) Raw ECoG signals from a patient for an electrode used for cursor control. Upper trace: ECoG signal when the patient was resting, which moves the cursor down. Lower trace: ECoG signals when the patient imagined saying the word "move" to make the cursor move up. (D) Amplitude spectra for rest (upper curve) and imagery (lower curve) for the experiment in (C) (from Leuthardt et al., 2004).

imagery tasks (this was done using r^2, the square of the correlation coefficient, sometimes also called the *coefficient of determination*). Patients then used the amplitude of these ECoG "features" to move a cursor up or down, for example, imagining right-hand movement to make the cursor move up and resting to move it down. Starting from the left edge of the screen, the cursor was traveling to the right at a constant velocity, and the task was to deflect the cursor up or down to hit a target randomly placed in the top or bottom half of the right edge of the screen.

The cursor's vertical position was updated every 40 ms, controlled by a translation algorithm based on a weighted linear summation of the amplitudes of the selected frequency bands from the selected electrodes for the previous 280 ms. The weights were chosen to move the cursor up with task execution (e.g., imagining hand movement) and down with rest. This relationship was explained to the patient prior to the experiments.

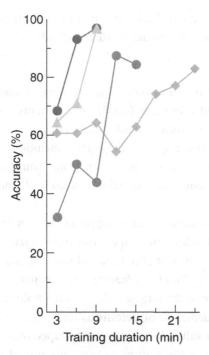

Figure 8.3. **Rapid learning of cursor control using ECoG.** The plot shows the improvement in cursor control over the course of several minutes of training in four patients. Cursor control was measured in terms of accuracy in hitting one of two targets (chance level accuracy is 50%). To control the cursor, patient 1 (upper circles) and patient 2 (triangles) imagined saying the word "move," patient 3 (diamonds) imagined opening and closing the right hand, and patient 4 (lower circles) imagined protruding the tongue (from Leuthardt et al., 2004).

After training periods lasting between 3–24 minutes, all four patients were able to successfully control the cursor, with accuracies ranging from 74% to 100% (Figure 8.3). Figure 8.2C illustrates the raw ECoG signal for one patient from an electrode used for cursor control when the patient rested to make the cursor go down (upper trace) and when the patient imagined saying the word "move" (lower trace) to make the cursor go up. There is a noticeable decrease in low-frequency oscillations during imagery – this is quantitatively verified in the amplitude spectra shown in Figure 8.2D. In this case, the cursor was controlled by the patient with an accuracy of 97% by changing the amplitude in the 20.5–22.5 Hz frequency band.

These early ECoG BCI results were later replicated in a set of experiments conducted in Seattle (Leuthardt et al., 2006), where four additional patients attained high accuracies in one-dimensional cursor control (73%–100%). More interestingly, the researchers observed a variety of changes in the ECoG signal features during online BCI control such as a spatial spread of significant ECoG features into adjacent cortex or the emergence of a markedly different set of significant features compared to the original screening task. In the latter case, switching to the newly significant ECoG features immediately improved accuracy from 71% to 94%. Additionally, the researchers also demonstrated cursor control for one patient based on an *epidural* ECoG electrode (compared to subdural electrodes in other patients).

Two-Dimensional Cursor Control

The one-dimensional cursor control results described above were extended to two dimensions by Schalk, Ojemann, and colleagues (2008). Five patients participated in a study in which 26–64 subdural electrodes (configured in grids or strips) were placed over the fronto-parietal-temporal region of the cortex, including the sensorimotor cortex. The study consisted of three stages: (1) screening using motor tasks to identify suitable BCI features, (2) one-dimensional cursor control, and (3) two-dimensional cursor control.

In the screening stage, subjects performed motor or motor imagery tasks such as opening or closing the hand, protruding the tongue, moving the jaw, saying the word "move," shrugging the shoulders, moving the legs, and moving individual fingers. As in the one-dimensional study, the ECoG features (i.e., amplitudes for particular electrodes and frequencies) with the largest task-related amplitude changes were identified by calculating the coefficient of determination r^2 between the two distributions of trial-averaged feature values for task and rest, respectively. This metric essentially measures the fraction of the feature variance accounted for by the task, reflecting how much control the subject has over a particular feature. Pairs of tasks independent of each other in spatial and spectral distributions and their most salient ECoG features were identified and assigned to control either horizontal or vertical cursor movement.

In the second stage, subjects trained first on horizontal and then vertical cursor control. They used one or more of the ECoG features identified above to control each dimension of movement. The subject was informed a priori about the type of imagery to use for the appropriate cursor movement based on the selected ECoG features. In each trial, the subject was presented with one of two targets (on the left/right edge or top/bottom edge), with the cursor at the center of the screen. The subject's task was to modulate the selected ECoG features to move the cursor to the target. Cursor movement was based on a weighted linear summation of values for 1 to 4 ECoG features. The weights were chosen manually and were usually either +1 or −1 so as to assign increase or decrease of feature change to the desired direction (up or down, left or right) of the cursor movement. The features were computed from the previous 280 ms (subjects A through D) or 64 ms (subject E). As in the previous study, subjects quickly acquired accurate one-dimensional control.

Two-dimensional control was implemented by combining ECoG features that the subject had previously learned to control independently in one-dimensional tasks, i.e., horizontal and vertical cursor movement was controlled continuously by the selected sets of horizontal and vertical ECoG features simultaneously. The subject's task was to move a computer cursor from the center of the screen to a target that appeared in one of four locations on the periphery of the screen. If the cursor failed

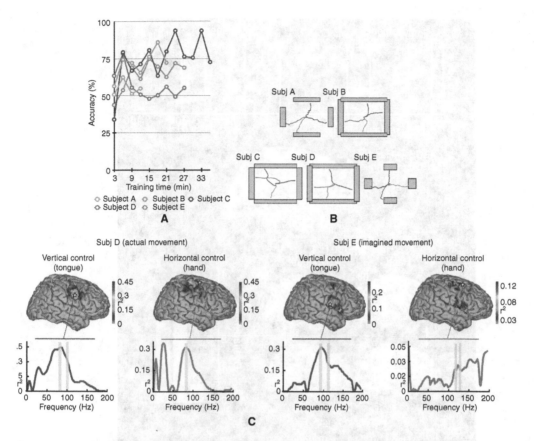

Figure 8.4.   **Two-dimensional cursor control using ECoG.** (See color plates for the same figure in color) (A) Improvement in performance for five subjects as a function of training time. (B) Average cursor trajectories to the four targets for each subject. (C) Correlation between cortical activity and vertical/horizontal cursor movement for subjects D and E. Correlation is depicted as r^2 values indicating the level of task-related control for different cortical areas. Subject D used actual tongue and hand movements for vertical and horizontal control respectively. Subject E used imagined versions of the same actions. The plots below show these correlation values as a function of frequency for the locations used for online cursor control (location indicated by a star). The frequency band used for online control is demarcated by two yellow bars (adapted from Schalk et al., 2008).

to reach a target within a predefined amount of time, the cursor and target disappeared and the trial was registered as a miss.

Figure 8.4A shows the learning curves for the five subjects demonstrating improved performance over a training period of 12–36 minutes. All five subjects successfully learned to control the cursor and guide it to the appropriate target with average hit rates in the range 53% –73% (chance target selection rate for this task is 25%). Figure 8.4B shows the average cursor trajectories for the five subjects. Figure 8.4C depicts the correlation between cortical activity at various locations on the brain

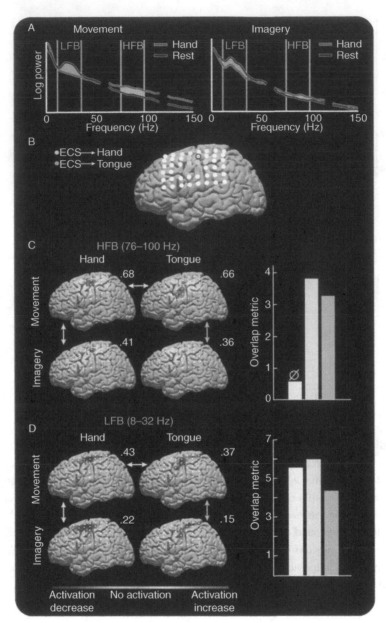

Figure 8.5.   **Comparison of ECoG activity during movement and imagery.** (See color plates for the same figure in color) (A) (Left panel) ECoG power spectrum for hand movement (red) and rest (blue). (Right panel) Same plot for hand imagery. The data are from an electrode in primary motor cortex (circled in B). Power at low frequencies ("LFB," 8–32 Hz, green) decreases with movement/imagery while power at high frequencies ("HFB," 76–100 Hz, orange) increases. Here, HFB increase with imagery is 32% that of movement (compare orange areas) while for the LFB decrease, it is 90% (green areas). (B) Electrodes for which stimulation produced movement of the hand (light blue) or tongue (light pink). Hand movement/imagery data in (A) is from the circled electrode. (C) (Left panel) Interpolated HFB brain activation maps for hand and tongue movement/imagery. Each is scaled to the maximum absolute value of

surface and cursor movement for two subjects. The plots below show this correlation as a function of frequency for the electrode used for cursor control. As seen in the plots, the features most useful for control are amplitudes of "high gamma" frequency (> 70 Hz) recorded from electrodes over sensorimotor cortex. The frequency band actually used for online control is demarcated by the two yellow bars. It can be seen that this location/frequency band, chosen on the basis of early screening, is not necessarily optimal for online cursor control.

Amplification of ECoG Activity through BCI Use

The ECoG studies discussed in the previous two sections relied on either motor imagery or actual movements to demonstrate brain-based cursor control. Does motor imagery activate similar areas as actual movement? Studies using EEG and fMRI have suggested a positive answer. That the same is true for ECoG was demonstrated by Miller, Rao, and colleagues (2010) in a study involving eight human subjects performing overt action and imagery of the same action.

The study focused on ECoG power in a "high frequency" (76–100 Hz) and a "low frequency" (8–32 Hz) band (Figure 8.5A). It was found that, as expected, the spatial distribution of ECoG activity during motor imagery mimics the spatial distribution of activity during actual motor movement (Figure 8.5B–D). However, the magnitude of imagery-induced cortical activity was less (approximately 25% of that associated with actual movement). More significantly, the high-frequency band (HFB) activity was much more localized compared to the lower-frequency band (LFB) activity (compare Figure 8.5C and 8.5D), motivating the use of the HFB in ECoG BCIs to exploit their greater spatial separability compared to the LFB.

The researchers then investigated how this imagery related activity is adapted when used in a BCI task that involved controlling a one-dimensional cursor (Figure 8.6A). The task was to move the cursor to a target randomly placed at the top or bottom edge of the screen. The cursor's velocity was determined by the power in the HFB (see equation in Figure 8.6A): increases in power above a baseline value moved the cursor up, and decreases in power moved the cursor down.

The four subjects who participated in the BCI study rapidly (in 5–7 minutes) learned to control the cursor using the power in the pre-selected HFB (Figures 8.6B and 8.6C). Subject 1 attained 94% accuracy using imagined word repetition

Figure 8.5. (continued)

activation (indicated by the number above each cortical map). (Right panel) Quantification of overlap between hand and tongue movement (yellow), hand movement and imagery (light blue), and tongue movement and imagery (light pink). (D) As in C but for the LFB. Note the lack of significant overlap (denoted by ∅ in the bar graph) between hand versus tongue movement in the HFB case, indicating greater localization compared to the LFB. Also note the significant overlap between movement and imagery in all cases (P-value < 10⁻⁴) (from Miller et al., 2010).

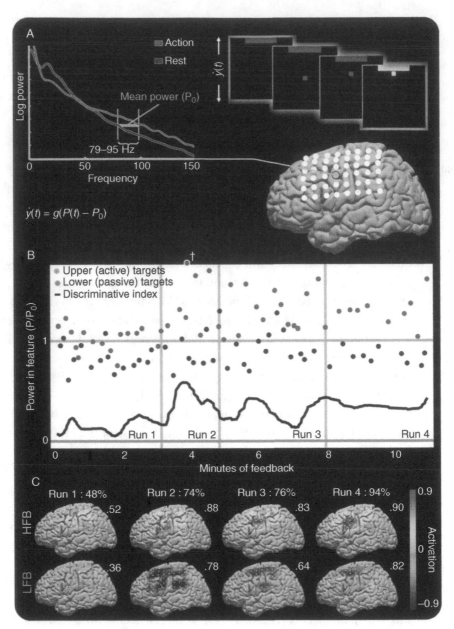

Figure 8.6.   **Amplification of cortical activity during learning of a BCI cursor task.** (See color plates for the same figure in color) (A) An initial motor-screening task was used to identify an ECoG "feature," i.e., a particular electrode-frequency-band combination (gold-colored electrode in the brain image, located in primary tongue cortex (see Figure 8.5B), HFB 79–95 Hz). The power $P(t)$ in this feature and the mean power P_0 across trials were used to control the velocity of a one-dimensional cursor using the linear equation shown. The subject was instructed to imagine saying the word "move" to move the cursor toward one target (the "active" target) and to rest (or "idle") to move the cursor to the other target (the "passive" target). (B) The relative power in the chosen ECoG feature is shown during four consecutive runs of the cursor

(imagining saying the word "move") while the other three subjects achieved 90%, 85%, 100% accuracies respectively using tongue, shoulder, and tongue imagery.

More interestingly, the spatial distribution of high-frequency ECoG activity was quantitatively conserved during learning, but the magnitude of the imagery-associated ECoG activity increased significantly (Figure 8.6C) – in most cases, this new activity even *exceeded* that observed during actual movement. In other words, coupling motor imagery with BCI feedback amplified imagery-related activity, analogous to the amplification of single neuron activity via operant conditioning in the experiments of Fetz and colleagues (Section 7.1.1). Furthermore, after 5–8 minutes of training, some subjects reported that motor imagery ceased and was replaced by directly thinking about moving the cursor up or down.

Using Classifiers to Decode ECoG Signals

The ECoG BCI studies above relied on manual selection of features (based on a screening task) and a direct linear mapping between feature value and cursor velocity. An alternate approach is to utilize a classifier (Section 5.1) that takes as input a large number of features and automatically decides how to weight these features to maximize accuracy. Shenoy, Rao, and colleagues (2008) explored this approach in eight patients implanted with 64–104 subdural ECoG electrodes. All eight subjects performed repetitive hand or tongue movements in response to a visual cue; six subjects also performed the corresponding motor imagery tasks.

For all subjects and for all ECoG channels, the same two frequency-band features, LFB (11–40 Hz) and HFB (71–100 Hz), were extracted from 1–3 seconds of data during task performance. As observed in the previous section, there is a decrease in the LFB and an increase in the HFB with movement as shown in Figure 8.7. The set of features across all channels was fed as input to four different linear binary classifiers (Section 5.1.1): regularized linear discriminant analysis (RLDA or RDA), support vector machine (SVM), and two "sparse" variants of these two methods called the Linear Programming Machine (LPM) and the linear sparse Fisher's discriminant (LSFD) respectively. Recall from Section 5.1.1 that a linear binary classifier is based on the equation:

$$y = sign(\mathbf{w}^T \mathbf{x} + w_0)$$

Figure 8.6.   (continue)
task. Red dots: mean power during active target trials. Blue dots: mean power during passive target trials (cross: outlier). Green line: mean power P_0 across passive/active trials. Black line: "discriminative index" (smoothed difference between mean power during previous three active target trials and previous three passive target trials). Target accuracies (shown in C) were highest when the subject found a middle dynamic range. (C) Spatial distribution of HFB and LFB activations, and target hit accuracies during each of the four runs. Number near each brain plot: maximum (absolute value) activation. Note that the final activations are most prominent at the electrode used for cursor control (from Miller et al., 2010).

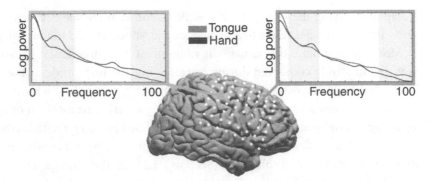

Figure 8.7.   **Comparing ECoG features for two movements.** (See color plates for the same figure in color) The two plots show average power spectra during tongue- and hand-movement tasks for two electrodes placed over the hand and tongue areas of the cortex. Similar to Figure 8.5A, movement causes a decrease in power in the LFB (left shaded region) and an increase in power in the HFB (right shaded region): (left plot) hand movement, (right plot) tongue movement (from Shenoy et al., 2008).

The components of the weight vector **w** can thus be used to judge which features in **x** are considered important by the classifier.

In a sparse linear classifier, the goal is to not only minimize classification error but also to obtain a sparse weight vector (i.e., a weight vector with most components at zero or close to zero). This is achieved by modifying the cost function being optimized (e.g., replacing the L2 norm on **w** in Equation 5.12 for the SVM with the L1 norm) to allow a trade-off between sparseness and training error. By examining the non-zero components of the weight vector after learning, one can automatically discover and use only the most important features from a large number of potentially irrelevant features in the input vector.

Figure 8.8 shows the performance of each classification method for distinguishing between actual tongue and hand movements as well as imagined tongue and hand movements. This performance was obtained from ECoG data lasting 1–3 seconds in each trial for only 30 trials. As seen in the figure, the best performance across the 8 subjects was obtained for the LPM classifier (average 6% error). Performance for motor imagery was worse (average 23% error for the LPM classifier) but significantly above chance levels (50%). The fact that such performance was obtained with as few as 30 data samples per class is worth noting.

The researchers also examined the weights **w** learned by the classifiers to see which input features (electrode and high or low frequency band combination) were deemed to be important by the classifier. Each subject's classifier weights were normalized to unit length and projected onto a standard brain using electrode positions estimated from X-rays. Figures 8.8C and 8.8D show the cumulative projection of all subjects' weight vectors onto the standard brain (spherical Gaussian kernels at each electrode location were used for interpolation across the brain). The plots

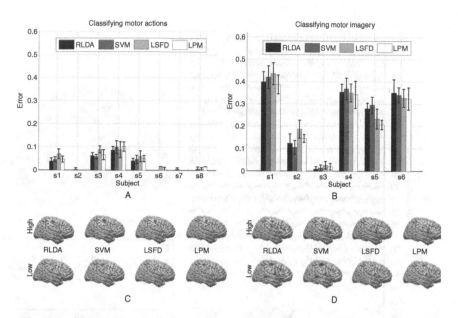

Figure 8.8. **Classifying ECoG signals for movement and imagery**. (See color plates for the same figure in color) (A) Hand versus tongue movement classification error for each classifier over eight subjects. Classification error was measured based on a cross-validation procedure (see Section 5.1.4). (B) Classification error for hand versus tongue motor imagery. (C) & (D) Cumulative weight vectors across all subjects for each classifier projected onto a standardized brain in separate low-feature and high-feature plots. The weights for movement are shown in (C) while those for imagery are shown in (D). Red denotes large positive values while blue denotes negative values. Note that the sparse methods (LPM and LSFD) select spatially more focused features (adapted from Shenoy et al., 2008).

show spatial clustering of important features across subjects at task-related soma-totopic locations. The sparse classifiers select more localized features, especially for the motor imagery task. This provides a method for *feature selection* based on classifier weights: indeed, the researchers were able to show that the number of features required for classification can be reduced to about 20% of the overall set of features without significantly impacting performance.

ECoG BCI for Arm Movement Control

We saw in Chapter 7 that the spiking activity of neurons in monkey motor cortex can be used to control a prosthetic arm by decoding the appropriate kinematic parameters such as hand position and velocity. Can such information also be decoded from ECoG signals?

In a study by Schalk and colleagues (2007), five patients implanted with ECoG electrodes used a joystick to move a two-dimensional cursor on a computer screen. The task was to track a target that was moving counter-clockwise in a circle. ECoG was recorded using a 48- or 64-electrode grid placed over the fronto-parietal-

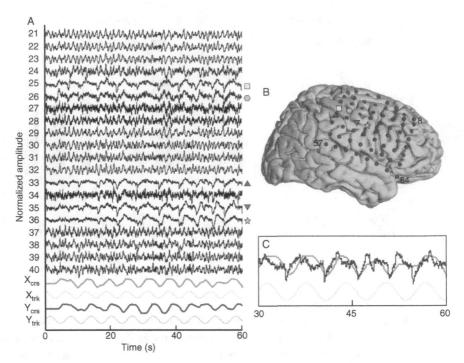

Figure 8.9.   **ECoG activity during a target tracking task.** (A) ECoG signals (channels 21–40) and X and Y positions of the subject-controlled cursor (crs) and the tracking target (trk). Channels correlated with cursor position (and exhibiting the LMP) are indicated with symbols. (B) Location of the ECoG electrodes (symbols denote locations showing LMP). (C) Magnification of ECoG LMP from channel 35 and the X position of cursor (thick dark curve) and target (thin light curve below) (from Schalk et al., 2007).

temporal region which included parts of sensorimotor cortex. The signal from each electrode was preprocessed using the common average referencing (CAR) method (Section 4.5.1).

The researchers found that ECoG voltage level in some channels appeared to directly correlate with kinematic parameters, i.e., the ECoG signals were amplitude-modulated in the time domain rather than in the frequency domain. The underlying neural signal is referred to as a *local motor potential (LMP)*. Examples of LMPs can be seen in Figure 8.9A which shows the ECoG signals for a subject and the position of the cursor over the course of 60 seconds. The LMPs, reflected in the channels over sensorimotor cortex (Figure 8.9B), show a clear correlation with cursor position. This correlation is especially evident in the magnified example shown in Figure 8.9C.

To quantify the decoding ability of the ECoG signal, the experimenters converted the ECoG signal for each 333 ms period (overlapping by 166 ms) into the frequency domain and calculated spectral amplitudes between 0 and 200 Hz in 1 Hz bins. These spectral amplitudes were then averaged in particular frequency

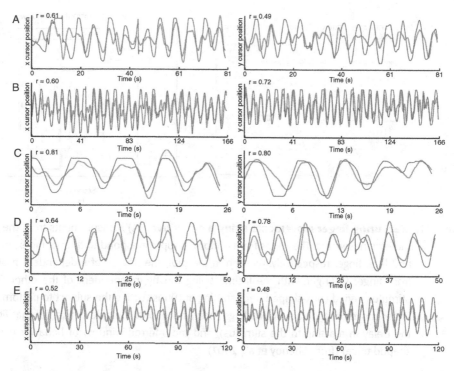

Figure 8.10. **Decoding kinematic parameters using ECoG.** (A) through (E) show examples of actual (thin traces) and decoded (thick traces) X and Y cursor position for 5 subjects (correlation coefficients r for these examples are shown at the top left corner) (from Schalk et al., 2007).

ranges (8–12 Hz, 18–24 Hz, 35–42 Hz, 42–70 Hz, 70–100 Hz, 100–140 Hz, 140–190 Hz) to obtain seven spectral features, to which was added a 333 ms running average of the raw unrectified signal to capture any LMPs. The ECoG features were used in four linear models (Section 5.2.1), one each for predicting each of the four kinematic parameters: vertical and horizontal cursor positions and vertical and horizontal cursor velocities. As illustrated by the examples in Figure 8.10, the positions and velocities predicted from ECoG correlate well with the actual cursor positions and velocities resulting from the circular hand movements for tracking the target. The average correlations over kinematic parameters ranged from 0.35 to 0.62 across subjects, which is within the range of correlations obtained using invasive electrode arrays in monkeys. The researchers also found that like single neurons in motor cortex, the LMP ECoG feature also showed cosine directional tuning, suggesting a direct link between ECoG LMPs and underlying motor neuronal activity.

The ability of ECoG signals to predict hand movements was further verified by experiments in which subjects used a manipulandum to move a cursor to one of nine possible target locations arranged in a 3 × 3 grid (Pistohl et al., 2008). For decoding, a Kalman filter (Section 4.4.5) was used in which the state vector comprised of the X- and Y- hand positions and velocities. As in the Kalman filter

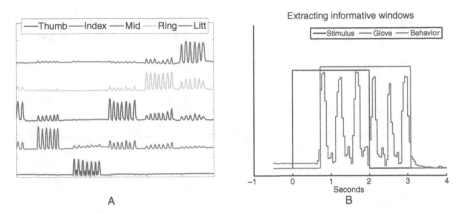

Figure 8.11. **Measuring finger movements using a dataglove.** (A) Measurements from the five-finger movement sensors. The traces from bottom to top correspond to thumb, index, middle, ring, and little finger respectively. As seen in the plot, the degree of independent motion varies from finger to finger, with the thumb being mostly independent of the other fingers. (B) Stimulus period (box-shaped trace starting at 0) instructing the subject to perform a specific finger movement, dataglove readings (noisy trace with multiple peaks) for that finger (note the delay in reacting to the stimulus), and the inferred window of behavior (second box-shaped trace) (from Shenoy et al., 2007).

models discussed in Section 7.2.1, the state vector at time t was linearly related to the observed neural data, which in this case was a low-pass filtered version of the ECoG signal from all electrodes at some time $t - \tau$ in the past. The researchers found that the Kalman filter approximately tracked the actually performed movements, with correlation coefficients between real and predicted positions in the range 0.16 to 0.45 across six subjects. The best correlations were obtained using a delay τ of approximately 94 ms.

ECoG BCIs for Prosthetic Hand Control

The experiments above demonstrated the ability to decode hand position and velocity from ECoG signals. Can ECoG also be used to decode individual finger movements?

To investigate this question, Shenoy, Rao, and colleagues (2007) conducted experiments in which six subjects implanted with 64-electrode ECoG grids moved the fingers of the hand contralateral to the grid placement, in response to visual cues on a computer screen. Subjects performed repeated movements of each individual finger for 2-second intervals, interspersed with rest periods. The instantaneous positions of the fingers was measured using a 5-sensor dataglove and written to disk simultaneously with the recorded ECoG signals. Each sensor measured the degree to which a finger was curled, providing a single measurement per finger. Figure 8.11 provides examples of finger position measurements during an experiment.

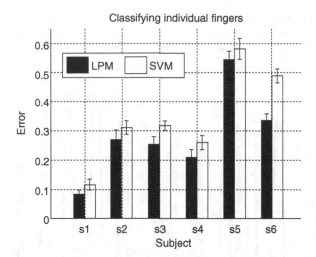

Figure 8.12. **Classifying finger movements using ECoG.** The plot shows the 5-class cross-validation error for LPM and SVM classifiers across 6 subjects (chance level error for 5-class classification is 0.8, or 80%) (from Shenoy et al., 2007).

The ECoG signal during finger movement was converted into the frequency domain and the power in the 11–40Hz, 71–100Hz, 101–150Hz bands were extracted for each of the 64 channels, resulting in a 192-dimensional feature vector. This feature vector was used as input to two classifiers: a support vector machine (SVM) and a linear programming machine (LPM) (see earlier section). The goal here is to predict which finger is moving, a multi-class classification task (Section 5.1.3). An all-pairs approach to multi-class classification was used: a separate classifier was trained for every pair of classes, resulting in a total of 10 classifiers. After training, a new input is run through each classifier, resulting in one vote for an output finger class, and the class with the maximum number of votes is selected as the output (*majority voting* as discussed in Section 5.1.3).

Figure 8.12 shows the 5-class error in classification of fingers across the six subjects. The error was measured using 5-fold cross-validation (see Section 5.1.4). As seen in the figure, the LPM classifier consistently outperformed the SVM classifier. The average error across 6 subjects was 23% for the LPM (chance classification error rate is 0.8 or 80%).

More interestingly, the researchers demonstrated that ECoG can be used to continuously track which finger is being moved. A sigmoid probabilistic output function was used for each pair-wise classifier to generate a single vector of class-conditional probabilities. The number of output classes was six, with rest periods as an additional class. One-second windows of data were used to compute ECoG features every 40 ms, and these features were classified using the probabilistic multi-class classifier. Figure 8.13 illustrates the output of the classifier over time along with the correct labels (i.e., which finger was being moved) as colored line segments at the top. It can

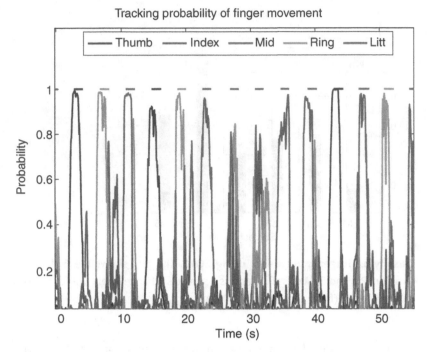

Figure 8.13. **Tracking finger movement using ECoG.** (See color plates for the same figure in color) (A) Continuous probabilistic output of the 6-class classifier on 1 second windows of ECoG, updated every 40 ms. Colored line segments at the top denote the true class labels (which finger was actually moved). Probabilities for the "rest" state are not shown. In most cases, the classifier correctly identifies the onset and termination of movement as well as which finger is being moved (from Shenoy, 2008).

be seen that the classifier accurately identifies movement onset and rest periods and outputs high probabilities for the correct finger (and sometimes adjacent fingers that may also be simultaneously moving, cf. Figure 8.11A). More recent work by the same group has demonstrated that ipsilateral hand movements can be discriminated from ECoG signals from a single hemisphere, suggesting the possibility of regaining ipsilateral movement control using signals from an intact hemisphere after damage to the other hemisphere (Scherer et al., 2009).

Other experiments have demonstrated that a principal component decomposition (see PCA, Section 4.5.2) of the ECoG power spectrum can reveal spatially distinct representations of individual fingers (Miller et al., 2009). Ten human subjects were asked to perform the finger movement task described above, and the movements were recorded using a dataglove (Figure 8.14A). From each ECoG electrode, the power spectrum was calculated from 1-second epochs centered at the time of maximum flexion during each movement. The spectra were normalized by dividing with the average at each frequency, and then the log was taken. For PCA, the covariance

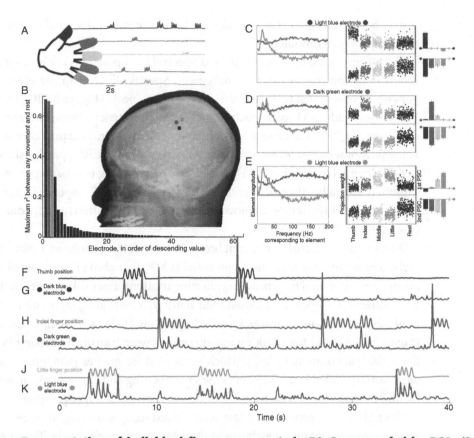

Figure 8.14. **Representation of individual finger movements in ECoG as revealed by PCA.** (See color plates for the same figure in color). (A) Finger positions measured by a dataglove during cued flexion-extension. (B) Cross-correlation between finger movement and sample projection weights for first principal spectral component (PSC) shows spatial specificity for different finger movements as indicated by the color code (dark blue: thumb, dark green: index finger, light blue: little finger). Same color code used in C-K. (C) Left panel: First (pink) and second (gold) PSCs for the dark blue electrode in (B). Middle panel: Projection magnitudes for each spectral sample from the first (top) and second (bottom) PSCs, sorted by movement type (black: rest periods). Each sample denotes the contribution of the PSC to the power spectrum from a 1 second epoch around a single movement. Note that the first PSC has a specific increase from rest for thumb movements. Right panel: Bar chart showing mean projection magnitudes for each finger-movement type, with mean from rest samples subtracted. Upper bars: first PSC, lower: second PSC. (D) and (E) Same as (C) except for the dark green and light blue electrodes in (B). (F), (H), and (J) Measured thumb, index, and little finger positions for a 40 second period. (G), (I), and (K) Projections to the first PSC for each of the three electrodes in (B) for the same 40 seconds as in (F), (H), (J). The plots show that each electrode is specifically and strongly correlated with one movement type (from Miller et al., 2009).

matrix between frequencies was calculated, and the eigenvalues and eigenvectors of this matrix were computed.

The eigenvectors, known as Principal Spectral Components (PSCs), captured the robust common features during movement. Specifically, two major spectral components were revealed by this analysis across all subjects (Figure 8.14C–E): the first PSC corresponds to a broad-spectral change at all frequencies between 5 and 200 Hz, and a second PSC reflecting a low-frequency narrow-band rhythm corresponding to the phenomenon of "event-related desynchronization" (ERD) previously reported in EEG studies (see Section 9.1.1). The PSC corresponding to broad-spectral change exhibited spatially discrete representation for individual fingers (Figure 8.14B) and reproduced the temporal movement trajectories of different individual fingers (Figure 8.14F–K).

Besides the relationship between broad-band spectral change and movements, it is also known that the local motor potential (LMP) (see above) is correlated with the position of individual fingers during grasping motions. Four subjects implanted with ECoG electrodes opened or closed their hand in a slow grasping motion (Acharya et al., 2010). This motion was recorded using an 18-sensor wireless CyberGlove (Figure 8.15A), and the resulting measurements were transformed using PCA. The first principal component (PC), which accounted for greater than 90% of the variance, corresponded in all subjects to the slow opening and closing movements of the hand. The next five PCs each corresponded to individual finger position variations.

Next, the ECoG signals were low-pass filtered using a moving average window 2 seconds long to obtain an estimate of the LMP for each electrode. The linear filter method (Equation 7.2) was used to predict each PC of hand motion from LMPs using a separate filter. The results, illustrated in Figure 8.15B, show that LMPs extracted from ECoG signals can be used to decode both opening and closing of the hand (first PC) as well as individual finger positions (other PCs). Additionally, the filters trained on data from any given session were robust in their performance across multiple sessions and days, and were invariant to changes in wrist angle, elbow flexion, and hand placement across these sessions.

Long-Term Stability of ECoG BCIs

One of the potential issues with invasive BCIs is signal degradation over a long period of time due to immunoreactive processes; ECoG has therefore been suggested as a better alternative for long-term BCI use. However, there have not been many studies investigating how an ECoG BCI performs over an extended period of time. Blakely, Ojemann, and colleagues (2009) examined BCI performance over multiple days using a *fixed set* of parameters for the BCI. A subject implanted with subdural electrodes used tongue imagery to control a cursor in a 1D BCI task identical to the one in Figure 8.6. The electrode-frequency band combination for control as well as the parameters g and P_0 (see Figure 8.6) were selected based on initial screening and kept fixed for 5 days. Performance remained robust throughout all

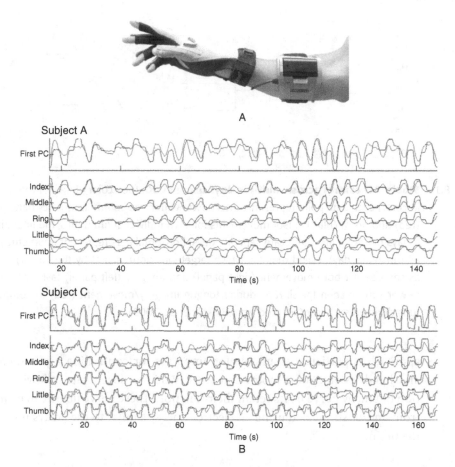

Figure 8.15. **Predicting grasping motions using ECoG.** (A) Wireless CyberGlove (Immersion Corp.) for tracking finger and wrist motion. The 18 sensors in the CyberGlove track flexions and extensions of finger joints as well as abductions and adductions of the fingers. (B) Comparison of actual (darker trace) and predicted (lighter trace) finger motion for two subjects. (Top traces for each subject) Linear decoding of the first PC of finger movement. (Other traces) Linear decoding of the individual fingers (adapted from Acharya et al., 2010).

days, with accuracies of 20/2 (hits/misses), 19/0, 19/5, 14/4, and 17/2 (chance level 50%). Figure 8.16 shows the total power for up/down cursor control in each run for the final trial on each day. The power levels remain relatively stable and well separated over the five days, suggesting that the ECoG BCI can be operated using a fixed set of parameters without the need for per-session adaptation of parameters as in some previous studies.

8.2 BCIs Based on Peripheral Nerve Signals

Rather than recording from the motor cortex, a less invasive approach to tapping motor-control signals from the brain is to record from peripheral nerves. This

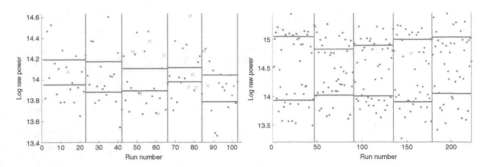

Figure 8.16. **Stable BCI control across multiple days using ECoG.** (See color plates for the same figure in color) Each data point represents total power within the control frequency band during up (red) and down (blue) cursor movements for each individual run during the final trial across 5 days (vertical bars demarcate separate days; horizontal bars represent geometric mean for all runs each day). Failed runs (in which target was not reached by the cursor) are shown as squares. For both movement (right panel) and imagery (left panel) tasks, an increase in power can be seen for all runs during tongue imagery/movement (red) in comparison to runs during rest (blue) (adapted from Blakely et al., 2009).

approach is particularly suitable for amputees for controlling a prosthetic arm-and-hand system. Some motor and sensory nerves degenerate following amputation but many nerve fibers retain their function. These nerve fibers can be recorded from and/or stimulated using an electrode array similar to the arrays implanted in the brain.

8.2.1 Nerve-Based BCIs

In the case of amputees, neural activity can be recorded from motor nerve fibers that previously targeted the muscles of the amputated body parts. For example when an upper-limb amputee desires to flex the elbow, wrist, or a particular finger, the volitionally evoked neural activity can be recorded from motor nerve fibers. Similarly, sensory information from sensors in a prosthetic hand and arm can be fed back to the subject by appropriately stimulating the sensory fibers that previously conveyed sensory inputs to the brain. Stimulating these fibers would provide feedback to the somatosensory parts of the brain about the consequences of the intended movements, thereby enabling natural closed-loop feedback control of prosthetic devices.

Median Nerve-Based BCIs

In one study (Warwick et al., 2003), a healthy human subject had an array of 100 individual needle electrodes surgically implanted into the median nerve fibers of the left arm. The 20 active electrodes in the array recorded the action potentials from small subpopulations of axons that surround each electrode. The electrodes could also be used to stimulate the axons. In one experiment, the blindfolded subject received feedback information via stimulation from force and slip sensors on a prosthetic hand. The subject was able to use the implanted device to control the hand by applying an appropriate force to grip an unseen object. In another experiment, the subject was able to control an electric wheelchair and select the direction of travel by opening and closing his hand. The subject reported no perceivable loss of hand sensation or motion control. The implant was extracted after 96 days because of mechanical fatigue of the percutaneous connection. No measurable long-term defects were found in the subject.

More extensive experiments by Dhillon and Horch (2005) have aimed to establish the feasibility of median nerve-based BCIs. Teflon-insulated platinum-iridium electrodes were implanted within fascicles of severed median nerves in six human subjects with upper limb amputations (amputation level at or below elbow). Short duration pulses were applied to individual electrodes to identify which electrodes could be used to elicit distally referred sensations of touch/pressure or proprioception. Conversely, motor-control channels were identified by connecting individual electrodes to a loudspeaker and asking the subject to attempt a missing limb movement (e.g., finger flexion) while listening to the nerve activity over the loudspeaker. For an electrode from which motor nerve activity could be recorded, the subject was asked to control the position of a cursor whose position was linearly related to the level of motor activity.

After becoming sufficiently proficient in the cursor control task, the subject was instructed to modulate the motor activity to control an artificial arm (Figure 8.17A). Subjects controlled actuators in the elbow and hand of the artificial arm using torque and force mode, respectively. A threshold level was set for detecting spikes, and each spike added a fixed increment to the output control signal, which decayed linearly over a selected time period (e.g., 0.5 second).

To test sensory performance, varying levels of indentation or force were applied to the strain gauge sensor on the thumb, and the subject was asked to rate them, without visual feedback, by using an open numerical scale for indentation or by squeezing a pinch-force meter for force. Subjects could quite accurately judge changes in indentation or force as seen in Figure 8.17B. For joint position sense, the elbow of the artificial arm was moved to different positions, and the subject was asked to match the perceived angle of elbow flexion/extension, again without visual feedback, through movements of the contralateral, intact arm. Subjects once again could consistently judge the static position of the elbow joint in the artificial arm (Figure 8.17B).

Motor control was assessed by asking subjects to control grip force or elbow position, without visual feedback. For grip-force control, the subjects were asked to match three or five force levels. In both cases, linear regression with a significant non-zero slope provided the best fit for the correlation between the target and the applied force or elbow flexion/extension angles (Figure 8.17C).

Finally, researchers have also explored the use of *"cuff" electrodes* that wrap around a peripheral nerve and record motor signals from the brain (Loeb and Peck, 1996;

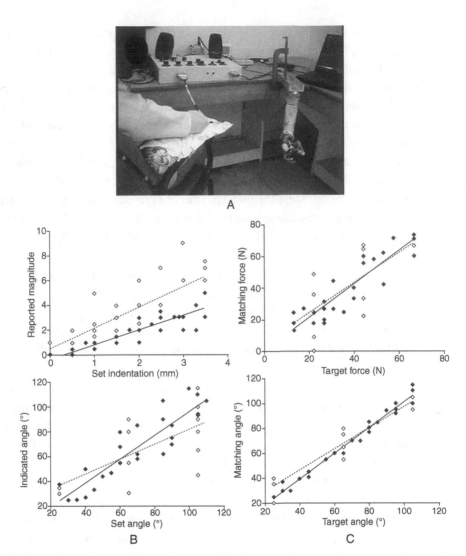

Figure 8.17. **Control and sensing of a robotic arm using nerve signals.** (A) Experimental setup showing subject with electrodes implanted in the median nerve connected to a differential amplifier and artificial arm-and-hand system. (B) Sensory performance. (Above) Sensation magnitude reported by subject versus indentation applied to the thumb sensor by the experimenter on day 1 (open symbols, dotted line) and day 7 (filled symbols, solid line). (Below) Position of the contralateral, intact elbow set by subject versus position of the artificial arm elbow set by the experimenter on day 1 (open symbols, dotted line) and day 4 (filled symbols, solid line). (C) Motor performance. (Above) Hand force applied by subject versus target force set by the experimenter on day 1 (open symbols, dotted line) and day 6 (filled symbols, solid line). (Below) Position of the artificial arm elbow set by subject versus target position of the contralateral, intact elbow set by the experimenter on day 1 (open symbols, dotted line) and day 5 (filled symbols, solid line) (adapted from Dhillon and Horch, 2005).

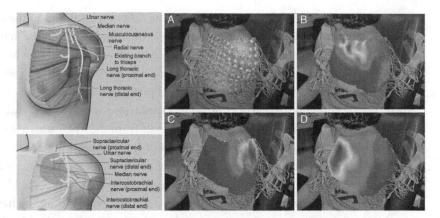

Figure 8.18. **Targeted muscle and sensory reinnervation.** (See color plates for the same figure in color) (Left panels) (Top) Depiction of the nerves transferred to the pectoralis muscle. (Bottom) Targeted sensory reinnervation. Cutaneous nerves were cut and transferred to the ulnar nerve and the median nerve. (Right panels) (A) Placement of EMG electrodes. (B) through (D) EMG patterns for elbow flexion, elbow extension, and hand closure respectively (adapted from Kuiken et al., 2007).

Wodlinger and Durand, 2010). Similar to the studies discussed above, they have demonstrated the use of such signals for controlling the elbow, wrist, and hand of a prosthetic arm as the patient imagines the movement.

8.2.2 Targeted Muscle Reinnervation (TMR)

A traditional method for controlling a prosthetic arm is to use EMG signals generated by intact muscles (e.g., EMG from biceps and triceps muscles to control a prosthetic hand). However, such a technique suffers from a lack of sufficient number of intact muscles to control both the body and the prosthetic device.

Targeted muscle reinnervation (TMR) is a surgical procedure that reroutes brain signals from nerves severed during amputation to intact muscles (Kuiken et al., 2007). After TMR, the intention of the subject evokes EMG signals in the reinnervated muscles, which are then amplified and used to control the actuators in the prosthetic arm. Sensory signals from the skin can also be routed to specific nerves for cutaneous sensory feedback, thereby allowing closed-loop feedback control.

As an example, in a subject whose left arm had been amputated, Kuiken and colleagues transferred the ulnar, median, musculocutaneous, and distal radial nerves to separate segments of the pectoral (chest) and serratus muscles (Figure 8.18, left panel). Two sensory nerves were cut, and the distal ends were connected to the ulnar and median nerves.

Three months after the surgery, the patient could feel her chest muscles twitching when she tried to close her hand or bend her elbow. Six months after surgery, EMG testing revealed differential EMG patterns for different types of imagined movements

(Figure 8.18, right panel). Additionally, touching different locations on the chest and other TMR areas resulted in touch sensation on the missing hand. The subject perceived different temperatures, sharpness of objects, vibrations, and pressures on the reinnervated skin as sensations on different fingers, the palm, etc.

The patient was fit with a new experimental prosthesis consisting of a motorized elbow with a computerized arm controller, a motorized wrist rotator, and a motorized hand. The patient trained to use EMG signals from the TMR sites to control the motorized hand and elbow. After seven weeks of training with the TMR-controlled prosthesis, the patient became proficient in the use of the prosthetic and was able to operate the hand, wrist, and elbow simultaneously. The patient reported being able to operate the hand and elbow very intuitively: thinking of opening the hand, closing the hand, bending the elbow, or straightening the elbow resulted in the corresponding motion of the prosthesis. Functional assessment tests using standardized tasks revealed that with TMR, the patient's control of prosthetic movements was almost four times faster than with a conventional prosthesis. More importantly, the patient was able to use her new TMR prosthesis for an average of four to five hours a day, five to six days per week, for daily living tasks ranging from cooking, putting on makeup and carrying things to eating, house cleaning, and doing the laundry.

8.3 Summary

In this chapter, we familiarized ourselves with semi-invasive BCIs, which avoid some of the risks and drawbacks of invasive BCIs (due to penetrating the blood-brain barrier and triggering immunoreactive processes that can reduce the quality of signals over time). At the same time, semi-invasive BCIs offer higher spatial resolution, better signal-to-noise ratio, a wider frequency range, and lesser training requirements than scalp-recorded EEG BCIs (see Chapter 9). We explored two types of semi-invasive BCIs: BCIs based on ECoG signals and BCIs based on nerve signals. ECoG BCIs have been typically demonstrated in epilepsy patients being monitored in the days prior to brain surgery. These BCIs can achieve high accuracies in cursor control tasks with relatively short training times. ECoG BCIs typically rely on the subject learning to modulate the spectral power in a high frequency band (e.g., 70–100Hz). The same spectral feature also allows finger movements to be differentiated, although precise manipulation and control of a multi-fingered robotic hand using ECoG remains to be demonstrated.

Nerve-based BCIs offer an even lesser invasive approach to BCI and prosthetic control. BCIs that tap voluntarily generated motor control signals from the median nerve have been used to control prosthetic arm–and-hand systems while sensory measurements from sensors on the artificial system can be conveyed through stimulation of pre-identified sensory fibers in the nerve. An alternate approach called TMR is based on diverting motor signals from nerves to intact muscles such as pectoral muscles and using EMG signals from these reinnervated muscles to control a prosthetic arm. TMR has significantly improved the quality of life of some amputees, allowing them to perform a range of daily living tasks not previously achievable through conventional prosthetics.

8.4 Questions and Exercises

1. Enumerate some of the advantages of using electrocorticography (ECoG) for recording neural activity compared to intracortical electrodes. What are some of the drawbacks?
2. In the monkey ECoG BCI discussed in Section 8.1.1, what information was extracted from the ECoG signal to allow control of a cursor? What evidence was observed that suggested neural plasticity while the monkey gained increasingly better control of the cursor?
3. Explain how the coefficient of determination r^2 is used in ECoG BCIs to select electrodes and frequency bands for control based on motor imagery.
4. In the ECoG BCI for cursor control described in Section 8.1.2, what were some of the changes in ECoG signal features observed, and how do these changes affect accuracy?
5. Describe the method used for achieving two-dimensional cursor control using ECoG as depicted in Figure 8.4. What features were found to be the most useful for online cursor control?
6. How does the spatial distribution of ECoG activation during motor imagery compare with ECoG activation during actual movement? How does this activation change after motor imagery is used for cursor control with feedback?
7. (♦ Expedition) Describe how the linear programming machine (LPM) used by Shenoy and colleagues in Section 8.1.2 differs from a standard SVM. What are the advantages of using the LPM compared to the SVM? How can the weights of the classifier be used for feature selection?
8. Explain how a classifier can be used for feature selection from a large number of features. (Hint: See Figure 8.8)
9. What is the local motor potential (LMP), and how is it related to movement?
10. Describe how the following techniques have been used to predict individual finger movements from ECoG:
    a. Classifiers such as LPM and SVM
    b. PCA applied to the ECoG power spectrum
    c. LMPs and PCA of hand motion
11. What is known about the long-term use and stability of ECoG BCIs? Describe some of the potential factors that can be expected to impact long-term use of ECoG implants.
12. Compare and contrast the potential advantages and disadvantages of using nerve recordings for controlling a prosthetic arm versus ECoG or intracortical recordings.

13. What nerve in the arm has been used for both conveying sensations as well as recording motor-control signals for a prosthetic arm? Which of the following quantities could be measured or controlled using nerves: joint position, grip force, indentation, torque?

14. (✶ Expedition) Find out what the state-of-the-art powered upper-limb prosthetic devices are, and discuss whether or how nerve-based BCIs such as those described in this chapter could be used to control and receive feedback from these devices.

15. (✶ Expedition) Explain how cuff electrodes work and discuss their strengths and weaknesses compared to more conventional electrodes.

16. What is targeted muscle reinnervation (TMR)? Can it be used to perceive sensations from a missing limb, control a prosthetic arm, or both?

17. What are the advantages and disadvantages of a BCI based on TMR compared to other nerve-based BCIs we discussed in the chapter?

9

Noninvasive BCIs

A holy grail of BCI research is to be able to control complex devices using noninvasive recordings of brain signals at high spatial and temporal resolution. Current noninvasive recording techniques capture changes in blood flow or fluctuations in electric/magnetic fields caused by the activity of large populations of neurons, but we are still far from a recording technique that can capture neural activity at the level of spikes noninvasively. In the absence of such a recording technique, researchers have focused on noninvasive techniques such as EEG, MEG, fMRI, and fNIR, and studied how the large-scale population-level brain signals recorded by these techniques can be used for BCI.

9.1 Electroencephalographic (EEG) BCIs

The technique of EEG involves recording electrical signals from the scalp (Section 3.1.2). The idea of using EEG to build a BCI was first suggested by Vidal (1973), but progress was limited until the 1990s when the advent of fast and cheap processors sparked a surge of interest in this area, leading to the development of a variety of EEG-based BCI techniques.

Since EEG signals reflect the combined input to large populations of neurons, methods for building BCIs from EEG signals rely on modulating the response of large neural populations either through subject training over a period of time or through external stimuli that can activate large populations of neurons. BCIs based on the former approach are called *self-paced* (or *asynchronous*) because the subject can voluntarily initiate control at any time without being tied to a stimulus. Self-paced BCIs typically utilize some form of imagery (motor or cognitive) that can generate a robust and reliable EEG response after a period of training. *Stimulus-based* BCIs (also called *synchronous* BCIs) rely on detecting a stereotypical brain response generated after the subject is presented with a stimulus (such as a flash) that is linked to a BCI command or choice. Control is thus not initiated by the subject but is tied to the presentation of stimuli by the BCI. Stimulus-based BCIs however are easier to use because they do not require training on the part of the subject, and relatively high accuracies can be obtained for naïve subjects, compared to imagery-based BCIs. We will now delve into both of these types of EEG BCIs and examine their capabilities in more detail.

9.1.1 Oscillatory Potentials and ERD

A number of successful imagery-based BCIs have relied on the subject learning to control specific brain rhythms, manifested as oscillatory EEG potentials at specific frequencies. It has been known that when a subject performs movement or imagines performing a movement, the power in low frequency bands such as the mu (8–12 Hz) or beta band (13–30 Hz) decreases, a phenomenon known as "desynchronization" (sometimes called *event-related desynchronization* or *ERD*). In a typical experiment, the power in the mu band is coupled to the movement of a cursor on a computer screen using a fixed mapping function; the goal is to move the cursor in a desired direction to hit a target. The subject starts by imagining a particular type of movement (e.g., opening and closing a hand) and over several training sessions, learns to control the movement of the cursor by being able to modulate the power in the mu band. The underlying physiology involves conditioning at the neural population level (see Section 6.2.1), wherein the subject learns to modulate a large number of neurons in concert to generate the appropriate change in power. The performance of noninvasive EEG BCIs based on ERD has been reported to be 10–29 bits/minute at 80–95% accuracy, after a dozen or so hour-long sessions. Note that these BCIs are self-paced.

Wadsworth BCI

One of the first BCIs based on the control of oscillatory potentials was developed by Wolpaw and colleagues (1991) at the Wadsworth Center in Albany, New York. They trained 4 subjects to use the 8–12 Hz mu rhythm in EEG over the central sulcus of one hemisphere to move a cursor from the center of a screen to a target located at the top or bottom edge (Figure 9.1). EEG was recorded using bipolar spatial filtering (Section 4.5.1) based on 2 electrodes placed 3 cm anterior and posterior to location C3 in the 10–20 system (Figure 3.7). The amplitude of the mu rhythm (calculated as the square root of the power at 9 Hz and measured in volts) was extracted using frequency analysis for every 333 ms time segment. The amplitude was compared to 5 preset amplitude ranges and translated to one of 5 possible cursor movements (see Figure 9.2C for an example), such that large mu amplitudes resulted in upward cursor motion and small mu rhythm amplitudes resulted in downward cursor motion.

To allow the subjects to learn to control their mu rhythm amplitude, initial training consisted of trials where only upward cursor movement was possible: the subject had to learn to relax, thereby increasing mu rhythm amplitude to cause the cursor to move up. After this initial training period, subjects trained on the top versus bottom target task described above. Over a period of several weeks, subjects learned

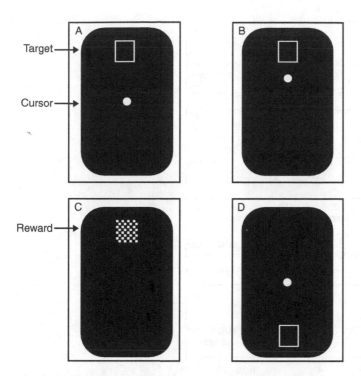

Figure 9.1.   **The first Wadsworth EEG BCI for one-dimensional cursor control.** The screen shots show an example run: (A) the cursor is at the center of the screen with the target at top; (B) subject uses mu rhythm amplitude to move the cursor toward the target; (C) cursor hits the target which flashes in a checkerboard pattern; (D) cursor reappears in center of screen and a new target appears (in case of an error, cursor reappears in the center, and the target remains where it was) (from Wolpaw et al., 1991).

to control their mu rhythm amplitude quite accurately, typically hitting the target within 3 seconds. Subjects reported that to move the cursor down, they adopted strategies such as imagining doing a certain activity (e.g., lifting weights), whereas to move the cursor up, they thought about relaxing. As training progressed, several reported that such imagery was no longer needed.

Figure 9.2 shows the mu rhythm amplitude distributions for the 4 subjects on the final training day when the target was at the top (dashed line) and bottom of the screen (solid line). The separation of the two distributions reflects the ability of the subjects to control the amplitude of their mu rhythms for upward or downward cursor movement. Figure 9.3A illustrates the frequency amplitude spectra for one subject, clearly showing the reduction in amplitude for the mu frequency band (8–12 Hz) when the target is at the bottom, compared to when the target is at the top. This reduction can also be seen in the sample EEG trace shown in Figure 9.3B. Such control of mu amplitude resulted in relatively high overall performance for the task (accuracy from 80% to 95%, with hit rates between 10 and 29 hits/minute).

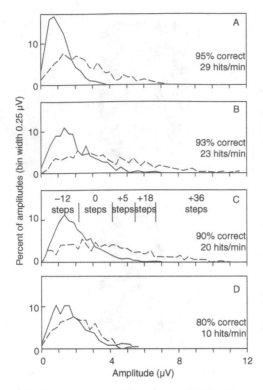

Figure 9.2.   **Distribution of mu rhythm amplitudes for 4 subjects on final training day.** The distribution when target was at the bottom is shown as a solid line. The distribution when the target was at the top is shown as a dashed line. Inset numbers show performance (accuracy = hits/(hits+errors)) and hit rate (hits/min). Vertical lines in (C) show the mapping from mu amplitude ranges to cursor movement in steps up (+) or down (-) for subject C (total number of steps from bottom to top was 76) (from Wolpaw et al., 1991).

In a follow-up study, Wolpaw and McFarland (1994) showed that subjects can control two-dimensional cursor movement using the same approach but with two channels of bipolar EEG. The two bipolar channels were recorded from the left and right hemispheres at pairs of locations across the central sulcus (i.e., using the FC3/CP3 pair and the FC4/CP4 pair in the 10–20 system – see Figure 9.4 (Left)). The task was to hit an L-shaped target at one of the corners of the screen (Figure 9.4 (Right)). The amplitudes for the mu band (5Hz bin centered at 10 Hz) for the left and right hemisphere channels were mapped to up/down and left/right cursor movements. The mapping was based on a linear equation where the sum of left and right amplitudes was mapped to vertical cursor movement while their difference (i.e., right minus left) was mapped to horizontal cursor movement. The slope and intercept of the equation were adjusted over time to optimize the subject's performance. Over a period of 6–8 weeks, 4 of 5 subjects acquired simultaneous control over the sum and difference of right and left hemisphere amplitudes, achieving accuracies that were 2–3 times chance levels (25%).

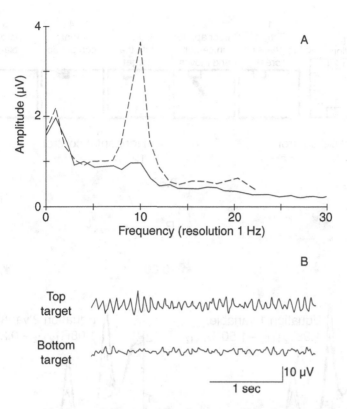

Figure 9.3.   **Control of mu rhythm amplitude in a subject during the cursor task.** (A) Frequency amplitude spectra for subject A in Figure 9.2 when the target is at the bottom (solid line) and at the top (dashed line). (B) Example EEG traces for the same subject for a top and a bottom target. Note the presence of the mu rhythm for the top target, which is reduced by the subject for the bottom target (from Wolpaw et al., 1991).

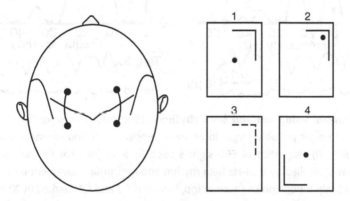

Figure 9.4.   **Bipolar EEG channels for two-dimensional cursor control.** (Left) One bipolar channel was recorded from each hemisphere from locations FC3/CP3 and FC4/CP4 across the central sulcus. (Right) Example run of two-dimensional cursor task showing cursor moving from the center of the screen to a target at the top right corner, followed by a new target at the bottom left corner (from Wolpaw and McFarland, 1994).

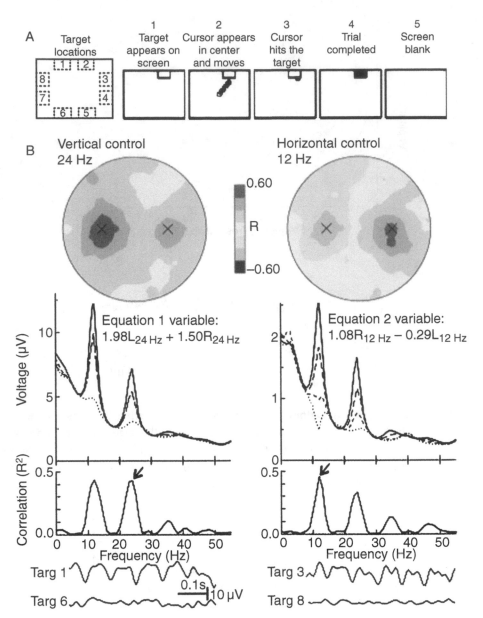

Figure 9.5. **2-D Cursor control using mu and beta rhythms.** (See color plates for the same figure in color) (A) The eight possible target locations (numbers 1–8) and example sequence of events in a trial. (B) Properties of EEG signals used by a subject. For this subject, vertical movement was controlled by a 24-Hz beta rhythm and horizontal movement by a 12-Hz mu rhythm. (*Top*) Scalp topographies (nose at top, locations C3 and C4 marked by X) of the correlations of the 2 rhythm amplitudes with the vertical and horizontal target coordinates. The topographies are for *R* rather than R^2 to show positive and negative correlations. (*Middle*) Amplitude (voltage) spectra (weighted combinations of right-side and left-side spectra) and their corresponding R^2 spectra. Different voltage spectra (dashed, dotted, etc.) are for the 4 vertical and 4 horizontal target coordinates. Arrows point to frequency bands used in vertical

How does the performance of these mu-rhythm-based EEG BCIs compare with invasive BCIs? Using a variation of the two-dimensional cursor task, Wolpaw and McFarland (2004) showed that their subjects could achieve a level of performance that falls within the range reported for invasive BCIs in monkeys. Subjects were required to use EEG signals to move the cursor to hit one of 8 targets placed on a computer screen (Figure 9.5A). EEG signals were recorded from 64 electrode locations distributed over the entire scalp, referenced to the right ear. The signals from locations C4 on the right and C3 on the left hemisphere were spatially filtered using a Laplacian filter (Section 4.5.1). The last 400 ms of spatially filtered EEG activity were used to compute the amplitudes in the mu (8–12 Hz) and beta (in this study, 18–26 Hz) frequency bands. Cursor movement was linearly determined using a weighted combination of the two amplitudes from the right side and two from left side. Specifically, vertical movement was determined using $M_V = a_V(w_{RV} R_V + w_{LV} L_V + b_V)$, where R_V is a right-side amplitude (either mu or beta, depending on the subject) and L_V is a left-side amplitude. The weights w_{RV} and w_{LV} as well as the parameters a_V and b_V were adapted online to optimize performance. A similar equation with a separate set of parameters governed horizontal cursor movement M_H. Positive and negative values of M_V and M_H moved the cursor up and down, and right and left, respectively. After each trial, the weights were adapted using a least mean-square (LMS) algorithm to minimize for past trials the difference between the actual target location and the target location predicted by the linear equations for M_V and M_H.

Over several weeks of training, subjects were able to gain control over their left/right mu and beta amplitudes (Figure 9.5B). The LMS algorithm was found to have adapted the weights so as to give more weight to those amplitudes that the user was best able to control. After training, the 4 subjects were able to reach a target within the 10-second allotted time in 89%, 70%, 78%, and 92% of the trials, respectively, with average movement times 1.9, 3.9, 3.3, and 1.9 seconds, respectively. Figure 9.6 illustrates the average cursor paths to the targets for each subject. The performance of the subjects was compared to the performance reported in the literature for invasive BCIs in nonhuman primates on point-to-point movement tasks. Three measures were compared: movement time, target size, and hit rate. Movement times and hit rates were found to be similar whereas target size was in between those used in the invasive studies. The researchers thus concluded that the performance of their noninvasive BCI falls within the range reported for invasive BCIs that use electrodes implanted in the cortex.

Figure 9.5.   (continued)

and horizontal movement variables, respectively. (*Bottom*) Sample EEG from single trials. (*Left*) Trace from electrode C3 (major contributor to vertical variable) for a target at the top (target 1) or target at bottom (target 6). (*Right*) Traces from electrode C4 (major contributor to the horizontal variable) for target on the right (target 3) or target on the left (target 8) (from Wolpaw and McFarland, 2004).

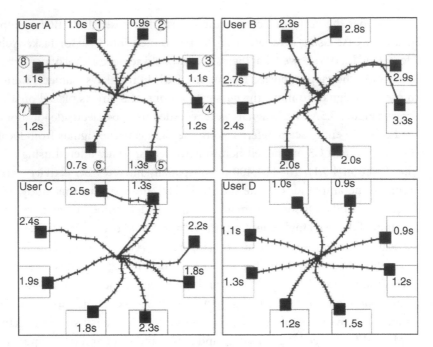

Figure 9.6.   **Average cursor paths to targets for 4 subjects.** Average paths were computed for all trials in which the cursor reached the target within 2 seconds for user A, 5 seconds for user B,
4 seconds for user C, and 2 seconds for user D. Short lines on paths denote tenths of time.
Numbers within targets denote average time to target (from Wolpaw and McFarland, 2004).

Graz BCI

The Graz BCI group, led by Pfurtscheller, has published a number of studies involving motor imagery-based BCIs. Like the approach of Wolpaw and colleagues at
Wadsworth, the Graz BCI system relies on low-frequency oscillations in EEG signals from sensorimotor areas to control cursors and prosthetic devices. A major
focus is on feature extraction and classification techniques to optimize subject
performance.

Early prototypes were based on EEG patterns during willful limb movement, such
as left hand, right hand or foot movement. Classification accuracy was optimized by
adapting input features, such as electrode positions and frequency bands, specifically for each subject. Later work demonstrated that primary sensorimotor areas are
also activated by movement *imagery*, with a circumscribed "event-related desynchronization" (ERD) for the contralateral and an "event-related synchronization"
(ERS) for the ipsilateral hemisphere (Figure 9.7). This fact is utilized by the Graz BCI
system using a classifier to exploit the left–right differences in sensorimotor rhythms
to classify imagery.

In one study (Pfurtscheller et al., 2000), subjects were provided continuous feedback of classification performance: a horizontal bar moved to the right or left boundary of the screen as the subject imagined moving the right or left hand. Three signal

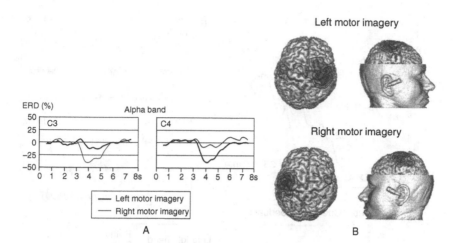

Figure 9.7.   **Oscillatory EEG activity used in the Graz BCI.** (A) Average power in the alpha band (here, 9–13 Hz; called the mu band over motor areas) during motor imagery based on EEG signals from the left (C3) and right sensorimotor cortex (C4). Positive and negative deflections, with respect to baseline (0.5 to 2.5 seconds), represent a band power increase (ERS) and decrease (ERD) respectively. The cue was presented at 3s for 1.25 seconds. (B) Distribution of ERD on the cortical surface calculated from a realistic head model, shown 625 ms after presentation of the cue (adapted from Pfurtscheller et al., 2000).

processing methods were tested: (1) band power in predefined, subject-specific frequency bands, (2) adaptive autoregressive (AAR) parameters estimated for each iteration using the recursive least squares algorithm, (3) common spatial patterns (CSP). For the first two methods, two closely spaced bipolar recordings from the left and right sensorimotor cortex were used, while the CSP method was based on a dense array of electrodes located over central areas. The resulting feature vectors were classified using linear discriminant analysis or LDA (Section 5.1.1). After 6 or 7 sessions, the lowest errors for three subjects (1.8%, 6.8%, and 12.5%) were obtained for the CSP method, with AAR yielding slightly higher rates and band power features performing the worst.

The Graz group has reported information transfer rates (ITR; see Section 5.1.4) of up to 17 bits/min obtained by real-time classification of oscillatory activity (Pfurtscheller et al., 2003). The group has also investigated the usefulness of ERD as a control signal for patients with spinal cord injury. A pilot project was performed in a tetraplegic patient with an electric hand orthosis (Pfurtscheller, Guger et al., 2000). After some months of training, the patient was able to operate the hand orthosis via imagery of specific motor commands (Figure 9.8).

Berlin BCI

Are months of training a necessity for learning to control an imagery-based EEG BCI? The Berlin Brain-Computer Interface (BBCI) project has explored this question and demonstrated that advanced feature extraction and machine learning

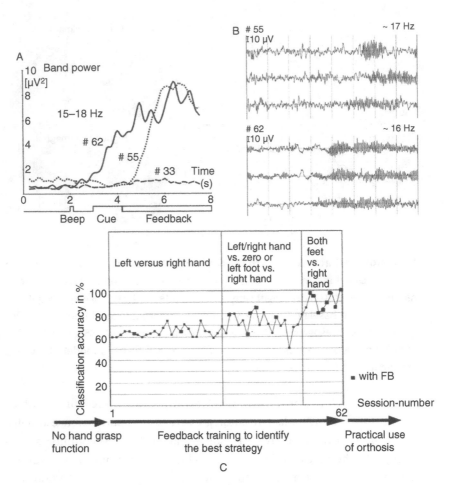

Figure 9.8.   **EEG-based BCI control of a hand orthosis using motor imagery.** (A) Average power in the beta frequency band (15–18 Hz, averaged over 80 trials each) for 3 motor imagery sessions (33, 55, 62) during the course of training over 5 months. EEG was recorded from the foot area (electrode position Cz), and imagery of foot movement was initiated by a visual cue-stimulus. Early sessions showed only small band power increases (due to ERS) whereas later sessions (e.g., #62) show larger and earlier increases due to learning. (B) Raw EEG signals from two sessions showing earlier onset of beta oscillations in session 62. (C) Classification accuracy of motor imagery over a period of 5 months for a tetraplegic patient with no hand grasp function. FB denotes feedback. (Adapted from Pfurtscheller, Guger et al., 2000).

techniques can allow naïve users to gain rapid control of external devices without extensive training.

For example, one study by Blankertz, Müller, and colleagues (2008) involved a one-dimensional cursor control task with 14 fully naïve subjects utilizing two of three kinds of motor imagery: left-hand imagery, right-hand imagery, or foot imagery. The two types of imagery were chosen for each subject in an initial "calibration" phase based on how much of the variance of power in a given frequency band could be explained by the imagery class affiliation (this was done using the r^2 method – see Chapter 8). Figure 9.9 illustrates the properties of the EEG signals for two subjects and the specific frequency bands chosen for these subjects. The chosen frequency band signals (from 55 electrodes) were then spatially filtered using filters learned with the common spatial patterns (CSP) method (Section 4.5.4). Between 2 and 6 CSP filters were used for each subject, resulting in a two- to six-dimensional feature vector which was input to a linear discriminant analysis (LDA) classifier (Section 5.1.1). The output of the classifier was used to move the cursor to the left or to the right to hit a target placed at the left or right edge of the screen.

Figure 9.10 summarizes the results: 8 out of the 14 BCI novices achieved > 84% accuracy in their first BCI session, and another 4 subjects performed at > 70%. Interestingly, in one of these subjects, the classifier used was actually trained on real movements, supporting the close relationship between real and imagined movements (cf. results from ECoG BCIs in Chapter 8). One subject (*cn* in Figure 9.10) performed at chance level (50%); for another, the EEG spectra showed no peaks and hence no classes could be distinguished.

These results are encouraging because they suggest that appropriate use of signal processing and machine learning techniques could ameliorate the need for long periods of training to achieve accurate EEG-based control.

9.1.2 Slow Cortical Potentials

Slow cortical potentials (SCPs) are slow *non-movement*-related changes in EEG amplitude lasting from 300 ms up to several seconds. They are thought to reflect a mechanism for local mobilization of excitation or inhibition in cortical populations, caused by inputs from the thalamus. The fact that humans can learn to voluntarily regulate these potentials based on feedback has led Birbaumer and colleagues to propose the use of SCPs for designing a BCI, which they call a thought translation device (TTD).

In one of their many studies on the TTD system (Kübler et al., 1999), 13 healthy subjects and 3 patients with total motor paralysis (due to amyotrophic lateral sclerosis or ALS) trained over several sessions to control their SCPs (in the case of patients, the training period lasted several months). EEG was recorded from electrode locations Cz, C3, and C4 (Figure 3.7), and two channels were extracted: a Cz-linked mastoid channel (i.e., 1/2 [(Cz-A1) + (Cz-A2)]) and a bipolar C3 minus C4 channel. The training task involved controlling a cursor to hit the top or bottom edge of the screen. The position of the cursor was proportional to the difference between average baseline EEG amplitude and the average EEG amplitude over the last 500 ms from the Cz channel. The baseline amplitude was calculated from an immediately preceding baseline period. Some subjects participated in a two-dimensional cursor task where the target could also be the left or right edge of the screen. In this case, the horizontal position of the cursor was proportional to the difference between average baseline EEG amplitude from the (C3–C4) channel and the average EEG amplitude from this channel over the last 500 ms.

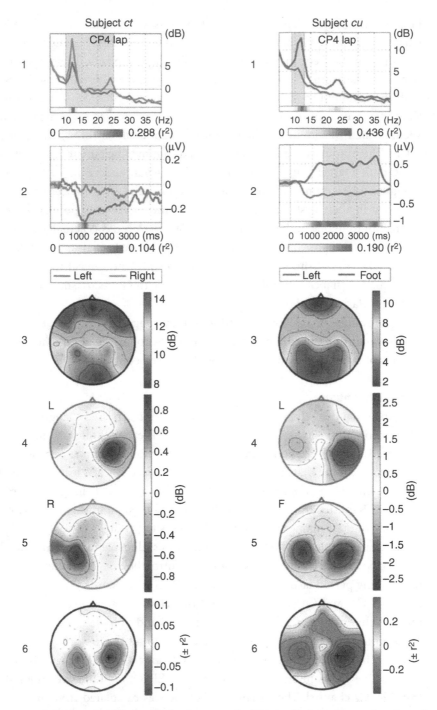

Figure 9.9.   **Modulation of EEG signals by imagery for the Berlin BCI.** (See color plates for the same figure in color) (1) Average spectra for two subjects for two motor imagery tasks (red: left hand, green: right hand; blue: right foot) for the Laplace-filtered CP4 channel ("CP4 lap") during the calibration phase. The r² values of the difference between imagery conditions are color coded; frequency band chosen is shaded gray. (2) Average amplitude envelope of

Figure 9.11 shows the average SCP waveforms generated by healthy subjects on cue after training. For both channels, a clear deviation from baseline activity in the positive or negative direction can be seen: this difference from baseline was used to proportionally move the cursor up/down or left/right. Out of the 13 subjects, 4 were able to produce significant positive-going responses, 3 generated significant negative-going responses, and 3 were able to generate both.

Figure 9.12 shows a similar result for one of the ALS patients MP. As seen in the figure, after several months of training, the patient was able to generate a negative-going SCP at Cz when required to hit the bottom target (deflections in vEOG indicate minor vertical eye movements). As the subject learned, there was a gradual increase in accuracy, as revealed by an increasing hit rate and decreasing false positive rate over time (Figure 9.12B). Overall, 2 patients achieved 70–80% accuracy in a spelling task, where a binary choice was made successively to select a letter from an alphabet.

9.1.3 Movement-Related Potentials

EEG signals show a small and slow potential drift prior to voluntary movements. These movement-related potentials (MRPs), sometimes also called *readiness potentials* (RPs) or *Bereitschaftspotentials* (BPs) (Jahanshahi and Hallet, 2002), show variation in distribution over the scalp with respect to the body part being moved. For example, the BP related to movement of left versus right arm shows a strong lateral asymmetry. This potentially allows one to not only estimate the intent to move, but also distinguish between left and right movement intention. This makes them attractive targets for BCI applications but since they are typically much smaller than other EEG phenomena such as alpha or beta rhythms, their detection is much harder. It has been suggested that while ERD may reflect changes in the background oscillatory activity in wide cortical sensorimotor areas, MRPs may represent increased, task-specific responses of supplementary and primary motor cortical areas (Babiloni et al., 1999).

An early demonstration of the utility of MRPs in BCI can be found in the work of Hiraiwa and colleagues (1990). They used a backpropagation neural network (see Section 5.2.2) to classify EEG patterns from 12 channels in 2 tasks: voluntary utterances of the syllables "a", "e", "i", "o", and "u" and moving a joystick in 1 of 4 directions: forward, back, left, or right. The input to the neural network consisted of 2 snapshots of the 12 EEG amplitudes at 0.66 and 0.33 seconds before speech or

Figure 9.9.　(continued)
chosen frequency band. Cue was presented at time 0. (3) Scalp maps showing log of power within chosen frequency band averaged over the calibration phase. (4) and (5) Log band power difference topographies for the imagery tasks (denoted L, R, or F). Global average (in 3) was subtracted for each. (6) r^2 values for the difference between the motor imagery tasks (row 4 minus row 5) (adapted from Blankertz et al., 2008).

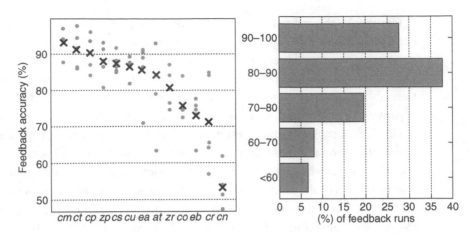

Figure 9.10. **Accuracy for naïve subjects using the Berlin BCI in a one-dimensional cursor task.** (Left) Each dot represents one run and each cross represents the average. (Right) Histogram of accuracies (from Blankertz et al., 2008).

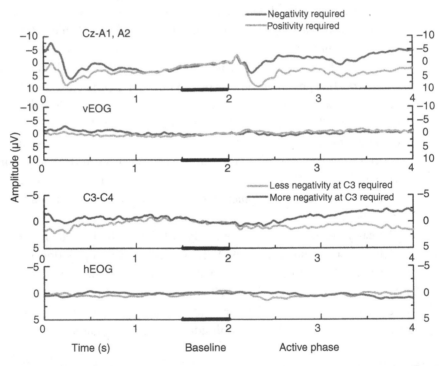

Figure 9.11. **Slow cortical potentials (SCPs) in healthy subjects.** (Top 2 panels) Average SCP at Cz and vertical electro-oculogram (vEOG), averaged during a single training session over 13 subjects. (Lower 2 panels) SCP difference between the left (C3) and right (C4) motor cortex and horizontal EOG (hEOG), averaged across last 3 training sessions for 5 subjects. Thick line between 1.5s-2s: baseline. Note that the y-axis has negative values at the top. (from Kübler et al., 1999).

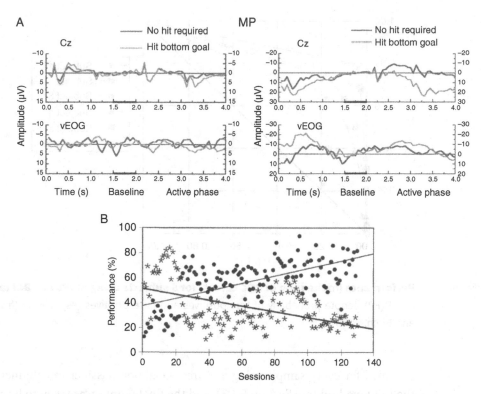

Figure 9.12. **SCP-based BCI in an ALS patient**. (A) SCP and EOG for an ALS patient MP at the beginning of training (left) and after training over several months (right). (B) Improvement in performance for the same patient over time, as revealed by an increasing percentage of hits (black dots) and decreasing percentage of false positive (asterisks) over sessions spanning several months (adapted from Kübler et al., 1999).

movement. The researchers found that for the speech task, 16 out of 30 new EEG patterns (i.e., 53%) were correctly classified into one of the 5 classes (chance performance: 20%). For the joystick task, 23 out of 24 new patterns (96%) were correctly classified (chance: 25%). These results are quite remarkable given the early date of these experiments.

One interesting application of voluntary MRPs is in the design of an "asynchronous switch" which allows a BCI to detect whenever the user voluntarily wants to transition from an idle state to an active control state to start using a BCI. Mason and Birch (2000) have proposed what they call a *low-frequency asynchronous switch design* (LF-ASD) for this purpose. They tested their method with 5 subjects using a task where the subject made fast index finger flexion movements to hit a moving ball with a second EEG-controlled ball on a computer screen. The EEG-controlled ball moved according to classification of MRPs extracted from bipolar EEG signals filtered in the 1–4 Hz range from electrode pairs over supplementary and primary motor areas. Wavelet analysis (Section 4.3) based on a "bi-scale" wavelet was used to extract a 6-dimensional feature vector from 6 electrode pairs. The feature vector was

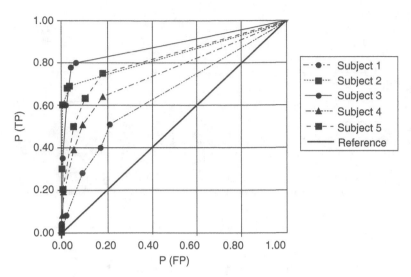

Figure 9.13. **Performance (in the form of ROC curves) for 5 subjects using MRPs in a BCI task.** P(TP) and P(FP) denote probability of true positives and false positives respectively (from Mason and Birch, 2000).

classified for every sample using a nearest neighbor classifier in conjunction with the LVQ method (see Section 5.1.3), and the final output was taken to be a moving average over the last five samples. Hit rates in the range of 38%–81% were achieved with corresponding false positive rates in the range of 0.3%–11.6% (see Figure 9.13 for the full ROC curve). The LF-ASD method was found to have lower mean error rates than methods based on mu band features (Section 9.1.1).

Another example of the use of MRPs is a BCI designed by Shenoy and Rao (2005) that uses a dynamic Bayesian network (DBN) (see Section 4.4.4) to infer probability distributions over brain- and body-states during planning and execution of actions. Their system used both EEG and EMG signals as inputs to the DBN, which inferred the probabilities of internal states such as intent to move, preparatory activity, and movement execution. The parameters of the DBN were learned directly from observed data. Unlike classification-based approaches, the advantage of using a DBN is that it allows the BCI to continuously track and predict a subject's internal states over time and generate control signals based on an entire probability distribution over states rather than binary yes/no decisions as in the case of classifiers. This allows the system to, for example, decide whether to commit to a decision or gather more information to reduce uncertainty. Such an ability to handle uncertainty is critical in real-world BCI applications (e.g., control of a wheelchair or other robotic device). Shenoy and Rao showed that the DBN can leverage MRPs generated before movement execution (Figure 9.14) to provide estimates of the current brain- and body-state during a self-paced left/right-hand movement task (Figure 9.15).

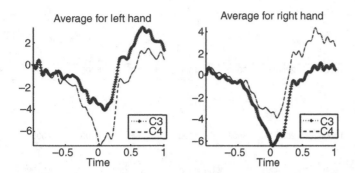

Figure 9.14. **Movement-related potentials (MRPs) during a left/right-hand movement task.** The plots show EEG signals bandpass-filtered in the 0.5–5Hz range and averaged over all trials from locations C3 and C4 (both referenced to averaged mastoids) for left (left panel) and right hand movement (right panel) respectively. Note the slow potential drift preceding the action at 0 and a return to the baseline potential after the action is performed. Note also the laterality of the MRPs with respect to the two movements (from Shenoy and Rao, 2005).

9.1.4 Stimulus-Evoked Potentials

A major class of EEG signals used in noninvasive BCIs are *evoked potentials* (EPs), which are stereotypical EEG responses generated by the brain when the subject is presented with a particular type of stimulus. For example, when a rare but task-relevant auditory, visual or somatosensory stimulus is interspersed with frequent and routine stimuli, the rare stimulus evokes a potential with a positive peak at about 300 ms after the stimulus is presented. This potential is called the P300 (or P3) potential (Section 6.2.4). Other types of responses include: visually evoked potentials (VEPs) generated by visual stimuli such as flashing lights, steady state visually evoked potentials (SSVEP) produced by a visual stimulus repeated at a rate greater than 5 Hz, auditory evoked potentials (AEPs) generated by auditory stimuli such as clicks and tones, and somatosensory evoked potentials (SSEPs) caused by somatosensory stimulation. In this section, we examine how such stimulus evoked responses can be used to build BCIs.

The P300 Potential

The P300 (or P3) signal is so named because it is a positive deflection in the EEG signal that occurs approximately 300 ms after a stimulus. The stimulus itself must be rare and unpredictable but relevant to the subject (e.g., sudden intensification of an attended target). The amplitude of the P300 depends directly on how relevant the stimulus is and varies inversely with the probability of the stimulus. The P300 is generally observed most strongly over the parietal lobe, although some components also originate in the temporal and frontal lobes. The exact neural mechanisms responsible for the P300 are as yet unclear, but brain structures such as the parietal cortex, cingulate gyrus, and the temporoparietal cortex as well as limbic structures (hippocampus, amygdala) have been implicated as possible substrates.

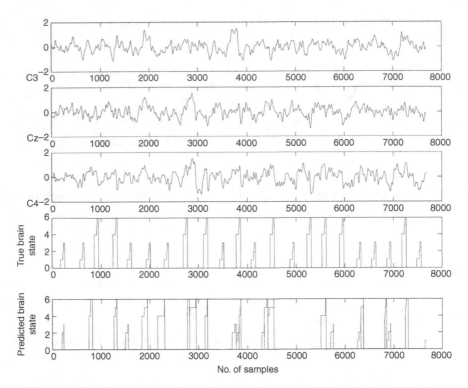

Figure 9.15. **Inference of brain state in a dynamic Bayesian network (DBN) using EEG.** (Top 3 panels) 1 minute of EEG data (sampled at 128Hz) for channels C3, Cz, C4. (Bottom two panels) The "true" brain state and the predicted brain state inferred using the DBN using only EEG. In the DBN, state 0 is the rest state, states 1 through 3 represent left hand movement, and 4 through 6 represent right hand movement (from Shenoy and Rao, 2005).

A famous example of an early BCI based on EEG is the P300 BCI proposed by Farwell and Donchin (1988). In their now-classic BCI "speller" based on the *odd-ball paradigm*, the 26 letters of the English alphabet (and some additional symbols/commands) are displayed in the form of a 6 × 6 matrix on a computer screen (Figure 9.16). In order to spell a word (or issue a command), the subject must select each letter comprising the word (or the command) by focusing attention on that letter (or command) in the matrix. While the subject is focusing on the letter or command, the rows and columns of the matrix are repeatedly flashed in random order. Each flash (or intensification) of a row or column lasts 100 ms, and the interval between flashes is fixed at either 500 ms or 125 ms.

Only when the row or column containing a subject's chosen letter or command is flashed is a large P300 generated by the subject's brain (Figure 9.17). This signal can be detected using a classifier such as linear discriminant analysis (LDA). The subject's choice of letter or command can thus be inferred by keeping track of which flashed row and column elicited the largest P300s. To help maintain attention, the subject is usually asked to count the number of times their choice was flashed. Note that the higher the number of flashes, the better the accuracy of detection, but this

MESSAGE

    BRAIN

Choose one letter or command

A	G	M	S	Y	*
B	H	N	T	Z	*
C	I	O	U	*	TALK
D	J	P	V	FLN	SPAC
E	K	Q	W	*	BKSP
F	L	R	X	SPL	QUIT

Figure 9.16. **The 6 × 6 matrix of characters and commands in the P300 "Speller" BCI.** To select a character or command, the subject focuses attention on its location, and the BCI flashes the rows and columns of the matrix in random order. The word "BRAIN" was constructed letter-by-letter by the BCI by detecting the P300s generated by the user's brain whenever the attended location was flashed (from Farwell and Donchin, 1988).

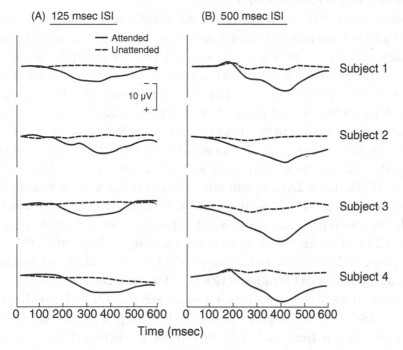

Figure 9.17. **The P300 signal in 4 subjects.** Each plot shows the average EEG response for 1 subject for flashes on attended (solid) and unattended (dashed) location. ISI = inter stimulus interval, i.e., interval between flashes (from Farwell and Donchin, 1988).

prolongs the spelling process – this is a classic example of the speed-accuracy trade-off typically found in detection systems.

In their first study in 1988, Farwell and Donchin used 4 able-bodied subjects. EEG was recorded from location Pz over parietal cortex and referenced to linked mastoids (see Section 3.1.2). In the training session, subjects attempted to spell a word that was sent to a voice synthesizer for feedback to the subject. All subjects were able to spell the word "brain" using their P300 signal, with occasional wrong selections being corrected using the BKSP (backspace) command. In the test session, subjects attended to individual letters of test words for a specific number of trials. The resulting data was analyzed offline.

Farwell and Donchin found that their BCI yielded an information transfer rate (ITR; see Section 5.1.4) of up to 0.20 bits/second at 95% accuracy, allowing subjects to communicate 12.0 bits, or 2.3 characters, per minute. In a more recent study, Sellers, Kübler, and Donchin (2006) studied a four-choice system that is easier to use for locked-in patients. This system is based on just 4 commands: yes, no, pass, and end, with the P300 evoked using an auditory, visual, or concurrent auditory/visual oddball task. Two ALS patients achieved average accuracies of 80% and 73% respectively using auditory stimuli while the other patient achieved 63% using concurrent auditory/visual stimuli (chance level: 25%).

Steady State Visually Evoked Potential (SSVEP)

Rather than detecting a transient evoked potential such as the P300, one can also design a BCI that detects the steady state evoked potentials caused by a continuously fluctuating stimuli (with repetition rate > 5 Hz). For example, consider a system where the goal is to decode one of two possible choices. One can then represent the two choices by visual stimuli (e.g., buttons on a screen or light emitting diodes – LEDs), each blinking at a different frequency. The subject focuses attention on the button corresponding to his or her choice (e.g., by looking at it). This results in an EEG signal in the early visual areas of the brain (the occipital region) oscillating at the stimulus frequency – this signal is called a *steady state visually evoked potential* (SSVEP) (Section 6.2.4). By performing a frequency decomposition of the EEG stimulus (e.g., using FFT – see Section 4.2), the BCI can detect the frequency of the stimulus the user is paying attention to and therefore, the user's choice (see Figure 9.18). A BCI based on these ideas (using buttons flashing at 17.56 and 23.42 Hz) was first explored by Middendorf and colleagues (Middendorf et al., 2000), building on the ideas of Calhoun and McMillan (1996) and Skidmore and Hill (1991).

Some of the highest information transfer rates for EEG BCIs have been obtained using SSVEP-based methods. In one study, Cheng, Gao, and colleagues (2002) reported results from an SSVEP BCI allowing selection from 13 buttons on a computer screen, representing a virtual telephone keypad with the digits 0–9, BACKSPACE, ENTER, and an ON/OFF button (Figure 9.19).

Each of the 13 buttons was flashed on and off at a different frequency between 6 Hz and 14 Hz. To reduce false positives due to alpha rhythms, a screening experiment with eyes closed was first performed, and frequencies with power more than twice the mean power between 4 Hz and 35 Hz were excluded from the stimulation frequencies. Additionally, all stimulation frequencies were odd multiples of the frequency resolution to prevent one stimulation frequency being twice another

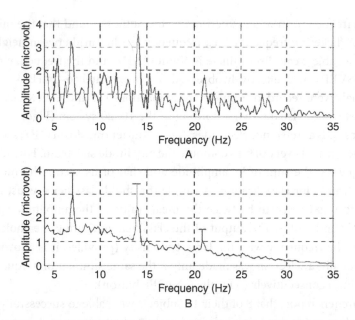

Figure 9.18. **Example of SSVEP evoked by 7 Hz visual stimulation.** The plots show amplitude spectra computed using FFT. (A) shows a single trial amplitude spectrum. (B) shows mean amplitude spectrum averaged over 40 trials (vertical lines: standard deviation). Note that there are three peaks, one at 7 Hz and one each at the harmonics 14 Hz and 21 Hz (from Cheng et al., 2002).

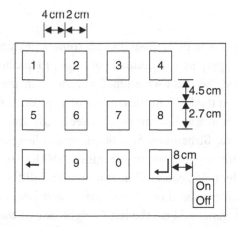

Figure 9.19. **An example of an SSVEP BCI.** Twelve buttons for a telephone keypad were arranged in a 3 × 4 matrix on a computer screen. The buttons were flashed at different frequencies in the range 6–14 Hz. An additional flashing on/off button was used to start or stop the flashing of the other buttons (from Cheng et al., 2002).

stimulation frequency. In other experiments, the authors found that the minimum difference in flickering frequency (i.e., frequency resolution) between neighboring targets that a subject can discriminate is about 0.2 Hz, and the frequency range in which the SSVEP can be effectively observed is approximately 6–24 Hz.

EEG signals were recorded from electrode locations O1 and O2 (which lie over occipital cortex, i.e., visual areas) according to the 10–20 system (Figure 3.7), with left/right mastoids as reference electrodes. A fast Fourier transform (FFT; see Section 4.2.3) was performed every 0.3s to compute the amplitude spectrum. For each stimulation frequency, the sum of its amplitude and that of its second harmonic was used as the feature for classification. A simple threshold classifier was used, where the threshold was chosen to be twice the mean value of the amplitude spectrum between 4 Hz and 35 Hz. The output of the classifier (indicating the choice of the subject) was the frequency with the largest intensity (provided it is above threshold). Additionally, a selection was made only if the same stimulation frequency was detected 4 times consecutively (6 for the ON/OFF button).

The researchers report that 8 of their 13 subjects were able to successfully use the SSVEP interface to type and ring a desired mobile phone number. An average ITR across all subjects of 27.15 bits/min was achieved, with the top 6 subjects attaining ITRs ranging from 40.4 to 55.69 bits/min. A follow-up study by the same researchers (Gao et al., 2003) with one subject demonstrated that an SSVEP BCI could distinguish at least 48 targets and provide an ITR of up to 68 bits/min (or 1.13 bits/sec). This ITR is among the highest reported for noninvasive BCIs, though lower than the ITR of 6.5 bits/sec reported by Santhanam and colleagues for their invasive BCI in monkeys (see Section 7.2.4).

Auditory Evoked Potentials

Adapting the approach used in P300 BCIs (see above), some researchers have explored BCI systems based on applying the oddball paradigm to auditory stimuli. We have already encountered the auditory oddball paradigm in the work of Donchin and colleagues, who used the P300 in the context of 4 spoken commands (yes, no, pass, and end) to obtain average accuracies between 63% and 80% in 3 ALS patients. In other work, Hill, Birbaumer, Schölkopf, and colleagues (2005) used ICA (see Section 4.5.3) with support vector machines (SVMs) (see Section 5.1.1) to classify the evoked potentials generated in response to auditory stimuli. In their case, the auditory stimuli consisted of 50 ms square-wave beeps of different frequencies. The beeps were generated on the left or right side of the subject. The stream of beeps contained frequent non-target beeps and occasional target beeps that were played independently in either ear. The subject's task was to pay attention to (by counting) the target stimuli occurring on either the left side or the right side. The BCI thus had to detect which of the targets (left or right) the user was attending to. EEG signals from 39 channels were averaged over many trials, unmixed using ICA, and classified using a linear SVM. Error rates in the range

5% to 15% were obtained for some subjects, with ITR in the 0.4 to 0.7 bits/trial (about 4 to 7 bits/min).

A different auditory evoked potential-based BCI was proposed by Furdea, Birbaumer, Kübler, and colleagues (2009) for spelling words: letters in a matrix were coded with acoustically presented numbers. Nine of the 13 participants presented with the auditory spelling system scored above a predefined criterion level control for communication. However, the researchers found that, compared to a visual BCI, users' performance was lower. In a subsequent study (Halder et al., 2010) involving an auditory BCI based on a 3-stimulus paradigm (i.e. 2 target stimuli, 1 frequent stimulus), 20 healthy participants achieved an average information transfer rate (ITR) of up to 2.46 bits/min and accuracies of 78.5%. The researchers suggest that due to its short latency per selection, the auditory BCI may constitute a reliable means of communication for patients who have lost all motor function and have a short attention span.

9.1.5 BCIs Based on Cognitive Tasks

Rather than imagining movements or detecting evoked potentials, one can also ask a human subject to perform a cognitive task such as mental arithmetic, mentally rotating a cube, or visualizing a person's face. If the cognitive tasks are sufficiently distinct, the brain areas that are activated will also be different, and the resulting brain activation can be discriminated using a classifier trained on an initial dataset collected from the subject. Each cognitive task can be mapped to one control signal (e.g., performing mental arithmetic is mapped to moving the cursor up, etc.). The approach thus relies strongly on being able to reliably discriminate the activity patterns for different cognitive tasks, making the choice of the cognitive tasks an important and tricky experimental design decision.

Early work on investigating the use of mental tasks for BCI was led by Anderson at Colorado State. In the approach proposed in (Anderson & Sijercic, 1996), the subject was asked to engage in one of 5 predetermined mental tasks: (1) a baseline task, where the subject was asked to relax, (2) a letter-composition task, where the subject was instructed to mentally compose a letter to a friend or relative without vocalizing, (3) a math task, where the subject had to mentally solve a nontrivial multiplication problem (e.g., 49 times 78), (4) a visual counting task, where the subject had to imagine a blackboard and visualize numbers being written on the board sequentially, and (5) a geometric figure rotation, where the subject visualized a particular three-dimensional object being rotated about an axis. EEG was recorded for 10 seconds from locations C3, C4, P3, P4, O1, and O2, as defined by the 10–20 system, and each task was repeated multiple times. Autoregressive (AR) models (Section 4.4.3) were used to preprocess the EEG signal. Two and three-layer backpropagation neural networks (Section 5.2.2) were trained to classify half-second segments of the 6-channel EEG data into 1 of the 5 task classes. 10-fold cross validation (Section 5.1.4) was used to prevent overfitting. The researchers found that average accuracy ranged from 71%

for one subject to 38% for another subject, both higher than chance performance (20%). A later study by the same group (Garrett et al., 2003) compared a linear classifier (linear discriminant analysis or LDA) with two nonlinear classifiers (neural networks and support vector machines, see Chapter 5). Nonlinear classifiers produced only slightly better classification results than linear classifiers.

Using cognitive tasks for control may not be as natural as, for example, using motor imagery to control a cursor or another device, but surprisingly good results can be achieved using this approach. For example, Galán, Milán, et al., (2008) used 3 mental tasks in a BCI for operating a simulated wheelchair from one point to another along a pre-specified path. The mental tasks were: (1) mentally searching for words starting with the same letter, (2) relaxing while fixating on the center of the screen, and (3) motor imagery of the left hand. Data from a calibration phase was used to select a set of subject-specific features (frequency-and-electrode combination) based on their performance using the LDA classifier (Section 5.1.1). In the test phase, a Gaussian classifier was used to map EEG features to 1 of 3 classes, which were in turn mapped to left, right, and forward commands for the wheelchair. Each subject participated in 5 experimental sessions, each consisting of 10 trials. In one experiment, two subjects were able to reach 100% (subject 1) and 80% (subject 2) of the final goals along the pre-specified trajectory in their best sessions. In a second experiment consisting of 10 trials with 10 different paths never tried before, subject 1 was able to reach the final goal in 80% of the trials.

9.1.6 Error Potentials in BCIs

A potentially critical component of a BCI is the ability to detect whether the BCI has committed an error (misclassification of a command that the user has given) by directly recognizing the brain's reaction to the error. This reaction manifests itself in EEG signals as a slow cortical potential called an *error potential* or ErrP (Figure 9.20).

ErrPs can be detected in single trials and can potentially be used to improve the accuracy of a BCI. In a study by Buttfield, Millán, and colleagues (2006), three subjects used a manual interface to move a robot to the left or right side of a room – they repeatedly issued commands to the robot by pressing keys. The experimenters configured the system to deliberately make errors 20% of the time to simulate a noisy BCI. Since ErrPs are typically manifest in frontocentral regions along the midline, EEG signals from locations Cz and Fz (Figure 3.7) were used and filtered using a 1–10 Hz bandpass filter. A mixture-of-Gaussians classifier (Section 5.2.3) was trained on EEG data from a window 50 to 650 ms after visual feedback from the user's action. A 10-fold cross validation analysis (Section 5.1.4) was performed on the collected data. Across the 3 subjects, the classifier detected the ErrP (i.e., the error trials) with an average accuracy of 79.9% and the absence of ErrP (i.e., the correct trials) with an average accuracy of 82.4%. These results are encouraging, but a study that combines the detection of ErrPs with a functioning BCI system remains to be conducted.

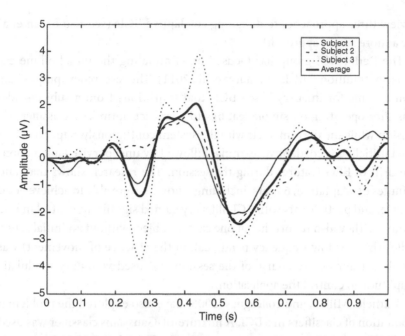

Figure 9.20. **Error potentials (ErrPs) in EEG.** The average ErrPs for 3 subjects are shown, along with the average ErrP across subjects. Visual feedback from the user's action was received at time 0 (from Buttfield et al., 2006).

9.1.7 Coadaptive BCIs

Traditional BCI systems like those discussed in the previous sections collect data from a subject and then use this data to train a classification (or regression) algorithm. The resulting learned function is then kept fixed in subsequent sessions. However, brain signals change over time, both between sessions and within a single session, due to internal factors (adaptation, change in user strategy, fatigue) as well as external factors (e.g., changes in electrode impedance or location due to slippage, etc.). This could be problematic because a classifier trained on data from a previous session will not be optimal for a new session due to the non-stationarity of the data. One solution is to periodically update the classifier offline with newly collected data; however, this leaves open the question of how often the classifier should be updated. A more attractive alternative is to let the BCI adapt to a user's brain signals continuously on an ongoing basis while the brain signals themselves are also adapting to the task at hand.

From a machine-learning perspective, the problem can be regarded as a *nonstationary learning* task where the system must continually adapt the function mapping inputs (brain signals) to outputs (control signals for devices). Such BCIs are called *coadaptive BCIs* because the BCI and the user adapt simultaneously and cooperatively to achieve desired goals. Coadaptive BCIs have been suggested as a solution to the BCI illiteracy problem because the burden of learning control does not rest entirely with the user – the BCI can assist the user through coadaptation. We briefly review three approaches to designing coadaptive BCIs (see also Bryan et al. (2013) for a more recent approach).

The Berlin BCI group has focused on eliminating the initial offline calibration phase of traditional BCIs (Vidaurre et al., 2011). The researchers propose an adaptation scheme for imagery-based BCIs that transitions from a subject-independent classifier operating on simple features to a subject-optimized classifier within one session while the user interacts with the system continuously. Supervised learning is used initially for coadaptive learning, followed by unsupervised adaptation to track the drift of EEG features during the session. The research shows that, after 3 to 6 minutes of adaptation, 6 users, including 1 novice, were able to achieve good performance, and participants with BCI illiteracy gained significant control in less than 60 minutes. They also report that in one case, a subject without an initial sensorimotor "idle" rhythm (low frequency band peak in the absence of movement) was able to develop it during the course of the session and used voluntary modulation of its amplitude to control the application.

Buttfield, Millán, and colleagues (2006) have also explored the problem of online adaptation of classifiers in a BCI. A mixture-of-Gaussians classifier was used to classify EEG patterns from 3 tasks: imagery of left- and right-hand movements, and mentally searching for words starting with the same letter. The feature vector consisted of the power for the frequencies in the range 8–30 Hz at 2-Hz resolution for the 8 centroparietal locations (C3, Cz, C4, CP1, CP2, P3, Pz, and P4 – see Figure 3.7). A gradient descent procedure (Section 5.2.2) was used to continuously adapt the parameters (mean and covariance) of the mixture-of-Gaussians classifier with individual learning rates for the parameters. The researchers found that the classification rates using online adaptation were significantly better (statistically) than a static classifier, with average performance improvements of up to 20.3% for 3 subjects.

A very different approach to coadaptive BCIs has been proposed by DiGiovanna, Sanchez, Principe, and colleagues (DiGiovanna et al., 2009). Their approach is based on the theory of reinforcement learning (RL) where an "agent" learns to map inputs to actions based on rewards and interactions with the environment, rather than an explicit training signal. In their approach, the brain signals from the user, together with the current state of the controlled device, form the input to the RL agent. The agent also receives rewards or punishments (positive/negative numbers) depending on whether an assigned task was achieved. The RL agent (the BCI) learns a "policy" i.e., a mapping from inputs to control outputs, that maximizes the expected sum of rewards.

Since the user is also presumably attempting to optimize performance (and hence the expected reward), both the BCI and the user are coupled through the reward function to cooperatively solve the task while adapting simultaneously and synergistically. The researchers present results from a BCI task involving rats that learn to complete a reaching task using a prosthetic arm in a three-dimensional workspace. They report successful closed-loop brain control over 6 to 10 days for 3 rats. All 3 rats co-adapted with the BCI to control the prosthetic arm at accuracy levels significantly above chance.

9.1.8 Hierarchical BCIs

As we have seen above, noninvasive EEG-based BCIs tend to have a limited bandwidth of control due to the lower signal-to-noise ratio of EEG; thus, such BCIs are better suited for high-level control of robots or other devices where commands are issued every few seconds rather than at the millisecond timescale. Invasive BCIs, on the other hand, can allow fine-grained control of devices such as prosthetic limbs, where a command is issued every few milliseconds (Section 7.2). However, such fine-grained control can leave users exhausted because of the amount of attention required in order to exert control on a moment-by-moment basis.

To addresses the trade-off between high- and low-level control in BCIs, the author's research group introduced the concept of *hierarchical BCIs* (Chung et al., 2011; Bryan et al., 2012): a user teaches the BCI system new skills on-the-fly using low-level control; these learned skills are later invoked directly as high-level commands, relieving the user of tedious lower-level control. This approach is inspired by the multiple levels of motor control in the human nervous systems, where skills that require a lot of attention when being learned eventually become automatic.

To illustrate the approach, a hierarchical BCI based on EEG was developed to control a humanoid robot (Chung et al., 2011). Four human subjects controlled the robot using an SSVEP-based interface in a simulated home environment. Each subject successfully used the BCI to teach the robot to navigate to different locations in the environment. The tasks were learned using RBF networks (Section 5.2.3) and Gaussian process models (Section 5.2.4). Subjects were later able to execute these tasks by selecting the newly learned command from the BCI's adaptive menu, avoiding the need to control the robot using low-level navigation commands. A comparison of the performance of the system under low-level and hierarchical control revealed that hierarchical control is both faster and more accurate. Further, the use of a Gaussian process model allowed the BCI to pass the control back to the user whenever uncertainty during task execution exceeded a particular threshold, thereby preventing potentially catastrophic accidents.

The general idea of hierarchical BCIs is equally applicable to invasive and noninvasive BCIs because it offers a way to achieve the dual goals of decreasing the cognitive load on the user while maintaining the flexibility to adapt to the user's needs. Such hierarchical approaches to control can be expected to become more prevalent as BCIs transition from the controlling cursors and menus to more complex prosthetic and robotic devices.

9.2 Other Noninvasive BCIs: fMRI, MEG, and fNIR

BCIs based on EEG remain the most popular class of noninvasive BCIs, but there has been growing interest over the last decade in exploring other noninvasive brain-

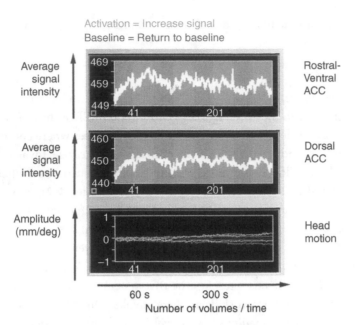

Figure 9.21. **Functional magnetic resonance imaging based BCI.** (Upper 2 panels) The experimental paradigm, showing the visual cues presented to the subject. Second, fourth, sixth, and eighth shaded bars: activation blocks, i.e., signal increase. First, third, fifth, and seventh darker shaded bars: relaxation blocks, return to baseline. The BOLD signal is shown superimposed as a white trace (upper panel: rostral–ventral ACC region, middle panel: dorsal ACC region). Note the increase in BOLD signal during activation blocks. (Lower panel) The subject's head motions (translation in mm and rotation in degrees) which were detected and corrected for (from Weiskopf et al., 2003).

imaging technologies for BCI. In this section, we briefly discuss some of these early attempts to build BCIs based on fMRI, MEG, and fNIR technologies.

9.2.1 Functional Magnetic Resonance Imaging-Based BCIs

The main question if one would like to use fMRI (Section 3.1.2) for BCI is whether a subject can learn to control changes in their blood oxygenation level dependent (BOLD) response. Weiskopf, Birbaumer, and colleagues (2003) investigated this question using a feedback paradigm. Visual feedback about local BOLD signals was continuously provided to the subject in the MRI scanner with a delay of less than 2 seconds from image acquisition. In particular, the mean signal of a region of interest was plotted superimposed on color-coded stripes to indicate to the subject whether to increase or decrease their BOLD signal (Figure 9.21).

The researchers report that their single subject was able to increase or decrease the local BOLD responses in the rostral–ventral and dorsal part of the anterior cingulate cortex (ACC). Across all sessions, the effect of signal increase was statistically highly significant for both dorsal ACC and rostral–ventral ACC (Figure 9.22A). The

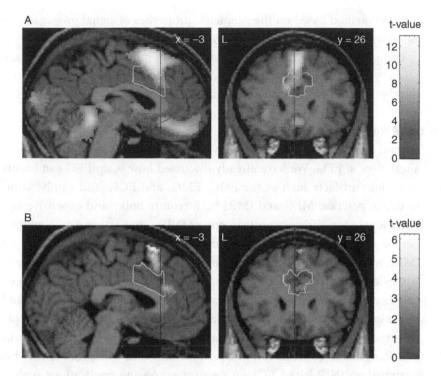

Figure 9.22. **Changes in BOLD signals in the fMRI BCI.** (See color plates for the same figure in color) (A) Signal increases during activation blocks, superimposed over individual three-dimensional MRI images and thresholded at significance level P < 0.05 and minimum spatial extent of 10 voxels. Signal increases were observed in rostral–ventral and dorsal ACC, besides activations in other areas such as supplementary motor area (SMA) and cerebellum. (B) Increase in signal change over the course of several feedback sessions, likely due to learning in the subject's brain. Increases were observed in rostral–ventral ACC, the SMA, and basal ganglia (from Weiskopf et al., 2003).

percent change in the BOLD signal increased as a result of feedback, suggesting learning over the training sessions (Figure 9.22B).

An advantage of fMRI over EEG is its spatial resolution and its ability to detect changes in neural activity deep in the brain (e.g., neural activity in the basal ganglia, cerebellum, and hippocampus). However, the fact that it takes several seconds for BOLD signals to develop and be detected implies that fMRI BCIs can only be used for high-level, coarse-grained control.

9.2.2 Magnetoencephalography-Based BCIs

MEG signals have been suggested to have higher spatiotemporal resolution than EEG – this could potentially translate to better performance in noninvasive BCIs. Mellinger, Kübler, Birbaumer, and colleagues (2007) investigated an MEG-based BCI based on voluntary amplitude modulation of sensorimotor mu and beta rhythms (see Section 3.1.2). To increase the signal-to-noise ratio, the BCI utilized a spatial filtering method based on the geometric properties of signal propagation in MEG, along with methods for reduction of MEG artifacts.

Using the MEG BCI, 6 subjects learned to communicate binary decisions using imagery of limb movements. In particular, subjects were able to gain control of their mu rhythm within 32 minutes of feedback training.

9.2.3 Functional Near Infrared and Optical BCIs

Several research groups have begun exploring optical imaging techniques as an alternative to EEG. We have already discussed how scalp EEG can be susceptible to various artifacts such as the EOG, EMG, and ECG, and can be cumbersome to use in practice. MEG and fMRI both require bulky and expensive equipment. Functional near infrared spectroscopy or fNIR (see Section 3.1.2), which captures hemodynamic response, has been suggested as an alternative to EEG, MEG, and fMRI, with the goal of developing a more practical, robust, and user-friendly BCI.

Coyle and colleagues (2004) have proposed a fNIR BCI that detects characteristic hemodynamic responses when subjects engage in motor imagery and utilizes this response to control an application. The researchers argue that such optical BCIs are easier to use than other noninvasive BCIs and require less user training (see also Ranganatha et al., 2005). Mappus, Jackson, and colleagues (2009) have demonstrated an fNIR-based BCI for creative-expression applications such as sketch drawing. In particular, they have developed a BCI that allows subjects to express themselves in an alphabetic letter-drawing task using continuous control of the cursor. Finally, Ayaz and colleagues (2009) evaluated an fNIR BCI using a closed-loop bar-size-control task with 5 healthy subjects across 2 days. The researchers reported that the average task versus rest period oxygenation changes were significantly different from each other, and the average task-completion time (reaching 90% accuracy) decreased with practice, with a day 1 mean of 52.3 seconds and a day 2 mean of 39.1 seconds. Although these results are promising, it remains to be seen whether fNIR BCIs can ultimately match the performance of EEG-based BCIs and emerge as a viable class of noninvasive BCIs.

9.3 Summary

In this chapter, we explored a variety of noninvasive BCIs. The dominant paradigm utilizes EEG and imagery or evoked potential methods to generate control signals. Imagery-based BCIs rely heavily on subjects being able to learn to modulate their brain signals in low-frequency bands. This is akin to learning a new motor skill. It has been reported that 15%–30% of subjects recruited for BCI studies are unable to gain control over the low-frequency band EEG signal despite a large number of training sessions. This inability to gain control in a BCI has been called *BCI illiteracy*. Solutions to this problem range from changing the experimental paradigm to non-imagery based modes of control (such as stimulus-based methods) to designing coadaptive BCIs.

BCIs based on evoked potentials remain the most popular alternative to imagery-based BCIs. Evoked potentials such as the P300 and SSVEP have been used for a variety of applications ranging from high-level robotic control to image processing (see Chapter 12). Their popularity stems from the fact that unlike imagery-based approaches, evoked potential-based BCIs do not require any extensive training and can achieve relatively high accuracies for naïve subjects. On the other hand, the subject cannot voluntarily initiate an action and must constantly pay attention to the stimulus, which are unnatural signals such as flashes. This puts a high cognitive load on the subject and could eventually lead to fatigue. Additionally, relying on responses to external stimuli invariably introduces delays in the BCI system, which can be avoided when imagery or other voluntarily generated brain responses are used. Hierarchical BCIs have been suggested as a way to optimize the trade-off between imagery-based low-level control, which is flexible but incurs high cognitive load, and evoked potential-based high-level control.

Among evoked potential-based methods, SSVEP-based approaches typically yield higher information rates than P300-based approaches. They also tend to produce higher accuracy because steady state frequencies can usually be detected more reliably than P300 signals. However, staring at the flashing stimuli in an SSVEP BCI can be quite strenuous and exhausting.

The highest information transfer rates (ITRs) among noninvasive BCIs have been obtained using SSVEP-based approaches (around 1.13 bits/sec), but these rates are still about 6 times lower than the highest ITRs reported using invasive BCIs in monkeys. Additionally, SSVEP and related approaches are not especially conducive for real-time control tasks such as moving a robotic arm or a wheelchair. Imagery-based approaches are more natural, but their ITRs are typically less than half those of SSVEP BCIs. Thus, many researchers believe that new, higher-resolution noninvasive methods for recording brain activity are needed in order to enable noninvasive BCIs to reach the level of performance of invasive BCIs.

9.4 Questions and Exercises

1. Explain the difference between asynchronous (or self-paced) and synchronous (or stimulus-based) BCIs. Compare the advantages and disadvantages of the two approaches.

2. What is ERD and how can it be used in a noninvasive BCI to control a cursor or prosthetic device?

3. How was the mu rhythm used to control a one-dimensional cursor in the first Wadsworth BCI? What was the training paradigm used for facilitating the learning of mu rhythm control by a subject?

4. Explain the linear method used in the Wadsworth BCI for achieving two-dimensional cursor control based on mu and beta rhythms. How does the performance of this BCI compare with invasive BCIs that use electrodes implanted in the cortex?

5. What is the difference between ERD and ERS? How are these two phenomena used in Graz BCI system? What is the ITR reported for this system?

6. The Berlin BCI group has achieved relatively high accuracies in novice BCI users in their very first session. Describe the approach used by this group and explain why such an approach is well-suited to reducing the time needed to learn BCI control.

7. What are slow cortical potentials (SCPs), what scalp locations are they typically recorded from, and how can they be used in a BCI to control a cursor?

8. What are movement-related potentials (MRPs) and how do they differ from oscillatory potentials that are modulated by movement or motor imagery?

9. Describe how MRPs have been used in BCIs in conjunction with:
    a. Backpropagation neural networks
    b. LVQ-based classifiers
    c. Bayesian networks

10. Compare and contrast the following types of evoked potentials (EPs): P300, VEP, SSVEP, AEP, and SSEP.

11. What is the oddball paradigm involving the P300, and how can it be used to build a speller for locked-in patients to communicate messages? How does the speed versus accuracy trade-off manifest itself in this paradigm?

12. Answer the following questions about SSVEP BCIs:
    a. What is the minimum difference in flickering frequency between targets that a subject can discriminate?
    b. What is the frequency range in which the SSVEP can be effectively observed?
    c. What electrode locations on the scalp are SSVEPs recorded from?

13. How does the ITR (in bits/sec) obtained using SSVEP BCIs compare with the best ITR obtained using an invasive BCI?

14. Give examples of some of the cognitive tasks that have been used for building EEG BCIs. How do these BCIs compare with motor imagery-based BCIs in terms of their accuracy and ease of use?

15. What are ErrPs and how can they potentially be used to make a BCI robust? What electrode locations are they typically measured from?

16. What are coadaptive BCIs and how can they help address the BCI illiteracy problem?

17. Describe and contrast the two main approaches to coadaptive BCIs discussed in this chapter, namely, supervised learning and reinforcement learning.

18. What are hierarchical BCIs? How do they help achieve the dual goals of decreasing the cognitive load on a user while maintaining flexibility to adapt to the user's needs?

19. Discuss some of the advantages and disadvantages of using fMRI as the source signal for a BCI compared to EEG. Consider the dimensions of spatial resolution, temporal resolution, portability, and cost.

20. (⚡ Expedition) Read the papers cited in Section 9.2.3 as well as more recent papers on fNIR BCIs. Write an essay comparing the signal processing and machine-learning methods used and the results achieved using these methods. Conclude with an assessment of whether fNIR BCIs can be regarded as an alternative to EEG BCIs in terms of performance, cost, and portability.

10

BCIs that Stimulate

We have thus far focused on BCIs that record signals from the brain and transform those signals to a control signal for an external device. In this chapter, we reverse the direction of control and discuss BCIs that can be used to stimulate and control specific brain circuits. Some of these BCIs have made the transition from the lab to the clinic and are currently being used by human subjects, such as cochlear implants and deep brain stimulators (DBS), while others are still in experimental stages. We divide these BCIs broadly into two classes: BCIs for sensory restoration and BCIs for motor restoration. We also consider the possibility of sensory augmentation.

10.1 Sensory Restoration

10.1.1 Restoring Hearing: Cochlear Implants

One of the most successful BCI devices to date is the cochlear implant for restoring or enabling hearing in the deaf. The implant is a good example of how one can convert knowledge of information processing in a neural system, in this case the cochlea, into building a working BCI that can benefit people.

Figure 10.1 illustrates the transformation of sound into neural signals in a functioning human ear. Sound pressure waves hitting the *tympanic membrane* are converted to mechanical vibrations by a series of bones – *malleus, incus*, and *stapes*. These mechanical vibrations are transformed into pressure variations in the fluid-filled cavity of the *cochlea* (see Figure 10.1). These in turn cause displacements of a flexible membrane in the cochlea called the *basilar membrane*. Cells known as *hair cells* are attached to the basilar membrane. Displacements of the basilar membrane cause deflections in the hair cells, which cause neurons of the cochlear nerve to fire. The cochlear nerve in turn conveys the information about the sound to the brain.

An important property of the cochlea is that it decomposes an input sound into its component frequencies. This is achieved by the properties of the basilar membrane. Different frequencies of sound cause maximum vibration at different locations along the basilar membrane. High-frequency sounds cause vibrations that do not propagate

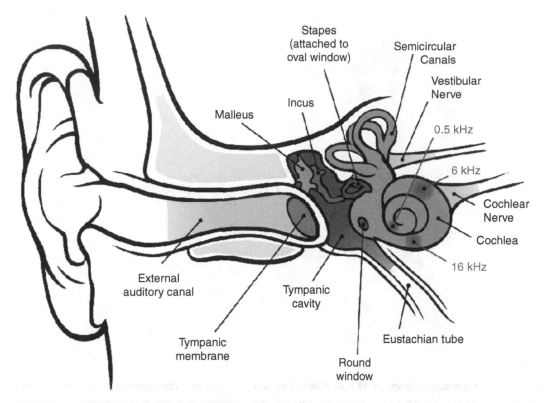

Figure 10.1. **Transformation of sound into neural signals in the cochlea.** (Image: Creative Commons).

very far along the membrane and cause the maximum displacement at the base of the membrane near the stapes (Figure 10.1). Low-frequency sounds on the other hand result in maximum displacement at the apex of the basilar membrane. This results in a "tonotopic" (or frequency-to-place) mapping of sound along the basilar membrane. The tonotopic organization is maintained by the cochlear nerve fibers that convey information to the brain, allowing the brain to infer the frequency composition of the sound based on which areas of the basilar membrane are resonating.

In a large number of cases, deafness is caused by the loss or absence of hair cells due to illnesses (e.g., meningitis), environmental factors, or genetic mutations. Cochlear implants provide an alternate pathway to conveying auditory information to the brain by stimulating cochlear nerves directly using electrical impulses. The implant exploits the tonotopic organization of nerve fibers by stimulating at different locations along the cochlea according to the frequencies of a sound. The implant thus attempts to mimic the function of lost or absent hair cells of the basilar membrane.

The basic components of a cochlear implant (Figure 10.2) include:

- A microphone (placed near the ear) that receives sounds from the environment;
- A signal processor (worn externally behind the ear) that implements a feature extraction or frequency analysis algorithm such as the fast Fourier transform

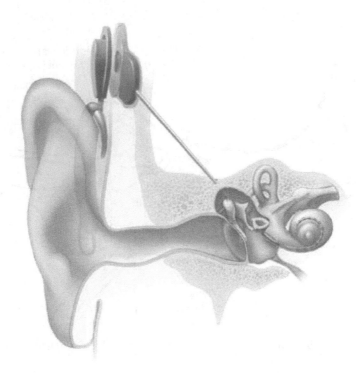

Figure 10.2. **Schematic diagram of a cochlear implant.** The external components consist of a micro-phone, a sound processor, and a transmitter of power and processed signals. The internal components consist of a receiver and stimulator, along with an array of electrodes that can be seen wound up within the cochlea in the figure. (Image: Creative Commons).

(see Section 4.2) to decompose a sound signal into its frequency components. The exact number of frequency components depends on the number of electrodes used in the implant and other factors. The output of the signal processor is sent to a transmitter via a thin cable;

- A transmitter (also worn externally near the ear) transmits power and processed sound signals across the skin to an internal receiver using a "radio frequency" (RF) link (this is based on the principle of electromagnetic induction – see Section 3.2.2).
- A receiver and stimulator embedded behind the ear in the skull which convert the received signals into electric pulses and transmit them to electrodes via an internal cable;
- An electrode array of up to 22 electrodes wound up and placed along the length of the cochlea (Figure 10.2): these electrodes deliver electrical pulses to nerve fibers at different locations along the cochlea, thereby conveying processed information about the sounds received by the microphone to the brain.

In the cochlear implant, the use of a radio frequency link means that no physical connection is needed between the external and internal components – this reduces the risk of post-surgical infection. The implant is customized for each user by setting the minimum and maximum current outputs for each electrode based on the user's reports of loudness as a function of stimulation. Additional customization involves selecting a user-specific speech-processing strategy and parameters for the sound processor. Post-implantation therapy is typically required as the brain adapts to hearing the sounds conveyed by the implant. In congenitally deaf children, training and speech therapy can continue for years.

Current cochlear implants have only about 22 electrodes compared to the approximately 20,000 hair cells used by a normal cochlea; thus the quality of sound perceived can be quite different from natural hearing due to the impoverished nature of information being conveyed to the brain. Nonetheless, the sound quality is often good enough that many users can understand speech without lip reading, especially in the absence of noise. Additionally, those who were born with normal hearing before progressively losing it tend to have better outcomes than those who were born deaf. Perception of complex stimuli such as music remains a topic of research.

According to the National Institute on Deafness and Other Communication Disorders, more than 200,000 people (as of 2012) have received cochlear implants worldwide, including about 42,600 adults and 28,400 children in the United States. Among these are post-lingually deaf persons who lost hearing after learning to speak as well as congenitally deaf children. Since being able to hear is critical to learning to speak language, having an implant can help a deaf child learn to speak. There are studies suggesting that congenitally deaf children who receive cochlear implants early (before they are 2 years old) are better able to learn to speak than those who receive implants at a later age. This raises the important ethical issue (Chapter 13) of whether parents should opt for an implant for their deaf child at an early age when the child cannot make that decision. Additionally, since implantation is a surgical procedure, the user must weigh a variety of risks such as infection, onset of ringing in the ears (tinnitus), vestibular malfunction, damage to facial nerves, and device failure.

Finally, there has been strong objection to cochlear implants from the pre-lingually deaf community whose first language is sign language. Objectors point out that the results of the cochlear implant and subsequent therapy are uncertain and often become the focus of the child's identity, and thus might be less desirable than the alternative of a possible future deaf identity and ease of communication in sign language. A recent trend in some educational programs has been to adopt a best-of-both-worlds approach by integrating cochlear-implant therapy with sign language.

10.1.2 Restoring Sight: Cortical and Retinal Implants

While cochlear implants have successfully made the transition from research to clinical application, efforts to build implants for the blind have lagged behind due to the complexity of information processing in the retina and the relatively low resolution of stimulating electrode arrays. The goal of these implants is to restore vision in individuals afflicted with photoreceptor degenerative diseases; these include *retinitis pigmentosa*, a major cause of inherited blindness, and age-related *macular degeneration*, a leading cause of blindness in adults older than 65. When these diseases cause the loss of a majority of photoreceptors in the retina, an implant offers one of the last hopes for restoring vision.

Implants for restoring sight transform light into electrical stimulation of neurons or nerve fibers. Several different sites for stimulation have been studied, ranging from the visual cortex and the optic nerve to the retinal surface itself. Of these options, stimulation of the optic nerve is the most difficult due to its dense structure and the inability to focally stimulate specific axons. Visual-prosthesis research has thus focused on cortical and retinal implants.

Cortical Implants

The fact that electrical stimulation of the visual cortex can cause "phosphenes" (perception of spots of light) was demonstrated early by Foerster (1929) and has been studied more recently by Brindley and Lewin (1968); Dobelle (2000); Javaheri et al. (2006), and others with the goal of building a visual prosthesis. For example, Dobelle implanted a 64-electrode array on the cortical surface of blind subjects and demonstrated that 6-inch-tall characters recorded by a camera could be recognized at a distance of about 5 feet by subjects receiving cortical stimulation (Dobelle, 2000). The possibility of using implants inside the visual cortex (rather than the cortical surface) are also being investigated by researchers but due to the risks involved, these studies are currently being conducted mainly in animal models. Although still in an early phase of research, visual cortical stimulation may eventually emerge as the most viable method for restoring sight, given its broad applicability.

Retinal Implants

An alternative to stimulating the cortex is to stimulate neurons in the retina, using either a *subretinal* or *epiretinal* approach. In the subretinal approach, a photodiode array is implanted in the retina between the bipolar cell layer and the retinal pigment epithelium (Figure 10.3). The motivation here is that such an implant could function as a simple solar cell and be powered entirely by light entering the eye, without the need for batteries. In the artificial silicon retina (ASR) proposed by Optobionics, a 2 mm chip containing 5,000 microelectrode-tipped photodiodes converts light into electrical pulses for stimulating retinal neurons. Experiments are underway to test this subretinal implant.

In the epiretinal approach (Figure 10.3), an external camera is used to capture and digitize images, which are translated to appropriate patterns of electrical stimulation delivered to viable retinal neurons. An example of such an approach is the intraocular retinal prosthesis (IRP) being developed by Humayun and others at the Doheny Eye Institute. The IRP consists of a small camera built into a pair of glasses, an external battery pack, and a visual-processing unit (Figure 10.3). The camera captures

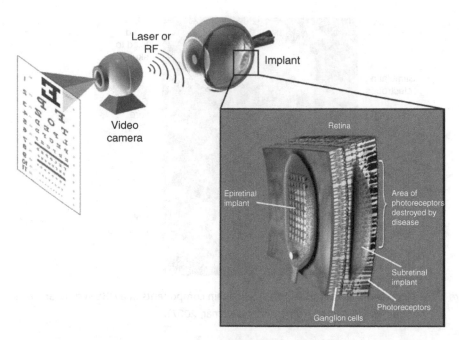

Figure 10.3. **Schematic diagram of a retinal implant.** Two types of retinal implants are depicted in the same figure. An epiretinal implant uses an external camera to capture images and transmit electrical stimulation patterns via telemetry (radio frequency (RF) or laser). The epiretinal implant, which is positioned on the surface of the retina, receives this pattern and stimulates retinal neurons. The subretinal implant is positioned below the surface of the retina. It uses microelectrode-tipped photodiodes to capture images for stimulation as well as obtain power from light (from Weiland et al., 2005).

an image, which is processed by the visual-processing unit and transformed into appropriate patterns of electrical pulses. These pulses are transmitted into the eye by magnetic coils via electromagnetic induction, similar to the approach taken in the cochlear implant. The transmitted pulses are conveyed via a cable to an array of 16 platinum microelectrodes, which stimulate retinal neurons according to the pattern of pulses.

In clinical trials, patients implanted with the 16-electrode IRP reported visual perception of spatially localized phosphenes in response to local stimulation. Brightness of their perception could be changed by changing the amount of stimulation. The patients were also able to distinguish the direction of motion of objects. In early 2013, the United States Food and Drug Administration (FDA) approved Argus II, an epiretinal implant containing 60 electrodes developed by Humayun and colleagues, which has allowed some patients to see color, navigate streets, locate bus stops, and enjoy concerts. These results are encouraging but for more complex visual tasks such as recognizing faces or driving, it is believed that a much larger number of stimulating electrodes (beyond 1,000) may be necessary.

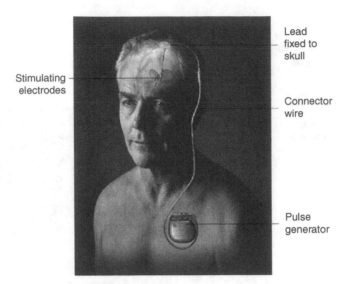

Stimulating electrodes

Lead fixed to skull

Connector wire

Pulse generator

Figure 10.4. **Deep brain stimulation (DBS).** The main components of a DBS system are labeled (see text for details) (adapted from Kern and Kumar, 2007).

10.2 Motor Restoration

10.2.1 Deep Brain Stimulation (DBS)

Besides the cochlear implant, deep brain stimulation (DBS) has emerged as one of the major clinical applications of brain-computer interfacing. DBS involves stimulating specific parts of the brain using a "brain pacemaker" in order to relieve some of the debilitating symptoms of movement and affective disorders such as Parkinson's disease and chronic pain. DBS is also being investigated as a technique for treating other conditions such as depression, epilepsy, Tourette's syndrome, and obsessive compulsive disorder (OCD).

A typical DBS system consists of a lead (terminating in stimulating electrodes) that is placed inside the brain, a pulse generator, and a connector wire that connects the pulse generator to the lead (Figure 10.4). All three components are surgically placed inside the body. The battery-powered pulse generator is usually placed under the skin below the collar bone. It is connected to the lead by the connector wire that runs under the skin from the head down the side of the neck (see Figure 10.4). The lead, which is implanted inside the head, is an insulated coiled wire that terminates in platinum electrodes (typically, four of them) for stimulating neurons in the implanted region.

The lead is implanted in different regions of the brain depending on the condition being treated. For symptoms associated with Parkinson's disease such as tremor, rigidity, bradykinesia (slow movement) and akinesia (inability to initiate movement), the lead is usually placed in the subthalamic nucleus or the globus pallidus in the basal ganglia. For chronic pain, the regions that have been targeted for stimulation include the hypothalamus and the thalamus.

The pulse generator produces stimulation pulses at a fixed frequency to reduce the symptoms of the neurological condition being treated. This frequency is tailored to the patient's specific needs. The neurologist or technician adjusts this frequency to achieve the best possible suppression of symptoms while at the same time mitigating any side effects.

The risks associated with DBS include infection, bleeding, and complications of surgery, as well as potential side effects of stimulation such as hallucinations, compulsive behavior, and impairment in cognitive function. Some of these side effects are a result of our lack of understanding of how DBS actually works to alter the behavior of abnormal neural circuits. As we gain a better understanding of brain function at the circuit level, one can expect more sophisticated "closed-loop" stimulation paradigms (rather than stimulation at one frequency) and simultaneous stimulation of multiple brain sites.

10.3 Sensory Augmentation

Given that the brain is plastic, one can imagine a scenario where artificial sensory signals could be used to stimulate particular sensory areas of the brain. For example, infrared or ultrasound signals could be converted to electrical stimulation patterns and streamed to cortical areas (visual or auditory). If there is sufficient statistical structure in the input signals and if the subject is required to solve tasks on the basis of these novel input signals, one might expect cortical areas to adapt and process these signals in a manner similar to other sensory signals such as visual signals from the optic nerve or auditory signals from the auditory nerve. If successful, such an approach would allow the subject's brain to process a wider range of sensory signals than made available through evolution. Is such sensory augmentation possible?

Experiments conducted in the laboratory of Sur at MIT (von Melchner et al., 2000) have shed some light on this question. In these experiments, researchers surgically diverted visual inputs from the retina to the auditory input pathway during early development in neonatal ferrets, and the normal auditory inputs to this pathway were removed (Figure 10.5). In particular, retinal axons were induced to innervate the auditory thalamus – specifically, the medial geniculate nucleus (MGN) – which provides inputs to the auditory cortex. The researchers found that during the course of development, the primary auditory cortex of the rewired ferrets developed many of the functional features of visual cortex. For example, neurons in the rewired auditory cortex developed a two-dimensional map of visual space and became selective to the orientation of visual stimuli and their direction of motion.

Additionally, the animals could use their rewired auditory cortex to solve visual tasks. In one task, four rewired adult ferrets were trained to go to a spout on the left for a reward following a sound stimulus and to a spout on the right for a light stimulus. The animals were trained using light only in the visual hemifield processed by

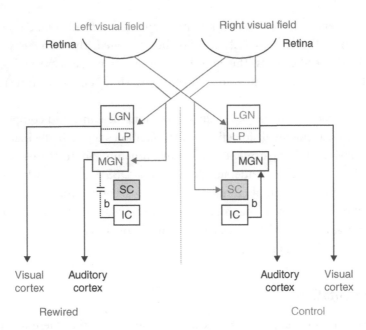

Figure 10.5. **Rewiring the auditory cortex to process visual information**. The diagram illustrates the routing of visual information from the two hemifields of the retina. In the experiment, visual information from the right visual field was conveyed to the left auditory cortex via the medial geniculate nucleus (MGN). Auditory inputs from the inferior colliculus (IC) were removed (dotted line from left IC). (SC: superior colliculus; b: brachium) (adapted from von Melchner et al., 2000).

the nonrewired visual hemisphere ("Control" in Figure 10.5). After training, the animals were tested using light presented in the other visual hemifield processed by the rewired auditory cortex. Inputs to the visual cortex from this hemifield (via LGN/LP) were removed, so that the animals could rely only on the visual information in the rewired auditory cortex to solve this task. The researchers found that the animals were able to respond correctly to the visual stimulus, indicating that they were able to perceive the light stimulus using their rewired auditory cortex. Furthermore, ablation of the rewired auditory cortex resulted in a significant reduction in responses at the visual reward spout, indicating that the animals were no longer able to perceive the visual stimulus.

These results demonstrate that neuronal networks in the neocortex are surprisingly plastic and their properties can be shaped to a considerable extent by their inputs even when those inputs are very different from those expected during normal development. This opens up the possibility that the brain's sensory capacity could be augmented by feeding to the neocortex inputs from novel types of sensors (e.g., ultrasonic, infrared, or millimeter-wave sensing devices). An example of such augmentation has recently been demonstrated by Thomson, Carra, and Nicolelis (2013).

10.4 Summary

The ability to electrically stimulate neurons allows a BCI to influence the operation of neural circuits and provide direct sensory input to the brain. In this chapter, we learned about cochlear implants, which are allowing a growing population of deaf individuals to hear sounds and in many cases, understand speech. Research is also being conducted on cortical and retinal implants to restore vision in the blind, with one retinal implant receiving recent FDA approval, but progress has been slow partly because of the complexity of visual processing and partly due to the low resolution offered by current electrode arrays. Implants for deep brain stimulation (DBS) are now being used for relieving the symptoms of debilitating diseases such as Parkinson's. These implants typically deliver high-frequency electrical pulses to nuclei deep in the brain, with the frequency customized to help relieve each individual patient's symptoms. More sophisticated paradigms for stimulation of brain regions will require a better understanding of each region's function and how regions interact to produce perception and behavior.

10.5 Questions and Exercises

1. Explain the various stages involved in the transformation of sound waves to electrical activity in the cochlear nerve. What stages of this transformation does the cochlear implant attempt to replace? What stage(s) need to be intact for the cochlear implant to function?

2. What is the "tonotopic" organization of sound in the cochlea, and how is it exploited by cochlear implants?

3. What are the basic components of a cochlear implant? What aspects of the implant are customized for each individual user?

4. Does the performance of the cochlear implant vary between congenitally deaf versus postlingually-deaf persons? What is the impact of age of implantation on the effectiveness of the implant?

5. (⚡ Expedition) Cortical implants for restoring sight have not yet made the transition from laboratory to clinical implantation in humans. Write a review of some of the progress made using this approach over the past ten years and identify the major obstacles, if any, to clinical use and commercialization.

6. What are the two main types of retinal implants? Compare their advantages and disadvantages, and identify the major obstacles, if any, to clinical use in humans.

7. Describe the major components used in a DBS system. What are some of the motor and affective disorders for which DBS has been used? List some of its risks and potential side effects.

8. (⚡ Expedition) Although DBS has been proved to be clinically useful for treating the symptoms of diseases such as Parkinson's, the exact neural mechanisms underlying the therapeutic effects of DBS remain unclear. Read recent review papers on

this topic (e.g., Kringelbach et al., 2007), and describe some of the hypotheses regarding how DBS affects neural circuits in the brain. Based on what you learned, suggest potential ways in which DBS could be improved using more sophisticated types of stimulation targeting one or more brain regions.

9. Describe the experiments conducted by Sur and colleagues involving the rerouting of visual information to auditory cortex in ferrets. What properties did auditory cortex neurons exhibit after rerouting? Describe the behavioral task used to verify that the animal could indeed use the rerouted information to solve a task.

10. (↟ Expedition) The experiments by Sur and colleagues were limited to "natural" modalities such as vision and audition. Suppose information from an artificial sensing device such as a laser range finder is fed as input to a cortical area instead of the area's natural inputs. What are some of the potential issues one might face when interfacing a brain with such an artificial input stream? How could these issues be resolved or alleviated using signal processing and machine-learning techniques?

11

Bidirectional and Recurrent BCIs

We have thus far studied BCIs that either record from the brain to control an external device (Chapters 7–9) or stimulate the brain to restore sensory or motor function (Chapter 10). The most general type of BCI is one that can simultaneously record from and stimulate different parts of the brain. Such BCIs are called *bidirectional (or recurrent) BCIs*. Bidirectional BCIs can provide direct feedback to the brain by stimulating sensory neurons to convey the consequences of operating a prosthetic device using motor signals recorded from the same brain. Furthermore, signals recorded from one part of the brain can be used to modulate the neural activity or induce plasticity in a different part of the brain.

In Chapter 1, we discussed the pioneering work of Delgado (1969) on an implantable BCI called the stimoceiver, which can be regarded as the first example of a bidirectional BCI. In this chapter, we briefly review a few more recent examples to illustrate the possibilities opened up by bidirectional BCIs and conclude by noting that the most flexible BCIs of the future will likely be bidirectional, though this flexibility will likely come at the cost and the associated risk of being invasive.

11.1 Cursor Control with Direct Cortical Instruction via Stimulation

One of the first studies to combine a BCI with cortical stimulation was by O'Doherty, Nicolelis, and colleagues (2009) who showed that a direct intracortical input can be added to a BCI to instruct a rhesus monkey which of two targets to move a cursor to, using either a joystick or direct brain control (Figure 11.1A). The idea here was to demonstrate that stimulation of somatosensory cortex could be used in conjunction with a BCI to control a cursor. Two electrode arrays (with 32 tungsten electrodes in each) were implanted in the primary motor cortex (area M1) and dorsal premotor cortex (PMd) to record neural activity, and a third electrode array was implanted in the primary somatosensory cortex (S1) for stimulation (Figure 11.1B and C). The area chosen for stimulation was in the hand area of S1, with receptive fields for stimulating electrode pairs as shown in Figure 11.1D.

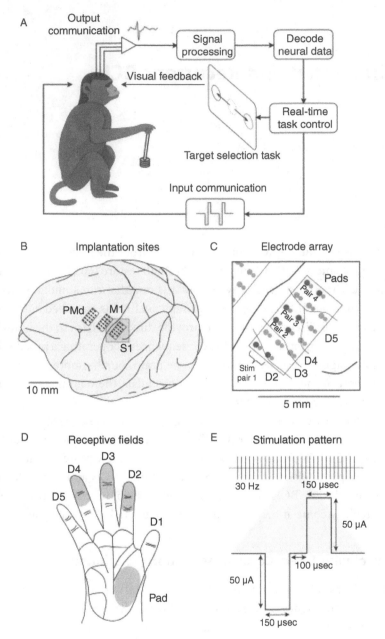

Figure 11.1. **Bidirectional BCI in a cursor control task.** (A) Experimental setup. The monkey moved the cursor to the right or left target either manually using a joystick or using a BCI that decodes motor cortical data. The target (left or right) is instructed by joystick vibration or by stimulating primary somatosensory cortex (S1). (B) The monkey was implanted with electrode arrays in its dorsal premotor (PMd) and primary motor cortex (M1) for recording and in the primary somatosensory cortex (S1) for stimulation. (C) Electrode array in S1. The darker shaded circles indicate electrode pairs used for stimulation. (D) Receptive fields on the monkey's hand for the electrode pairs used for stimulation. (E) Parameters of the stimulation pulse (from O'Doherty et al., 2009).

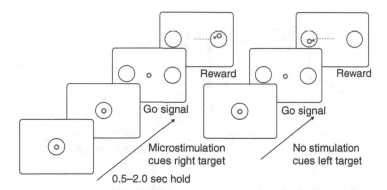

Figure 11.2. **BCI cursor task with stimulation.** The screens show the different stages in the cursor task. Either joystick vibration or stimulation of S1 served as the cue for the monkey to move the cursor (via the BCI) to the target on the right; lack of vibration/stimulation indicated the left target (adapted from O'Doherty et al., 2009).

Figure 11.2 illustrates the experimental paradigm. The monkey first moves the cursor (using a joystick or neural control) to the circle in the center of the screen. This initiates an "instruction period" of 0.5–2 seconds during which the monkey is stimulated using either a vibration in the joystick handle or direct stimulation in S1 using electrical pulses of the form shown in Figure 11.1E. This is followed by the appearance of two targets, one on the left and another the right (Figure 11.2). In any particular trial, if stimulation was delivered, the animal had to move the cursor to the target on the right; if no stimulation was delivered, the cursor had to be moved to the target on the left (and vice versa for other sessions).

The monkey was first trained to use a joystick to control the cursor in the standard center-out and pursuit tasks (Figure 7.19). This data was used to learn the weights for two linear (Weiner) filters (Equation 7.2), one for predicting the X-coordinate of the cursor and the other for the Y-coordinate. These predictions were made based on the firing rates of neurons in M1 and PMd in the past 10 time-steps, each time-step corresponding to 100 ms. These filters were later used to allow the monkey to control the cursor directly using M1 and PMd activity.

Once the monkey had learned to control the cursor using brain activity, it was tested in the stimulation task. The monkey was first trained to use the vibration in the joystick to infer which target to move the cursor to. The monkey achieved 90% accuracy in this task in 12 sessions. Then, vibration was replaced with direct stimulation of S1. The monkey initially performed at chance levels, but after about 15 sessions and 2 weeks of training, the monkey rapidly improved performance and again achieved 90% accuracy, this time with stimulation alone (Figure 11.3).

These results suggest that it may be possible to convey information about tactile stimuli directly to somatosensory cortex via intracortical stimulation, and use this information within a BCI. However, these experiments used only stimulation to instruct a target at the beginning of BCI control and leave open the question

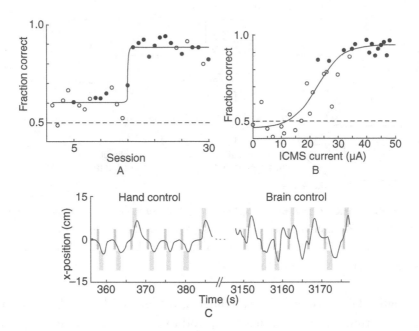

Figure 11.3. **Performance of a bidirectional BCI**. (A) Improvement in accuracy of discriminating and hitting the correct target when target information was delivered via stimulation of S1. (B) Performance of the monkey as a function of stimulation pulse train amplitude. (C) X-coordinate of cursor position under joystick (left) and BCI control (right). Thin rectangles: period of target instruction (stimulation or absence of stimulation); thick rectangles: location of correct target (adapted from O'Doherty et al., 2009).

of whether recording and stimulation can be done simultaneously in a closed-loop manner. This question has been addressed using other paradigms as described in the following sections.

11.2 Active Tactile Exploration Using a BCI and Somatosensory Stimulation

The bidirectional BCI discussed in the previous section used only stimulation to instruct the monkey which target to move the cursor to. A more realistic scenario would involve using tactile information, delivered via stimulation, to actively explore objects using a BCI and select a desired target object based only on its tactile properties as conveyed through stimulation. O'Doherty, Nicolelis, and colleagues (2011) explored such a bidirectional BCI using a virtual reality setup.

Monkeys were trained to move a cursor or a virtual image of an arm to explore objects on a computer screen (Figure 11.4A). The task was to use brain control to search for the object with particular artificial tactile properties conveyed via stimulation. Microwire arrays were implanted in the primary motor cortex (M1) for recording and in the primary somatosensory cortex (S1) for stimulation (Figures 11.4B and 11.4C). The monkeys explored the virtual objects first using hand control and

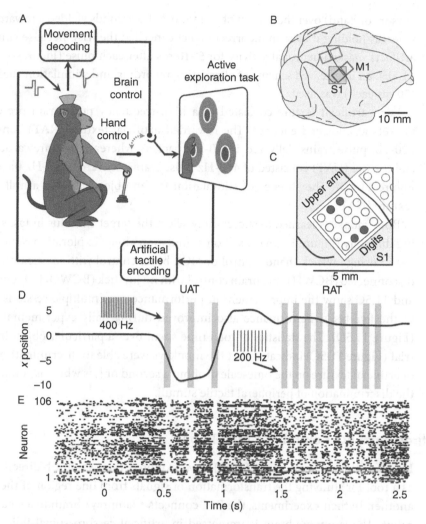

Figure 11.4. **Bidirectional BCI for tactile exploration.** (A) A cursor or virtual hand is controlled by joystick or activity from primary motor cortex (M1) to explore circular objects on a computer screen. Artificial tactile feedback about an object is delivered to primary somatosensory cortex (S1) via electrical stimulation. (B) Location of microwire arrays implanted in areas M1 and S1. (C) Microwires used for stimulation are shown as shaded circles. (D) Solid line: Example of actuator movement in a trial in which the monkey explores an unrewarded object (UAT) before moving over and selecting the rewarded target (RAT). Gray bars: stimulation patterns. Insets: stimulation frequency. (E) Spiking activity of ensemble of M1 neurons recorded during the same trial as (D) (from O'Doherty et al., 2011).

then using brain control based on M1 ensemble activity (Figure 11.4E) and Kalman filtering (see Sections 4.4.5 and 7.2.3).

Objects consisted of a central "response" zone and a peripheral feedback zone. When the cursor or virtual hand entered the feedback zone, artificial tactile feedback was delivered directly to the brain via stimulation of S1 (Figure 11.4D). Holding the cursor (or hand) over the correct object for 0.8–1.3 seconds yielded a reward (juice), whereas holding it over an incorrect object cancelled the trial. Because stimulation artifacts masked neuronal activity for 5–10 ms after each pulse (Figures 11.4D and 11.4E), an interleaved scheme of alternating recording and stimulation subintervals (50 ms each) was used.

Each artificial texture consisted of a high-frequency pulse train presented in packets at a lower frequency. The rewarded artificial texture (RAT) consisted of 200-Hz pulse trains delivered in 10-Hz packets whereas the unrewarded artificial texture (UAT) consisted of 400-Hz pulse trains delivered in 5-Hz packets (see Figure 11.4D). The absence of stimulation for an object denoted a null artificial texture (NAT).

Both monkeys learned to successfully select the target stimulus in tasks of varying difficulty (Figure 11.5A) based on stimulation alone. Exploration of targets was tested using joystick (hand control or HC), brain control with joystick present but disconnected (BCWH), and brain control with no joystick (BCWOH). Figures 11.5B and 11.5C show the improvement in performance over multiple sessions for each of the five tasks. Performance also improved during daily experimental sessions (Figure 11.5D). The statistics of total time spent over a particular object in a given trial (Figure 11.5C) indicated that the monkeys were able to discriminate each type of artificial texture on the timescale of about a second or less which is comparable to the discrimination of peripheral tactile stimuli.

11.3 Bidirectional BCI Control of a Mini-Robot

Mussa-Ivaldi and colleagues (2010) have explored the use of a bidirectional BCI as a tool for studying the transformation of signals from one region of the brain to another. In their experiments, the BCI connects a lamprey's brain to a small mobile robot. The lamprey's brain is immersed in artificial cerebro-spinal fluid within a recording chamber. Signals from optical sensors on the robot are translated to electrical stimuli that are used to stimulate the right and left vestibular neural pathways. The frequency of stimulation is linearly proportional to light intensity.

The neural responses to electrically delivered stimuli are recorded from another brain region known as the posterior rhombencephalic reticular nuclei (PRRN). Recorded signals from right and left PRRNs are decoded by the BCI which generates the commands to the robot's wheels. These commands are set to be proportional to the estimated average PRRN firing rate on the corresponding side of the lamprey's brainstem: higher firing rates make the corresponding wheel turn faster and cause the robot to turn in the opposite direction.

The robot was placed in a circular arena with light sources on the periphery (Figure 11.6A), and the behavior of the neural-robot system was studied by turning on each light source. The transformation implemented by the neural system

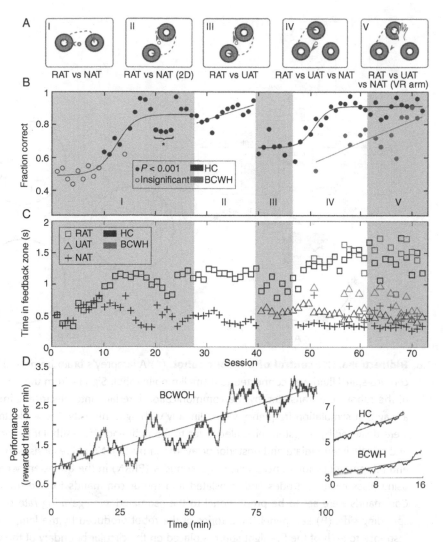

Figure 11.5. **Learning to use a bidirectional BCI.** (A) Five tasks of varying difficulty levels. (B) Fraction of correctly performed trials for each task as a function of session number. Open circles: chance performance. HC: Hand control. BCWH: Brain control with joystick present but disconnected. (C) Squares, triangles, and crosses represent mean times spent over different types of objects (RAT, UAT and NAT – see text for details). (D) Improvement in performance within daily experimental sessions. BCWOH: Brain control without hand movements (i.e., joystick removed) (from (O'Doherty et al., 2011).

between the stimulation and recording electrodes determined how the robot moved in response to a light source (Figure 11.6B). Mussa-Ivaldi and colleagues studied this transformation by substituting it with mathematical models such as polynomials of varying degrees and autoregressive models (Section 4.4.3) with inputs. They found that polynomials of degree 3 outperformed linear models (Figure 11.6B) in

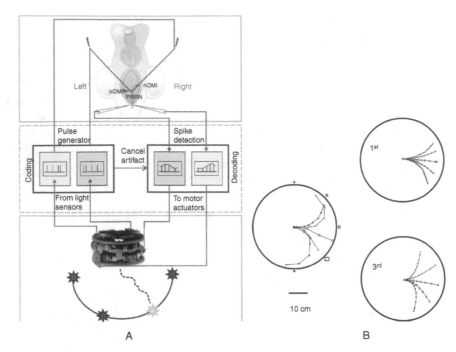

Figure 11.6. **Bidirectional BCI control of a mobile robot.** (A) A lamprey's brain immersed in artificial cerebro-spinal fluid was connected to a small mobile robot. Signals from the optical sensors of the robot were translated by the communication interface into electrical stimuli in such a way that stimulation frequency varied linearly with light intensity. These electrical stimuli were delivered by tungsten microelectrodes to the right and left vestibular pathways (nOMI and nOMP: intermediate and posterior octavomotor nuclei). Neural responses from the right and left posterior rhombencephalic reticular nuclei (PRRN) in the brainstem were recorded using glass microelectrodes and translated into motor commands for the robot's wheels. Commands were set to be proportional to the estimated average firing rate on the corresponding side. (B) Left panel: Trajectories of the robot produced by the lamprey's brain in response to each of the five light sources placed on the circular boundary of the workspace. The robot tended to move toward the light. The two panels on the right show the results of fitting a linear and third degree polynomial to the neural transformation function controlling the robot (adapted from Mussa-Ivaldi et al., 2010).

approximating the neural transformation function, but the best performance was achieved using a first-order autoregressive model with inputs.

A question of considerable importance to the future use of bidirectional BCIs left open by the study is whether neural plasticity can be harnessed to create a desired behavior of an external device such as a robot. In other words, rather than the robot acting according to the fixed neural transformation in the lamprey's brain, can an arbitrary behavior be generated using neural plasticity? This question has been partly addressed by studies targeting cortical control of muscles and creation of connections between brain areas, discussed in the following two sections.

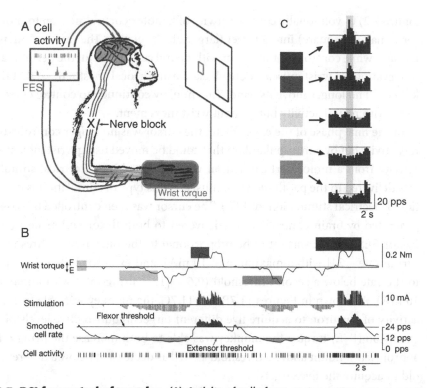

Figure 11.7. **BCI for control of muscles.** (A) Activity of cells from motor cortex was converted into electrical stimuli for functional electrical stimulation (FES) of wrist muscles. The resulting wrist torque was used to move a cursor (gray square) on a computer screen into a target (black square). (B) Examples of the monkey modulating the activity of a cell in its motor cortex to acquire targets at five levels of flexion-extension (F–E) torque (indicated by different shades of gray). FES was delivered to both flexor and extensor muscles. Flexor FES was proportional to the rate above a threshold (0.8 × [firing rate – 24] with a maximum of 10 mA), and extensor FES was proportional to the rate below a second threshold (0.6 × [12 – firing rate] with a maximum of 10 mA). (C) Histograms of firing rate used to acquire the five target levels (gray shaded boxes at left). Horizontal lines indicate FES thresholds for flexor (dark gray) and extensor (light gray) stimulation (adapted from Moritz et al., 2008).

11.4 Cortical Control of Muscles via Functional Electrical Stimulation

A different type of bidirectional BCI seeks to restore movement in people who are paralyzed due to spinal cord injury. The idea, first explored by Moritz, Perlmutter, and Fetz (2008), is to use neural signals from an area of the brain (such as the motor cortex) to stimulate the spinal cord or muscles, thereby bypassing the spinal block and reanimating the limb. Moritz and colleagues demonstrated this approach in two monkeys by translating the activity of single motor cortical neurons into electrical stimulation of wrist muscles to move a cursor on a computer screen (Figure 11.7A). The monkey was initially trained using operant conditioning (Section 7.1.1 and

Figure 7.2) to volitionally control activity of a motor cortical neuron to move a cursor (small red square) into a target (larger black square). The monkey often moved its hand while controlling the cursor with neural activity. Next, the peripheral nerves innervating the wrist muscles were blocked using a local anesthetic so that the monkey could no longer move its hand. The monkey continued to control cursor movement with neural activity but without wrist movement.

In the final phase of the experiment, the cursor was no longer controlled by neural activity but by a manipulandum that could be moved using wrist movement. The activity from a motor cortical neuron was converted into electrical stimuli which was delivered to the paralyzed wrist muscles (this type of stimulation is called functional electrical stimulation, or FES). The cursor was then controlled by wrist torque generated by brain-controlled FES delivered to both flexor and extensor muscles. Flexor FES current was set to be proportional to the rate above a threshold ($0.8 \times$ [firing rate – 24] with a maximum of 10 mA), and extensor FES was proportional to the rate below a second threshold ($0.6 \times$ [12 – firing rate] with a maximum of 10 mA). As shown in Figures 11.7B and 11.7C, the monkey was able to control the activity of a neuron to acquire five different targets requiring five levels of flexion-extension (F–E) torque: the monkey was able to both increase the firing rate by an appropriate amount above a threshold as well as decrease it below a different threshold to acquire the five targets.

A potential shortcoming of this approach is the well-known fact that continued electrical stimulation of muscles beyond a few minutes generally results in muscle fatigue, rendering the technique impractical for day-long use. An alternate approach that could turn out to be more practical is using brain signals to stimulate neurons in the spinal cord. Several research groups, including the group above, are actively exploring this alternative, both for arm-hand reanimation as well as for reactivating spinal circuits (van den Brand et al., 2012) responsible for gait control in order to restore mobility in paralyzed individuals.

11.5 Establishing New Connections between Brain Regions

Bidirectional BCIs can also be used to directly stimulate one brain region using input from another. Such an artificial connection can be useful in cases where the biological connection between brain regions has been damaged due to stroke or neurological disease. Additionally, establishing an artificial connection between brain regions can also induce neural plasticity and functional reorganization, as shown by Jackson, Fetz, and colleagues (2006). The *Hebbian* principle of plasticity (Section 2.6) states that the connections from one group of neurons to another are strengthened if there is a persistent causal relationship between pre- and postsynaptic activity. Jackson and colleagues investigated whether Hebbian plasticity could be induced by creating an artificial connection between two sites in the motor cortex of freely behaving primates.

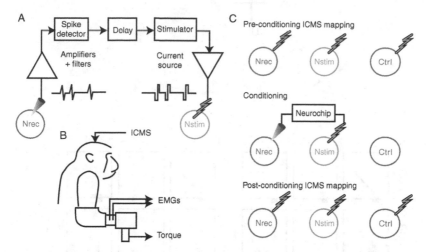

Figure 11.8. **Inducing plasticity using a bidirectional BCI.** (A) Schematic diagram of the bidirectional BCI. Spikes recorded from a recording electrode (Nrec) were converted to electrical stimuli which were delivered to the Nstim electrode after a predefined delay. (B) Changes in the properties of neurons were monitored by delivering intracortical microstimulation (ICMS) to each electrode and measuring output effects on the right wrist. (C) Top to bottom: Experimental sequence of testing, conditioning using the Neurochip, followed by testing after conditioning (from Jackson et al., 2006).

The Neurochip implant (Section 3.3.2) was implanted in the wrist area of the primary motor cortex (M1) of two monkeys. The chip's microprocessor detected spikes from a recording electrode (labeled Nrec in Figure 11.8A) and instructed a stimulator circuit to deliver, after a specific delay, biphasic, constant-current pulses (25–80μA, 0.2 ms per phase) via a stimulating electrode (Nstim in Figure 11.8A). Once the chip was programmed with appropriate recording and stimulation parameters, it operated autonomously over the course of one to four days of unrestrained behavior. The researchers studied the effects of conditioning caused by artificial connections between 17 different pairs of neurons with delays of 0, 1, and 5 ms between spike and stimulus. These effects were studied using daily intracortical microstimulation (ICMS) of the various electrodes and measuring the torque produced in the contralateral wrist (Figure 11.8B and 11.8C).

As shown in the example in Figure 11.9, after two days of continuous operation, the output generated by stimulating the recording site (Nrec) shifted to resemble the output torques from the corresponding stimulation site (Nstim) in a manner consistent with the potentiation of synaptic connections between the artificially synchronized populations of neurons (in this case, the synaptic connections that may have existed from Nrec to Nstim – see Figure 11.10). This change in the functional output of Nrec lasted in some cases for more than one week (Figure 11.9E).

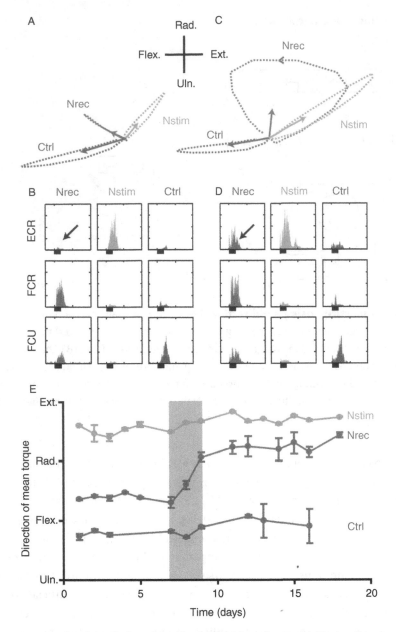

Figure 11.9. **Motor plasticity induced by the bidirectional BCI.** (A) Preconditioning average trajectories of isometric wrist torque (dashed lines) after electrical stimuli (ICMS) were delivered separately to each of three electrodes: recording (Nrec), stimulation (Nstim), and control (Ctrl) electrodes. The mean torque (solid arrows) was toward the flexion direction (Flex.) for Nrec and Ctrl, and in the radial-extension direction (Rad.-Ext.) for Nstim. (B) Average rectified electromyogram (EMG) responses to ICMS in three wrist muscles: extensor carpi radialis (ECR), flexor carpi radialis (FCR), and flexor carpi ulnaris (FCU). The black shaded bars below denote the ICMS duration. (C) and (D) Data after two days of conditioning with an artificial connection between Nrec and Nstim mediated by the Neurochip. Arrows indicate change in EMG response from Nrec after conditioning. (E) Direction of mean torque response over eighteen days, showing persistence of new torque response for Nrec several days after conditioning. Shaded region: conditioning period. Error bars: s.e.m. ICMS parameters: 13 pulses at 300 Hz; current: 30 mA (Nrec), 40 mA (Nstim), and 50 mA (Ctrl) (from Jackson et al., 2006).

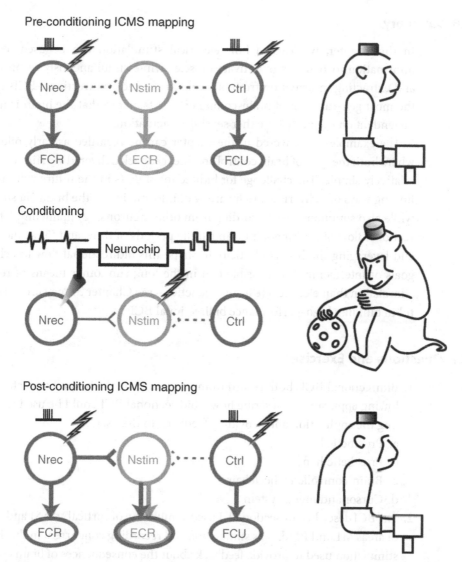

Figure 11.10. **Possible mechanism for plastic changes caused by the bidirectional BCI.** (Top) Before conditioning, ICMS predominantly activates distinct descending projections from electrodes Nrec, Nstim, and Ctrl to their respective wrist muscles. (Middle) Conditioning using the Neurochip artificial connection during unrestrained behavior causes a strengthening of horizontal connections between Nrec and Nstim. (Bottom) Post-conditioning ICMS of Nrec now activates the ECR muscle via the strengthened horizontal connections (from Jackson et al., 2006).

The changes in the functional output of neurons in the Nrec site suggest that the Neurochip was successful in inducing functional reorganization in vivo using physiologically derived stimulus trains. Although not yet demonstrated, such a method could be potentially quite useful for neurorehabilitation and restoration of connections between brain areas after damage or injury.

11.6 Summary

In this chapter, we learned how electrical stimulation can be used to provide information to neurons or activate muscles while simultaneously recording from and extracting information from other neurons. Such bidirectional BCIs represent the most general form of brain-computer interfacing in that the brain is no longer dependent on the body for either sensing or actuation.

The examples we covered in the chapter can be regarded as early pilot studies where both the type of brain control and the feedback delivered via stimulation were relatively simple. The challenge for bidirectional BCIs in the future will involve (1) finding ways of delivering a rich variety of information to the brain via stimulation while also simultaneously recording from other neurons, (2) maintaining this bidirectional flow of information for indefinite periods of time, and (3) acknowledging and leveraging the brain's plasticity to shape this bidirectional flow to achieve the goals of interfacing. It is possible that in the long run, other means of recording/ stimulation than electrical (e.g., optogenetics – see Chapter 3) may prove more useful in building high-performance bidirectional BCIs.

11.7 Questions and Exercises

1. Bidirectional BCIs both record from and stimulate the brain. For each of the following applications, describe how a bidirectional BCI could be used for controlling the application and providing feedback to the user:
   a. Prosthetic leg
   b. Prosthetic hand
   c. Brain-controlled wheelchair
   d. Cursor and menu system
2. The BCI described in Section 11.1 used stimulation of cortical area S1 and recording of areas M1 and PMd. Was stimulation and recording concurrent in this BCI? Was stimulation used to provide feedback about the consequences of brain control?
3. Describe the experimental setup and active exploration task used in Section 11.2 to demonstrate bidirectional BCIs in monkeys.
4. The BCI in Section 11.2 provided visual feedback to the monkey to allow it to guide the cursor to various targets on a screen. How would you modify the BCI to replace visual feedback with direct cortical feedback via stimulation?
5. Explain how bidirectional BCIs can serve as a tool for studying the transformation of signals from one brain region to another, based on the experiments by Mussa-Ivaldi and colleagues described in Section 11.3.
6. (⚡ Expedition) The experiment in Section 11.3 was inspired by Braitenberg's "vehicles" (Braitenberg, 1984), which were originally proposed as simple examples of intelligent behavior emerging from sensorimotor interaction between an "agent" and its environment without any internal memory or representation of

the environment. Describe the different types of Braitenberg's vehicles and specify which vehicle the bidirectional BCI in Section 11.3 resembles the most.

7. Describe the approach proposed by Moritz and colleagues for reanimating a limb using cortical activity for functional electrical stimulation (FES). What is a potential drawback of this method for long-term use, and how can this weakness be addressed?

8. What is Hebbian plasticity, and how can it be exploited for restoring connectivity between cortical regions using a recurrent BCI?

9. In the experiment performed by Jackson and colleagues (Section 11.5), how was the Neurochip used, and for how long? How were the behavioral effects of using the chip experimentally ascertained? What conclusions were drawn from the results and on what basis?

10. (♠ Expedition) Brainstorm about other ways in which one could use a recurrent BCI for connecting different regions of the brain for sensory and motor restoration or augmentation. For example, could a recurrent BCI be used to convey auditory information to visual or somatosensory cortex to bypass a malfunctioning auditory cortex? What about connecting an area implicated in memory such as the hippocampus with sensory areas to treat memory disorders? Consider also the implications of allowing on-chip and cloud-based memory storage and processing capacity.

Part IV

Applications and Ethics

12

Applications of BCIs

In this chapter, we explore the range of applications for BCI technology. We have already touched upon some medical applications such as restoration of lost motor and sensory function when we examined invasive and noninvasive BCIs in previous chapters. Here we briefly review these applications before exploring applications in other areas such as entertainment, robotic control, gaming, security, and art.

12.1 Medical Applications

The field of brain-computer interfacing originated with the goal of helping the paralyzed and the disabled. It is therefore not surprising that some of the major applications of BCIs to date have been in medical technology, particularly restoring sensory and motor function.

12.1.1 Sensory Restoration

One of the most widely used commercial BCIs is the cochlear implant for the deaf, discussed in Section 10.1.1. The cochlear implant is an example of a BCI for sensory restoration, as are retinal implants being developed for the blind (Section 10.1.2).

There has not been much research on two other possible types of purely sensory BCIs, namely, BCIs for somatosensation and BCIs for olfaction and taste. In the case of the former, the need for a BCI is minimized because it is often possible to restore tactile sensation through skin grafting. However, as we saw in Chapter 11, there is considerable interest in somatosensory stimulation as a component of bidirectional BCIs for allowing paralyzed individuals and amputees to, for example, sense objects being grasped or touched by prosthetic devices.

In the case of BCIs for olfaction and taste, there have been efforts to build "artificial noses" and chips that can sense various types of odors, but these devices have been built more with an eye toward security and robotics applications than BCIs. The lack of interest in developing BCIs for olfaction and taste is mostly due to the lack of a large population of individuals in need of such BCIs, compared to the population of visually or hearing impaired persons.

12.1.2 Motor Restoration

Another major motivation for BCI research over the last two decades has been the goal of developing prosthetic devices for amputees and paralyzed individuals that can be controlled using neural signals. Perhaps closest to being commercialized are prosthetic arms that can be controlled by intact nerve signals (Section 8.2). Further into the future are prosthetic arms and hands that can be controlled directly using cortical neurons – the early prototypes for such BCIs are currently being tested in monkeys (Section 7.2.1) and humans (Section 7.3.1; see also Hochberg et al., 2012 and Collinger et al., 2012 for the state of the art in BCIs for prosthetic control).

Perhaps the most challenging to realize are lower-limb prosthetics controlled by brain signals. In this case, the BCI/prosthetic system needs to be able to maintain stability and allow the user to maintain balance while obeying commands from the brain and providing feedback by stimulating somatosensory neurons appropriately. We briefly reviewed BCI research on lower-limb control in monkeys in Section 7.2.2. An approach based on hierarchical BCIs (Section 9.1.8) based on a mix of autonomy and user control may provide the most flexible way of controlling lower-limb prosthetics.

12.1.3 Cognitive Restoration

BCIs could potentially be used to treat a number of cognitive neurological disorders. For example, several groups are working on methods to predict seizures or detect their onset. If successful, such methods could be incorporated into a BCI that monitors the brain for the onset of a seizure and when the onset of a potential seizure is detected, delivers appropriate drugs or stimulates the vagus nerve to stop the seizure before it spreads to other parts of the brain.

Similarly, deep brain stimulation (DBS) has been used not only for treating the symptoms of Parkinson's disease (see Section 10.2.1) but also to relieve chronic pain and depression. Finally, BCIs that can record memories and stimulate appropriate memory centers of the brain could potentially help counter memory impairment from diseases such as Alzheimer's disease, though the development of such BCIs will require a much deeper understanding of how memories are created and stored in the brain than what we know today.

12.1.4 Rehabilitation

Another potentially significant application of BCIs is in rehabilitating patients recovering from a stroke, surgery, or other neurological conditions. The BCI would be part of a closed-loop feedback system that converts brain signals into a stimulus on a computer screen or into movements of a rehabilitative device. Such a neurofeedback system can enable patients to learn to generate the appropriate type of neural activity for accelerating their rehabilitation. The interested reader is referred to (Birbaumer & Cohen, 2007; Dobkin, 2007; and Scherer et al., 2007) for examples.

12.1.5 Restoring Communication with Menus, Cursors, and Spellers

A major motivation for the development of noninvasive EEG-based BCIs has been the restoration of communication for locked-in patients suffering from progressive motor diseases such as amyotrophic lateral sclerosis (ALS, also known as Lou Gehrig's disease). In cases where patients are unable to even blink or suck on a straw to indicate a "yes" or "no" answer, a BCI becomes the only possible mode of communication.

One approach to restoring communication is to build a BCI to control a cursor in a menu system, allowing the patient to select an option from a set of choices. A nested menu system allows for the composition of arbitrarily long sentences or sequences of commands. The cursor in such a system could be controlled by any of the methods for self-paced BCIs described in Chapter 9, for example, via voluntary control of oscillatory potentials (Section 9.1.1) or slow cortical potentials (Section 9.1.2), as well as any of the invasive methods described in Chapter 7.

Alternately, a stimulus-evoked method such as the P300 BCI speller (Section 9.1.4) can be used to select letters to spell out words. Both the speller and the cursor-based approaches can be quite slow and tedious for the patient. A more natural BCI for communication would entail tapping into the speech centers of the brain. Some early results have been published on decoding phonemes from neural activity recorded from the speech region (Broca's area) of the cerebral cortex (Blakely et al., 2008), but a more in-depth understanding of speech processing in the brain is required before a BCI can be developed for translating linguistic thoughts.

12.1.6 Brain-Controlled Wheelchairs

Paralyzed patients are sometimes able to control a wheelchair using parts of their body still under voluntary control. Others may be able to use speech to issue commands to a semi-autonomous wheelchair. A natural question to ask is whether one may ultimately be able to control a wheelchair directly using brain signals. Several research groups have developed solutions to this problem using varying degrees of robotic autonomy.

The simplest approach is to use a BCI to select high-level commands (e.g., go to kitchen, go to bedroom, etc.) and endow the wheelchair with sufficient knowledge and autonomy to be able to execute these commands in an autonomous fashion. The high-level commands can be selected using a synchronous BCI, such as a P300-based BCI (Rebsamen et al., 2006; Bell et al., 2008; Iturrate et al., 2009). This approach can be made flexible and adaptive to the individual user's needs using a *hierarchical BCI* (Chung et al., 2011; Bryan et al., 2012) as described in Section 9.1.8.

A different approach proposed by Millán and colleagues (Galán et al., 2008; Millán et al., 2009) relies on the concept of *shared control* (see Figure 12.1). In this approach, the user continually generates commands for the robot that are then probabilistically combined with pre-wired behaviors. The wheelchair is assumed

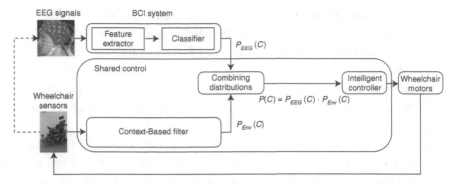

Figure 12.1. **BCI control of an intelligent wheelchair.** Commands from a self-paced EEG BCI based on mental tasks were probabilistically (i.e., multiplicatively) combined with environmental constraints to achieve shared control of a wheelchair (from Galán et al., 2008).

to have sensors such as a laser range scanner. If the goal of the user is to move smoothly forward through the environment, information from the wheelchair's sensors can be used to construct a "contextual filter" in the form of a probability distribution $P_{Env}(C)$ over a set of possible mental steering commands, e.g., $C = \{left, right, forward\}$. The EEG-based BCI system estimates the probabilities $P_{EEG}(C)$ for the different mental commands from the user's brain signals. The wheelchair is controlled using a "filtered" estimate of the user's intent: $P(C) = P_{EEG}(C)\, P_{Env}(C)$. The command with the highest probability is used to control the wheelchair. The BCI is based on three mental tasks: (1) searching for words starting with the same letter, (2) relaxing while fixating on the center of the screen, and (3) motor imagery of the left hand. A subject-specific set of features (frequency-and-electrode combination) is used with a Gaussian classifier to map EEG features to one of the three commands. Using such an approach, two subjects achieved between 80%–100% accuracy in navigating to pre-specified goals.

Although these early results are promising, a practical BCI-controlled wheelchair for day-to-day use remains hard to achieve due to the lack of a reliable, easy-to-use, and portable recording system (EEG or other modality) as well as the lack of robust, semi-autonomous robotic wheelchairs that can function safely in human environments.

12.2 Nonmedical Applications

There has been a steady rise in the number of nonmedical applications of BCI technology. Many of these applications have been driven by commercial factors such as the potential for a novel interface for gaming and entertainment. Most of these applications are still in their infancy and being investigated in research laboratories, though some have been applied to real-world problems such as triaging large quantities of images and lie detection.

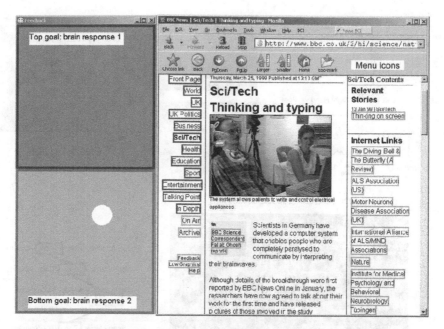

Figure 12.2. **The BCI-controlled Web browser Nessi.** Links on a Web page are framed by either red or green colored boxes (shown here as dark and light gray boxes respectively). The user selects a desired link by successively producing brain responses (e.g., slow cortical potentials, SCPs) to prune the set of selectable links via binary selection until the desired link is selected. During each binary selection, feedback is provided in the form of a cursor (yellow circle, shown here as a white circle) that is moved upward into a red goal (dark gray box) or down-ward into a green goal (light gray box) (from Bensch et al., 2007).

12.2.1 Web Browsing and Navigating Virtual Worlds

We have already discussed in previous chapters a variety of efforts aimed at building a BCI for controlling a cursor on a computer screen. A natural extension of such efforts is to build BCIs for browsing the Internet and navigating virtual worlds.

An example of a BCI-controlled Web-browser interface is *Nessi* (Neural Signal Surfing Interface; Bensch et al., 2007), which allows a user to select any link on a Web page and access Web-based services see (Figure 12.2). Nessi is a platform-independent, open-source software that can be used with different types of BCIs. One demonstration (Bensch et al., 2007) used a two-class BCI based on slow cortical potentials (SCPs; see Section 9.1.2). Red or green frames were placed around links on a Web page: red frames were selected by producing negative SCP shifts and green frames were selected by positive SCP shifts. Feedback was provided in the form of a cursor that was moved upward into a red goal or downward into a green goal using the SCP-based BCI. The user only had to observe the color of the desired link's frame to know what type of brain response to produce, thereby successively pruning the set of selectable items via binary decisions until the desired link was selected.

Another example is an imagery-based BCI developed by the Graz BCI group (Scherer et al., 2008) for navigating virtual environments and Google Earth. The

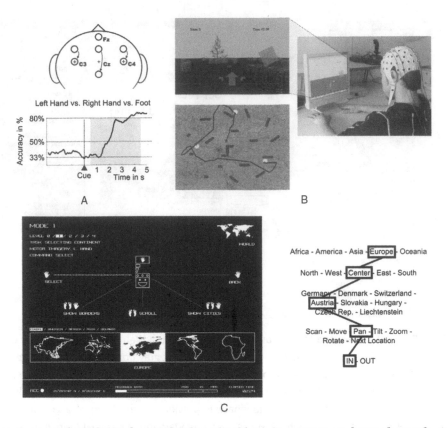

Figure 12.3. **Imagery-based BCI for navigating virtual environments and Google Earth.** (A) Top: Three bipolar channels used in the BCI. Bottom: Classification performance for one subject during cue-guided feedback training. (B) Example of navigation by a subject (right panel) using the 3-class imagery-based BCI in a virtual environment containing trees and hedges (top left panel). The subject successfully picked up coins (bright circles) dispersed in the environment (bottom left panel). (C) Example of interaction with Google Earth using the 3-class BCI for choosing one of the commands, "scroll," "select," and "back." The panel on the right shows the sequence of selections made to choose the map for Austria and zoom in (adapted from Scherer and Rao, 2011).

user generates commands for moving left, right, or forward by imagining left-hand, right-hand, and foot (or tongue) movements: as we saw in Section 9.1.1, such motor imagery causes a decrease or increase in power in particular frequency bands, which can be detected by a classifier. Only three subject-specific bipolar EEG channels, recorded from six electrodes, were used (Figure 12.3A). Features used to quantify the EEG activity were computed by bandpass filtering, squaring, and averaging the samples collected over the past one second.

To achieve three-class classification, a scheme based on 3 binary LDA classifiers (Section 5.1.1) with majority voting (Section 5.1.3) was used. For self-paced operation, the BCI needs to detect whether the user wants to use the BCI or not at any point in time. For this purpose, an additional LDA classifier was trained to discriminate between motor imagery (all 3 tasks pooled together) and other brain activity. Self-paced operation was achieved by combining the 2 types of classifiers: whenever motor imagery activity was detected by the individual LDA, the majority vote of the group of 3 classifiers was used as the BCI's output signal. For three subjects, after a total training time of about 5 hours, the accuracy of the 3-class classifier was higher than 80%. Subjects were able to use the BCI to navigate in a virtual world containing trees and hedges to find and pick up scattered coins (see Figure 12.3B).

The Graz BCI system has also been used to interact with the Google Earth virtual globe program (Scherer et al., 2007). As shown in Figure 12.3C, the user's current selection is represented by an icon positioned in the middle of the screen, and the user can use the 3-class BCI to select the commands "scroll," "select," and "back." By browsing through the available menu options ("scroll"), the desired menu entry can be selected ("select"). Google Earth's virtual camera position is then repositioned accordingly. Countries of the world were hierarchically grouped by continent and continental area to allow fast sequential selection, as shown in Figure 12.3C for zooming into Austria. After additional training of about 10 hours, one subject from the 3-class self-paced experiment successfully operated Google Earth in front of a public audience. The average time to select a desired country was about 20 seconds.

Before concluding the section, it is worth mentioning that there have been other non-imagery-based approaches to controlling virtual environments using EEG signals – these have typically relied on evoked potentials such as the P300 (see, for example, Bayliss, 2003).

12.2.2 Robotic Avatars

Brain-controlled telepresence, or the idea of controlling a remote robotic avatar directly with the human mind, has been the subject of Hollywood movies such as *Avatar* and *Surrogates*, but advances in robotics and BCI technology are bringing this idea closer to reality. We have already discussed research efforts currently underway to build BCIs that can control robotic wheelchairs. A parallel line of research has targeted the development of assistive robots and avatars that can be remotely controlled via brain signals. Besides telepresence, such robots could assist paralyzed and disabled individuals in performing various tasks in day-to-day life, such as getting a cup of water from the kitchen or fetching a bottle from the medicine cabinet.

One approach to robotic avatars, explored in the author's laboratory, has focused on EEG-based BCI systems for controlling humanoid robots (Bell et al., 2008; Chung et al., 2011; Bryan et al., 2012). In one of the first demonstrations of a brain-controlled "avatar" (Bell et al., 2008), a P300-based BCI (Section 9.1.4) was used to command a humanoid robot to go to desired locations and fetch desired objects. The user had a robot's eye view of the environment, which provided an immersive experience. The robot had the ability to autonomously move and pick-up/

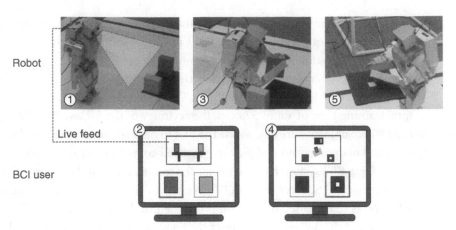

Figure 12.4. **A brain-controlled robotic avatar for remote interaction.** (See color plates for the same figure in color) The top panel shows images of the humanoid robot in action. The bottom row depicts the user's computer screen. The user receives a live feed from the robot's cameras, thereby immersing the user in the robot's environment and allowing the user to select actions based on objects seen in the robot's cameras (screen marked "2"). Objects are found using computer vision techniques. The robot transmits the segmented images of the objects (in this case, a red and a green object) and queries the user about which one to pick up. The selection is made by the user using a P300 BCI. After picking up the object selected by the user (image marked "3"), the robot asks the user which location to bring the selected object to. Images of the possible locations (blue tables on the left and right sides) from an overhead camera are presented to the user (screen marked "4"). Again, the selection of the destination is made by the user by means of the P300. Finally, the robot walks to the destination selected by the user and places the object on the table at the selected location (image marked "5") (from Rao and Scherer, 2010; based on Bell et al., 2008).

release objects. The robot also possessed some computer-vision capabilities, such as being able to segment objects it saw on a table and use vision to navigate to a destination.

EEG signals were used to select the two main types of commands for the robot: which object to pick among those in the images transmitted by the robot and which location to choose as the destination from among a set of known locations. The images of the possible choices (objects or destination locations) were scaled and arranged as a grid on the computer screen of the user. Figure 12.4 illustrates the case for two objects, one red and one green, and two locations (two blue tables, one with a white square in the center). The oddball paradigm (Section 9.1.4) was used to evoke the P300 response. The user focused his or her attention on the image of choice while the border of a randomly selected image was flashed every 250 ms. When the flash occurred on the attended object, a P300 was elicited (Figure 12.5); this response was then detected by the BCI and used to infer the user's choice. In order to focus their attention, users were asked to mentally count the number of flashes on their image of choice.

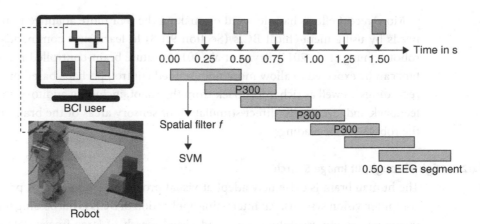

Figure 12.5. **Using the P300 response to command the robot.** (See color plates for the same figure in color) (Left panel) When the robot finds objects of interest (in this experiment a red and a green cube), segmented images are sent to the user and arranged in a grid format in the lower part of the BCI user's screen. (Right panel) The oddball paradigm is used to evoke the P300 response. The colored objects at the top show a random temporal order of flashed images. EEG segments of a 0.5-second duration from flash onset were spatially filtered and classified by a soft margin SVM into either segments containing a P300 or not containing a P300. After a fixed number of flashes, the object associated with the most P300 classifications was selected as the user's choice (in this case, the red object) (adapted from Rao and Scherer, 2010; based on Bell et al., 2008).

Thirty-two EEG channels were recorded, and a linear soft margin support vector machine (SVM) classifier (see Section 5.1.1) was trained to discriminate between the P300 response generated by a flash on a desired object and EEG responses due to flashes on other objects. The feature vectors used in classification were based on a set of spatial filters similar to CSP filters (Section 4.5.4). Like LDA (Section 5.1.1), these spatial filters were chosen to maximize the distance between the means of the filtered data from each class while minimizing the within-class variance of the filtered data.

To learn the filters and train the classifier for a given user, a 10-minute data-collection protocol was used prior to operating the BCI. After training on the labeled data, the BCI was used to infer the user's choice regarding an object or destination location. The choices (objects or locations) were presented in a grid format (e.g., 2×2 grid for 4 object images), and the borders flashed in random order. EEG data for the 500 ms duration after each image flash was classified as a P300 response or a non-P300 response. The image with the highest number of P300 classifications after all flashes was selected as the user's choice. The results, based on 9 able-bodied subjects, showed that an accuracy of 95% can be achieved for discriminating between 4 classes (chance classification level is 25%). With the implemented rate of 4 flashes per second, the selection of 1 out of 4 options takes 5 seconds, yielding a bit rate of 24 bits/min at 95% accuracy.

More recent efforts have focused on making the BCI more adaptive to the user's needs by using hierarchical BCIs (Section 9.1.8) to learn new commands for the robot (Chung et al., 2011; Bryan et al., 2012). Future brain-controlled robotic avatars can be expected to allow more fine-grained control, perhaps based on invasive recordings, as well as richer feedback from the robot, including auditory and tactile feedback and, eventually, direct stimulation of sensory areas of the brain based on the robot's sensor readings.

12.2.3 High Throughput Image Search

The human brain is extremely adept at visual processing compared to present-day computer-vision systems. An interesting application of BCIs is harnessing the brain's image-processing capabilities for rapid visual search of large image datasets. The idea, explored by Sajda and colleagues (2010), is to use single-trial analysis to rapidly detect neural signatures correlated with visual recognition.

Suppose the goal is to sort images (e.g., satellite images) such that the images most likely to contain objects of interest (e.g., tanks) are placed at the beginning of the sequence of images for further examination. Sajda and colleagues (Gerson et al., 2006; Sajda et al., 2010) developed a real-time EEG BCI for triaging such imagery using the paradigm of rapid serial visual presentation (RSVP). Their technique, called *cortically coupled computer vision* (CCCV), is based on the oddball paradigm (Section 9.1.4) for eliciting a P300: a target image that occurs in a sequence of non-target distractor images will cause a P300 response.

In each trial, the subject was presented with a continuous sequence of 100 images, each image lasting 100 ms (Figure 12.6, top panels). The sequence contained 2 target images with 1 or more people in a natural scene; these were designated as target images. The sudden appearance of a target image in the sequence typically elicited a P300, which was detected by a classifier. The output of the classifier was used to reprioritize the image sequence, placing detected target images at the front of the image stack (Figure 12.6, bottom panels).

Linear discriminant analysis (LDA, see Section 5.1.1) was used to recover a spatial filter $\mathbf{w}$ whose output emphasized differences in the EEG signal $\mathbf{x}_t$ at time t across 59 electrodes between target and non-target images:

$$y_t = \sum_i w_i x_{it}$$

Several such spatial filters were calculated for the different 100 ms time windows following an image presentation. Figure 12.7A illustrates the output of these different spatial filters in terms of correlation maps over the scalp for each time window.

The output of each filter was summed over time within each window to get a value y_k for the kth time window:

$$y_k = \sum_t \sum_i w_{ki} x_{it}$$

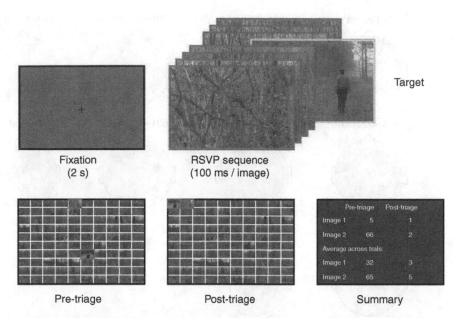

Figure 12.6. **Rapid image search and triaging using a P300-based EEG BCI.** The panels depict the RSVP experimental paradigm. A fixation cross lasting 2 seconds is followed by a sequence of 100 images containing 2 target images with people occurring at any position within the sequence. After the image sequence, the subject sees the same images arranged in a 10×10 grid with the target images outlined. After the user presses the space bar, the images are sorted according to EEG, with the target images ideally moving to the top. Pressing the space bar again results in a summary slide being displayed that shows the position of target images before and after triage. The next trial begins when the subject presses the space bar again (from Gerson et al., 2006).

Finally, a linear weighted sum of the y_k's for each image was used as the final "interest score" (y_{IS}) for that image:

$$y_{IS} = \sum_k v_k y_k$$

The weights v_k were calculated from training data using regression. Figure 12.7B illustrates the distribution of these interest scores for a subject: there appears to be a good separation between these EEG-based scores for target images versus non-targets. Figure 12.7C shows the ROC curve (Section 5.1.4) for the method: the ROC curve depicts performance as one varies the threshold used to classify EEG signals based on y_{IS}. In their study, Gerson et al. (2006) found that for 5 subjects and a sequence of 2,500 images, their method moved 92% of target images from a random position to the first 10% of the sequence.

12.2.4 Lie Detection and Applications in Law

An application of BCIs that has evoked considerable interest (and controversy) in the law and criminal-justice communities is lie detection or detection of possession

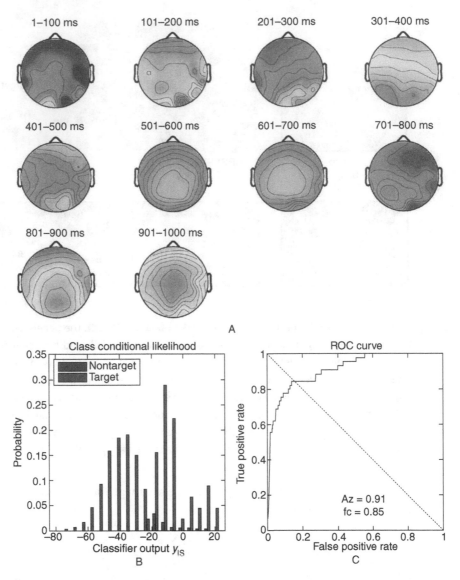

Figure 12.7. **Performance of the EEG-based BCI for image search.** (See color plates for the same figure in color) (A) Scalp maps of normalized correlation between the output of the spatial filter for a given time window and the EEG data across all electrodes (red: positive values, blue: negative values). The map at 301–400 ms has a spatial distribution which is characteristic of a type of P300 known as "P3f," while the parietal activity at 501–700 ms is consistent with a "P3b" potential thought to be indicative of attentional orienting. (B) The distribution of y_{IS}, the overall interest score for each image, for target images versus non-targets. There is a clear separation between the two distributions. (C) ROC curve obtained by varying the position of the classification threshold along the y_{IS} axis (from Sajda et al., 2010).

of guilty knowledge. The traditional technique is the *polygraph*, which measures a subject's bodily reactions such as changes in blood pressure, skin conductivity, and heart rate while he or she answers a series of questions during an interrogation. The premise is that deceptive answers will produce physiological responses different from those associated with truthful answers. Although polygraphy is used by many law-enforcement agencies, it is generally considered to be unreliable by most scientists because it is thought to measure anxiety rather than deception, and its accuracy levels are considered to be little better than chance.

To overcome the shortcomings of the polygraph, BCI researchers have explored the use of brain responses as a way to detect whether a subject has previously encountered or possesses knowledge about a specific person, place, or object. The challenge is to design a BCI for *memory detection* that could be used to directly interrogate the brains of suspects and witnesses. The goal is to find neural evidence, if it exists, of recognition of a person, place, or object linked to a crime scene.

An early example of a "lie detector" BCI based on the P300 event-related potential (ERP, Section 6.2.4) was investigated by Farwell and Donchin (1991) (see also Rosenfeld et al., 1988). In this paradigm, the subject is asked to discriminate between predesignated targets and irrelevant stimuli. Embedded among the irrelevant stimuli are a set of diagnostic items called "probes," which are indistinguishable from the irrelevant items if the subject does not possess guilty knowledge. For subjects who do possess guilty knowledge, the probes are perceived differently from the irrelevant items and are likely to elicit a P300, which can be detected by a BCI.

How reliable can such a P300-based lie detection test be? Farwell and Donchin tested their idea in two experiments. In the first, 20 subjects participated in 1 of 2 mock espionage scenarios. Six critical 2-word phrases associated with a scenario were learned by the subject. The subject was then tested for knowledge of both scenarios, one that they were familiar with and the other that they were unaware of. The stimuli for the P300 experiment consisted of 2-word phrases presented for 300 ms, at an interstimulus interval of 1.55 seconds. A set of prespecified "target" phrases appeared 17% of the time, and probes related to the scenarios also appeared 17% of the time. The rest of the stimuli were irrelevant phrases. Subjects were instructed to press one switch whenever they saw a target and another switch following irrelevant items. ERPs were recorded from electrode locations Fz, Cz, and Pz in the 10–20 system (see Figure 3.7).

As expected, targets elicited large P300s in all subjects (Figure 12.8). More interestingly, probes associated with a given scenario also elicited a P300 in subjects who had been exposed to that scenario (Figure 12.8A) whereas subjects not exposed to the scenario did not exhibit the P300 response to the probes (Figure 12.8B). To classify a subject as "guilty," "innocent," or "indeterminate," it must be determined whether the probe response is closer to the target response or the irrelevant response. The researchers used a bootstrapping method (see Farwell and Donchin, 1991) to estimate the distribution of two correlations: the correlation between the average probe

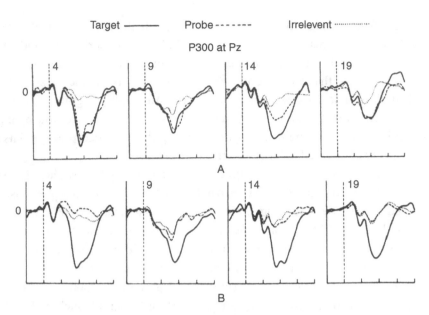

Figure 12.8. **EEG BCI for "guilty knowledge" detection**. (A) Data for 4 subjects under the "guilty" condition. Each plot compares the average EEG response from electrode Pz for a target stimulus (solid line), a probe stimulus (dashed), and an irrelevant stimulus (dotted). The probe
response is closer to the response for target stimuli than irrelevant stimuli, indicating possession of "guilty knowledge" associated with the probe. (B) The plots show the same comparison under the "innocent" condition, where the subject was not exposed to the scenario
associated with the probe stimuli (adapted from Farwell and Donchin, 1991).

response and average target response, and the correlation between the average probe
response and irrelevant response. Two criteria were used for classification, one to
declare a subject guilty and another to declare a subject innocent; cases falling in
between were declared indeterminate. This method classified 12.5% of the subjects
as indeterminate. For the rest of the subjects, a decision was made, with no false
positives and no false negatives.

In a second experiment, the researchers tested their method on 4 subjects who had
committed minor crimes (e.g., being arrested for underage drinking). The experiment in this case investigated whether a subject generated a P300 response to probe
stimuli associated with their previously committed crime. Again, in 87.5% of the
cases, the system correctly classified guilty subjects as guilty and innocent subjects
as innocent, the rest being classified as indeterminate.

The above research has led to commercialization of EEG-based systems for "brain
fingerprinting" (Farwell, 2012), with proposed applications in detection of a specific
crime, terrorist act, or specialized knowledge and training (such as knowledge possessed by undercover agents, terrorists, or bomb makers). Results from a P300-based
system for brain fingerprinting were admitted into evidence in a U.S. court case in
the state of Iowa in 2001 (*Harrington v. State*, Case No. PCCV 073247). In this case,

the EEG results were presented as exculpatory evidence for an individual who had served 24 years in prison for a murder he said he did not commit. The individual was subsequently released on other grounds after a new trial. In another case, reported in Dalbey (1999), the same technique was used to show that an accused had possession of knowledge of specific details about a murder, which led to a confession by the individual and a guilty plea. In India, results from a different EEG technique known as *brain electrical oscillation signature* (BEOS) profiling were admitted as evidence in a murder trial to establish that the suspect's brain contained knowledge that only the murderer could possess (Giridharadas, 2008).

EEG-based techniques such as those described above have come under criticism because they suffer from a number of weaknesses (Bles and Haynes, 2008), ranging from the lack of rigorous demonstrations in the field to their susceptibility to countermeasures (Rosenfeld et al., 2004), such as deliberately performing covert acts to make presumed irrelevant stimuli relevant. To overcome some of these problems, researchers are exploring other brain-recording techniques such as fMRI for detection of concealed information. In particular, the better spatial resolution of fMRI (Section 3.1.2) could provide a more precise signature of the spatially distributed pattern of brain activity evoked by a stimulus or a cognitive state. Investigations of fMRI-based systems for lie detection (and more generally, memory detection) are currently underway, with recent results indicating that fMRI may be useful in detecting neural correlates of *subjective* remembering of individual events but is less useful in revealing the veridical experiential record (Rissman et al., 2010).

12.2.5 Monitoring Alertness

A potentially important application of BCIs is monitoring the alertness of humans during the performance of critical but potentially monotonous tasks such as driving or surveillance. Many catastrophic accidents are caused each year by drivers who are tired, drowsy, or even asleep at the wheel. Such accidents can be prevented by monitoring brain signals for any transitions from an alert and awake state to a state indicating lack of alertness. While drowsiness or sleep states can be detected by monitoring eyelid closure, such detection may occur too late to prevent an accident. Brain-based detection of diminished alertness also has applications in education and learning (see Section 12.2.7) where such detection could be used to gauge the degree to which a student is engaged during a lesson.

Researchers have sought to find correlates of a decrease in attention and alertness in brain signals, especially EEG. It has been known for some time that an increase in power in certain frequency bands (such as alpha, 8–13 Hz) in EEG correlates with a decrease in concentration, as measured by higher error rates in detection tasks. An early study by Jung, Makeig, and colleagues (1997) explored the use of EEG for monitoring the alertness of 15 human subjects under laboratory conditions during a dual auditory and visual target-detection task. The auditory task involved detecting target noise bursts (on average 10 per minute) embedded in a continuous

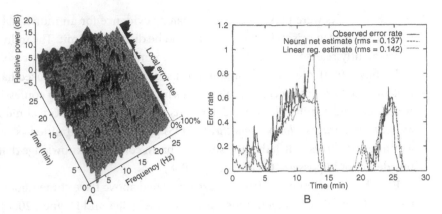

Figure 12.9. **Predicting alertness from EEG.** (A) Plot of EEG log power spectra at location Cz and error rate as a function of time during a test session. There is an increase in power, especially near 4–6 Hz and 14 Hz, when the subject's error rate increases, signaling periods of reduced alertness. (B) Running estimate of error rate in a test session for the same subject as in (A), predicted from PCA-reduced EEG log spectra (see text). The 3-layer neural network provided better predictions of error rate compared to linear regression (rms = root mean square error) (adapted from Jung et al., 1997).

white-noise background. The visual task involved detecting a line of white squares embedded in a television-noise ("snow") background. The mean target rate was 1 per minute. The visual and auditory stimuli were presented simultaneously (not correlated with each other) and the subject had to press a visual or auditory response button each time a visual or auditory target was detected. EEG signals were recorded from 2 locations: central (Cz) and midway between parietal and occipital (Pz/Oz), referenced to the right earlobe. The EEG power spectrum during the task was computed for a moving window with 50% overlap, and a measure of alertness, the "local error rate," was calculated as the percentage of auditory targets (10/min) missed by the subject within a moving 33-seconds exponential time window. Error rate was based only on auditory targets and not the visual targets (whose purpose was mainly to increase the difficulty of the task).

The researchers found a correlation between increased error rate and increased EEG log power near 4–6 Hz (theta band) for both electrodes (Figure 12.9A). They also noticed sharp increases in EEG power for electrode Cz near 14 Hz, related to the "sleep spindling" frequency, during peak error rate periods.

To ascertain whether alertness could be predicted in real time based on EEG from just 2 electrodes, the researchers applied PCA (Section 4.5.2) to the EEG log power spectra from each electrode and extracted the first 4 eigenvectors. Input EEG log spectral vectors were projected onto these 4 eigenvectors, and the resulting eight-dimensional feature vectors (4 PCA features from each electrode) were used as input to a neural network and a linear regression algorithm (Chapter 5). These were trained to map the EEG log power spectrum at any point in time to the corresponding error rate based on training data from one session. The algorithms were then tested on data from a different session (Figure 12.9B). The researchers found that a 3-layer neural network (Section 5.2.2) with 3 hidden units predicted the error rate better than linear regression, as measured by the root mean square error between predicted and actual error rates in the test session ("rms" in Figure 12.9B). In a more recent follow-up study, Liang, Jung, and colleagues (2005) measured the level of alertness of drivers in a 45-minute highway-driving task using a virtual-reality-based driving simulator. Alertness level was indirectly quantified as the deviation between the center of the vehicle from the center of the cruising lane: when the driver is drowsy (checked from video and self-reports), deviation increased and vice versa. The researchers showed that log EEG power, PCA, and linear regression can be used to estimate the driver's alertness level from EEG (Liang et al., 2005).

The Berlin BCI group (Section 9.1.1) has also explored the application of BCI technology to monitoring task engagement and alertness (Blankertz et al., 2010). Their experiment simulated a security surveillance system that required sustained attention in a monotonous task where subjects rated 2,000 simulated X-ray images of luggage as either dangerous or harmless by pressing keys with the left or right index finger (see Figure 12.10A for example images). There were a lot more "harmless" than "dangerous" images (oddball paradigm), and each trial lasted about 0.5 seconds. The goal was to use EEG to recognize and predict mental states that correlate with a high or a low number of performance errors of the subject. EEG was recorded from 128 channels, and a Laplacian spatial filter (Section 4.5.1) was applied to the channels. 8–13 Hz band power values were computed from 2 second windows, and these features from all channels were concatenated to get an input vector for an LDA classifier (Section 5.1.1). To obtain training data, the number of errors made by the subject across trials was smoothed over time to obtain an "error index" (Figure 12.10B). A high and a low threshold on the error index yielded the class labels of "high concentration" versus "low concentration." The output of the classifier was interpreted as a *concentration insufficiency index* (CII), with high values corresponding to more errors and hence lower concentration and alertness.

The researchers found that decreased concentration was correlated with an increase of power in the 8–13Hz (alpha) band. The CII values output by the classifier based on EEG data correlated well with the subject's true error index, predicting the increase in errors (decreased alertness) over time inside each block of trials and predicting more errors for later blocks (Figure 12.10B).

These results suggest that it may be possible to develop noninvasive BCIs for monitoring alertness by tracking changes in EEG power in particular frequency bands. However, most of these studies have been conducted under laboratory conditions. It remains to be seen if the ability of these techniques to predict alertness levels can be replicated in real-world conditions, such as those experienced by truck drivers or security personnel when on duty.

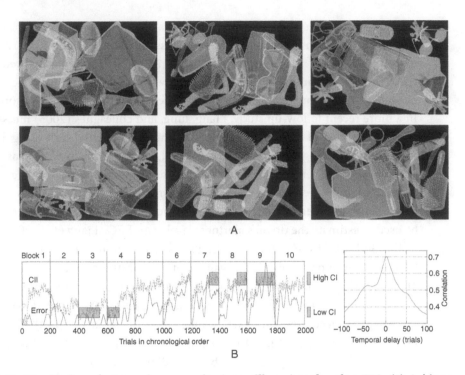

Figure 12.10. **Monitoring alertness in a security (surveillance) task using EEG.** (A) Subjects were asked to indicate whether a (simulated) X-ray image of a suitcase was harmless or danger-ous (contained a weapon). The upper row shows examples of images that do not contain a weapon and the lower row images contain a weapon (machine gun, knife, and axe). (B) Left: Plot of the output of the classifier ("concentration insufficiency index" or CII; dotted curve) and the error index (solid line) for a subject across blocks of trials. The error index (number of errors smoothed over time) indirectly reflects lack of alertness. Right: Correlation coefficient between the CII and error index for different time shifts. There appears to be increased correlation even before the error appears, suggesting a possible predictive capac-ity of the classifier (adapted from Blankertz et al., 2010).

12.2.6 Estimating Cognitive Load

When designing devices and systems to be operated by humans, it is important that the cognitive load placed on the user be kept to a manageable level and for the sys-tem to adapt in case the load becomes too high. For example, if a car manufacturer intends to redesign the driver's console or add new features, it is important to know whether the new console increases the driver's cognitive load to the point that it hinders driving. Additionally, if the driver's cognitive load can be estimated in real time, it could be used to reduce potential distractions (such as turning off an enter-tainment system) automatically when the load becomes high (e.g., due to hazardous road conditions).

Researchers have explored the use of noninvasive BCIs for monitoring cognitive load during the performance of a task under laboratory conditions. Grimes, Tan,

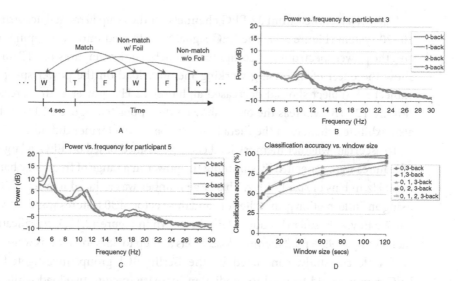

Figure 12.11. **Measuring cognitive load using EEG.** (See color plates for the same figure in color) (A) Schematic depiction of a 3-back task. The subject must match the current stimulus with the one they saw 3 stimuli ago. Examples of a match and 2 non-matches are shown. A foil is a stimulus within the last 2 that matches the current. Subjects saw all 3 cases shown. (B) & (C) Power spectra for 2 subjects as a function of increasing working memory load. 3-back required storing the last 3 items seen in memory whereas in 0-back, only the very first item seen in the series needed to be memorized and compared to the current one. Increasing the amount of memory (0-back to 3-back) decreased alpha (8–12 Hz) power in one subject (B) while increasing it in the other (C) (along with increasing theta, 4–8 Hz, power). (D) Classification of memory load based on EEG. Different curves correspond to discriminating between different amounts of load. Increasing the size of the window of EEG data used for classification increased accuracy to levels of up to 99% in some cases (adapted from Grimes et al., 2008).

and colleagues (2008) explored using EEG to classify different amounts of cognitive (or working memory) load when subjects performed a task known as the *n-back* task. In this task, subjects saw a sequence of stimuli (e.g. letters), one at a time (Figure 12.11A) and pressed the left or right arrow key to indicate whether or not the stimulus was the same as or different from the one that they saw n stimuli ago ($n = 1, 2, 3, \ldots$).

Figure 12.11A shows an example of a 3-back task. Each letter (from a set of 8 possible letters) was shown for 1 second followed by a blank screen for 3 seconds during which the subject made a decision, before the next letter appeared. Note that for each trial, the subject needed to remember the last n stimuli, perform a matching task, and then update the sequence in memory with the new stimulus. Task difficulty could thus be increased by increasing the value of n which requires keeping more items in working memory. In addition to letters, experiments were also conducted using images and spatial locations as stimuli.

Data was recorded from 32 EEG channels on the scalp arranged according to the 10–20 system (Figure 3.7). The EEG signal was divided into overlapping windows, and the power spectrum was computed for each window. Figures 12.11B and 12.11C show the effect of increasing working memory load on the power spectrum of 2 subjects: 1 subject showed decreased alpha (8–12 Hz) power with increasing load (Figure 12.11B) whereas the other showed the opposite (Figure 12.11C). The latter also exhibited changes in the theta (4–8 Hz) band; the former did not.

To ascertain whether memory load can be classified based on EEG, a large number of features were generated by summing the power in a range of frequency bands, from 4–50 Hz in bins of size 1–4 Hz. This large number was reduced to a set of 30 features using an "information gain" criterion, and this vector of 30 features was used as input to a naïve Bayes classifier (Section 5.1.3). As shown in Figure 12.11D, classification accuracies of up to 99% for 2 memory load levels and up to 88% for 4 levels were achieved.

A different study, conducted by the Berlin BCI group, investigated whether EEG signals could be used to predict an increase in cognitive load while a subject was driving on a public German highway (B10 between Esslingen am Neckar and Wendlingen) at a speed of 100 km/hr (Blankertz et al., 2010). A secondary task was introduced to mimic interaction with an electronic device: the driver had to press 1 of 2 buttons mounted on the left and right index fingers in response to a "left" or "right" vocal prompt. Finally, in every second block of 2 minutes, an increase in cognitive load was introduced by asking the subject to perform 1 of 2 tertiary tasks (Figure 12.12A): a mental calculation (successively subtracting a fixed number (the number 27) from a random number between 800 and 999) or an auditory comprehension task (following the story in an audiobook while ignoring a simultaneous news broadcast and then answering a question pertinent to the story).

LDA classifiers based on subject-specific frequency bands, spatial filters, and EEG channels were used for classifying high versus low cognitive load (extra task versus no extra task, respectively) during driving. After training, these classifiers were able to continuously predict high versus low cognitive load periods (see Figure 12.12B) with an average accuracy of around 70% and a best detection result of around 95.6%. The output of the classifier was used to implement a "mitigation" strategy: whenever the classifier predicted mental workload as being high, the secondary task ("left" vs. "right" button press on vocal prompt) was turned off, which resulted in faster reaction times in the tertiary task (Kohlmorgen et al., 2007).

These results illustrate the possibility of developing a "mental workload-detecting" BCI that can intervene whenever the user's cognitive load becomes high, automatically turning off nonessential options and even potentially taking over some of the functions under the user's control.

12.2.7 Education and Learning

We have already discussed how noninvasive BCI techniques are useful in measuring the level of alertness and cognitive load during the performance of a task. Similar

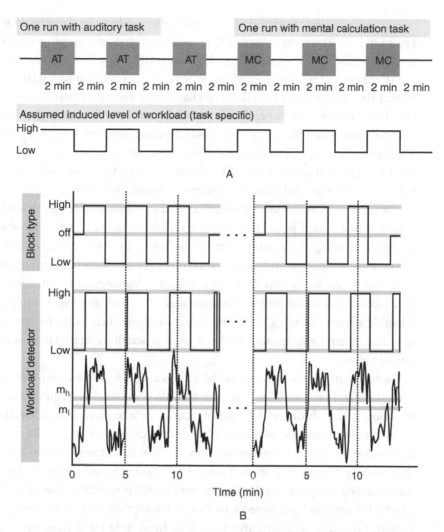

Figure 12.12. **Detecting cognitive load during a driving task using EEG.** (A) Schematic diagram of the experimental paradigm. Besides driving on a highway at 100 km/hr, the subject had to perform a secondary task involving a button press. A tertiary task involving an auditory task or mental calculation task (AT or MC) was used in blocks of 2 min (high workload condition) interleaved with blocks without a tertiary task (low workload condition). (B) The lowest trace shows the classifier output for the best performing subject while driving and performing the secondary task and the auditory tertiary task (AT). This output was thresholded to yield a continuous prediction of high or low workload (middle panel). The prediction compares well with the true high or low workload labels (upper panel) (adapted from Blankertz et al., 2010).

ideas can be applied to assess the degree of engagement, attention, and cognitive load of a student listening to a lecture or completing an assigned exercise. For example, the company Neurosky has developed a BCI application that attempts to measure the user's level of attention during a math exercise. The BCI is based on Neurosky's MindWave headset which measures EEG from a frontal dry electrode.

A recent study by Szafir and Mutlu (2012) also used a frontal electrode at location Fp1 in the 10–20 system (Figure 3.7) to monitor a student's attention level while the student listened to a Japanese folktale being recited by a humanoid robot. During the 10 minutes of robotic storytelling, whenever the system detected (from the EEG signal) that the student's attention level had fallen, the robot raised its voice or executed arm movements to regain the student's attention. The researchers found that students who heard the story from a robot whose behavior was contingent on the attention-detecting BCI were much better at answering questions about the folktale, answering an average of 9 out of 14 questions correctly, compared to students for whom the robot did not exhibit attention-contingent behavior.

The early results discussed above, if verified in subsequent in-depth studies, indicate that BCIs could potentially provide valuable feedback to educators as well as students, allowing appropriate steps to be taken to tailor educational strategies, interaction paradigms, and lessons according to each student's current attentional state and needs. Being able to detect a student's engagement or attention level can be especially useful for online educational efforts (such as those being pursued by Khan Academy, Coursera, EdX, and Udacity) where there is no human teacher to gauge a student's engagement as the student is watching material presented in an online video.

Students can additionally use the BCI as an assistive device to improve their concentration and performance. The BCI may also be useful in helping students with attention-deficit disorders by catching lapses of attention and redirecting focus. As advances in neuroscience provide a deeper understanding of the mechanisms involved in learning and comprehension, one can expect new BCIs to be developed that leverage these advances and accelerate learning by adapting to each student's learning style and pace. Teachers and parents could potentially determine the degree to which a student has learned a particular concept directly from changes in brain signals, providing an alternative to standardized tests for measuring competency and learning.

12.2.8 Security, Identification, and Authentication

BCIs are beginning to be applied to problems in security such as biometric identification for information retrieval from databases and authentication for access control (e.g., for airport security, account login, or electronic banking).

As an example, the distinctive alpha rhythm activity from an individual's EEG signal has been proposed as a biometric signature for identification. In one study (Poulos et al., 1999), subjects were asked to relax and close their eyes while EEG was recorded from electrodes O2 and Cz in the 10–20 system (see Figure 3.7). The bipolar signal obtained from the difference between O2 and Cz was bandpass filtered in the 7.5–12.5 Hz frequency band (alpha band) using FFT and inverse FFT. An AR model of order $p = 8$ (see Section 4.4.3) was constructed for the resulting signal, and the AR parameters were used as input to a learning vector quantizer (LVQ) classifier

(Section 5.1.3). Classification accuracies between 72% and 84% were obtained for distinguishing each of 4 subjects from a pool of 75 other subjects. The usefulness of AR parameters from EEG alpha rhythms was also verified in (Paranjape et al., 2001) where accuracies of up to 85% correct were reported in identifying a subject from a pool of 40 subjects.

While identification involves recognizing one person from a large pool of individuals, the problem of authentication involves verifying whether the person claiming an identity is indeed that person or an imposter. Researchers are beginning to explore the use of EEG-based BCIs for authentication. In a study by Marcel and Millán (2007), subjects were asked to perform 1 of 3 mental tasks (imagination of left- or right-hand movements and word generation). The EEG signals were spatially filtered using a Laplacian filter (Section 4.5.1), and power spectral features in the 8–32 Hz range were extracted using the FFT (Section 4.2.3). These features were used to construct a probabilistic model of the data. Specifically, training data was collected to train a mixture-of-Gaussians model for the likelihood $P(X|C)$ that EEG feature vector X was generated by a client C and the model $P(X|NC)$ that X could have been generated by a generic non-client (imposter). The trained probabilistic model was used for authentication as follows: given a claim for client C's identity and a set of EEG features X purporting to support the claim, the system computes the log likelihood ratio: $L(X) = \log P(X|C) - \log P(X|NC)$. The claim is accepted if $L(X) \geq t$ where t is pre-chosen threshold and rejected otherwise.

The authentication method above was evaluated on 9 subjects using the half total error rate (HTER), defined as the average of the false positive rate (FPR) and the false negative rate (FNR) (see Table 5.1). An average HTER of 6.6% was obtained for the imagined left-hand movement task, with higher error rates for the other two tasks (Marcel and Millán, 2007). Such an error rate is still too high for a practical authentication system, but it is likely that other methods for recording brain signals (e.g., invasive or semi-invasive) or the combination of brain signals with other types of biometrics (e.g., voice, iris scans, or fingerprints) could yield robust and practical authentication systems in the future.

12.2.9 Physical Amplification with Exoskeletons

Many a comic-book villain has relied on amplifying the power of the human body to achieve superhuman strength (cf. Dr. Octopus in Spiderman). Powered exoskeletons offer the means to achieve amplification of the human body beyond what evolution has gifted us. While researchers have explored control mechanisms for exoskeletons based on self-generated motion or muscle signals (EMG), BCI researchers have recently begun exploring the use of brain signals to directly control an exoskeleton.

As an example, the European Mindwalker project seeks to use EEG signals recorded from custom-designed dry electrodes and recurrent neural networks to control a robotic exoskeleton attached to the subject's legs. The dual goals of the project are to enable people with spinal cord injuries to achieve mobility and to help in the recuperation of astronauts after a prolonged mission in space.

A number of companies such as Cyberdyne, Ekso Bionics, and Raytheon have developed powered exoskeletons that amplify the strength of users, allowing them to lift and carry up to 200 pounds of weight with little or no effort. In the future, full-body exoskeletons could potentially be used by rescue workers, firepersons, and soldiers to move faster, jump higher, carry heavier loads, and perform other physical feats that cannot be performed by a normal human body. These exoskeletons could potentially be controlled by brain signals, and feedback from the exoskeleton could be used to directly stimulate appropriate somatosensory centers in the brain to allow accurate control, to the extent that the exoskeleton could become incorporated as part of the body map in the user's brain.

12.2.10 Mnemonic and Cognitive Amplification

The storyline of the movie *Johnny Mnemonic* revolves around the protagonist acting as a courier with secret data implanted in his brain. Other science-fiction plots have relied on machines that can selectively inject or erase memories. These abilities have yet to be demonstrated in a BCI, but researchers have recently begun exploring the possibility of restoring memory and amplifying cognitive functions via neural recording and stimulation.

In one such set of experiments, Berger, Deadwyler, and colleagues (2011) demonstrated a brain implant in rats that can restore lost memory function and strengthen recall of new information. The rats were trained to remember which of 2 identical levers to press to receive water as reward. In each trial of this *delayed-nonmatch-to-sample* (DNMS) task, 1 of 2 levers appeared first, and the rats had to memorize this fact. After a delay of between 1 and 30 seconds, both levers appeared, and the rat had to press the lever *that was not presented earlier* to be rewarded. The researchers found that the rats learned this general rule and were able to consistently pick the correct lever.

Two electrode arrays (Figure 12.13) were then implanted in both hemispheres of each rat to record from neighboring areas, CA1 and CA3 respectively, in the hippocampus, a structure long implicated in the formation of new memories. The dynamics underlying spike-train-to-spike-train transformations from CA3 to CA1 as the rats solved the task were modeled using a set of nonlinear filtering equations. These equations were used to predict output firing patterns of CA1 from input patterns of CA3 neural activity. In a subsequent trial, the researchers used a drug (glutamatergic antagonist MK801) to suppress activity in CA3 and CA1 (Figure 12.14A). Though the rats still remembered the general rule (push the opposite lever of the one that first appeared), the rats performed poorly because, in the absence of CA3/CA1 activity, they presumably could not remember which lever appeared first.

The researchers then stimulated CA1 with electrical pulse patterns derived from the nonlinear filtering model based on previous successful trials. The CA1 stimulation

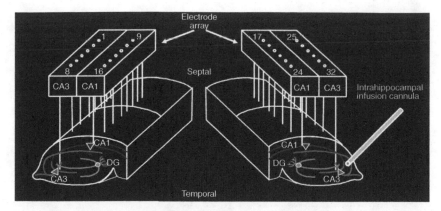

Figure 12.13. **BCI for restoring and enhancing memory.** Two identical array electrodes, each consisting of 2 parallel rows of 20-micron steel wires, were implanted in the CA3 and CA1 regions of the hippocampus in both hemispheres. For memory restoration and enhancement (see text), CA1 was stimulated with patterns derived from previous trials. The "cannula" was used in the experiments to deliver a drug to block neural activity and prevent memory formation in order to test the implant (adapted from Berger et al., 2011).

caused the rats' performance to improve significantly, reaching levels close to normal performance (Figure 12.14A). The implant thus effectively substituted for the CA3–CA1 transformation, restoring lost mnemonic function. Additionally, the researchers found that even rats that did not receive the activity-suppressing drug sometimes performed poorly in trials in which they had to maintain the memory of the initial lever for long durations (> 10s). By stimulating CA1 neurons with patterns derived from previous high-performance trials, the researchers were able to *enhance* the rats' memory and significantly improve their performance for these longer duration trials (Figure 12.14B).

Although yet to be tested in humans, memory implants such as these offer a ray of hope for those suffering from Alzheimer's, amnesia, and other devastating memory disorders. Additionally, the ability to store and amplify certain memories opens the door to new forms of memory enhancement and cognitive amplification for able-bodied individuals. For example, memories could be stored offline (e.g., on the "cloud") and retrieved on an as-needed basis through wireless implants. Although humans today routinely use the Internet, books, smartphones, computers, and other devices as external memory stores, memory implants would make accessing such information essentially seamless by enabling storage and retrieval through thought alone. The important issues of safety, security, and privacy engendered by such technology are discussed in the next chapter.

12.2.11 Applications in Space

Astronauts could benefit from BCIs that augment their physical abilities (Rossini et al., 2009). For example, a BCI could help in operating tools or robotic devices

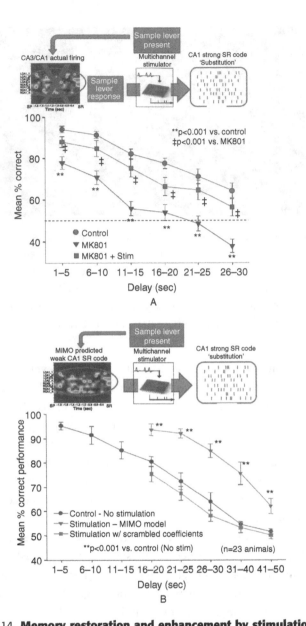

Figure 12.14. **Memory restoration and enhancement by stimulation of hippocampal area CA1.** (A) Top panel depicts the experimental paradigm for memory restoration. CA3/CA1 activity was blocked using a drug (MK801) and the implanted array was to stimulate CA1 neurons with electrical pulse patterns ("CA1 strong SR code") derived from previous high-performance trials. The bottom panel shows the increase in performance (% trials correctly performed) with stimulation by the implant ("MK801 + Stim") as a function of the time ("Delay") that the sample lever has to be kept in memory. (B) Top panel: Experimental paradigm for memory enhancement. In trials in which poor performance was predicted due to a "weak CA1 SR code," CA1 was stimulated with electrical pulse patterns derived from previous high-performance trials ("CA1 strong SR code"). The bottom panel shows that CA1 stimulation significantly increased the performance of the rat compared to the "no stimulation" condition, suggesting that the effect of stimulation was to enhance the rat's ability to store task-relevant information in memory for the longer duration trials (adapted from Berger et al., 2011).

when an astronaut's hands are otherwise occupied while he or she is performing a space walk to repair a space station module. BCIs could also be used by recuperating astronauts in conjunction with exoskeletons after long space missions. Additionally, BCI-controlled exoskeletons could be used in space exploration, for example, to walk on uneven terrain or counter the effects of gravity.

An important question regarding the potential use of BCIs in space is whether zero gravity alters the brain signals of competent BCI users to the point where these users can no longer control a device they were previously able to control on earth. Millán and colleagues (2009) investigated this question by recording EEG signals in 2 experienced BCI users during parabolic flight on a jet airplane on earth. Subjects experienced 5 different gravity conditions lasting 20 seconds each during each parabola of the flight in the following sequence: normal gravity (1g), hypergravity (1.8g), zero gravity (0g), hypergravity (1.8g), and normal gravity (1g). Subjects performed 2 mental tasks: imagination of left-hand movements and a word-association task involving mentally searching for words beginning with a randomly chosen letter. The researchers found that the different gravity conditions did not alter either the frequency bands or the electrode locations that were previously found to be relevant to the 2 tasks when performed on the ground (Millán et al., 2009).

These early results are promising, but it remains to be seen whether online BCI control can be achieved in space, especially when the astronaut is simultaneously engaged in other activities and movements. Another challenge that will need to be addressed is designing BCIs that can adapt to the neural plasticity in the brain caused by long-term exposure to zero gravity.

12.2.12 Gaming and Entertainment

Many traditional BCI paradigms (e.g., cursor control) have a game-like flavor. For medical applications such as menu selection or rehabilitation based on neurofeedback, using a game-like interaction paradigm helps in sustaining the interest of the patient. These applications were not designed with entertainment purposes in mind, but gaming for able-bodied individuals is nonetheless one of the most rapidly growing nonmedical application areas of BCI. One reason for this growth is the huge market that currently exists for video games, dwarfing the market for medical applications of BCIs. A second reason is that unlike in medical applications such as BCI-controlled wheelchairs or prosthetics, faulty performance of a BCI in a game may annoy a user but typically does not cause bodily harm or injury to either the user or individuals nearby, thereby lessening concerns of liability. Finally, BCIs can be used in gaming as an interface that augments other more traditional interfaces such as joysticks, gamepads, gesture recognition systems, and so forth. Thus, unlike medical BCI applications such as communication systems for locked-in patients, BCIs for gaming may actively rely on a mixture of brain signals (e.g., EEG), muscle signals (EMG), and hand/body movements to achieve a novel mode of human-computer interaction.

In one of the first studies exploring this direction, Cheung, Rao, and colleagues (2012) demonstrated that subjects could control the two-dimensional motion of a

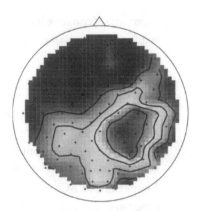

Figure 12.15. **EEG BCI for the game of Tetris.** Left: User playing the BCI-controlled Tetris game. Left- or right-hand motor imagery is used to move a falling piece to the left or right respectively, mental rotation to rotate it clockwise and foot motor imagery to let it drop. Right: Cortical activation map when the subject engages in mental rotation to rotate a Tetris piece. The activation map shows event-related desynchronization (ERD; see Section 9.1.1) in the beta band (here, 18–24 Hz) in the right parietal cortex, which is consistent with previous findings from mental rotation tasks (from Blankertz et al., 2010).

cursor using a joystick simultaneously with hand motor imagery in an EEG BCI. Subjects learned to use imagery to control the up-down motion of the cursor and simultaneously used the joystick to the control the cursor's left-right motion. These results suggest that it may be possible to use BCIs to augment normal motor capabilities in able-bodied individuals.

A large number of brain-controlled games have been introduced over the past decade or so. Brainball (Hjelm and Browall, 2000) was an early BCI game where users learned to control their relaxation level by controlling their alpha rhythm (Section 3.1.2). MindGame (Finke et al., 2009) is a more recent game based on the P300 (Section 9.1.4) that involves moving a character on a three-dimensional game board. Other game applications have relied on SSVEP (Lalor et al., 2005) and motor imagery (e.g., BCI-PacMac; see Krepki et al., 2007) as well as EEG-based virtual navigation (Scherer et al., 2008). An interesting demonstration of real-time control of a physical gaming device involved a BCI-controlled pinball machine (Tangermann et al., 2009) where the paddle was controlled by a 2-class BCI based on imagery (e.g., left- and right-hand motor imagery). The BCI parameters were tuned individually for each user. The researchers reported that the game was perceived as highly immersive and motivating.

There has also been a BCI-controlled version of the popular video game Tetris (Blankertz et al., 2010). The EEG-based BCI game relies on a "natural" set of controls: the gamer uses left- or right-hand motor imagery to move a falling Tetris piece to the left or right respectively, mental rotation to rotate the piece clockwise, and foot motor imagery to drop the piece (Figure 12.15). A 4-class classifier

(3 motor imagery commands and mental rotation) was trained in an offline calibration phase and then applied online during the gaming phase to achieve control of a falling piece.

Several commercial systems have recently appeared on the market that attempt to measure EEG-like signals from the scalp. These systems typically use a small number of dry electrodes (in contrast to traditional "wet" EEG electrodes that require gel to make contact with the scalp). The measurements made by these dry electrodes are used to control objects on a computer screen or real objects such as a foam ball. Examples include systems manufactured by Emotiv (EPOC headset) and Neurosky (MindWave headset), and toys such as Mindflex by Mattel. These new systems are a lot cheaper than traditional gel-based EEG systems used in research and clinical settings and are easier to wear and operate. However, one problem with these new systems is that there is no guarantee that they are capturing true EEG signals. In uncontrolled settings, such systems may be capturing a mix of EEG and EMG activity caused by facial and neck muscle activation, eye movements, changes in skin resistance, or in some cases, even electrical noise. On the other hand, as mentioned above, the use of a hybrid EEG/EMG or other type of voluntarily generated signal may be fine for gaming applications if it constitutes a novel and potentially entertaining mode of control in a game.

12.2.13 Brain-Controlled Art

There is a tremendous potential for BCIs to enhance the way humans can enjoy the arts. For example, BCIs can be used as a vehicle to create art, as exemplified by the fNIR-based sketch drawing program created by Mappus, Jackson, and colleagues (2009) discussed in Section 9.2.3.

More interestingly, BCIs can be used to close the loop between an art installation and a user's experience of the same art. In particular, as the user begins experiencing the art, his or her brain signals can be used to change appropriate elements of the art installation, initiating a novel interaction between the human and the work of art. This turns experiencing art on its head by making the work of art dynamic, rather than the classic static work of art that hangs on a wall in a museum or art gallery. The artist's job becomes one of anticipating the various ways in which an observer might react to the work of art and incorporate the ability for the work of art to adapt to the observer's brain signals on an ongoing basis. One can also imagine the work of art responding to brain signals from multiple observers experiencing the artwork at the same time.

An early example of brain-controlled art is a participatory theatrical performance titled "The Ascent" and created by Yehuda Duenyas. It debuted at the Experimental Media and Performing Arts Center at Rensselaer Polytechnic Institute in New York on May 12, 2011. The interactive art installation is experienced by a participant and an audience who watch from an observation deck. The participant wears a three-dimensional theatrical flying harness and a dry electrode headset (the EPOC

Figure 12.16. **Brain-controlled performance art "The Ascent."** The performer is levitated in the air by a harness controlled by brain signals, triggering a dynamically changing display of sound and light (image from http://news.rpi.edu/update.do?artcenterkey=2866).

headset manufactured by Emotiv). Signals from the headset are used to control the harness, allowing the performer to "ascend" by modulating the recorded signals (Figure 12.16). The BCI works by detecting alpha and theta band oscillations in EEG (see Section 3.1.2). When a performer closes his or her eyes and relaxes, there is typically an increase in alpha band power and a decrease in theta. These events are detected by the BCI and used as a trigger to elevate the performer more than 30 feet into the air through dynamically responsive displays of sound and light. The performance thus incorporates the paradox that the performer's calm mental state generates a spectacle of light and sound. As described on the art installation's Web site, theascent.co, "As an audience watches, the rider's concentration begins to lift her into the air. A storm of stimuli conspires to distract her from reaching her goal: levitating into 'transcendence' and 'winning' by unleashing a climactic, firework-filled, grand-prize explosion, immortalizing the rider in an ephemeral blinding moment of super-human glory."

12.3 Summary

From the diversity of BCI applications we have reviewed in this chapter, it seems that we are limited only by our imagination when it comes to developing new ways of harnessing the power of BCIs. The field in many ways owes its genesis to the promise offered by medical applications such as developing implants for the deaf (the cochlear implant), neural prosthetics for the paralyzed (such as the BrainGate implant discussed in Section 7.3.1), and electrical stimulators for treating the symptoms of debilitating motor diseases such as Parkinson's (deep brain stimulation or DBS). Faster computers and cheaper noninvasive recording systems for EEG and fNIR have opened the door to an increasing number of nonmedical applications for able-bodied individuals, ranging from BCIs for security, education, and gaming to robotic avatars, lie detection, and physical, sensory, or cognitive augmentation. The proliferation of BCI applications also makes it imperative that we address the many ethical and moral issues engendered by these disruptive technologies. We discuss some of these issues in the next chapter.

12.4 Questions and Exercises

1. Enumerate four applications of BCI technology to sensory and motor restoration. For each, specify whether these applications are clinically available, and if not, describe why not.
2. What are some of the possible applications of BCIs for cognitive restoration?
3. (✳ Expedition) Read some of the references cited in Section 12.1.4. Write a brief essay on the various ways in which BCI technology could be used to speed up rehabilitation and recovery from stroke or surgery.
4. Compare the advantages and disadvantages of the two main approaches to BCI-based communication for locked-in patients: cursor-controlled menu systems based on oscillatory potentials versus spellers based on stimulus-evoked potentials such as P300.
5. Compare and contrast the following approaches to brain-controlled wheelchairs: hierarchical BCIs versus shared control. What are some of the obstacles to making such wheelchairs available for day-to-day use in the real world?
6. The BCI-controlled Web browser Nessi uses binary selection via SCPs to prune away links until the user's desired link is selected. Discuss the strengths and weaknesses of this approach to browsing and suggest an alternate scheme based on either oscillatory potentials or evoked potentials.
7. The Graz BCI allows self-paced navigation of Google Earth using imagery. Describe how the system uses multiple LDA classifiers to achieve this self-paced operation.
8. Describe how the soft margin SVM was used in the P300-based robotic avatar application described in Section 12.2.2.

9. What are some of the advantages and drawbacks of using evoked potentials such as P300 for controlling a robotic avatar? Describe how some of the drawbacks could be addressed using oscillatory potentials and/or hierarchical BCIs.

10. What is cortically coupled computer vision (CCCV) and what is its purpose? What is the role of the following in CCCV?
    a. RSVP
    b. P300
    c. LDA

11. Describe how evoked potentials can be used for "lie detection" or detection of "guilty knowledge." Compare this approach to the traditional method of polygraphy.

12. (⋔ Expedition) Read articles that have been published recently on "brain finger-printing" and memory detection (see Section 12.2.4). What are some of the aspects of the proposed technology that have engendered controversy and why?

13. Describe how changes in EEG power could potentially be used to monitor alertness during driving or surveillance. What are some of the obstacles to practical application of the technique to real-world scenarios?

14. What is the n-back task and why is it useful for studying memory load? How well can memory load in the n-back task be predicted using EEG? Is there a single EEG frequency band whose power varies with memory load, or is the phenomenon subject-specific?

15. Describe the signal processing and machine-learning techniques used by the Berlin BCI group to predict cognitive load in their highway-driving task. Discuss whether the system that was used is practical enough for commercial applications.

16. Discuss the ways in which BCIs could be used in education and learning, focusing on the following aspects:
    a. Gauging student engagement and focus
    b. Customizing presentation of material
    c. Evaluation and testing

17. Explain the difference between the problems of identification and authentication in security. How can BCIs be used for these two problems? Provide details on the type of tasks used, and the signal-processing and machine-learning algorithms that have been explored. Describe the performance reported for these systems and comment on whether they are ready for use in real-world applications.

18. (⋔ Expedition) Read about the current state-of-the-art technology in powered exoskeletons (e.g., the systems being developed by Cyberdyne, Ekso Bionics, and Raytheon) and write an essay describing their capabilities, mode of control, and feedback (if any) provided to the user. Then discuss whether and how these exoskeletons could potentially be controlled using (i) muscle signals (EMG), (ii) noninvasively recorded brain signals such as EEG, (iii) nerve signals (e.g., from the limbs), and (iv) invasive brain signals (e.g., spiking activity from multielectrode arrays).

19. Describe the experiment performed by Berger and colleagues to demonstrate their implant for restoration and enhancement of memory function (Section 12.2.10). How was memory storage of task-relevant information prevented experimentally, and how was performance restored using the implant? In other rats with normally functioning memory circuits, how was memory performance enhanced?

20. Discuss three ways in which BCIs could be used by astronauts in space or on earth. Is there any evidence for or against the claim that zero gravity can have detrimental effects on BCI performance?

21. (∦ Expedition) Compare and contrast currently available commercial dry electrode systems such as those being manufactured by Emotiv and Neurosky in terms of number of electrodes, electrode locations, cost, portability, and infrastructure provided for software development. Then, pick your favorite video game and explain how one of the degrees of control in the game could be replaced with input from a commercial dry electrode system. Make sure your proposed control paradigm takes into account the electrode locations available in the device as well as any potential interference due to muscle activation.

22. Section 12.2.13 described "The Ascent," an example of BCI-controlled performance art. Propose BCIs for enhancing the experience of the following forms of art for the artist and/or the audience:
    a. Painting
    b. Music
    c. Theater
    d. Literature

13

Ethics of Brain-Computer Interfacing

Among the most important aspects of brain-computer interfacing are ethical issues – issues pertaining to the medical use of BCIs, the use of BCIs for human augmentation and other applications, and the potential for their misuse. Some of these issues fall under the rubric of *neuroethics*, but other issues are specific to technological aspects of BCIs.

BCI conferences and workshops sometimes include sessions on ethics, and there have been several articles discussing ethical aspects of BCIs and neural interfaces (e.g., Clausen, 2009; Haselager et al., 2009; Tamburrini, 2009; Salvini et al., 2008; Warwick, 2003). However, there are currently no official regulations or guidelines on BCI use, aside from conventional laws regarding medical and legal ethics. As with other technologies in the past, one can expect that as BCIs become more prevalent in society, laws and ethics pertaining to BCI use will likely be codified by medical and governmental regulatory agencies. In the meantime, this chapter surveys the variety of ethical issues and dilemmas surrounding BCI research and BCI use.

13.1 Medical, Health, and Safety Issues

13.1.1 Balancing Risks versus Benefits

Perhaps the most important issue concerning the use of BCIs by any particular user is whether the risks associated with the BCI are acceptable compared to the benefits to be gained from its use. This issue becomes especially critical when the BCI is invasive, and the risk of damage or infection is non-negligible. For patients who are considering a BCI for improving their quality of life, the questions are similar to those ones faced by patients deciding on potentially risky surgical interventions such as an organ transplant or a heart pacemaker implant. In fact, such a risk-benefit analysis is already part of the protocol used in hospitals today to determine whether a BCI, such as a cochlear implant or a deep brain stimulator, should be implanted. As other types of BCIs are developed and commercialized, the protocols used for cochlear implants and DBS could potentially be modified to apply to these new types of invasive BCIs.

In general, the company designing a BCI and the doctor who will implant it can be expected to advise the patient about the risks and benefits associated with the device. The decision to opt for the implant would ultimately rest with the patient and the family of the patient, as with other medical procedures today. Questions to consider include the potential side effects of BCI use, the potential for patient expectations not being met, and the effect of BCI use on family and caregivers.

Another dimension to consider in a risk-benefit analysis is whether a noninvasive BCI might be sufficient for a particular subject instead of an invasive option so as to mitigate the risks. We have seen in previous chapters that noninvasive BCIs may be inferior to invasive BCIs in terms of performance and duration. The relevant question then would be: does the increase in performance provided by an invasive BCI justify, for this particular subject, the increase in risk associated with invasive BCIs? The broader guidelines for clinical use of invasive BCIs will ultimately need to be set by government regulatory agencies after a thorough assessment of the efficacy and safety of each implantable device.

13.1.2 Informed Consent

An important aspect of the use of BCIs for both medical and nonmedical purposes is to ensure that informed consent has been obtained from the subject – that is, the subject has been made aware of:

- the risks and benefits associated with the BCI technology being suggested versus alternatives,
- the information being extracted from the brain, and
- the consequences of extracting this information: could it lead to embarrassment or, worse, legal consequences such as incrimination?

As with other experiments involving humans, the subject must have the freedom to end BCI use at any time. Complications may arise in some cases:

(a) in the case of children, is it sufficient to get consent from the parents?
(b) in the case of locked-in patients who are unable to communicate, who should give informed consent? (Is informed consent from a caregiver sufficient?) and
(c) can consent be obtained from patients suffering from cognitive deficits that prevent them from fully understanding the risks versus benefits?

13.2 Abuse of BCI Technology

Like any new technology, BCIs can and probably will be abused for a variety of purposes, ranging from crime, war, and terrorism to subverting the law and manipulating brain processes for profit. Physical augmentation (e.g., neurally-controlled exoskeletons, vehicles, and weapons) will potentially change the way crime or terrorism is committed and wars are fought. Marketing agencies could attempt to manipulate customers through subliminal advertising during BCI use ("neuromarketing").

Additionally, consider the fact that in the not-too-distant future, one may see the commercialization of sophisticated, wireless BCIs that can both record and stimulate the brain. The advent of such BCIs will bring with it the potential for some alarming scenarios, potentially turning science fiction to reality. In particular, wireless communication from or to a brain could be intercepted if encryption is not used or if the encryption method used is not sufficiently strong. Such interception of brain signals could potentially lead to:

- **Mind reading or "brain tapping"**: Depending on the type of signals being transmitted from the brain, a person's thoughts, reflections, and beliefs could be intercepted, recorded, and exploited by criminals, terrorists, commercial enterprises, and spy agencies as well as legal, law enforcement, and military entities.
- **Coercion or "mind control"**: The ability of a BCI to stimulate a user's brain opens up the dangerous possibility that the BCI may be hijacked and used to coerce a person to perform objectionable acts (e.g., commit a crime or sign a document such as a will).
- **Memory manipulation**: A BCI that can stimulate the brain could also potentially be hijacked to selectively erase memories or write in false memories, leading to the possibility of "brainwashing."
- **Viruses**: Malicious entities could send a "virus" as part of a communication from a machine, resulting in cognitive impairment or cognitive manipulation.

These possibilities place utmost importance on the need for extremely secure channels for BCI communications as well as security algorithms that can detect a breach and take the necessary preventative actions. We delve into the issue of BCI security and privacy in more detail in the next section.

BCI technology could also be tampered with to bias an outcome. For example, "brain fingerprinting" methods for lie detection could potentially be manipulated to align an outcome in favor of or against a defendant. BCIs for human augmentation could be tampered with to cause significant harm to the user and/or other individuals and property. Once again, such scenarios can be minimized if sufficiently strong security measures are put in place.

13.3 BCI Security and Privacy

Surreptitious mind reading and "brain hacking" have been popular topics in many science-fiction novels and movies. However, even in present-day BCI research, it is important to consider the question of security and privacy: What kind of neural data is being recorded in an experiment? Could the data reveal something personal that the subject may not want revealed? Will the data be stored and, if so, for how long and for what purpose? Will a subject's data be shared with other researchers? Such questions are typically part of the human subjects review process conducted by the Institutional Review Board (IRB) at research institutions. Experiments are approved only if they meet national (or international) guidelines for ethical human subjects research.

We have already discussed the potential for unprecedented abuse and malicious attacks on future wireless BCIs that can record and stimulate a brain in sophisticated ways. Before the deployment of such BCIs, it is therefore imperative that strong legal and technological safeguards are put in place. Activities that violate BCI security and privacy should be made illegal, with stringent punishments for breaking the law. Encryption techniques and security methods will need to have much stronger guarantees against attacks than current techniques and methods, given that the consequences of a successful attack can be quite devastating to the BCI user. An opportunity exists for new research into possible hybrid security techniques that rely on both neural mechanisms and computer algorithms to safeguard against attacks and invasion of privacy during BCI use. Approaches to security (e.g., Gollakota et al., 2011; Paul et al., 2011) in implantable biomedical devices such as insulin pumps and heart pacemakers may also be relevant to BCIs, but their applicability to BCI security and "neurosecurity" (Denning et al., 2009) in general has not yet been fully explored.

13.4 Legal Issues

A host of new legal issues will need to be tackled as BCI use becomes widespread. First, as mentioned, lawmakers will need to pass sufficiently nuanced legislation to prescribe what type of BCI-related activities are legal and what are not. Courts will need to decide who should be responsible for unlawful acts involving a BCI, the fundamental question being where does the human end and the machine begin? Since BCIs will likely possess a degree of autonomy and the ability to learn, it may not be clear if the law was broken due to a voluntary command issued by the BCI user or if the BCI autonomously performed the action at a subconscious level for the user.

One way to resolve this issue is to place the responsibility entirely on users by asking them to sign a waiver before using the BCI, absolving the BCI company from liability except for manufacturing defects. This is similar to the situation of a human driving a car, where the manufacturer is not held liable for injury caused by a driver unless the injury was due to a manufacturing defect in the car. However, things may not be as clear cut in the case of BCIs (or adaptive systems in general) because it could be argued that the manufacturer should be held liable not only for bugs in the software, but also for unforeseen consequences resulting from a self-learning and adaptive BCI. Clearly, there is a need for discussion, followed by appropriate changes to the current set of laws governing liability and insurance to make them apply to the case of users operating BCIs.

13.5 Moral and Social Justice Issues

Whether or not a BCI should even be used can become a moral dilemma, as seen in the case of the cochlear implant. Many in the deaf community have rejected cochlear implants because they do not regard deafness as a disability. For them, deafness is an integral part of who they are and their culture. The moral question thus becomes whether deafness should even be considered a "disease" that requires "treatment." If it is not, then there is no need for parents of a deaf child to obtain a cochlear implant for their child. The opposing viewpoint contends that willfully depriving a child of a cochlear implant is unethical because this decision deprives the child of the opportunity to learn to speak, hear, and enjoy aspects of human life such as music.

A number of moral issues arise when BCIs are used for augmenting the physical and mental capabilities of able-bodied human beings. First, the integration of a BCI into the brain fundamentally redefines what it means to be human. Over the course of more than 500 million years, evolution sculpted the brain to control the biological body for interaction with the physical environment. BCIs have now opened the door for the brain to directly exert control over objects in the environment without using the body as an intermediary. How will this escape from the limitations imposed by our biological bodies shape human evolution? Cyborgs have been a staple of science fiction for a long time, but will some humans forego the advantages of augmenting their physical and mental capabilities and choose to live a BCI-free existence or become "BCI luddites?"

The fact that BCIs in the future could allow mnemonic, sensory, and physical augmentation leads to the possibility that society may be divided along the lines of a new type of "haves" and "have-nots." For example, the rich might have their children implanted at an early age to give them an edge in mental and/or physical capabilities. Those who are unable to afford such implants will certainly be left behind with potentially drastic social consequences. This could lead to a much greater divide between the rich and the poor. Similarly, nations that can equip their citizens and soldiers with BCIs would have a distinct advantage over nations that are unable to do so, potentially leading to a bigger divide between developed and underdeveloped countries.

These important social justice issues need to be addressed well before powerful augmentative BCIs are developed and go on the market. One potential solution is for governments to subsidize certain basic types of BCIs for those who otherwise would not be able to afford them – this would be similar to government programs in many countries today that provide free public education and healthcare for all citizens. However, there is still the distinct possibility that market forces will put some of the higher-end BCIs out of reach of many people.

Another moral dilemma arises from the observation that to be proficient in operating a sophisticated, general-purpose BCI, a person will need to start at an early age, very likely as a child. Parents will thus be faced with the difficult decision of whether or not to implant their child with a BCI to augment the child's future mental and/or physical capabilities. Is it ethical for parents to decide what type of augmentation a child should have? Is it ethical for them to opt out of implanting a BCI in their child, potentially leaving the child at a significant disadvantage compared to implanted children?

Finally, the widespread availability of different types of BCIs could stratify society into different classes of people. We have already mentioned the dilemma of the BCI haves and have-nots. Should there be different schools for students with and without BCI-assisted augmented memory and cognitive enhancement? For athletes who have augmented their physical abilities, should there be special leagues or differently-special Olympics?

These, and other questions arising from a society of diverse BCI users, challenge our current conceptions of what it means to be human and point to the urgent need for a comprehensive discussion of the moral and ethical issues surrounding BCI development and use. It is thus incumbent on the BCI research community to engage with lawmakers, colleagues in the humanities and other disciplines, and public stakeholders in such a discussion, and arrive at a consensus on a set of ethical guidelines governing BCI use and commercialization.

13.6 Summary

It has been said that any great human advance in technology brings with it great moral and ethical responsibility. BCIs are no exception. BCIs have already started transforming the lives of people for the better (e.g., DBS for Parkinson's patients), but there is much potential for abuse as BCIs make the transition from the laboratory to the real world. Although existing medical practices such as informed consent and risks-versus-benefits analysis may guide BCI use in the near term, appropriate ethical guidelines and laws are not yet in place to regulate future, more advanced types of BCIs that could be used for human augmentation.

The purpose of this chapter was to make the reader aware of the range of ethical and moral issues permeating BCI research, ranging from various ways in which BCI technology could be abused to the need for BCI security and a discussion of legal and social justice issues. We conclude the chapter with the hope that this and other discussions on the topic may help in the formulation of an internationally accepted code for BCI ethics in the near future.

13.7 Questions and Exercises

1. Perform a risk-benefit analysis for each of the following cases:
   a. A person paralyzed from the neck down considering an invasive implant (such as BrainGate – see Section 7.3.1) to control a prosthetic arm
   b. An amputee with a missing right arm considering a semi-invasive ECoG interface for controlling a robotic hand-arm prosthetic.

    c. An amputee with a missing right arm considering a semi-invasive nerve-based BCI (Section 8.2.1) for controlling the same robotic system as in (b)

    d. A locked-in patient considering an EEG P300 speller (Section 9.1.4) for communication

2. For each of the cases (a) through (d) in Question 1, draft an informed consent form for a patient containing the following information: the nature and purpose of the BCI, risks and benefits, alternatives (regardless of cost), risks and benefits of alternatives, and risks and benefits of not receiving or using the BCI.

3. For each of the following BCI technologies (some currently available and some not yet available), identify potential ways in which the technology could be abused or subverted:

    a. Implant for restoring or enhancing memory storage and retrieval

    b. BCIs for physical amplification

    c. Brain-controlled remote robotic avatar

    d. Brain fingerprinting and lie detection

    e. BCIs for cognitive monitoring (alertness, cognitive load, etc.)

    f. Brain-powered computing such as CCCV (Section 12.2.3)

4. (⚡ Expedition) Review some of the current security and encryption techniques that have been proposed for wireless communication from personal devices, such as wearable health-monitoring sensors or medical devices such as pacemakers, implantable cardioverter-defibrillators (ICDs), or insulin pumps. Discuss whether these techniques are directly applicable to wireless BCIs and, if not, whether they could be modified to achieve BCI security.

5. (⚡ Expedition) Research what the liability law in your country states about the extent to which a car manufacturer is liable for an accident versus the driver of the car. Discuss whether such a law could be modified to account for liability of a BCI manufacturer versus the human user of the BCI in the following cases:

    a. An implanted BCI for controlling an exoskeleton

    b. A hierarchical BCI for controlling a remote robotic avatar

    c. A wireless memory implant for amplifying memory storage and retrieval

6. Discuss the moral and social justice issues surrounding the possible future use of BCIs for human augmentation, focusing on the dimensions of:

    a. Societal stratification ("cyborgs" versus "BCI luddites," rich versus poor)

    b. Stratification according to national boundaries and wealth

    c. Parental choices regarding BCI implantation in children

14

Conclusion

The field of brain-computer interfacing has witnessed tremendous growth over the past decade. Invasive BCIs based on multielectrode arrays have allowed laboratory animals to precisely control the movement of robotic arms. Implants and semi-invasive BCIs have enabled human subjects to quickly acquire control of computer cursors and simple devices. Noninvasive BCIs, particularly those based on EEG, have allowed humans to control cursors in multiple dimensions and issue commands to semi-autonomous robots. Commercially available BCIs such as cochlear implants and deep brain stimulators have helped improve the quality of life of hundreds of hearing-impaired individuals and patients suffering from debilitating neurological diseases.

The achievements of the field thus far are impressive, but many obstacles remain. As pointed out by Gilja, Shenoy, and colleagues (2011), invasive BCIs have yet to achieve the same levels of performance, multidecade robustness, and naturalistic proprioception and somatosensation as able-bodied people. Furthermore, invasive BCIs remain risky for humans and are used only as a last resort in severely disabled patients. The most popular noninvasive BCIs, based on EEG, suffer from a number of problems:

- Electrode placement is cumbersome and setup time is typically long (up to half an hour depending on the number of electrodes).
- Results of training and learning may not be transferable from one day to the next due to shifts in electrode locations, noisy contacts with scalp, etc.
- Low signal-to-noise ratio and on-line adaptation in subjects necessitate the availability of powerful amplifiers as well as efficient machine-learning and signal processing algorithms.
- Signal attenuation and summation between the brain and the scalp, together with sparse sampling of activity, limits the range of useful control signals that can be extracted.

To minimize risk, one would ideally like to noninvasively record the activities of several thousands of neurons with high signal-to-noise ratio. This would require advances in both biophysics and engineering in order to discover better methods of brain imaging than EEG and MRI. In the case of invasive BCIs, there is a need for *biocompatible* implantable chips that can remain implanted for years and even decades without being rejected while still providing reliable signals from the targeted brain areas. Such chips will ideally contain circuitry for amplification and wireless telemetry. On the software end, the field will need to go beyond traditional methods such as Fourier analysis, neural networks, and linear regression to more robust and co-adaptive algorithms such as those based on probabilistic models for inferring, tracking, and predicting brain state.

The field of brain-computer interfacing offers unprecedented possibilities for transforming how we as a species interact with the physical world and with each other. The field began with the goal of enhancing communication and control for paralyzed and disabled individuals. The rapid progress made by the field has thrown open the doors to radically new ways for the brain to exert control on objects other than the human body and for objects to provide feedback directly to the brain.

Thus, one can envision a not-too-distant future in which it may become routine to augment one's physical and mental capabilities through BCI technology, overcoming the limitations on physical and mental prowess imposed by evolution and one's own genes. "Telekinesis," the ability to manipulate and move certain objects by thought, and "telepathy," the ability to communicate with others through thought, also become distinct possibilities.

Are we as a species ready to make such a radical jump in our evolution? Are the governments and regulatory agencies of the world willing to work together to ensure a safe, equitable, and mutually beneficial transition for all to such a future? Humans have successfully negotiated and embraced other transformational technologies in the past, from stone tools and gunpowder to the steam engine and nuclear fission. One can therefore be optimistic that we as a species will successfully incorporate BCI technology into our lives in ways that enhance and enrich our experiences as human beings. BCIs offer us the potential to break out of the evolutionary confines of our biological bodies and brains. One can thus nurture the hope that BCIs will usher a new era of human creativity and achievement, brought about by an intimate fusion of brains, machines, and computer technology.

Appendix: Mathematical Background

To understand many of the technical ideas discussed in this book, the reader needs to have a working knowledge of some basic mathematical concepts learned in the second or third year of college, mainly in linear algebra, probability theory, and calculus. For background in calculus, such as the concepts of limits, integration, and differentiation, we refer the reader to standard calculus textbooks such as (Riddle, 1979). Here, we review some of the mathematical notation and units of measurement used in the book as well as fundamental ideas in linear algebra and probability theory.

A.1 Basic Mathematical Notation and Units of Measurement

We use $s(t)$ to denote the fact that s is a *function* of the variable t (e.g., time). If t is discrete (e.g., $t = 1, 2, 3 \ldots$), we sometimes also use subscript notation to represent the function, i.e., s_t for $t = 1, 2, 3 \ldots$

To denote the sum of a sequence of variables, we use the sigma (Σ) notation:

$$s_1 + s_2 + s_3 + \ldots + s_N = \sum_{i=1}^{N} s_i$$

We use the notation $|x|$ to denote the *absolute value* function:

$$|x| = \begin{array}{ll} x & \text{if } x \geq 0 \\ -x & \text{if } x < 0 \end{array} \tag{A.1}$$

The following abbreviations are commonly used to denote various units of measurement:

Unit	Quantity being measured	Value
mV (millivolts)	Voltage or potential difference	10^{-3} volts
μV (microvolts)	Voltage or potential difference	10^{-6} volts
mW (milliwatts)	Power	10^{-3} watts
ms (millisecond)	Time	10^{-3} seconds
mm (millimeter)	Length	10^{-3} meter
cm (centimeter)	Length	10^{-2} meter
Hz (Hertz)	Frequency (number of cycles/second)	1/second
kHz (kilohertz)	Frequency (number of cycles/second)	10^3/second
MHz (Megahertz)	Frequency (number of cycles/second)	10^6/second

A.2 Vectors, Matrices, and Linear Algebra

A.2.1 Vectors

We define a *vector* as an ordered sequence of values. For example, a four-dimensional vector can be written as:

$$\begin{bmatrix} a \\ b \\ c \\ d \end{bmatrix}$$

where *a, b, c,* and *d* are called *elements* of the vector. In this book, we will be concerned mostly with vectors whose elements are real numbers (e.g., $a = 17.6$, $b = -120.5$, $c = 150$, $d = -0.917$).

Vectors are useful because you can use them to represent any set of measurements or attributes simultaneously. For example, *a, b, c,* and *d* could represent electric potentials you have measured from four different locations on the scalp using EEG (see Chapter 3). We will use the four-dimensional vector above as an example throughout our discussion below. However, keep in mind that the concepts discussed apply to vectors of arbitrary dimensionality.

Vector names are usually represented using boldface characters. For example, we can use **x** to represent the four-dimensional vector above:

$$\mathbf{x} = \begin{bmatrix} a \\ b \\ c \\ d \end{bmatrix}$$

The elements of a vector **x** are identified using subscripts, i.e., $x_1 = a$, $x_2 = b$,   etc. A one-dimensional vector is just a single value and is called a *scalar*, e.g., the value $a = 17.6$.

Two vectors of the same size can be added by adding their corresponding elements, for instance, given:

$$\mathbf{x} = \begin{bmatrix} x_1 \\ x_2 \\ x_3 \\ x_4 \end{bmatrix} \text{ and } \mathbf{y} = \begin{bmatrix} y_1 \\ y_2 \\ y_3 \\ y_4 \end{bmatrix},$$

their sum $\mathbf{x} + \mathbf{y}$ is given by:

$$\mathbf{x} + \mathbf{y} = \begin{bmatrix} x_1 + y_1 \\ x_2 + y_2 \\ x_3 + y_3 \\ x_4 + y_4 \end{bmatrix}$$

Another simple operation you can apply to vectors is *scalar multiplication*, i.e., multiplying a vector by a scalar – this multiplies each element of the vector by the scalar. For example, if c is a scalar value and $\mathbf{x}$ is the vector above, then

$$c\mathbf{x} = \begin{bmatrix} cx_1 \\ cx_2 \\ cx_3 \\ cx_4 \end{bmatrix}$$

A useful type of multiplication involving two vectors is the *dot product*. This involves taking two vectors of the same size, such as the vectors $\mathbf{x}$ and $\mathbf{y}$ above, multiplying them elementwise, and adding up the products to get a single scalar value:

$$\mathbf{x} \cdot \mathbf{y} = \sum_i x_i y_i = x_1 y_1 + x_2 y_2 + x_3 y_3 + x_4 y_4$$

As a concrete example, if:

$$\mathbf{a} = \begin{bmatrix} 3 \\ -1 \\ 0.5 \\ 2 \end{bmatrix} \text{ and } \mathbf{b} = \begin{bmatrix} -2 \\ -4 \\ 2 \\ 0.5 \end{bmatrix},$$

their dot product is given by:

$$\mathbf{a} \cdot \mathbf{b} = 3(-2) + (-1)(-4) + (0.5)2 + 2(0.5) = -6 + 4 + 1 + 1 = 0$$

The *length* (or *magnitude*) of a vector $\mathbf{x}$, also known as its *L2 norm*, is represented by $\|\mathbf{x}\|$ and is defined as the square root of the sum of squares of all its elements. For example, for a four-dimensional vector $\mathbf{x}$,

$$\|\mathbf{x}\| = \sqrt{x_1^2 + x_2^2 + x_3^2 + x_4^2}$$

Note that the length of a vector is equal to the square root of the dot product of the vector with itself: $\|\mathbf{x}\| = \sqrt{\mathbf{x} \cdot \mathbf{x}}$.

Geometrically, it is useful to visualize an n-dimensional vector as an arrow (or straight-line segment with a length and a direction) in an n-dimensional "Euclidean" space. For example, the vector:

$$\begin{bmatrix} 4 \\ 3 \end{bmatrix}$$

can be thought of as a line segment that starts at the origin (0,0) in two-dimensional space and ends at the coordinates (4,3). Here, (0,0) is called the *tail* of the vector and (4,3) the *head* of the vector. Note that like all vectors, this vector has both a direction and a length, the length being given by $\sqrt{4^2 + 3^2} = \sqrt{25} = 5$. Addition of two vectors $\mathbf{x}$ and $\mathbf{y}$ can be visualized as placing the tail of $\mathbf{y}$ at the head of $\mathbf{x}$ and drawing an arrow from the tail of $\mathbf{x}$ to the head of $\mathbf{y}$. Furthermore, in such a setting, the dot product $\mathbf{x} \cdot \mathbf{y}$ can be shown (using the law of cosines) to be equal to

$$\mathbf{x} \cdot \mathbf{y} = \|\mathbf{x}\| \ \|\mathbf{y}\| \ \cos\theta \tag{A.2}$$

where θ is the angle between $\mathbf{x}$ and $\mathbf{y}$.

Two vectors are said to be *orthogonal* if they are perpendicular to each other. This happens when the angle between them θ is 90°, i.e., when:

$$\mathbf{x} \cdot \mathbf{y} = \|\mathbf{x}\| \ \|\mathbf{y}\| \ \cos 90° = 0 \tag{A.3}$$

i.e., when the dot product between the vectors is zero.

A vector $\mathbf{x}$ is said to be a *normalized (or unit) vector* if its length $\|\mathbf{x}\| = 1$. Any vector $\mathbf{y}$ can be normalized by dividing the vector by its length, i.e., $\dfrac{\mathbf{y}}{\|\mathbf{y}\|}$ is a normalized (or unit) vector.

A set of vectors is said to be *orthonormal* if they are all unit vectors and orthogonal to each other, i.e., for any two vectors $\mathbf{x}_i$ and $\mathbf{x}_j$ in the set:

$$\mathbf{x}_i \cdot \mathbf{x}_j = \begin{matrix} 0 \ \ \text{if } i \neq j \\ 1 \ \ \text{if } i = j \end{matrix} \tag{A.4}$$

A.2.2 Matrices

The concept of a vector can be generalized to a rectangular array of values called a *matrix*. You can think of a matrix in terms of vectors of the same size stacked next to each other column by column, or in terms of rows of values ("row vectors") arranged one below the other. A matrix is usually represented by a capital letter. Consider, for example, the matrix:

$$M = \begin{bmatrix} M_{11} & M_{12} & M_{13} \\ M_{21} & M_{22} & M_{23} \\ M_{31} & M_{32} & M_{33} \\ M_{41} & M_{42} & M_{43} \end{bmatrix}$$

The matrix M is of size 4×3 because it contains 4 rows and 3 columns. The values M_{ij} are the elements of the matrix, where i specifies the row and j the column of the element. A matrix is said to be a *square matrix* if it has the same number of rows and columns.

Matrices are useful for the study of BCIs because they arise time and again in operations such as filtering (see Chapter 4), classification (Chapter 5), and probability theory (e.g., the multivariate Gaussian distribution – see Section A.3).

Note that a vector is just a special type of matrix where the number of columns is 1, i.e., a vector is an $n \times 1$ matrix, where n is the number of elements in the vector.

The *transpose* M^T of a matrix M is obtained by taking the rows of the matrix and turning them into columns, i.e., $M_{ij}^T = M_{ji}$. For example, if A is the matrix:

$$A = \begin{bmatrix} a & b & c \\ d & e & f \end{bmatrix}, \text{then its transpose is given by:}$$

$$A^T = \begin{bmatrix} a & d \\ b & e \\ c & f \end{bmatrix}$$

Just as we did with vector addition, we can add two matrices of the same size by adding their corresponding elements: $(A + B)_{ij} = A_{ij} + B_{ij}$. For example,

$$\begin{bmatrix} 2 & -5 \\ -1 & 3 \\ 4 & 2 \end{bmatrix} + \begin{bmatrix} 3 & 5 \\ -2 & -1 \\ 1 & 2 \end{bmatrix} = \begin{bmatrix} 5 & 0 \\ -3 & 2 \\ 5 & 4 \end{bmatrix}$$

Similarly, scalar multiplication of a matrix A with a scalar c involves multiplying each element of the matrix with the scalar: $(cA)_{ij} = cA_{ij}$.

We can also multiply one matrix with another, an operation known as *matrix multiplication*, provided the first matrix has the same number of columns as the number of rows in the second matrix. Specifically, if A and B are matrices, we can multiply them to get a new matrix $C = AB$ only if the size of A is $a \times b$ and the size of B is $b \times c$. The resulting product matrix C will be of size $a \times c$, and is defined as:

$$C_{ij} = (AB)_{ij} = \sum_{k=1}^{b} A_{ik} B_{kj} \tag{A.5}$$

In other words, each element of the new matrix C is obtained by taking a row from the first matrix and a column from the second matrix and computing a dot product (this also explains why the rows of the first matrix and the columns of the second must be of the same size). To make this more concrete, consider the following example:

$$A = \begin{bmatrix} 2 & -5 \\ -1 & 3 \\ 4 & 2 \end{bmatrix} \text{ and } B = \begin{bmatrix} 3 & -2 & 1 \\ 5 & -1 & 2 \end{bmatrix}$$

A is of size 3×2 and B is of size 2×3, so they can be multiplied, giving us a 3×3 matrix:

$$C = AB = \begin{bmatrix} 2(3)+(-5)5 & 2(-2)+(-5)(-1) & 2(1)+(-5)2 \\ (-1)3+3(5) & (-1)(-2)+3(-1) & (-1)1+3(2) \\ 4(3)+2(5) & 4(-2)+2(-1) & 4(1)+2(2) \end{bmatrix} = \begin{bmatrix} -19 & 1 & -8 \\ 12 & -1 & 5 \\ 22 & -10 & 8 \end{bmatrix}$$

Note that unlike multiplication with real numbers, matrix multiplication is *not commutative*, i.e., even if A and B are square and both AB and BA exist, AB is not generally equal to BA (check this with some examples yourself!).

Matrix multiplication also allows us to multiply matrices with vectors, which we will find useful in several places in this book, such as in the sections on PCA and ICA (Chapter 4) as well as in LDA (Chapter 5). Multiplying a matrix with a vector is a special case of matrix multiplication – we just need to make sure the number of columns of the matrix is equal to the size of the vector. The result of the multiplication will be a vector. Specifically, if we multiply an $a \times b$ matrix A with a $b \times 1$ vector $\mathbf{x}$, we will get an $a \times 1$ vector $\mathbf{y}$, whose elements are the dot products of the rows of A with the vector $\mathbf{x}$. As an example, consider the 2×3 matrix B above and the following 3×1 vector $\mathbf{c}$:

$$\mathbf{c} = \begin{bmatrix} 3 \\ -1 \\ 0.5 \end{bmatrix}$$

We can multiply B and $\mathbf{c}$ to get the 2×1 vector $\mathbf{d}$:

$$\mathbf{d} = B\mathbf{c} = \begin{bmatrix} 3 & -2 & 1 \\ 5 & -1 & 2 \end{bmatrix}\begin{bmatrix} 3 \\ -1 \\ 0.5 \end{bmatrix} = \begin{bmatrix} 3(3)+(-2)(-1)+1(0.5) \\ 5(3)+(-1)(-1)+2(0.5) \end{bmatrix} = \begin{bmatrix} 11.5 \\ 17 \end{bmatrix}$$

Note that when you multiply a *square* matrix B (of size $b \times b$) with a vector $\mathbf{x}$ (of size $b \times 1$), the result is another $b \times 1$ vector $\mathbf{y} = B\mathbf{x}$. Thus, the effect of the multiplication in this case is to effectively perform a *rotation* of the original vector $\mathbf{x}$ to point in the direction $\mathbf{y}$ (and possibly change its magnitude also).

An interesting observation is that we can define the dot product between two vectors of the same size in terms of matrix multiplication using the transpose operation:

$$\mathbf{x} \cdot \mathbf{y} = \sum_i x_i y_i = \mathbf{x}^T \mathbf{y}$$

This form of the dot product is useful in derivations involving multiplication of matrices and vectors.

A square matrix A is said to be *symmetric* if $A^T = A$. A symmetric $n \times n$ matrix A is said to be *positive definite* if for all nonzero $n \times 1$ vectors $\mathbf{x}$, $\mathbf{x}^T A \mathbf{x} > 0$. The matrix A is *positive semidefinite* if for all $n \times 1$ vectors $\mathbf{x}$, $\mathbf{x}^T A \mathbf{x} \geq 0$.

A *diagonal matrix* D is a matrix whose elements are all zeros except along the diagonal, i.e., $D_{ij} = 0$ for all $i \neq j$.

One example of a diagonal matrix is the *identity matrix I*, which is a square matrix such that:

$$I_{ij} = \begin{array}{l} 1 \ \text{if } i = j \\ 0 \ \text{otherwise} \end{array}$$

The identity matrix is so called because $AI = A$ for all matrices A of the same size as I.

The *inverse* of a square matrix A is another square matrix A^{-1} such that $AA^{-1} = I$. Not all square matrices have inverses. In particular, a matrix must be "nonsingular" to have an inverse (see Strang [2009] for more details).

A.2.3 Eigenvectors and Eigenvalues

We have already noted above how the effect of multiplying a square matrix with a vector is to basically rotate the vector and change its magnitude. There are however some "special" nonzero vectors for which the effect of multiplying with the matrix is to simply scale the vector (multiply the vector by a scalar). Such vectors are called *eigenvectors* of the matrix, and the scalar values are called *eigenvalues*. This relationship is captured by the following equation:

$$M\mathbf{e} = \lambda\mathbf{e} \tag{A.6}$$

where $\mathbf{e}$ is called an eigenvector of the square matrix M and λ is the corresponding eigenvalue. Equation A.6 is called the *eigenvector-eigenvalue equation* for the matrix M.

The eigenvectors and eigenvalues can be obtained by solving the following polynomial equation (also called the *characteristic equation*) for λ:

$$\det(M - \lambda I) = 0 \tag{A.7}$$

where $\det(A)$ is the determinant of the matrix A (see Strang [2009] for further details). If M is an $n \times n$ matrix, there can be up to n distinct eigenvalues and eigenvectors. The eigenvalues can be real or complex depending on the characteristic equation, as can the eigenvectors. If M is symmetric (e.g., a covariance matrix – see Section A.3), the eigenvalues are guaranteed to be real, and the eigenvectors are real and orthogonal to each other. If the eigenvectors are further normalized to be of length 1, they form an orthonormal set of vectors, which is useful in applications such as PCA (see Chapter 4).

A.2.4 Lines, Planes, and Hyperplanes

We conclude our linear algebra review by highlighting the connection between vectors and equations for lines, planes, and hyperplanes – this turns out to be essential for understanding binary classification methods such as perceptrons, LDA, and SVMs (Chapter 5) where we are trying to find a line, plane, or hyperplane that can separate points belonging to one class from points belonging to another.

Consider a point P_0 on a p-dimensional hyperplane and let $\mathbf{x}_0$ be the vector from the origin to that point. Let $\mathbf{w}$ be a vector that is perpendicular to the hyperplane, i.e., the "normal vector" to the hyperplane. Let $\mathbf{x}$ be the vector from the origin to *any* point $(x_1,\ldots,x_p)$ on the hyperplane. Then, as discussed above, the dot product between normal vector $\mathbf{w}$ and the vector $(\mathbf{x}\text{-}\mathbf{x}_0)$ (which lies on the hyperplane) should be zero because they are orthogonal:

$$\mathbf{w}\cdot(\mathbf{x}-\mathbf{x}_0)=\mathbf{w}^T(\mathbf{x}-\mathbf{x}_0)=0$$

This can be simplified to get the *general equation for a hyperplane*:

$$\mathbf{w}^T\mathbf{x}+w_0=0 \qquad (A.8)$$

where w_0 is a constant scalar value $(=-\mathbf{w}^T\mathbf{x}_0)$. It is instructive to examine what Equation A.8 reduces to in the two-dimensional case, where the vector $\mathbf{x}$ is determined by the coordinates (x, y):

$$\mathbf{w}^T\mathbf{x}+w_0=\begin{bmatrix} w_1 & w_2 \end{bmatrix}\begin{bmatrix} x \\ y \end{bmatrix}+w_0=w_1 x+w_2 y+w_0=0$$

This equation can be rearranged to get a familiar form:

$$y=mx+b \quad \text{where } m=-\frac{w_1}{w_2} \text{ and } b=-\frac{w_0}{w_2} \qquad (A.9)$$

This is the classic *slope-intercept equation* for a straight line in two-dimensional space, where m is the slope and b the y-intercept of the line.

A.3 Probability Theory

The notion of probability is at the heart of machine learning, artificial intelligence, and much of information processing in today's data-rich world. Any system that interacts with the real world with humans as partners requires methods for quantifying uncertainty and reasoning using probabilities. It is therefore not surprising that probability theory is playing an increasingly important role in brain-computer interfacing.

A.3.1 Random Variables and Axioms of Probability

Probability theory relies on two concepts: a *sample space* S of mutually exclusive possible events and a "*measure*" defined over these events. We consider first a finite sample space S. This can be, for example, events associated with flipping a coin. There are two possible events: heads (h) or tails (t). As another example, consider the weather tomorrow – the possible outcomes could be sunny, rainy, or cloudy, and every subset of these outcomes could be an event (e.g., rainy and cloudy).

We use a *random variable* to represent an event. For example, we can use the random variable X to represent the outcome of flipping a coin. There are two possible values for X: $X = h$ or $X = t$. As a convention, uppercase letters such as X and Y are used to represent random variables, and lowercase letters such as h and t are used to represent their values.

A probability can be formally defined as a measure (a number) assigned to each event in the sample space S that satisfies the following 3 axioms ("the *axioms of probability*"):

1. The measure is between 0 and 1, i.e., $0 \le P(X = x) \le 1$ for all events x. For instance, in the example of flipping a coin, we may have $P(X = h) = 0.5$ and $P(X = t) = 0.5$, both of which are between 0 and 1.

2. The measure of all of the events is 1, i.e., $\sum_x P(X = x) = 1$. In our example above of flipping a coin, we have $P(X = h) + P(X = t) = 0.5 + 0.5 = 1$.

3. The probability of a union of mutually exclusive events is the sum of the probabilities of the individual events, i.e., $P(X = x_1 \cup X = x_2 \ldots \cup X = x_n) = \sum_{i=1}^{n} P(X = x_i)$ where the x_i are mutually exclusive events. In our coin-flipping example, the probability for getting heads or tails is 1 (those are the only two possible events), i.e., $P(X = h \cup X = t) = 1$, which is equal to $P(X = h) + P(X = t)$.

To simplify notation, it is common to use $P(x)$ as a shorthand for $P(X = x)$.

A.3.2 Joint and Conditional Probability

The *joint probability* of two events x and y is written as $P(x, y)$ and is the probability that x and y both occur. For example, if we use X to represent the weather on one day and Y to represent the weather the previous day, $P(X = \text{rainy}, Y = \text{cloudy})$ is the joint probability that it will rain on one day and is cloudy the previous day.

Suppose we want to calculate the probability that it will rain *given that* it was cloudy the previous day. To answer such questions, we need the notion of conditional probability. The *conditional probability* $P(x \mid y)$ ("probability of x given y") is the probability that an event x occurs ("it will rain") given that another event y has already occurred ("cloudy the previous day"). This conditional probability is defined as:

$$P(x \mid y) = P(x, y) / P(y) \qquad (A.10)$$

Two or more random variables are *independent* if their joint probability is equal to the product of their individual probabilities. For example, X and Y are independent if:

$$P(X = x, Y = y) = P(X = x)P(Y = y) \qquad (A.11)$$

for all x and y.

Or equivalently, X and Y are independent if:

$$P(X|Y) = P(X,Y)/P(Y) = P(X)P(Y)/P(Y) = P(X) \qquad (A.12)$$

for all values of X and Y.

A.3.3 Mean, Variance, and Covariance

In many cases, we use a random variable such as X to represent numbers, e.g, the number of heads obtained when you flip a coin 5 times (in this case, X can take on the values 0, 1, 2, 3, 4, 5). In such cases, we may be interested in calculating the mean (or average value) of the random variable and its variance.

The *mean* (or *expectation*) of a discrete random variable X is defined as:

$$E(X) = \sum_x P(X=x)x \qquad (A.13)$$

We sometimes use μ_x to represent the mean $E(X)$.

The *variance* of X is defined as:

$$\mathrm{var}(X) = E\left((X - \mu_x)^2\right) = E(X^2) - \mu_x^2 = \sum_x P(X=x)x^2 - \mu_x^2 \qquad (A.14)$$

The *standard deviation* of X is defined as:

$$\sigma_x = \sqrt{\mathrm{var}(X)} \qquad (A.15)$$

Given this relationship, it is common to use σ_x^2 to represent the variance.

The above definitions of mean and variance can also be applied to random variables that are vectors. Suppose we have an n-dimensional random variable:

$$\mathbf{x} = \begin{bmatrix} x_1 \\ x_2 \\ \vdots \\ x_n \end{bmatrix}$$

The *mean vector* for $\mathbf{x}$ is the vector:

$$\boldsymbol{\mu}_\mathbf{x} = E(\mathbf{x}) = \begin{bmatrix} E(x_1) \\ E(x_2) \\ \vdots \\ E(x_n) \end{bmatrix} = \begin{bmatrix} \mu_1 \\ \mu_2 \\ \vdots \\ \mu_n \end{bmatrix} \qquad (A.16)$$

The analog of variance for vector random variables is the *covariance matrix*:

$$\text{cov}(\mathbf{x}) = E((\mathbf{x} - \boldsymbol{\mu}_x)(\mathbf{x} - \boldsymbol{\mu}_x)^T)$$

$$= \begin{bmatrix} E((x_1 - \mu_1)(x_1 - \mu_1)) & E((x_1 - \mu_1)(x_2 - \mu_2)) & \cdots & E((x_1 - \mu_1)(x_n - \mu_n)) \\ E((x_2 - \mu_2)(x_1 - \mu_1)) & E((x_2 - \mu_2)(x_2 - \mu_2)) & \cdots & E((x_2 - \mu_2)(x_n - \mu_n)) \\ \vdots & \vdots & \vdots & \vdots \\ E((x_n - \mu_n)(x_1 - \mu_1)) & E((x_n - \mu_n)(x_2 - \mu_2)) & \cdots & E((x_n - \mu_n)(x_n - \mu_n)) \end{bmatrix} \quad (A.17)$$

Note that the diagonal of the covariance matrix contains the variances of the elements of the vector $\mathbf{x}$: $\text{var}(x_i) = E((x_i - \mu_i)^2)$.

A.3.4 Probability Density Function

We have thus far been discussing random variables that are discrete, i.e., they can take on one of a finite number of values. Under suitable conditions, a random variable X can also take on continuous values such as real numbers. In this case, we can define a *probability density function* as follows:

$$P(X = x) = \lim_{\Delta x \to 0} \frac{P(x \leq X \leq x + \Delta x)}{\Delta x}$$

We can then define the mean, variance, and covariance using the same definitions as above, except that we replace the sums over probabilities with integrals over probability densities.

We conclude our review of probability theory by going over some commonly used probability distributions. We first consider discrete distributions, followed by continuous ones.

A.3.5 Uniform Distribution

The simplest discrete distribution is the *uniform distribution*, which assumes that all events are equally likely. Thus, if there are N possible events, the uniform distribution assigns to each event x the probability:

$$P(X = x) = \frac{1}{N} \quad (A.18)$$

In the coin-flipping example, a uniform distribution would assign the probabilities $P(X = h) = 1/2$ and $P(X = t) = 1/2$ for the two possible outcomes. For rolling a six-sided die, the probability of each outcome under the uniform distribution would be 1/6.

A.3.6 Bernoulli Distribution

The Bernoulli distribution is used to model situations involving binary random variables, i.e., when there are only two possible outcomes: $X = 0$ or $X = 1$. We could, for example, use 1 to represent heads and 0 to represent tails in a coin-flipping experiment where the two outcomes are not necessarily equally likely (perhaps the coin is damaged). We can use a parameter μ to denote the probability of $X = 1$:

$$P(X=1|\mu)=\mu$$

where $0 \leq \mu \leq 1$. Then, $P(X=0|\mu)=1-\mu$. We can therefore write the probability distribution over the binary random variable X as:

$$P(X|\mu)=\text{Bern}(X|\mu)=\mu^X(1-\mu)^{1-X} \tag{A.19}$$

This distribution is known as the *Bernoulli distribution*. The reader can verify that this distribution is normalized (sums to 1). Using the definitions of mean and variance shown in Equations A.13 and A.14, we obtain the following results for the mean and variance of a Bernoulli distribution:

$$E(X)=P(X=1|\mu)\cdot 1 + P(X=0|\mu)\cdot 0$$
$$=\mu$$
$$\text{var}(X)=P(X=1|\mu)\cdot(1-\mu)^2 + P(X=0|\mu)\cdot(0-\mu)^2 = \mu(1-\mu)^2 + (1-\mu)\mu^2$$
$$=\mu(1-\mu)((1-\mu)+\mu)$$
$$=\mu(1-\mu)$$

A.3.7 Binomial Distribution

A closely related distribution is the *binomial distribution*, which characterizes the probability of observing the event $X = 1$ m times out of a total of N observations (e.g., N coin flips) where $m = 0, 1, 2, \ldots, N$:

$$P(m|N,\mu)=\text{Binom}(m|N,\mu)=\binom{N}{m}\mu^m(1-\mu)^{N-m} \tag{A.20}$$

where $\binom{N}{m}$ is the number of possible ways of choosing m items out of N identical items.

A.3.8 Poisson Distribution

The Poisson distribution is a special case of the binomial distribution where the number of observations or trials N is not given and neither is μ, the probability of "success" (i.e., observing the event $X = 1$). Instead, we are given the expected number of successes, which is:

$$\lambda=N\mu \tag{A.21}$$

The above equation comes from the fact that if we run N trials and the success probability in each trial is μ, then we will observe $N\mu$ successes on average.

Rewriting Equation A.21 as $\mu = \dfrac{\lambda}{N}$, substituting this value for μ in Equation A.20 for the binomial distribution above, and taking the limit as N becomes large and approaches infinity, we get:

$$\lim_{N \to \infty} \text{Binom}(m \mid N, \mu) = \lim_{N \to \infty} \binom{N}{m} \left(\frac{\lambda}{N}\right)^m \left(1 - \frac{\lambda}{N}\right)^{N-m}$$

After some mathematical simplification, we obtain the following expression for the *Poisson distribution*:

$$P(m \mid \lambda) = \text{Poisson}(m \mid \lambda) = \frac{\lambda^m}{m!} \exp(-\lambda) \tag{A.22}$$

where $m = 0, 1, 2, \ldots$ It can be shown that the mean and variance of the Poisson distribution are both equal to λ.

The Poisson distribution is useful because it can be used in BCIs (and neuroscience in general) to model the spiking activity of a neuron: if we know the neuron's average firing rate r, then the expected number of spikes ("successes") in a time period T is $\lambda = rT$. It has been found that for many biological neurons, the Poisson distribution provides a good approximation to the probability of observing m spikes in the time interval T.

A.3.9 Gaussian Distribution

The distributions we have discussed thus far pertain to discrete random variables. Perhaps the most important distribution associated with *continuous* random variables is the *Gaussian distribution* (also called the *normal distribution*).

Consider first the case of a scalar random variable X that can take on arbitrary real number values. The Gaussian distribution in this case is determined by two parameters, a mean μ and a variance σ^2, and takes the form:

$$P(X = x \mid \mu, \sigma^2) = \frac{1}{\sqrt{2\pi}\sigma} \exp\left(-\frac{1}{2}\left(\frac{x-\mu}{\sigma}\right)^2\right) \tag{A.23}$$

Note that the Gaussian assumes its highest value at the mean μ, and the standard deviation σ determines the spread around the mean (a larger value results in a larger spread).

A.3.10 Multivariate Gaussian Distribution

The Gaussian distribution can also be defined for continuous *vector* random variables. Consider an n-dimensional vector random variable $\mathbf{X}$ that can take on real-valued vectors $\mathbf{x}$ as values. We can define a *multivariate Gaussian distribution* for $\mathbf{X}$ that is determined by two parameters: an n-dimensional *mean vector* $\boldsymbol{\mu}$ and an $n \times n$ *covariance matrix* Σ (see Equations A.16 and A.17 for definitions of the mean vector and covariance matrix). The multivariate Gaussian distribution for $\mathbf{X}$ is defined as:

$$P(\mathbf{X} = \mathbf{x} \mid \mu, \Sigma) = \frac{1}{(2\pi)^{\frac{n}{2}} \sqrt{\det(\Sigma)}} \exp\left(-\frac{1}{2}(\mathbf{x} - \mu)^T \Sigma^{-1}(\mathbf{x} - \mu)\right) \qquad \text{(A.24)}$$

where $\det(\Sigma)$ denotes the determinant of the covariance matrix Σ. Note that Equation A.23 for the Gaussian distribution for a scalar variable is a special case of the multivariate Gaussian equation above for $n = 1$. Note also that the exponent $(\mathbf{x} - \mu)^T \Sigma^{-1}(\mathbf{x} - \mu)$ is a measure of the square of the distance between the input vector $\mathbf{x}$ and the mean vector μ. This distance is called the *Mahalanobis distance* (see Chapter 5 for an example of its use).

References

Acharya S, Fifer MS, Benz HL, Crone NE, Thakor NV. Electrocorticographic amplitude predicts finger positions during slow grasping motions of the hand. *J Neural Eng.* 2010 Aug;7(4):046002.

Andersen RA, Hwang EJ, Mulliken GH. Cognitive neural prosthetics. *Annu Rev Psychol.* 2010;**61**:169–90, C1–3.

Anderson C, Sijercic Z. Classification of EEG signals from four subjects during five mental tasks. In *Solving Engineering Problems with Neural Networks: Proceedings of the Conference on Engineering Applications in Neural Networks (EANN'96)*, 1996, Bulsari, AB, Kallio, S, and Tsaptsinos, D (eds.), pp. 407–14.

Ayaz H, Shewokis PA, Bunce S, Schultheis M, Onaral B. Assessment of cognitive neural correlates for a functional near infrared-based brain computer interface system. *Augmented Cognition*, HCII, 2009;LNAI 5638, pp. 699–708.

Babiloni C, Carducci F, Cincotti F, Rossini PM, Neuper C, Pfurtscheller G, Babiloni F. Human movement-related potentials vs desynchronization of EEG alpha rhythm: a high-resolution EEG study. *Neuroimage.* 1999 Dec;**10**(6):658–65.

Barber D. *Bayesian Reasoning and Machine Learning.* Cambridge University Press, 2012.

Bayliss JD. Use of the evoked potential P3 component for control in a virtual apartment. *IEEE Trans Neural Syst Rehabil Eng.* 2003;**11**(2):113–16.

Bear MF, Connors BW, Paradiso MA. *Neuroscience: Exploring the Brain.*, 3rd ed., Lippincott Williams & Wilkins, Baltimore, MD, 2007.

Bell AJ, Sejnowski TJ. An information-maximization approach to blind separation and blind deconvolution. *Neural Computation.* 1995;**7**:1129–59.

Bell CJ, Shenoy P, Chalodhorn R, Rao RPN. Control of a humanoid robot by a noninvasive brain-computer interface in humans. *J Neural Eng.* 2008 Jun;**5**(2):214–20.

Bellavista P, Corradi A, Giannelli C. *Evaluating filtering strategies for decentralized handover prediction in the wireless internet.* Proc. 11th IEEE Symposium Computers Commun., 2006.

Bensch M, Karim A, Mellinger J, Hinterberger T, Tangermann M, Bogdan M, Rosenstiel W, Birbaumer N. Nessi: an EEG controlled web browser for severely paralyzed patients. *Comput. Intell. Neurosci.* 2007;Article ID 71863.

Berger H. Über das Elektroenkephalogram des Menschen. *Arch. f. Psychiat.* 1929;**87**: 527–70.

Berger T, Hampson R, Song D, Goonawardena A, Marmarelis V, Deadwyler S. A cortical neural prosthesis for restoring and enhancing memory. *Journal of Neural Engineering.* 2011; **8**(4):046017.

Birbaumer N, Cohen LG. Brain-computer interfaces: communication and restoration of movement in paralysis. *J Physiol.* 2007;**579**(Pt 3):621–36.

Bishop CM. *Pattern Recognition and Machine Learning.* Springer, New York, 2006.

Blakely T, Miller KJ, Rao RPN, Holmes MD, Ojemann JG. Localization and classification of phonemes using high spatial resolution electrocorticography (ECoG) grids. *Conf Proc IEEE Eng Med Biol Soc.* 2008;4964–67.

Blakely T, Miller KJ, Zanos SP, Rao RPN, Ojemann JG. Robust, long-term control of an electrocorticographic brain-computer interface with fixed parameters. *Neurosurg Focus.* 2009 Jul;**27**(1):E13.

Blankertz B, Losch F, Krauledat M, Dornhege G, Curio G, Müller KR. The Berlin brain-computer interface: accurate performance from first-session in BCI-naïve subjects. *IEEE Trans Biomed Eng.* 2008 Oct;**55**(10):2452–62.

Blankertz B, Tangermann M, Vidaurre C, Fazli S, Sannelli C, Haufe S, Maeder C, Ramsey L, Sturm I, Curio G, Müller KR. The Berlin brain-computer interface: non-medical uses of BCI technology. *Front Neurosci.* 2010;**4**:198.

Blankertz B, Tomioka R, Lemm S, Kawanabe M, Müller KR. Optimizing spatial filters for robust EEG single-trial analysis. *IEEE Signal Processing Magazine.* 2008;**25**(1):41–56.

Bles M, Haynes JD. Detecting concealed information using brain-imaging technology. *Neurocase.* 2008;**14**:82–92.

Blumhardt LD, Barrett G, Halliday AM, Kriss A. The asymmetrical visual evoked potential to pattern reversal in one half field and its significance for the analysis of visual field effects. *Br. J. Ophthalmol.* 1977;**61**: 454–61.

Boser BE, Guyon IM, Vapnik VN. A training algorithm for optimal margin classifiers. *Proceedings of the fifth annual workshop on computational learning theory,* ACM, New York, 1992, 144–52.

Braitenberg V. *Vehicles: Experiments in synthetic psychology.* MIT Press, Cambridge, MA, 1984.

Breiman L. Random Forests. *Machine Learning.* 2001;**45**(1):5–32.

Brindley GS, Lewin WS. The sensations produced by electrical stimulation of the visual cortex. *J Physiol.* 1968;**196**(2):479–93.

Bryan M, Nicoll G, Thomas V, Chung M, Smith JR, Rao RPN. Automatic extraction of command hierarchies for adaptive brain-robot interfacing. *Proceedings of ICRA 2012,* 2012 May 5–12.

Bryan MJ, Martin SA, Cheung W, Rao RPN. Probabilistic co-adaptive brain-computer interfacing. *Proceedings of Fifth International Brain-Computer Interface Meeting, Asilomar, CA, 2013 June 3–7.*

Bryson AE, Ho YC. *Applied optimal control.* New York: Wiley, 1975.

Burges CJC. A tutorial on support vector machines for pattern recognition. *Data Mining and Knowledge Discovery.* 1998;**2**:121–67.

Buttfield A, Ferrez PW, Millán J del R. Towards a robust BCI: error potentials and online learning. *IEEE Trans Neural Syst Rehabil Eng.* 2006;**14**(2):164–68.

Calhoun GL, McMillan, GR. EEG-based control for human computer interaction. *Proc. Annu. Symp. Human Interaction with Complex Systems.* 1996, pp. 4–9.

Chapin JK, Moxon KA, Markowitz RS, Nicolelis MA. Real-time control of a robot arm using simultaneously recorded neurons in the motor cortex. *Nat Neurosci.* 1999 Jul;**2**(7):664–70.

Cheng M, Gao X, Gao S, Xu D. Design and implementation of a brain-computer interface with high transfer rates. *IEEE Trans Biomed Eng.* 2002 Oct;**49**(10):1181–86.

Cheung W, Sarma D, Scherer R, Rao RPN. Simultaneous brain-computer interfacing and motor control: expanding the reach of non-invasive BCIs. *Conf Proc IEEE Eng Med Biol Soc.* 2012;**2012**:6715–8.

Chung M, Cheung W, Scherer R, Rao RPN. A hierarchical architecture for adaptive brain-computer interfacing. *Proceedings of IJCAI.* 2011, pp.1647–52.

Citri A, Malenka RC. Synaptic plasticity: multiple forms, functions, and mechanisms. *Neuropsychopharmacology.* 2008;**33**: 18–41.

Clausen J. Man, machine and in between. *Nature.* 2009;**457**(7233): 1080–81.

Collinger JL, Wodlinger B, Downey JE, Wang W, Tyler-Kabara EC, Weber DJ, McMorland AJ, Velliste M, Boninger ML, Schwartz AB. High-performance neuroprosthetic control by an individual with tetraplegia. *The Lancet.* 2013 Feb 16;**381**(9866):557–64.

Cooper R, Osselton JW, Shaw JC. *EEG Technology*, 2nd ed., London: Butterworths, 1969.

Cortes C, Vapnik V. Support-Vector Networks. *Machine Learning.* 1995;**20**:273–297.

Coyle S, Ward T, Markham C, McDarby G. On the suitability of near-infrared (NIR) systems for next-generation brain computer interfaces. *Physiol Meas.* 2004;**25**:815–22.

Croft RJ, Chandler JS, Barry RJ, Cooper NR, Clarke AR. EOG correction: a comparison of four methods. *Psychophysiology.* 2005;**42**:16–24.

Dalbey B. *Brain fingerprinting testing traps serial killer in Missouri.* The Fairfield Ledger. Fairfield, IA, 1999 August, p. 1.

Delgado J. *Physical Control of the Mind: Toward a Psychocivilized Society.* Harper and Row, New York, 1969.

Denk W, Strickler JH, Webb WW. Two-photon laser scanning fluorescence microscopy. *Science.* 1990;**248**, 73–76.

Denning T, Matsuoka Y, Kohno T. Neurosecurity: security and privacy for neural devices. *Neurosurg Focus.* 2009;**27**(1):E7.

Dhillon GS and Horch KW. Direct neural sensory feedback and control of a prosthetic arm. *IEEE Trans Neural Syst Rehabil Eng.* 2005;**13**:468–72.

Diester I, Kaufman MT, Goo W, O'Shea DJ, Kalanithi PS, Deisseroth K, Shenoy KV. *Optogenetics and brain-machine interfaces. Proc. of the 33rd Annual International Conference IEEE EMBS.* 2011, Boston, MA.

DiGiovanna J, Mahmoudi B, Fortes J, Principe JC, Sanchez JC. Coadaptive brain-machine interface via reinforcement learning. *IEEE Trans Biomed Eng.* 2009;**56**(1):54–64.

Dobelle WH. Artificial vision for the blind by connecting a television camera to the visual cortex. *American Society for Artificial Internal Organs Journal.* 2000;**46**:3–9.

Dobkin BH. Brain-computer interface technology as a tool to augment plasticity and outcomes for neurological rehabilitation. *J Physiol.* 2007;**579**(Pt 3):637–42.

Donoghue JP, Nurmikko A, Black M, Hochberg LR. Assistive technology and robotic control using motor cortex ensemble-based neural interface systems in humans with tetraplegia. *J Physiol.* 2007 Mar 15;**579**(Pt 3):603–11.

Dornhege G, Millán JR, Hinterberger T, McFarland DJ, Müller KR. (eds.) *Towards Brain-Computer Interfacing.* MIT Press, Cambridge, MA, 2007.

Duda R, Hart P, Stork D. *Pattern Classification (2nd ed.).* Wiley Interscience, New York, 2000.

Fagg AH, Ojakangas GW, Miller LE, Hatsopoulos NG. Kinetic trajectory decoding using motor cortical ensembles. *IEEE Trans Neural Syst Rehabil Eng.* 2009 Oct;**17**(5):487–96.

Farwell LA, Donchin E. Talking off the top of your head: toward a mental prosthesis utilizing event-related brain potentials. *Electroencephalogr Clin Neurophysiol.* 1988 Dec;**70**(6):510–23.

Farwell LA, Donchin E. The truth will out: interrogative polygraphy ("lie detection") with event-related brain potentials. *Psychophysiology.* 1991;**28**(5):531–47.

Farwell LA. Brain fingerprinting: a comprehensive tutorial review of detection of concealed information with event-related brain potentials. *Cognitive Neurodynamics.* 2012;**6**: 115–54.

Fatourechi M, Bashashati A, Ward RK, Birch GE. EMG and EOG artifacts in brain computer interface systems: A survey. *Clin Neurophysiol.* 2007 Mar;**118**(3):480–94.

Fetz EE. Operant conditioning of cortical unit activity. *Science.* 1969 Feb 28;**163**(870):955–58.

Fetz EE. Volitional control of neural activity: implications for brain-computer interfaces. *J Physiol.* 2007 Mar 15;**579**(Pt 3):571–9. Epub 2007 Jan 18.

Finke A, Lenhardt A, Ritter H. The mindgame: a P300-based brain-computer interface game. *Neural Networks* 2009;**22**: 1329–33.

Fitzsimmons NA, Lebedev MA, Peikon ID, Nicolelis MA. Extracting kinematic parameters for monkey bipedal walking from cortical neuronal ensemble activity. *Front Integr Neurosci.* 2009;**3**:3.

Foerster O. Beitrage zur pathophysiologie der sehbahn und der spehsphare. *J Psychol Neurol.* 1929;**39**:435–63.

Fork RL. Laser stimulation of nerve cells in Aplysia. *Nature.* 1971;**171**, 907–08.

Freund, Yoav, Schapire, Robert E. A decision-theoretic generalization of on-line learning and an application to boosting. *Journal of Computer and System Sciences,* 55(1):119–139, 1997.

Friedman JH. Regularized discriminant analysis. *J Amer Statist Assoc.* 1989;**84** (405):165–75.

Furdea A, Halder S, Krusienski DJ, Bross D, Nijboer F, Birbaumer N, Kübler A. An auditory oddball (P300) spelling system for brain-computer interfaces. *Psychophysiology.* 2009;**46**(3):617–25.

Galán F, Nuttin M, Lew E, Ferrez PW, Vanacker G, Philips J, Millán J del R. A brain-actuated wheelchair: asynchronous and non-invasive brain-computer interfaces for continuous control of robots. *Clin Neurophysiol.* 2008;**119**(9):2159–69.

Ganguly K, Carmena JM. Emergence of a stable cortical map for neuroprosthetic control. *PLoS Biol.* 2009 Jul;**7**(7):e1000153.

Gao X, Xu D, Cheng M, Gao S. A BCI-based environmental controller for the motion-disabled. *IEEE Trans Neural Syst Rehabil Eng.* 2003 Jun;**11**(2):137–40.

Garrett D, Peterson DA, Anderson CW, Thaut MH. Comparison of linear, nonlinear, and feature selection methods for EEG signal classification. *IEEE Trans Neural Syst Rehabil Eng.* 2003 Jun;**11**(2):141–44.

Georgopoulos AP, Kettner RE, Schwartz AB. Primate motor cortex and free arm movements to visual targets in three-dimensional space. II. Coding of the direction of movement by a neuronal population. *J of Neurosci.* 1988;**8**(8):2928–37.

Gerson AD, Parra LC, Sajda P. Cortically coupled computer vision for rapid image search. *IEEE Trans Neural Syst Rehabil Eng.* 2006;**14**(2):174–79.

Gilja V, Chestek CA, Diester I, Henderson JM, Deisseroth K, Shenoy KV. Challenges and opportunities for next-generation intra-cortically based neural prostheses. *IEEE Transactions on Biomedical Engineering.* 2011;**58**:1891–99.

Gilmore RL. American Electroencephalographic Society guidelines in electroencephalography, evoked potentials, and polysomnography, *J. Clin. Neurophysiol.* 1994;**11**.

Giridharadas A. India's novel use of brain scans in courts is debated. *New York Times.* 2008 Sept. 15. Section A, p10.

Gollakota S, Hassanieh H, Ransford B, Katabi D, Fu K. They can hear your heart-beats: non-invasive security for implantable medical devices. In *Proceedings of the ACM SIGCOMM 2011 conference* (SIGCOMM '11). 2011. ACM, New York, NY, pages 2–13.

Graimann B, Allison B, Pfurtscheller G. (eds.) *Brain-Computer Interfaces: Revolutionizing Human-Computer Interaction.* Springer, Berlin, 2011.

Grimes D, Tan DS, Hudson S, Shenoy P, Rao RPN. Feasibility and pragmatics of classifying working memory load with an electroencephalograph. In *Proceedings of ACM SIGCHI Conference on Human Factors in Computing Systems* (CHI 2008). 2008;835–44.

Halder S, Rea M, Andreoni R, Nijboer F, Hammer EM, Kleih SC, Birbaumer N, Kübler A. An auditory oddball brain-computer interface for binary choices. *Clin Neurophysiol.* 2010;**121**(4):516–23.

Hanks TD, Ditterich J, Shadlen MN. Microstimulation of macaque area LIP affects decision-making in a motion discrimination task. *Nat Neurosci.* 2006;**9**: 682–89.

Haselager P, Vlek R, Hill J, Nijboer F. A note on ethical aspects of BCI. *Neural Networks.* 2009;**22**: 1352–57.

Hill NJ, Lal TN, Bierig K, Birbaumer N, Schölkopf B. An auditory paradigm for brain-computer interfaces. In *Advances in Neural Information Processing Systems* **17**, 569–76. (Eds.) Saul, L.K., Y. Weiss and L. Bottou, MIT Press, Cambridge, MA, USA (2005).

Hinterberger T, Kübler A, Kaiser J, Neumann N, Birbaumer N. A brain-computer interface (BCI) for the locked-in: comparison of different EEG classifications for the thought translation device. *Clin Neurophysiol.* 2003;**114**(3): 416–25.

Hiraiwa A, Shimohara K, Tokunaga Y. EEG topography recognition by neural networks. *Engineering in Medicine and Biology.* 1990;**9**(3): 39–42.

Hjelm S, Browall C. Brainball – Using brain activity for cool competition. *In Proceedings of NordiCHI, Stockholm.* 2000.

Hochberg LR, Bacher D, Jarosiewicz B, Masse NY, Simeral JD, Vogel J, Haddadin S, Liu J, Cash SS, van der Smagt P, Donoghue JP. Reach and grasp by people with tetraplegia using a neurally controlled robotic arm. *Nature.* 2012;**485**(7398):372–75.

Hochberg LR, Serruya MD, Friehs GM, Mukand JA, Saleh M, Caplan AH, Branner A, Chen D, Penn RD, Donoghue JP. Neuronal ensemble control of prosthetic devices by a human with tetraplegia. *Nature.* 2006 Jul 13; **442**(7099):164–71.

Hwang EJ, Andersen RA. Cognitively driven brain machine control using neural signals in the parietal reach region. *Conf Proc IEEE Eng Med Biol Soc.* 2010;3329–32.

Hyvärinen A, Oja E. Independent component analysis: algorithms and applications. *Neural Networks.*2000;**13**(4–5): 411–430.

Hyvärinen A. Fast and robust fixed-point algorithms for independent component analysis. *IEEE Transactions on Neural Networks.* 1999;**10**(3): 626–34.

Iturrate I, Antelis J, Minguez J. Synchronous EEG brain actuated wheelchair with automated navigation. In *Proc. 2009 IEEE Int. Conf. Robotics Automation, Kobe, Japan.* 2009.

Jackson A, Mavoori J, Fetz EE. Long-term motor cortex plasticity induced by an electronic neural implant. *Nature.* 2006;**444**(7115):56–60.

Jahanshahi M, Hallet M. The Bereitschaftspotential: movement related cortical potentials. *Kluwer Academic.* 2002. New York.

Jasper HH. Report of the Committee on Methods of Clinical Examination in Electroencephalography. *Electroenceph. Clin. Neurophysiol.* 1958;**10**:370–71.

Javaheri M, Hahn DS, Lakhanpal RR, Weiland JD, Humayun MS. Retinal prostheses for the blind. *Ann Acad Med Singapore.* 2006;**35**(3):137–44.

Jung TP, Humphries C, Lee TW, Makeig S, McKeown MJ, Iragui V, Sejnowski TJ. Extended ICA removes artifacts from electroencephalographic recordings. *Adv Neural Inf Process Syst.* 1998;**10**:894–900.

Jung TP, Makeig S, Stensmo M, Sejnowski TJ. Estimating alertness from the EEG power spectrum. *IEEE Transactions on Biomedical Engineering.* 1997;**44**:60–69.

Kandel ER, Schwartz JH, Jessell TM. *Principles of Neural Science.* Third edition. Elsevier, New York, 1991.

Kandel ER, Schwartz JH, Jessell TM, Siegelbaum SA, Hudspeth AJ. *Principles of Neural Science.* Fifth Edition. McGraw Hill, New York, 2012.

Kern DS, Kumar R. Deep brain stimulation. *The Neurologist.* 2007;**13**: 237–52.

Kherlopian AR, Song T, Duan Q, Neimark MA, Po MJ, Gohagan JK, Laine AF. A review of imaging techniques for systems biology. *BMC Syst Biol.* 2008;**2**:74.

Kim SP, Simeral JD, Hochberg LR, Donoghue JP, Black MJ. Neural control of computer cursor velocity by decoding motor cortical spiking activity in humans with tetraplegia. *J Neural Eng.* 2008 Dec;**5**(4):455–76.

Kohlmorgen J, Dornhege G, Braun M, Blankertz B, Müller K-R, Curio G, Hagemann K, Bruns A, Schrauf M, Kincses W. Improving human performance in a real operating environment through realtime mental workload detection. In *Toward Brain–Computer Interfacing* (eds. G. Dornhege, J. del R. Millán, T. Hinterberger, D. J. McFarland, and K.-R. Müller). MIT Press, Cambridge, MA. 2007;409–22.

Koller, D., Friedman, N. *Probabilistic Graphical Models: Principles and Techniques*, MIT Press, 2009.

Krepki R, Blankertz B, Curio G, Müller KR. The Berlin brain–computer interface (BBCI): towards a new communication channel for online control in gaming applications. *J Multimed. Tool Appl.* 2007;**33**:73–90.

Kringelbach ML, Jenkinson N, Owen SLF, Aziz TZ. Translational principles of deep brain stimulation. *Nature Reviews Neuroscience.* 2007;**8**:623–35.

Kübler A, Kotchoubey B, Hinterberger T, Ghanayim N, Perelmouter J, Schauer M, Fritsch C, Taub E, Birbaumer N. The thought translation device: a neurophysiological approach to communication in total motor paralysis. *Exp Brain Res.* 1999 Jan;**124**(2):223–32.

Kuiken TA, Miller LA, Lipschutz RD, Lock BA, Stubblefield K, Marasco PD, Zhou P, Dumanian GA. Targeted reinnervation for enhanced prosthetic arm function in a woman with a proximal amputation: a case study. *Lancet.* 2007;**369**:371–80.

Lalor EC, Kelly SP, Finucane C, Burke R, Smith R, Reilly R, McDarby G. Steady-state VEP-based brain-computer interface: Control in an immersive 3D gaming environment. *EURASIP Journal on Applied Signal Processing.* 2005;**19**:3156–64.

Leuthardt EC, Miller KJ, Schalk G, Rao RPN, Ojemann JG. Electrocorticography-based brain computer interface – the Seattle experience. *IEEE Trans Neural Syst Rehabil Eng.* 2006 Jun;**14**(2):194–98.

Leuthardt EC, Schalk G, Wolpaw JR, Ojemann JG, Moran DW. A brain-computer interface using electrocorticographic signals in humans. *J Neural Eng.* 2004 Jun;**1**(2):63–71.

Li Z, O'Doherty JE, Hanson TL, Lebedev MA, Henriquez CS, Nicolelis MA. Unscented Kalman filter for brain-machine interfaces. *PLoS One.* 2009 Jul 15;**4**(7):e6243.

Liang SF, Lin CT, Wu RC, Chen YC, Huang TY, Jung TP. Monitoring driver's alertness based on the driving performance estimation and the EEG power spectrum analysis. *Conf Proc IEEE Eng Med Biol Soc.* 2005;**6**:5738–41.

Lins OG, Picton TW, Berg P, Scherg M. Ocular artifacts in recording EEGs and event-related potentials. II: source dipoles and source components. *Brain Topogr.* 1993;**6**:65–78.

Loeb GE, Peck RA. Cuff electrodes for chronic stimulation and recording of peripheral nerve activity. *J Neurosci Methods.* 1996 Jan;**64**:95–103.

Makeig S, Enghoff S, Jung TP, Sejnowski TJ. Moving-window ICA decomposition of EEG data reveals event-related changes in oscillatory brain activity. In *Proc. Second International Workshop on Independent Component Analysis and Signal Separation.* 2000; 627–32.

Malmivuo J, Plonsey R. *Bioelectromagnetism – Principles and Applications of Bioelectric and Biomagnetic Fields,* Oxford University Press, New York, 1995.

Mappus RL, Venkatesh GR, Shastry C, Israeli A, Jackson MM. An fNIR based BMI for letter construction using continuous control. *ACM CHI 2009 Human Factors in Computing Systems Conference Work in Progress Paper.* 2009;**2**:3571–76.

Marcel S, Millán J del R. Person authentication using brainwaves (EEG) and maximum a posteriori model adaptation. *IEEE Trans Pattern Anal Mach Intell.* 2007;**29**(4):743–52.

Mason SG, Birch GE. A brain-controlled switch for asynchronous control applications. *IEEE Trans Biomed Eng.* 2000 Oct;**47**(10):1297–307.

Mavoori J, Jackson A, Diorio C, Fetz E. An autonomous implantable computer for neural recording and stimulation in unrestrained primates. *J Neurosci Methods.* 2005;**148**(1):71–77.

Mellinger J, Schalk G, Braun C, Preissl H, Rosenstiel W, Birbaumer N, Kübler A. An MEG-based brain-computer interface (BCI). *Neuroimage.* 2007;**36**(3):581–93.

Middendorf M, McMillan G, Calhoun G, Jones KS. Brain computer interfaces based on the steady-state visual-evoked response. *IEEE Trans. Rehab. Eng.* 2000;**8**:211–14.

Millán JJ del R, Galán F, Vanhooydonck D, Lew E, Philips J, Nuttin M. Asynchronous non-invasive brain-actuated control of an intelligent wheelchair. *Conf. Proc. IEEE Eng. Med. Biol Soc.* 2009;3361–64.

Millán JR, Ferrez PW, Seidl T. Validation of brain-machine interfaces during parabolic flight. In L. Rossini, D. Izzo, L. Summerer (eds.), "Brain-machine interfaces for space applications: enhancing astronauts' capabilities." *International Review of Neurobiology.* 2009;**86**.

Miller KJ, Leuthardt EC, Schalk G, Rao RPN, Anderson NR, Moran DW, Miller JW, Ojemann JG. Spectral changes in cortical surface potentials during motor movement. *J Neurosci.* 2007;**27**(9):2424–32.

Miller KJ, Schalk G, Fetz EE, den Nijs M, Ojemann JG, Rao RPN. Cortical activity during motor execution, motor imagery, and imagery-based online feedback. *Proc. Natl. Acad. Sci. USA.* 2010 Mar 2;**107**(9):4430–35.

Miller KJ, Zanos S, Fetz EE, den Nijs M, Ojemann JG. Decoupling the cortical power spectrum reveals real-time representation of individual finger movements in humans. *J Neurosci.* 2009 Mar 11;**29**(10):3132–37.

Moritz CT, Fetz EE. Volitional control of single cortical neurons in a brain-machine interface. *J Neural Eng.* 2011;**8**(2).

Moritz CT, Perlmutter SI, Fetz EE. Direct control of paralysed muscles by cortical neurons. *Nature.* 2008;**456**, 639–42.

Müller KR, Anderson CW, Birch GE. Linear and nonlinear methods for brain-computer interfaces. *IEEE Trans Neural Syst Rehabil Eng*. 2003;**11**(2):165–69.

Müller KR, Tangermann M, Dornhege G, Krauledat M, Curio G, Blankertz B. Machine learning for real-time single-trial EEG-analysis: From brain-computer interfacing to mental state monitoring. *J Neurosci Methods*. 2008;**167**(1):82–90.

Musallam S, Corneil BD, Greger B, Scherberger H, Andersen RA. Cognitive control signals for neural prosthetics. *Science*. 2004 Jul 9;**305**(5681):258–62.

Mussa-Ivaldi FA, Alford ST, Chiappalone M, Fadiga L, Karniel A, Kositsky M, Maggiolini E, Panzeri S, Sanguineti V, Semprini M, Vato A. New perspectives on the dialogue between brains and machines. *Front Neurosci*. 2010;**4**:44.

Nunez PL. *Electric Fields of the Brain: The Neurophysics of EEG*, Oxford University Press, New York, 1981.

O'Doherty JE, Lebedev MA, Hanson TL, Fitzsimmons NA, Nicolelis MA. A brain-machine interface instructed by direct intracortical microstimulation. *Front Integr Neurosci*. 2009;**3**:20.

O'Doherty JE, Lebedev MA, Ifft PJ, Zhuang KZ, Shokur S, Bleuler H, Nicolelis MA. Active tactile exploration using a brain-machine-brain interface. *Nature*. 2011;**479**(7372):228–31.

Ohki K, Chung S, Ch'ng YH, Kara P and Reid RC. Functional imaging with cellular resolution reveals precise microarchitecture in visual cortex. *Nature*. 2005;**433**:597–603.

Ojakangas CL, Shaikhouni A, Friehs GM, Caplan AH, Serruya MD, Saleh M, Morris DS, Donoghue JP. Decoding movement intent from human premotor cortex neurons for neural prosthetic applications. *J Clin Neurophysiol*. 2006 Dec;**23**(6):577–84.

Onton J, Makeig S. Information-based modeling of event-related brain dynamics. In C. Neuper and W. Klimesch, (eds.) *Progress in Brain Research*. 2006;**159**. Elsevier, Amsterdam.

Orbach HS, Cohen LB, Grinvald A. Optical mapping of electrical activity in rat somatosensory and visual cortex. *J Neurosci*. 1985;**5**:1886.

Paranjape RB, Mahovsky J, Benedicenti L, Koles Z. The electroencephalogram as a biometric. In *Proceedings of the Canadian Conference on Electrical and Computer Engineering*. 2001;**2**:1363–66.

Paul N, Kohno T, Klonoff DC. A review of the security of insulin pump infusion systems. *J Diabetes Sci Technol*. 2011;**5**(6):1557–62.

Pfurtscheller G, Guger C, Müller G, Krausz G, Neuper C. Brain oscillations control hand orthosis in a tetraplegic. *Neurosci Lett*. 2000 Oct 13;**292**(3):211–14.

Pfurtscheller G, Neuper C, Guger C, Harkam W, Ramoser H, Schlögl A, Obermaier B, Pregenzer M. Current trends in Graz brain-computer interface (BCI) research. *IEEE Trans Rehabil Eng*. 2000 Jun;**8**(2):216–19.

Pfurtscheller G, Neuper C, Müller GR, Obermaier B, Krausz G, Schlögl A, Scherer R, Graimann B, Keinrath C, Skliris D, Wörtz M, Supp G, Schrank C. Graz-BCI: state of the art and clinical applications. *IEEE Trans Neural Syst Rehabil Eng*. 2003 Jun;**11**(2):177–80.

Pierce JR. *An Introduction to Information Theory*. Dover, New York, 1980.

Pistohl T, Ball T, Schulze-Bonhage A, Aertsen A, Mehring C. Prediction of arm movement trajectories from ECoG-recordings in humans. *J Neurosci Methods*. 2008 Jan 15;**167**(1):105–14.

Poulos M, Rangoussi M, Chrissicopoulos V, Evangelou A. Person identification based on parametric processing on the EEG. In *Proceedings of the Sixth International*

Conference on Electronics, Circuits and Systems (ICECS99), Pafos, Cyprus. 1999;**1**:283–86.

Pregenzer M. *DSLVQ*. PhD thesis, Graz University of Technology, 1997.

Puikkonen J, Malmivuo JA. Theoretical investigation of the sensitivity distribution of point EEG-electrodes on the three concentric spheres model of a human head – An application of the reciprocity theorem. *Tampere Univ. Techn., Inst. Biomed. Eng., Reports.* 1987;**1**(5):71.

Ramoser H, Muller-Gerking J, Pfurtscheller G. Optimal spatial filtering of single trial EEG during imagined hand movement. *IEEE Trans. on Rehab.* 2000;**8**(4):441–46.

Ranganatha S, Hoshi Y, Guan C. Near infrared spectroscopy based brain-computer interface. *Proceedings of SPIE Exp. Mech.* 2005;**5852**:434–42.

Rao RPN, Scherer R. Brain-computer interfacing. *IEEE Signal Processing Magazine.* 2010;**27**(4).

Rao RPN, Scherer R. Statistical pattern recognition and machine learning in brain-computer interfaces. In K. Oweiss (ed.), *Statistical Signal Processing for Neuroscience and Neurotechnology.* Academic Press, Burlington, MA, 2010.

Rao RPN. An optimal estimation approach to visual perception and learning. *Vision Research.* 1999;**39**(11):1963–89.

Rebsamen B, Burdet E, Teo CL, Zeng Q, Guan C, Ang M, Laugier C. A brain control wheelchair with a P300-based BCI and a path following controller. In *Proc. 1st IEEE/RAS-EMBS Int. Conf. Biomedical Robotics and Biomechatronics*, Pisa, Italy, 2006.

Riddle DF. *Calculus and Analytic Geometry*, 3rd ed., Wadsworth Publishing, Belmont, CA, 1979.

Rissman J, Greely HT, Wagner AD. Detecting individual memories through the neural decoding of memory states and past experience. *Proc. Natl. Acad. Sci. USA.* 2010;**107**(21):9849–54.

Rosenfeld JP, Cantwell G, Nasman VT, Wojdac V, Ivanov S, Mazzeri, L. A modified, event-related potential-based guilty knowledge test. *International Journal of Neuroscience.* 1988;**24**:157–61.

Rosenfeld JP, Soskins M, Bosh G, Ryan A. Simple, effective countermeasures to P300-based tests of detection of concealed information. *Psychophysiology.* 2004;**41**(2):205–19.

Rossini L, Izzo D, Summerer L (eds.). *Brain-machine interfaces for space applications: enhancing astronauts' capabilities. International Review of Neurobiology.* 2009;**86**, Elsevier, Amsterdam.

Rouse AG, Moran DW. Neural adaptation of epidural electrocorticographic (EECoG) signals during closed-loop brain computer interface (BCI) tasks. *Conf Proc IEEE Eng Med Biol Soc.* 2009;5514–17.

Rush S, Driscoll DA. EEG-electrode sensitivity – An application of reciprocity. *IEEE Trans. Biomed. Eng.* 1969;BME-**16**:(1) 15–22.

Russell S, Norvig P. *Artificial Intelligence: A Modern Approach*, 3rd ed., Prentice Hall, Upper Saddle River, NJ, 2009.

Sajda P, Pohlmeyer E, Wang J, Parra LC, Christoforou C, Dmochowski J, Hanna B, Bahlmann C, Singh MK, and Chang SF. In a blink of an eye and a switch of a transistor: cortically coupled computer vision. *Proc. IEEE.* 2010;**98**:462–78.

Salvini P, Datteri E, Laschi C, Dario P. Scientific models and ethical issues in hybrid bionic systems research. *AI & Society.* 2008;**22**:431–48.

Santhanam G, Ryu SI, Yu BM, Afshar A, Shenoy KV. A high-performance brain-computer interface. *Nature.* 2006 Jul 13;**442**(7099):195–98.

Schalk G, Kubánek J, Miller KJ, Anderson NR, Leuthardt EC, Ojemann JG, Limbrick D, Moran D, Gerhardt LA, Wolpaw JR. Decoding two-dimensional movement trajectories using electrocorticographic signals in humans. *J Neural Eng.* 2007 Sep;**4**(3):264–75.

Schalk G, Miller KJ, Anderson NR, Wilson JA, Smyth MD, Ojemann JG, Moran DW, Wolpaw JR, Leuthardt EC. Two-dimensional movement control using electrocorticographic signals in humans. *J Neural Eng.* 2008;**5**(1):75–84.

Scherer R, Lee F, Schlögl A, Leeb R, Bischof H, Pfurtscheller G. Towards self-paced brain-computer communication: Navigation through virtual worlds. *IEEE Trans Biomed Eng.* 2008;**55**(2):675–82.

Scherer R, Mohapp A, Grieshofer P, Pfurtscheller G, Neuper C. Sensorimotor EEG patterns during motor imagery in hemiparetic stroke patients. *International Journal of Bioelectromagnetism.* 2007;**9**(3):155–62.

Scherer R, Schlögl A, Lee F, Bischof H, Janša J, Pfurtscheller G. The self-paced Graz brain-computer interface: Methods and applications. *Computational Intelligence and Neuroscience.* 2007;Article ID 79826: 9 pages.

Scherer R, Zanos SP, Miller KJ, Rao RPN, Ojemann JG. Classification of contralateral and ipsilateral finger movements for electrocorticographic brain-computer interfaces. *Neurosurg Focus.* 2009;**27**(1):E12.

Scherer R, Rao RPN. Non-manual control devices: Direct brain-computer interaction. In J. Pereira (ed.), *Handbook of Research on Personal Autonomy Technologies and Disability Informatics.* IGI Global, Hershey, PA, 2011.

Sellers EW, Kübler A, Donchin E. Brain-computer interface research at the University of South Florida Cognitive Psychophysiology Laboratory: the P300 Speller. *IEEE Trans Neural Syst Rehabil Eng.* 2006 Jun;**14**(2):221–24.

Serruya MD, Hatsopoulos NG, Paninski L, Fellows MR, Donoghue JP. Instant neural control of a movement signal. *Nature.* 2002 Mar 14;**416**(6877):141–42.

Shannon CE, Weaver W. *The Mathematical Theory of Communication.* Univ. Illinois Press, Urbana, IL, 1964.

Sharbrough F, Chatrian G-E, Lesser RP, Lüders H, Nuwer M, Picton TW. American Electroencephalographic Society guidelines for standard electrode position nomenclature. *J. Clin. Neurophysiol.* 1991;**8**:200–202.

Shenoy P. *Brain-computer interfaces for control and computation.* PhD thesis, Department of Computer Science and Engineering, University of Washington, 2008.

Shenoy P, Miller KJ, Ojemann JG, Rao RPN. Generalized features for electrocorticographic BCIs. *IEEE Trans Biomed Eng.* 2008 Jan;**55**(1):273–80.

Shenoy P, Miller KJ, Ojemann J, Rao RPN. Finger movement classification for an electrocorticographic BCI. In *Proc. of 3rd International IEEE EMBS Conf. Neur Eng* 2007; 192–195.

Shenoy P, Rao RPN. Dynamic Bayesian networks for brain-computer interfaces. In L.K. Saul, Y. Weiss, and L. Bottou (eds.), *Advances in Neural Information Processing System* (NIPS). 2005;**17**:1265–1272, MIT Press, Cambridge, MA.

Simeral JD, Kim SP, Black MJ, Donoghue JP, Hochberg LR. Neural control of cursor trajectory and click by a human with tetraplegia 1000 days after implant of an intracortical microelectrode array. *J Neural Eng.* 2011 Apr;**8**(2):025027.

Skidmore TA, Hill Jr., HW. The evoked potential human-computer interface. *Proc. Annu. Conf. Engineering in Medicine and Biology.* 1991:407–408.

Stosiek C, Garaschuk O, Holthoff K, Konnerth A. In vivo two-photon calcium imaging of neuronal networks. *Proc. Natl Acad. Sci. USA.* 2003;**100**, 7319–24.

Strang G. *Introduction to Linear Algebra*, 4th ed., Wellesley-Cambridge Press, Wellesley, MA, 2009.

Suihko V, Malmivuo JA, Eskola H. Distribution of sensitivity of electric leads in an inhomogeneous spherical head model. *Tampere Univ. Techn., Ragnar Granit Inst.* 1993;Rep. 7:(2).

Suminski AJ, Tkach DC, Fagg AH, Hatsopoulos NG. Incorporating feedback from multiple sensory modalities enhances brain-machine interface control. *J Neurosci.* 2010 Dec 15;**30**(50):16777–87.

Szafir D, Mutlu B. Pay attention! Designing adaptive agents that monitor and improve user engagement. *In Proceedings of ACM SIGCHI Conference on Human Factors in Computing Systems* (CHI 2012). 2012;11–20.

Tamburrini G. Brain to computer communication: Ethical perspectives on interaction models. *Neuroethics* 2009;**2**: 137–49.

Tan DS, Nijholt A. (eds.) *Brain-Computer Interfaces: Applying our Minds to Human-Computer Interaction*. Springer, London, UK, 2010.

Tangermann M, Krauledat M, Grzeska K, Sagebaum M, Blankertz B, Vidaurre C, Müller KR. Playing pinball with non-invasive BCI. In *Advances in Neural Information Processing Systems*, 2009;21:1641–48. MIT Press, Cambridge, MA.

Thomson EE, Carra R, Nicolelis MA. Perceiving invisible light through a somatosensory cortical prosthesis. *Nature Commun.* 2013;**4**:1482.

Tufail Y, Matyushov A, Baldwin N, Tauchmann ML, Georges J, Yoshihiro A, Tillery SI, Tyler WJ. Transcranial pulsed ultrasound stimulates intact brain circuits. *Neuron.* 2010 Jun 10;**66**(5):681–94.

Van den Brand R, Heutschi J, Barraud Q, DiGiovanna J, Bartholdi K, Huerlimann M, Friedli L, Vollenweider I, Moraud EM, Duis S, Dominici N, Micera S, Musienko P, Courtine G. Restoring voluntary control of locomotion after paralyzing spinal cord injury. *Science.* 2012;**336**:1182–85.

Vapnik, V. *The Nature of Statistical Learning Theory*. Springer-Verlag, New York, 1995.

Vargas-Irwin CE, Shakhnarovich G, Yadollahpour P, Mislow JM, Black MJ, Donoghue JP. Decoding complete reach and grasp actions from local primary motor cortex populations. *J Neurosci.* 2010 Jul 21;**30**(29):9659–69.

Velliste M, Perel S, Spalding MC, Whitford AS and Schwartz AB. Cortical control of a prosthetic arm for self-feeding. *Nature.* 2008; **453**:1098–1101.

Vidal JJ. Toward direct brain-computer communication. *Annu. Rev. Biophys. Bioeng.* 1973;**2**:157–80.

Vidaurre C, Scherer R, Cabeza R, Schlögl A, Pfurtscheller G. Study of discriminant analysis applied to motor imagery bipolar data. *Med Biol Eng Comput.* 2007; **45**(1):61–68.

Vidaurre C, Sannelli C, Müller KR, Blankertz B. Machine-learning-based coadaptive calibration for brain-computer interfaces. *Neural Comput.* 2011;**23**(3):791–816.

Von Melchner L, Pallas SL, Sur M. Visual behaviour mediated by retinal projections directed to the auditory pathway. *Nature.* 2000;**404**(6780):871–76.

Warwick K, Gasson M, Hutt B, Goodhew I, Kyberd P, Andrews B, Teddy P, Shad A. The application of implant technology for cybernetic systems. *Arch Neurol.* 2003;**60**:1369–73.

Warwick K. Cyborg morals, cyborg values, cyborg ethics. *Ethics and Information Technology.* 2003;**5**:131–37.

Weiland JD, Liu W, Humayun MS. Retinal prosthesis. *Annu Rev Biomed Eng.* 2005;**7**:361–401.

Weiskopf N, Veit R, Erb M, Mathiak K, Grodd W, Goebel R, Birbaumer N. Physiological self-regulation of regional brain activity using real-time functional magnetic resonance imaging (fMRI): methodology and exemplary data. *Neuroimage*. 2003;**19**(3):577–86.

Wessberg J, Stambaugh CR, Kralik JD, Beck PD, Laubach M, Chapin JK, Kim J, Biggs SJ, Srinivasan MA, Nicolelis MA. Real-time prediction of hand trajectory by ensembles of cortical neurons in primates. *Nature*. 2000 Nov 16;**408**(6810):361–65.

Wodlinger B, Durand DM. Peripheral nerve signal recording and processing for artificial limb control. *Conf Proc IEEE Eng Med Biol Soc*. 2010:6206–09.

Wolpaw JR, Wolpaw EW. (eds.) *Brain-Computer Interfaces: Principles and Practice*. Oxford University Press, 2012.

Wolpaw JR, Birbaumer N, Heetderks WJ, McFarland DJ, Peckham PH, Schalk G, Donchin E, Quatrano LA, Robinson CJ, Vaughan TM. Brain-computer interface technology: a review of the first international meeting. *IEEE Trans Rehabil Eng*. 2000;**8**(2):164–73.

Wolpaw JR, McFarland DJ, Neat GW, Forneris CA. An EEG-based brain-computer interface for cursor control. *Electroencephalogr Clin Neurophysiol*. 1991 Mar;**78**(3):252–59.

Wolpaw JR, McFarland DJ. Control of a two-dimensional movement signal by a noninvasive brain-computer interface in humans. *Proc Natl Acad Sci USA*. 2004 Dec 21;**101**(51):17849–54.

Wolpaw JR, McFarland DJ. Multichannel EEG-based brain-computer communication. *Electroencephalogr Clin Neurophysiol*. 1994 Jun;**90**(6):444–49.

Wolpaw JR, Birbaumer N, McFarland D, Pfurtscheller G, Vaughan T. Brain-computer interfaces for communication and control. Clinical Neurophysiology. 2002;**113**:767–91.

Wu W, Gao Y, Bienenstock E, Donoghue JP, Black MJ. Bayesian population decoding of motor cortical activity using a Kalman filter. *Neural Comput*. 2006 Jan;**18**(1):80–118.

Zhuang J, Truccolo W, Vargas-Irwin C, Donoghue JP. Decoding 3-D reach and grasp kinematics from high-frequency local field potentials in primate primary motor cortex. *IEEE Trans Biomed Eng*. 2010;**57**(7):1774–84.

Index

Printed in the United States
By Bookmasters